The Days of
Wee Willie, Old Cy
and Baseball War

The Days of Wee Willie, Old Cy and Baseball War

Scenes from the Dawn of the Deadball Era, 1900–1903

CHUCK KIMBERLY

McFarland & Company, Inc., Publishers
Jefferson, North Carolina

LIBRARY OF CONGRESS CATALOGUING-IN-PUBLICATION DATA

Kimberly, Chuck, 1940–
The days of Wee Willie, Old Cy and baseball war : scenes from the dawn of the Deadball Era, 1900–1903 / Chuck Kimberly.
    pages cm
Includes bibliographical references and index.

ISBN 978-0-7864-9401-9 (softcover : acid free paper) ∞
ISBN 978-1-4766-1551-6 (ebook)

1. Baseball—United States—History—20th century. I. Title.

GV863.A1K53 2014   796.357'64097309041—dc23
                     2014030830

BRITISH LIBRARY CATALOGUING DATA ARE AVAILABLE

© 2014 Chuck Kimberly. All rights reserved

No part of this book may be reproduced or transmitted in any form or by any means, electronic or mechanical, including photocopying or recording, or by any information storage and retrieval system, without permission in writing from the publisher.

On the cover: Wee Willie Keeler (National Baseball Hall of Fame Library, Cooperstown, New York)

Printed in the United States of America

McFarland & Company, Inc., Publishers
Box 611, Jefferson, North Carolina 28640
www.mcfarlandpub.com

Table of Contents

Preface 1

Chapter One. 1900, National League
A Gem of a Season 5 • The Iron Man to the Rescue: Brooklyn 10 • Putting It Together Too Late: Pittsburgh 14 • A Formidable Batting Order: Philadelphia 17 Faded Glory: Boston 18 • Spoiled Broth: St. Louis 21 • A Team of Fighters: Chicago 22 • Good Idea, Bad Timing: Cincinnati 23 • Polishing the Big Apple's Team 27 • Big Ed Decided to Bunt 29 • Wee Willie Was Big 30 • Kip's Bad Rep 36 • Intersecting Career Paths: Pink Hawley and Joe McGinnity 37 • A Loud Noise in Brooklyn: Roaring Bill Kennedy 43

Chapter Two. 1901, National League
The Baseball War's Opening Salvo 46 • A New Powerhouse: Pittsburgh 47 More Ginger: Philadelphia 51 • Please, Please—Not Toward Third: Brooklyn 53 Addition by Subtraction: St. Louis 55 • Battle Damage: Boston, Chicago, New York and Cincinnati 57 • A Fine Utility Player: Honus Wagner 61 • There Was Something About Harry: Harry Wolverton 64 • A Rising Star: Jimmy Sheckard 65 • He Doesn't Need the Money: Emmet Heidrick 66 • A Tale of Two Lefties: Lefty Davis 69 • The Toast of New York: Christy Mathewson 70 Rambling Rube 73 • Harsher Times 77

Chapter Three. 1901, American League
The New Major League 81 • The Defending—and New—Champions: Chicago 82 • A Gentleman's Team: Boston 86 • A Thrilling Start: Detroit 89 Mack Cobbles Together a Winner: Philadelphia 91 • McGraw's Orioles, Act II 94 • A Considerable Trick: Washington 96 • Cleveland Still Had the Blues 98 Losing Brews Fan Discontent 102 • In a Class by Himself: Napoleon Lajoie 104 A Designated Hitter Born Too Soon: Bill Keister 108 • Davey Crockett in Detroit 110 • Adjusting Successfully: Cy Young 111 • A Logical Decision: Frank DeHaas Robison 115

Chapter Four. 1902, National League

A Desperate Counterattack 117 • Like Men Among Boys: Pittsburgh 121 • Hanlon's Projects: Brooklyn 123 • End of the Road for a Star: Boston 127 • Refreshing Changes: Cincinnati 129 • New Nickname, New Manager, New Players: Chicago 130 • Why Rebuilding Is Difficult: St. Louis 133 • Seventy-Five Percent Good: Philadelphia 136 • The Fourth Estate Gets Its Chance: New York 138 • A Fielding Wonder: Fred Tenney 141 • A Wee Bit of a Slugger: Tommy Leach 143 • The Future King of Sluggers: Sam Crawford 144 • Setting the Standard: Bill Bergen 149 • "Noodles": Frank Hahn 150

Chapter Five. 1902, American League

Mixed Luck and Rube Waddell: Philadelphia 156 • Dashed Hopes: St. Louis 161 • Misplaced Charity: Boston 164 • Comiskey's Machine Sputters 166 • A Team Transformed: Cleveland 168 • Not As Good As Advertised: Washington 170 • A Team Too Fiery: Detroit 173 • Orioles and Patriots 176 • A Golden Glove: Jimmy Collins 180 • "Scoops": George Carey 184 • An All-American Guy: Dave Fultz 186 • Welcome to the Big Leagues, Mr. Joss 189

Chapter Six. 1903, National League

Stumbling Toward Peace 193 • Still Good Enough: Pittsburgh 199 • A Successful "Con" Job: New York 202 • Selee Builds a Contender: Chicago 205 • Costly Altruism: Cincinnati 208 • The Stars Said "Goodbye": Brooklyn 210 • A Painful Season: Boston 214 • Tragedy and Disappointment: Philadelphia 216 • At Least the Grandstand Didn't Collapse: St. Louis 218 • Poor Control: Mike Donlin 221 • A Quiet Hero: Deacon Phillippe 227

Chapter Seven. 1903, American League

Paying More, Getting Less 232 • A Nebraska Cyclone in Boston 233 • Not Enough Pixie Dust: Philadelphia 238 • Too Many E's: Cleveland 240 • Not Quite Ready: New York 243 • Kerosene: Detroit 245 • Seriously Off-Track: St. Louis 248 • Playing Ugly: Chicago 250 • The Passing of a Great Player: Washington 253 • The Man They Fought Over: George Davis 255 • Bill Bradley, B.I. 259 • Count Your Cows: Kid Elberfeld 262 • "Socks": Ralph Seybold 265 • Don't Tread on Griff: Clark Griffith 267

Chapter Notes   273
Bibliography   281
Index   283

Preface

The period covered by this book, the early Deadball Era (1900 through 1903), came at an eventful time in baseball history. The National League quit trying to make a success of its awkward 12-team format after the 1899 season, and contracted to eight teams in 1900. The contraction left four of the country's most populous cities without a major league team and created an opportunity for other baseball people to organize a rival major league. In 1901, a group of owners from the American League moved into three of the four abandoned markets and placed rival teams in three other National League cities. It raided the older league for some of its players. The conflict between the two leagues shaped the next three seasons, and the league structures that emerged from the "baseball war" remained unchanged for five decades.

The early Deadball Era served as a bridge between the 1890s, when batting averages reached an all-time high, and the middle of the next decade, when they plunged to an all-time low. It was a time when game strategy was quite different from the modern approach. Teams played "small ball" and some of the best players were small men. Players were expected to be able to bunt and execute the hit-and-run play. Managers commonly chose to give up an out to move a batter up one base. Today these strategies are employed mostly when a manager believes scoring one run will be crucial to his team's chances of winning a game, rather than throughout the contest.

The prominent players of the period occupy a special place in baseball lore. When the Baseball Hall of Fame was established in 1936, four of the first eight players inducted were active during the early Deadball Era, as were managers John McGraw and Connie Mack and American League president Ban Johnson, who were also among the Hall's first inductees. The award now presented annually to the top pitcher in each major league is named after Cy Young, who enjoyed two of his best years in 1901 and 1902. Perhaps the most widely known batting advice ever offered by a player is, "Hit 'em where they ain't." That concise "treatise" on hitting (described by the player in just that way) came, of course, from Wee Willie Keeler. During these years Keeler's batting style was considered the model young players should seek to emulate.

There were also a number of players who were genuine baseball characters. Outfielder Davy Jones later said of his contemporaries, "Baseball attracted all sorts of people in those days. We had stupid guys, smart guys, tough guys, mild guys, crazy guys, college men, slickers from the city and hicks from the country. And back then a country kid was likely to *really* be a country kid. We'd call them hayseeds or rubes."[1] The players featured in this book include quite a few who fall into at least one of Jones' categories.

This book's approach is intended to reflect the fact that every baseball season presents not one story or theme but a multitude of them. Each chapter contains team-oriented vignettes, as well as several that provide a more in-depth look at some of the players of the era. For the top teams, vignettes focus on a team's leading players and its fate in the race for the league championship. That is what the team's fans would almost certainly have been focusing on at the time. For second-division teams, a vignette might be devoted to promising young players, weaknesses that led to a fall in the standings, or a development affecting the team's performance. As in modern times, the fans of those teams likely would have been paying more attention to such matters than to the team's fanciful pennant chances.

A common strand running through many of the team vignettes is the baseball war between the American and National leagues. The war is addressed primarily at the field level. The inter-league conflict essentially made free agents of all the players. For three seasons every team was deeply affected by its players' sense of loyalty to the team or by the lack of it. The American League succeeded because it was able to attract a large percentage of the better players. The warring ended when it did because owners in both leagues came to believe they could no longer afford the escalating cost of the fight.

Team vignettes include tables summarizing the records of team members. The tables offer a succinct summary of a team's makeup and the contributions of individual team members. Position players are listed by the place they were most often assigned in the batting order during the season. Managers of the early Deadball Era seldom made dramatic changes in their lineups; therefore, for most teams the tables present a reasonably accurate representation of their batting order. For a few teams—usually ones who finished near the bottom of the league—constant player movement made it difficult to determine a "typical" lineup. Even for those teams, though, the tables show whether a player was placed at the top, middle or bottom of the batting order. For the 1900 and 1901 seasons, the order shown in the tables was determined based on my own notes. For the remaining two seasons the order is based on the lineups contained in *Deadball Stars of the National League* and *Deadball Stars of the American League*, two books by the Deadball Era Committee of the Society for American Baseball Research.

Although the players whose records appear in this book have not thrown a pitch or hit a ball for many decades, their records have been subject to periodic revision for roughly the last forty years. The researchers who put together the original Macmillan *Baseball Encyclopedia* in the late 1960s found many mistakes in baseball's official records. Errors are still being discovered. Researchers' findings, have in fact brought about pushback from Organized Baseball. Ty Cobb is still officially the American League batting champion for the 1910 season, despite recalculations indicating that Nap Lajoie ended up with a higher batting average. Christy Mathewson has, and presumably will always have, 373 career victories and Cy Young will always have 511, regardless of what baseball researchers might discover.

Other aspects of these legends' records, however, have been subject to change, as have the records of lesser players. In almost every case the revisions are minor, an inning or two added to a year's innings pitched total, a win added or subtracted, a hit or RBI added or subtracted. It is only when a revision, however minor, affects a well-known statistic that we hear anything about it.

The statistical tables appearing in this book were generated using the *Bill James Electronic Baseball Encyclopedia for Windows,* which was complete through the 1995 season. The figures were then compared with more recent listings, such as those appearing in *Total Baseball* and on Internet sites hosted by Retrosheet, Baseball Reference, and Major League Baseball. Where discrepancies were found, the numbers in the tables were updated to reflect the newer listing.

The player vignettes generally focus on well-known figures of the period. A few depict relatively obscure players who are interesting for reasons unique to the player. For some of the top stars, the contours of whose careers are familiar to serious fans, the emphasis is squarely on the seasons of 1900 through 1903. For other, lesser-known players a broader view is taken.

The research for the book included scanning game summaries and box scores for each of the major league teams for the seasons from 1900 through 1903, reading issues of *The Sporting News* from 1892 through 1903, and performing online word searches in *Sporting Life* for relevant years. This required hundreds of hours of staring at a microfilm reader. That seemingly simple task could not be completed without the support and assistance of many people, to whom I wish to express my gratitude.

First I wish to thank my wife, Ana, and my son, Danny, who offered their encouragement even though it meant long periods of absence from home. I also wish to thank the staffs of the Fairfax County, Virginia, regional libraries, and especially to the technicians who kept the rickety old microfilm readers and printers operating despite periodic budget cutbacks. That is also true for workers at the Library of Congress reading rooms I frequented over a three-year period. More broadly, together with other people who are interested in baseball research, I owe a debt of gratitude to the Society for American Baseball Research, which has been instrumental in expanding the availability of resources for the study of baseball history.

Finally, a small army of researchers working over the last several decades have produced a wealth of statistical data reaching back to the earliest years of organized baseball. In this book I have drawn on data contained in Macmillan's *Baseball Encyclopedia,* John Thorn, Peter Palmer, and Michael Gershman's *Total Baseball,* and the *Bill James Electronic Baseball Encyclopedia,* along with information from the Internet sites *retrosheet.org* and *baseball-reference.com.* Our knowledge of baseball history is much richer as a result of the effort that went into compiling the data in these reference works.

One

1900, National League

A Gem of a Season

Suppose major league baseball eliminated ten of its thirty teams all at once. Lots of very good baseball players would suddenly be available to strengthen the remaining twenty teams. Several cities would field veritable All-Star teams. And the Yankees, naturally, would use their 40-man roster to stock their Triple-A franchise with a reserve team of players just below the All-Star level. Of course, a drastic league contraction such as this would not happen nowadays. First, the players' union would get a court injunction to suspend it, and then Congress would step in and pass a law prohibiting it. But at the end of the nineteenth century, something very similar occurred.

From 1892 to 1899 the National League was an awkward organization composed of 12 survivors of a ruinous war between the major league players and the owners of the two major leagues of that time, the National League and the American Association. Several franchises in the new 12-club National League did not do well in the rough economic times prevailing during most of the 1890s. By 1898 the National League magnates in the larger, more prosperous cities decided they could no longer continue with the 12-club format. Four franchises suffering from poor attendance were marked for "league reduction." Those franchises were Baltimore, Cleveland, Louisville, and Washington.

The reduction proceeded in two phases. The first, implemented before the 1899 season, imposed "syndicate baseball" upon four of the National League teams. The owners of the Baltimore and Brooklyn teams merged their holdings so the players of the two teams were controlled by one group of owners. The St. Louis and Cleveland teams also came under a single ownership when Frank DeHaas Robison and his brother, Stanley, who already owned the Cleveland team, obtained control of the St. Louis franchise. Both ownerships gave one of the cities the pick of the players under their control, while saddling the other with the leftovers.

For the Brooklyn-Baltimore combine the move worked out pretty well, partially because two of Baltimore's best players, John McGraw and Wilbert Robinson, refused to go to Brooklyn. They were allowed to stay in Baltimore. McGraw's inspired play and managing led a group of journeyman players to a fourth-place finish. The Brooklyn team, meanwhile, was a powerhouse. Three future Hall-of-Famers—Willie Keeler,

Joe Kelley, and Hughie Jennings—were among the players moving over from Baltimore. Brooklyn easily won the 1899 pennant.

The St. Louis-Cleveland combine, on the other hand, proved to be a disaster. It was an amalgamation of a woeful tail-end team with a fifth-place team that was aging rapidly. The result was another fifth-place team that continued to decline and a last-place team whose ineptitude reached historic levels. The Cleveland team—nicknamed the "Misfits" in 1899—went 20–134, accruing the lowest winning percentage in major league history (.130) and finishing 84 games behind the champion Brooklyn team.[1]

The second phase of the National League's reduction came after the 1899 season. It began with another two-team amalgamation. The principal owner of the Pittsburgh Pirates had let it be known that his stock was for sale. Barney Dreyfuss, whose Louisville club was marked for elimination, opened negotiations for the Pittsburgh team, using his Louisville interests as leverage. The deal was finalized in December. Dreyfuss became a minority owner of the Pittsburgh team, owning 47 percent of the stock and serving as the team's president. Shortly afterwards a deal was announced in which Pittsburgh sent five players and $25,000 in cash to Louisville in exchange for Louisville's 14 best players. Strictly speaking, this may not have been "syndicate baseball." But whatever we call it, Dreyfuss put together a two-team combination that was about as good as the Brooklyn-Baltimore syndicate.[2]

At the annual National League meeting, held in December, the Louisville, Washington, and Cleveland owners agreed to sell their teams to the league. A circuit committee was formed to negotiate the terms of the sale with the owners of those three teams and with the Baltimore owners, who were insisting they would not relinquish their franchise at the price offered by the league. Negotiations continued over the winter. League officials threatened to saddle Baltimore with undesirable playing dates and high travel costs if its owners insisted on playing the 1900 season and promised to freeze it out of the league after the 1901 season, when the agreement forming the 12-club league expired. On March 5, 1900, the Baltimore owners conceded. A settlement was reached by which the four franchises and their playing grounds were sold to the league. The deal with Washington also transferred that team's players to the league.[3]

In keeping with the magnates' prevailing credo of "do unto your fellow owners before they can do unto you," the Washington owners sold the team's best two players to Boston before the settlement. After March 5, the remaining Washington players and surplus players from the Brooklyn, St. Louis, and Pittsburgh teams were put on the market. Of the five non-syndicate teams, only two were interested buyers. Chicago and Philadelphia both picked up a few players to add depth to already solid teams. Boston had already raided the Washington franchise for the players it wanted. Cincinnati's owners declined to go after any of the available players, they had embarked upon a rebuilding program. Cincinnati had been the only team really active in purchasing minor league players for the 1900 season. It had purchased several of the best minor league players of 1899 and its ownership was committed to using them in 1900.[4]

New York was a special case. Its owner, Andrew Freedman, had purchased controlling stock in the team in 1895. He was an arrogant man who insulted newspapermen, berated umpires, and quarreled with the other magnates. He fired his manager nearly every season. His antics and the mediocre performance of his teams alienated the team's fans. The relatively poor attendance in New York hurt the league. Several owners who were allied with Freedman in the league's internal squabbles urged him to strengthen his team for the 1900 season. As encouragement, the league offered him the pick of the Washington players at no cost. Freedman chose pitcher Win Mercer off a list of players shown to him and said he would consult with manager Buck Ewing before choosing any of the others. Before he could respond, Philadelphia swooped in and grabbed Jimmy Slagle, a promising young outfielder. Freedman became enraged. He insisted Slagle should be given to him. When Philadelphia refused, Freedman turned down all of the other Washington players. He also refused McGraw and Robinson when the Brooklyn syndicate offered to sell them to the Giants. The two ex–Orioles, both of whom were still very good players, were instead sold to St. Louis. Freedman later accepted several other journeyman players as gifts, but none of them possessed the talent or drawing power of McGraw and Robinson.[5]

Most of the ex–Washington players ended up being sold to minor league clubs, as did many of the players displaced from the Brooklyn, St. Louis, and Pittsburgh teams. About two dozen well-established major league players found themselves working for minor league teams in 1900. They were, of course, quite unhappy with the cut in pay accompanying their move to the minor league ranks, as well as the manner in which it happened.

While the National League reduction was a disaster from a player's point of view, from a fan's it promised to be a treat. All the National League teams were strengthened, even the ones that weren't trying very hard to take advantage of the situation. Lineups were filled with proven veterans. Even the pitching staffs were for the most part made up of experienced hurlers, which was not often the case in this era when pitchers' arms frequently gave out under the typical heavy workload. A broad indicator of the concentration of talent in the National League in 1900 is the relatively high number of players on each team who eventually entered the Baseball Hall of Fame.

Every 1900 National League team had at least one future Hall of Fame player. In fact, if Christy Mathewson's six-game tryout with the Giants is counted, each team had at least two. Boston, a powerful team throughout the nineties, had five players (Kid Nichols, Jimmy Collins, Hugh Duffy, Billy Hamilton, and Vic Willis) and their manager (Frank Selee) inducted into the Hall of Fame. St. Louis also had five (Cy Young, Bobby Wallace, Jesse Burkett, John McGraw, and Wilbert Robinson). Brooklyn had four players (Joe McGinnity, Hughie Jennings, Joe Kelley, and Willie Keeler) and their manager (Ned Hanlon) inducted. Pittsburgh had four (Honus Wagner, Fred Clarke, Rube Waddell, and Jack Chesbro); Philadelphia three (Ed Delahanty, Nap Lajoie, and Elmer Flick); Chicago two (Clark Griffith and Frank Chance); Cincinnati two (Jake Beckley and Sam Crawford); and New York one (George Davis). Near the end of the season, another future Hall of Famer, Roger Bresnahan, appeared in two games for Chicago.

Newspaper reporters saw the 1900 season as being fundamentally different from previous National League seasons. "Every baseball magnate and every player believes the playing will be faster [better] and the race closer than for many years," wrote Hugh S. Fullerton of the *Chicago Tribune*. "As a matter of fact, the teams are so evenly matched every prediction is a guess. One slump, one player injured, one run of 'hard luck' may make a tail-ender out of any club, and a few scratch hits made at the right time might give the weakest team the victory." As for the home team, Fullerton mused, "the team is the best that has represented Chicago in the last six years, but the question is, will it prove strong when compared with the seven other improved clubs." Chicago manager Tom Loftus expressed similar views. "We are going to see faster ball playing this season and more brainy playing than we have seen for many years," he said. "There will be eight strong clubs."[6]

Once the season started, players and writers noted the game was being played at a higher level than before.

The hitting was better. After being knocked out of the box in a game, Philadelphia's Red Donahue said, "The hitting is remarkable all over the league this year. I don't know why it is, but no pitcher, no matter what he has up his sleeve can go into a game and bet his life that he will fool his opponents. On numerous occasions this season pitchers have been knocked out of the box while doing splendid work. The fact that a man is pitching his best ball does not seem to cut any figure this spring."[7]

The fielding was better. Veteran Pittsburgh shortstop Fred Ely explained why there seemed to be less teamwork at bat in 1900—that is, why the hit-and-run and other situational hitting strategies weren't working as well. "In the first place there are no weak infields and no easy pitching, and when a batsman makes a move to bunt or to hit to right field to advance a runner the opposition lines up to stop him, and he finds himself up against nine men in every game." Before, it had been different, Ely said. "Last season only one or two clubs had any system for stopping teamwork at the bat, but this year all have effective methods."[8]

The pitching was better. "This is a bad year for the sluggers of the league," the *Chicago Tribune* noted. "[Ed] Delahanty and [Jesse] Burkett, [Fred] Clarke and many others are down in the lists.... The reason is the pitching all around the circuit has so improved the big batters are but little better than the weak ones. The fast runners and the good bunters are the men who are getting the base hits and winning the games. The great batters are the especial marks of the pitchers and their slump in hitting is the more noticeable. As a matter of fact, a man who is batting .300 this season is better than the man who batted .330 last year, for he has made the hits off real pitchers and earned most of what he has made."[9]

In 1900 the National League magnates succeeded in their goal of giving every city a good team. There really were eight pretty good teams in the league. The Brooklyn team was somewhat better than the others and, for the first part of the season, New York was a lot worse. But the six teams in the middle found themselves in a real dogfight. They took turns beating up on each other. They were so close in talent none of them could sustain a winning streak for very long. When the hops went their way, they won; when the breaks went against them, they lost.

Getting over .500 was a real challenge. On June 19, after roughly 50 games, only Brooklyn and Philadelphia were over .500. The Pirates held third place with a 24–26 record. Four weeks later Chicago was in second place with a 36–31 record, while Boston, in seventh place, was only six games behind Chicago with a 30–37 record. New York was the doormat of the league on July 13, having won 21 and lost 41. The owners fired the manager, the team was shored up in a couple of weak positions, and its players focused more on winning games than undermining their manager. Over the rest of the season they went 39–37.

The race for first place was an interesting one. Philadelphia took the lead with a strong start and held it for two months. They were overtaken by the favored Brooklyn Superbas near the end of June. Although the Superbas held the lead the rest of the way, they were never able to build an overwhelming lead. The writers and fans, however, were so sure the Superbas were going to win they started declaring the pennant race over in July, even though the Superbas usually had only a six- or seven-game lead. Pittsburgh, which was only three games over .500 the last week of July, got its act together in August and September. The Pirates put on a strong finishing kick and came within a game of catching the Superbas before falling back to 4½ games off the pace.

1900 National League Standings

Team	W	L	Pct.	GB
Brooklyn	82	54	.603	—
Pittsburgh	79	60	.568	4.5
Philadelphia	75	63	.543	8
Boston	66	72	.478	17
Chicago	65	75	.464	19
St. Louis	65	75	.464	19
Cincinnati	62	77	.446	21.5
New York	60	78	.435	23

From the eyewitness statements quoted above and based on the logic of league consolidation, it seems clear that the fans of 1900 were watching professional baseball played at a distinctly better level than they had witnessed before. It could be assumed they cherished the treat. But while baseball fans like to see good baseball, they are mostly interested in seeing the home team win. For the fans all this parity on the field was frustrating. In each city the fans knew the local team was filled with good ballplayers, but the "bums" kept losing. In Boston the fans felt the former champions were playing "dopey ball." In Chicago, the Orphans turned victory into defeat by "dumb work on the bases." New York lost because "their efforts to field were infantile and their hitting but little better." On the young Cincinnati team, "the new men do not fit in well and fail to take advantage of the openings." Pittsburgh "lacked a leader." St. Louis lost because there "was no harmony in the team." Philadelphia had great players but didn't win. Why didn't the Phillies win? "There is certainly something wrong with this team, or else they are a lot of quitters. The latter, most likely, is the case." Those were the seven teams that failed to win the pennant. The team that won? It got the same treatment: "Hanlon's men seem more interested in horse racing than in baseball, although on the road they will cut that out to a great extent. In Brooklyn they are too near the racetrack to do good work."[10]

The season was a disappointment financially. Only Pittsburgh and Philadelphia drew well. New York—by far the most important city to the league financially—did poorly, and the champion Brooklyn team drew embarrassingly small crowds at home. The National League magnates could not understand why attendance was so poor, but they were largely responsible for the negative fan reaction. Their backroom manipulations had cold-bloodedly stripped teams from four cities and offered their fans nothing in return. Indignation was felt among fans throughout the league. Writers and fans were also upset because the magnates had been so busy stabbing each other in the back that they had ignored the league's most serious problem—uncontrolled rowdy behavior on the field. Summing up the season, the *Chicago Tribune* said, "The people were tired of the way baseball was being handled. The weakness of the magnates, their bickerings and the ceaseless and senseless delays on the field helped irritate conditions already bad." The keen competition among the teams hurt, rather than helped the situation. "The clubs were so evenly matched that for most of the season the people of seven cities regarded their teams as losers," the *Tribune* noted. "It was four months before the people of Pittsburgh realized the team was a winning one. Rowdyism in Brooklyn and bad conditions in New York deadened interest all over the boroughs, and before July the men who handle baseball realized they were going to lose."[11]

It is a bit sad to see that those who watched the 1900 season unfold felt so disappointed. They had no way of knowing that the highly skilled players performing for the 1900 teams would soon be dispersed among twice as many teams. They failed to realize what appears apparent to us more than 100 years later: The clinker of a season they thought they were witnessing was in fact a gem.

The Iron Man to the Rescue: Brooklyn

Possibly because of the unsavory way it was put together, this team has received far less attention than the 1894–96 Baltimore Orioles or the Boston Beaneaters of the 1890s. But the 1899–1900 Superbas were a powerful team. The 1899 team cruised to the pennant. In the spring of 1900, the Superbas had so many good players to choose from they could afford to let McGraw and Robinson virtually auction themselves off to the highest bidder while Brooklyn made no effort to sign them. Before the season opened they sold, released or farmed out eight players who had started regularly in 1899. They also farmed out two promising young pitchers who in normal circumstances would probably have started regularly with a major league team.

Brooklyn (82–54)

Regular Lineup	AVG	OBP	SLG	R	RBI	SB
Fielder Jones, cf	.310	.383	.393	106	54	33
or Jimmy Sheckard, lf	.300	.416	.454	74	39	30
Willie Keeler, rf	.362	.402	.449	106	68	41
Hughie Jennings, 1b	.272	.348	.347	61	69	31
Joe Kelley, lf	.319	.398	.485	90	91	26
Bill Dahlen, ss	.259	.364	.344	87	69	31
Lave Cross, 3b*	.293	.329	.368	79	73	21
Tom Daly, 2b	.312	.403	.414	72	55	27
or G. Demontreville, 2b	.244	.283	.286	34	28	21
Duke Farrell, c	.275	.310	.352	33	39	3
or Deacon McGuire, c	.286	.348	.365	20	34	2

Leading Pitchers	W	L	PCT	IP	H	ERA
Joe McGinnity	28	8	.778	343	350	2.94
Bill Kennedy	20	13	.606	292	316	3.91
Frank Kitson	15	13	.536	253.3	283	4.19
Harry Howell	6	5	.545	110.3	131	3.75

*Includes record with St. Louis

Most impressive of all, the 1900 Superbas won the pennant despite losing the services (except for ten games) of three pitchers who had a combined record of 70–34 for them the previous year. Jim Hughes had gone 28–6 in 1899 and was generally considered the best pitcher in baseball upon entering the 1900 season. During spring training he announced that he had chosen to open a saloon in Sacramento, California, and pitch on weekends for the local semi-professional team, rather than go east to play for the Superbas. At nearly the same time, Doc McJames, who won 19 games in 1899, decided to retire from baseball to practice medicine with his father. Then Jack Dunn, who had a 23–13 record in 1899, blew out his arm six weeks into the 1900 season. Even with the loss of these three star pitchers, the Superbas still had three pitchers remaining who had won 20 games in 1899. (They entered spring training with *six* pitchers on their roster who had won at least 19 games the previous year.) Joe McGinnity had been 28–16 and Frank Kitson 22–16 with the Orioles, and Bill Kennedy, Brooklyn's top pitcher during most of the 1890s, had been 20–13 with the Superbas.[12]

At each position in the field the Superbas started a player who was considered among the best in the league. In the outfield future Hall of Famers Willie Keeler and Joe Kelley were joined by Fielder Jones, an outstanding defensive outfielder who hit higher than .300 every year but one from 1896 to 1902. The infield had four highly respected veterans. Hughie Jennings, the Hall of Fame shortstop for the great Orioles teams of the mid-nineties, had moved to first base in 1899 after hurting his arm. While Jennings' batting had begun to tail off, his fielding at first base was sensational. Reliable veteran Tom Daly was at second base. Bill Dahlen was the shortstop. Dahlen's accomplishments during his 19-year career were so distinguished that some current baseball historians consider him the "best ballplayer not in the Hall of Fame."[13] Third baseman

Brooklyn manager Ned Hanlon was noted for his knowledge of "scientific baseball" (National Baseball Hall of Fame Library, Cooperstown, New York).

Lave Cross was purchased from St. Louis in May. Cross had started his major league career as a catcher in 1887. He switched to third in the mid-nineties and continued playing until 1907, when he was 41 years old. Although he turned 34 in 1900, some of his best years were still in the future, and he was considered one of the league's top third basemen. The catchers were Deacon McGuire and Duke Farrell, who excelled both offensively and defensively.

The team's two primary substitutes were young players who had been regulars before 1900. Outfielder Jimmy Sheckard had come to Brooklyn from the minors at the age of 18 near the end of the 1897 season. He was a starter for Brooklyn in 1898 and with the Orioles in 1899, when he batted .295 and led the league in stolen bases. Infielder Gene DeMontreville had hit .343, .341, and .328 from 1896 to 1898. DeMontreville was an outstanding defensive second baseman but only adequate when moved to the left side of the infield.

Manager Ned Hanlon was considered the foremost tactician and teacher of "scientific baseball." Like Hanlon's Baltimore teams, the Superbas were noted for their ability to play smart baseball. They were aggressive in running the bases, proficient at the hit-and-run game, and quick-thinking on defense. An example of Hanlon's style of play came early in the season when the Superbas scratched out a 2–0 win over the Giants by manufacturing two runs.

In the first inning Sheckard led off with a walk. On the next play Keeler dragged a bunt between the pitcher and first baseman. Keeler was out at first base, but Sheckard went all the way to third on the sacrifice. He scored on a grounder to the shortstop. In the fifth DeMontreville led off with a bunt hit. On a hit-and-run play McGuire grounded to first. McGuire was put out, but as the first baseman flipped the ball to the pitcher covering first, DeMontreville raced to third. He scored when the Giants' shortstop fumbled a grounder. After the game, Hanlon commented on the two plays. "I have been working for some time to get the boys to go from first to third on a bunt and they have got it right. It can only be done when the pitcher and first baseman are mixed up in the play, because neither can recover in time to get a fast man. Sheckard and DeMont were good examples."[14]

For the Superbas the season was marked by two key series. The first came against the Phillies in late June. The Phillies, propelled by a powerful attack featuring future Hall of Famers Ed Delahanty, Nap Lajoie, and Elmer Flick, had grabbed the lead early in the season. The Superbas soon settled into second place but remained a few games behind the Phillies. On June 19 the Superbas moved past the Phillies into first place by a half-game. The next day the two teams began a three-game series.

The Phillies flexed their batting muscles in the first game of the series. In the fifth inning, with his team holding a slim 2–1 lead, Flick smashed a three-run home run over the right field fence. The Phillies held on to beat the Superbas, 5–4, and regained first place. The next day the Phillies were on the verge of moving further ahead in the standings. They led Brooklyn, 6–3, going into the ninth inning. But the Superbas rapped out six hits and scored five runs to win the game, 8–6, and regain first place. The following day the Superbas again beat the Phillies to increase their lead to 1½ games.

Over the next two months the Superbas built a solid lead that ranged from six to nine games. Many baseball reporters assumed the Superbas would cruise to the 1900 pennant, as they had the preceding year. They praised the team for its baseball savvy. "The Brooklyn club has more veterans than any club playing ball," remarked the *Boston Globe*. "While this crowd of old-timers have lost a little in the way of getting over ground, they have more than made up by their inside knowledge of the game. They are not satisfied with playing good ball themselves, but they have a faculty of figuring out the weak points of their opponents until it becomes very annoying." "Brooklyn looks to be the pennant winner," the *Chicago Tribune* observed. "The champions are playing ball in a manner that would be suicide for any other club to attempt, yet by the craziest sort of baserunning they win games and get away with tricks that would be laughable in a miserable baserunning club like Chicago. It is simply the brains and quick wits of the champions pitted against the slower thinking of the opposition."[15]

Although the Superbas continued to win regularly, trouble was brewing for them, both within the team and in the opposition. On the mound, the Superbas were getting great seasons from Joe McGinnity and Bill Kennedy. McGinnity won thirteen of his first fourteen decisions. On August 6 his record was 18–2. He added two more victories to that total before losing three in a row. Kennedy was 16–7 on August 6, but was beginning to lose his effectiveness. A sign of potential trouble could be seen in the fact that the next biggest winner on the Brooklyn staff was Kitson, whose record stood at 7–9 on August 6. At the beginning of the season Hanlon had worked Jack Dunn regularly as the fourth starter and given spot starts to Harry Howell and Jerry Nops. Dunn's injury meant that either Howell or Nops had to step up as a regular. Neither pitched well enough to gain Hanlon's confidence. Both were inconsistent, Howell because his stuff was not quite good enough, Nops because he couldn't control his fondness for alcoholic beverages. Dissatisfied with the makeup of his staff, Hanlon released Dunn and Nops on August 8 and signed Gus Weyhing, a 33-year-old veteran who had just been released by St. Louis. Weyhing turned out to be just one more inconsistent starter, alternating good games with disastrous ones.[16]

On August 31, Kennedy walked six men in the second inning as the Phillies pounded the Superbas, 9–4. He was again erratic in his next start, although he managed to beat Chicago, 9–5. Hanlon and the Brooklyn fans became worried. The Pittsburgh Pirates, who had moved into second place a month earlier but had not been able to threaten the Superbas' lead, had just swept Boston. They still trailed Brooklyn by five games, but they were red-hot. The Pirates came into Brooklyn on September 6 to open a five-game series. This was the second key series of the season for the Superbas, and it came at a time when Hanlon had only one pitcher, McGinnity, who was pitching effectively.

Kennedy pitched the opening game of the series and was again wild. He gave up four runs in two innings and was replaced by Kitson. The Superbas lost, 9–2. Worried that the team's season could go down the drain in this key series, Hanlon turned to McGinnity. The "Iron Man" was a willing worker. During spring training he had told a reporter he could work three times a week if necessary. Hanlon was thinking more along the lines of three times during the remaining four games of this series and about one game every three days after that. He huddled with McGinnity and the two came to an agreement.

McGinnity started the next game and battled the Pirates to a 6–6 tie. Keeler, who had four hits in the opening game of the series, had two hits and scored three runs. A doubleheader was scheduled for the next day. In the first game Pittsburgh knocked Weyhing out of the box, scoring six runs in four innings. They then roughed up Kennedy for nine more runs to win, 15–7. McGinnity pitched the second game, which was called after six innings because of darkness with Brooklyn ahead, 6–5. He gave up four runs in the fourth to lose a four-run lead but hung on as Keeler scored the winning run on a triple by Sheckard. In the final game of the series, Kitson, nursing a 5–3 lead in the eighth inning, threw a changeup to Tommy Leach. The pint-sized Leach smashed it for a three-run home run to win the game. Meanwhile, McGinnity continued his "Iron Man" stint, pitching a scoreless ninth in relief of Kitson.[17]

When Pittsburgh left town the Superbas still held a three-game lead. The momentum, however, had seemed to shift to the Pirates' favor. The two teams sparred on even terms for a week before the Superbas stumbled again. From September 18 through September 25, they lost six out of seven games, their only win coming in a game forfeited by St. Louis in the third inning after an argument with the umpire. Brooklyn's lead had dropped to one game, their record being 73–51 to Pittsburgh's 73–53. The Superbas were to close the season playing all but three of their twelve remaining games against Philadelphia and Boston, the third- and fourth-place teams, while Pittsburgh closed out against the weaker western teams. The Pirates' next series was a five-game set against Cincinnati, which had lost 17 of its last 22 games.

Looking disaster in the face but remaining unfazed, Hanlon's veterans responded by bombing the Phillies, 12–0, while Pittsburgh lost to Cincinnati. The Superbas proceeded to beat Boston three times in their next five games, while losing one and tying one. The Pirates, meanwhile, lost three of their next four games to the Reds. While the Pirates were idle the first five days of October, the Superbas thumped Boston four more times while again losing one and tying one. At that point the Superbas' lead was 5½ games. On October 6, the Superbas beat Philadelphia while Pittsburgh lost to St. Louis and the pennant race was over.

During the 27 days from September 5 through October 1, McGinnity appeared in 13 of the Superbas' 27 games. He started ten games and relieved in three, winning five, losing three, tying one, and getting a no-decision in the game forfeited by St. Louis. Hanlon used McGinnity when there was a good chance for a game to be called by darkness. Twice McGinnity pitched the second game of a doubleheader, one lasting six innings and the other five. A third game was called after seven innings. He went three innings in the forfeited game. While the team was waiting to board a train for Boston on October 1, McGinnity showed reporters a check for $100—Hanlon's side of the agreement reached at the beginning of the Pittsburgh series.[18]

Putting It Together Too Late: Pittsburgh

This was essentially the team that would win the National League pennant each of the next three seasons. Indeed, some observers attributed the Pirates' first two pennants to the fact that they retained most of the players from their 1900 team while other clubs lost strength due to the American League raids. The pennant-winning Pirates of 1901–03 were built around great pitching, the immortal Honus Wagner, and several mere mortals who were star players: Manager/left fielder Fred Clarke, center fielder Ginger Beaumont, second baseman Claude Ritchey, third baseman Tommy Leach, and first baseman Kitty Bransfield. The pitchers, Wagner, and all the other stars except Bransfield were with the team in 1900. Bransfield joined the team in 1901. The addition of Bransfield, however, was largely offset by the loss of third baseman Jimmy Williams, who jumped to Baltimore in 1901.

Pittsburgh (79–60)

Regular Lineup	AVG	OBP	SLG	R	RBI	SB
Ginger Beaumont, cf	.279	.331	.362	105	50	27
Fred Clarke, lf	.276	.368	.396	84	32	21
Jimmy Williams, 3b	.264	.323	.389	73	68	18
Honus Wagner, ss	.381	.434	.573	107	100	38
Tom O'Brien, 1b	.290	.349	.404	61	61	12
or Duff Cooley, 1b	.201	.243	.241	30	22	9
Claude Ritchey, 2b	.292	.339	.368	62	67	18
Chief Zimmer, c	.295	.361	.395	27	35	4
or Jack O'Connor, c*	.235	.271	.268	19	25	5
Fred Ely, ss	.244	.272	.282	60	51	6
Leading Pitchers	W	L	PCT	IP	H	ERA
Deacon Phillippe	20	13	.606	279	274	2.84
Jesse Tannehill	20	6	.769	234	247	2.88
Sam Leever	15	13	.536	232.7	236	2.71
Jack Chesbro	15	13	.536	215.7	220	3.67
Rube Waddell	8	13	.381	208.7	176	2.37

*Includes record with St. Louis

At the outset of the 1900 season, most baseball writers recognized that the Pirates were a very talented team. But many of them questioned whether Clarke could bring them together as a cohesive unit.[19] As it turned out, much of the season passed by before the Pirates began winning with any great consistency. They were still at .500 on June 29, and were only four games over .500 as late as August 5. They struggled largely because they encountered problems at three key positions—first base, left field, and Rube Waddell's spot in the pitching rotation.

Both Pittsburgh and Louisville had been weak at first base in 1899. When the two teams merged, the weakness was still there. Clarke thought he had solved the problem when he acquired Duff Cooley from the Phillies at the end of April. Cooley was a smart veteran who had always hit well and fielded adequately in center field and first base. But for the Pirates he hit .201. It wasn't until August, when Clarke moved substitute outfielder Tom O'Brien to first, that the position was adequately filled.

Although Clarke was one of the best outfielders in the league, both defensively and at the bat, he was terrible at the beginning of the 1900 season. Clarke had hit .342 in 1899, but he didn't get his first hit until the sixth game of the season. After 22 games he was batting .138, and was suffering from a debilitating kidney illness. On June 7 he left the team to recuperate at a health spa. By then almost one-third of the season had passed and he had raised his batting average only to .153. He returned to the lineup on June 26, well-rested and once again capable of playing at his best. From then until the end of the season he hit .327 and scored 67 runs in 98 games.[20]

The third problem area involved Waddell's personality. He and Clarke were incompatible. Clarke was a disciplinarian, an intense competitor, and very serious about professional baseball. Waddell was almost childlike in his approach to life. He had very little self-discipline. Rube was very competitive but he could lose his focus. He would hold up a game to watch fire wagons go by, show up late for a start because he was busy playing marbles with kids under the stands, or respond to the opposing team's razzing by making a pick-off throw to first when no baserunner was there. And Rube had a very busy nightlife, often frequenting bars in Pittsburgh and elsewhere. By July Clarke's patience with Rube's act had run out. He suspended Rube indefinitely. Rube pitched semi-pro ball for three weeks and then was farmed to Milwaukee, where he won ten games while losing only three for Connie Mack.[21]

At the end of July Clarke expressed regret over Rube's absence, saying, "If Waddell had acted right with us, we would have been either tied with or ahead of Brooklyn. He can pitch great ball when he is right."[22] On September 1, Clarke decided to "pull the string" on Rube's contract. He brought him back from Milwaukee, and Rube pitched regularly from then until the end of the season. For the most part he pitched well, but he couldn't provide the spark needed to propel the team ahead of the Superbas.

One position that caused no problems for the Pirates in 1900 was right field. Honus Wagner played regularly there, the only year he would be allowed to settle into one position until 1903, his seventh major league season. Wagner responded with one of his greatest years. He got off to a great start. In mid–May, after 24 games, he was batting .490. Five weeks later his average was at .446, with 16 doubles, 12 triples and one home run in 168 at-bats. A "slump" in late July and early August brought his average down into the .370s, but he was back at the .400 level as late as the last week of September. At season's end he led the league in batting with a .381 average. He also led in doubles (45), triples (22), and slugging percentage (.573).

Wagner's talents, of course, extended to all aspects of the game. The outfield allowed him to show his speed and great throwing arm. After one game, a Brooklyn reporter wrote, "There are ballplayers who can pose with better effect before the camera than Hans Wagner, but he can give many of the fashion plates a big handicap when it comes to all-around ability on the diamond. He covers acres of territory and the Pittsburgh reporters have become accustomed to put down as an out anything that goes in the direction of the Flying Dutchman. He is as ungainly as an elephant when chasing flies, but he manages to get under the ball, as five Brooklyn batters will testify as a result of yesterday's game."[23]

On the bases Wagner was smart and aggressive. He stole 38 bases in 1900, fifth-best in the league. But his value on the basepaths went beyond stolen bases. He looked for any opportunity to take an extra base, and was usually successful. In a game against Cincinnati he scored from second base after the catcher and third baseman collided while catching a foul pop-up. Against Boston he stole second base and then came all the way home when the catcher's throw bounced about a dozen feet from the bag. A month later he victimized the same catcher by scoring from third on a short passed ball.[24]

Wagner was at his best during the Pirates' late drive for the pennant. In the first game of their series against Boston, the Pirates trailed, 7–5, entering the ninth. The first two batters singled. The next batter sacrificed, bringing up Wagner. Honus drove the first pitch over Boston's short left field fence to win the game. Two blow-out victories followed. Wagner scored the winning run as the Pirates took the fourth game, 6–5, and two more runs in a 5–2 victory to cap the five-game sweep. Wagner played in only four of the five games in the key Brooklyn series that followed. In those games he got nine hits and scored eight runs.

On September 10, Wagner's mother died. He took the next week off for her funeral. When he returned, he resumed his outstanding play, going 4-for-5 in a victory over New York. He continued to hit well until the last week of September, when he cooled off against Cincinnati in the series that doomed the team's pennant chances.

A Formidable Batting Order: Philadelphia

As a team the Phillies of the 1890s weren't too interested in "scientific baseball." No "baby bunt" for them. They played in the Baker Bowl, a hitter's park, and they loved to smash the ball.[25] The 1900 team departed from that model somewhat. It had three of the league's top sluggers, but added speed and some finesse to its attack.

The first two batters in the Phillies' lineup, Roy Thomas and Jimmy Slagle, were little guys who, fittingly, played "little ball." Their game was to get on base, move around through the sacrifice, hit-and-run or steal, and wait for the sluggers to bring them in. Following those two speedsters were three of the league's premier power hitters. Until Honus Wagner asserted himself with his great 1900 season, most baseball fans thought the top slugger in the league was the Phillies' number three batter, Ed Delahanty. Those who didn't think Delahanty was the best slugger usually considered Nap Lajoie to be the best. He batted cleanup for the Phillies. And in 1900 the Phillies' number five hitter, Elmer Flick, outhit both Delahanty and Lajoie.

Philadelphia (75–63)

Regular Lineup	AVG	OBP	SLG	R	RBI	SB
Roy Thomas, cf	.316	.451	.335	132	33	37
Jimmy Slagle, lf	.287	.358	.347	115	45	34
Ed Delahanty, 1b	.323	.378	.430	82	109	16
Nap Lajoie, 2b	.337	.362	.510	95	92	22
Elmer Flick, rf	.367	.441	.545	106	110	35
Ed McFarland, c	.305	.364	.392	50	38	9
or Klondike Douglass, c	.300	.360	.406	23	25	7
Harry Wolverton, 3b*	.279	.322	.368	44	58	5
Monte Cross, ss	.202	.289	.258	59	62	19
Leading Pitchers	W	L	PCT	IP	H	ERA
Al Orth	14	14	.500	262	302	3.78

Red Donahue	15	10	.600	240	299	3.60
Chick Fraser	15	9	.625	223.3	250	3.14
Bill Bernhard	15	10	.600	218.7	284	4.77
Wiley Piatt	9	10	.474	160.7	194	4.65

*Includes record with Chicago

Midway through the season a Cincinnati writer saluted these five, as well as Ed McFarland, who followed them in the lineup. "It is doubtful if there was ever a team in the League that presented such a formidable batting front as the Phillies," the writer claimed. "The first six batsmen are about as expert with the stick as it is possible for men to become. Thomas, who reaches first about as often as any man in the business, owing to his ability to foul off the ball and his speed in getting to first on infield hits, leads, Slagle coming next with his ability for bunting and place hitting, and sprinting ability added. Delahanty is next, the acknowledged long distance hitter. Lajoie, equally as hard a hitter and almost as scientific, follows. Flick, who has speed on the bases, ability to bunt or line them out and an eye for placing the ball, comes next, while McFarland, with his famous and effective one-handed swing, brings up the rear of this sextette of the greatest batting line-up in the League."[26]

Their formidable offense enabled the Phillies to jump off to a good start. They looked like possible pennant winners. At the end of May, however, Lajoie and Flick got into an argument in the dressing room and wound up trading punches. Flick did little damage to Lajoie, but Lajoie did major harm. To himself, that is. One of his punches missed Flick but hit the wall behind Flick, breaking Lajoie's thumb. Lajoie missed the next six weeks because of the injury.[27]

Phillies fans were sure the fight was the beginning of their team's annual collapse. The collapse never came. But on June 20, the Phillies dropped behind the Superbas and slowly slipped further behind as the season progressed. Pittsburgh passed them in mid–August, but Philadelphia held off challenges from Boston and Chicago to finish third.

Faded Glory: Boston

When the 1900 season opened on April 19, Boston fans had every reason to believe their team would be in the thick of a lively pennant race. The Beaneaters had finished second in 1899, eight games behind Brooklyn. Their key players were all returning in 1900 and the team had added two potential stars in Buck Freeman and Bill Dinneen. The team boasted the best pitcher of the 1890s (Charles "Kid" Nichols), a pitcher coming off a 27-win season (Vic Willis), the best third baseman in baseball (Jimmy Collins), a man considered the league's best defensive first baseman (Fred Tenney), a great shortstop (Herman Long), and the home run sensation of 1899 (Freeman). What could go wrong?

As it turned out, just about everything. The Beaneaters' opening game seemed to foreshadow the miseries that would plague the team throughout the season. Attendance was so large that the overflow ringed the outfield, bringing about a game rule that any ball hit into the crowd on the fly was limited to a single. The visiting team, the slugging Philadelphia Phillies, took liberal advantage of the rule, scoring five runs in each of the first two innings off Willis. The Beaneaters battled back gamely. Going into the bottom of the ninth, they trailed, 17–8. To lead off the inning, Selee sent up "Home Run Freeman" as a pinch-hitter. He drilled a pitch over the right field fence. An avalanche of hits followed, as eight more runs came in, tying the game, 17–17. In the tenth Nichols, pitching in relief, walked the first batter, Ed Delahanty. The next batter hit an apparent double-play grounder to Bobby Lowe, Boston's sure-handed second baseman. The ball went through Lowe's hands for a two-base error. A double followed for two runs and a heart-breaking 19–17 loss for the Beaneaters.

Boston (66–72)

Regular Lineup	AVG	OBP	SLG	R	RBI	SB
Billy Hamilton, cf	.333	.449	.396	103	47	32
Herman Long, ss	.261	.325	.391	80	66	26
or Shad Barry, ut	.260	.301	.366	40	37	9
Chick Stahl, lf	.295	.336	.421	88	82	27
Fred Tenney, 1b	.279	.346	.339	77	56	17
Jimmy Collins, 3b	.304	.352	.394	104	95	23
Buck Freeman, rf	.301	.355	.452	58	65	10
Bobby Lowe, 2b	.278	.323	.342	65	71	15
Boileryard Clarke, c	.315	.344	.359	35	30	0
or Billy Sullivan, c	.273	.302	.399	36	41	4
Leading Pitchers	**W**	**L**	**PCT**	**IP**	**H**	**ERA**
Bill Dinneen	20	14	.588	320.7	304	3.12
Vic Willis	10	17	.370	236	258	4.19
Kid Nichols	13	16	.448	231.3	215	3.07
Ted Lewis	13	12	.520	209	215	4.13

As if to emphasize that a new era had dawned for Beaneater fans, the next day Lowe repeated his performance. With one out in the eleventh inning of a 4–4 game, he again booted a double-play grounder to let in the winning run. Long got into the act a few days later when he threw the ball away twice to give New York three runs in a 4–3 loss. Catcher Bill Clarke, suffering from a sore shoulder, regularly made poor throws to the bases. After one game the *Boston Globe* reporter commented, "Clarke managed to make his usual wild throw to center field after having a passed ball."[28] In their first nine games, the Beaneaters committed 35 errors.

Boston's pennant-winning teams had been built around a solid defense and great pitching. Now, their vaunted "Stonewall Infield" was seemingly full of holes and their pitching staff became riddled with injuries. On April 28, Nichols strained a ligament in his pitching arm, which sidelined him for six weeks. Willis complained of shoulder and back soreness but continued to pitch and was hit hard. On May 1, Long, playing with his usual exuberance, injured his ankle sliding into first base while trying to beat out a grounder. He was out of the lineup for a month. His replacement, all-purpose utility man Shad Barry, had little range at shortstop. This put more pressure on the already-shaky pitching staff.

During the first three weeks of May, Boston won whenever it was able to score at least ten runs in a game. That was three games. By May 22, the Beaneaters were in last place with a 5–17 record. It seemed like they would go from pennant winners to cellar dwellers in two short years. "There was a time a few years ago, when a bad start such as the Bostons got this year did not put them out of the race," observed Brooklyn manager Ned Hanlon. "But it is different now, and I do not expect any trouble from that source this year."[29]

Hanlon's analysis eventually proved correct. But the Beaneaters were not ready to be pronounced dead. On May 23, Freeman blasted a two-run homer to beat St. Louis, 3–2. The team went to Cincinnati, where it took two of three, and then returned home. There Long rejoined the team. He played inspired ball; nearly every game featured a great stop or catch by the "King of Shortstops." He stood out in a 3–1 victory over Pittsburgh on June 12. "Herman Long made one more of his phenomenal catches," reported the *Boston Globe*. "Williams, one of the heaviest hitters in the league, met the ball with a smash that sounded like the breaking of a bedslat in a garret. Long, ever on the alert, ran two steps and went into the air like a man on a springboard. His bare hand went across his face high over his head, and then he came back to earth with a header, clinging to the ball. As the baserunners had started on the round a double play was easy. The play was cheered to the echo."[30] The Beaneaters ran off eight straight wins and won 16 of 19 games. On June 14, they were in third place, one game over .500 (21–20), and looking forward to a four-game series with the second-place Brooklyn Superbas.

Entering the series the Beaneaters' revival was the talk of the baseball world. But it was not to be the beginning of a storybook comeback. The Superbas swept the series. Worse yet, they beat the Beaneaters at their own game. The 1893 Boston team had either invented or popularized the hit-and-run tactic, depending upon how one wishes to interpret the claims of players who were "old-timers" in the 1890s. By 1900 everyone used the tactic, but none better than the Superbas in their June 15–19 sweep of the Beaneaters. After the last game, a 10–4 drubbing, the *Globe* lamented, "The baseball fans were very much disappointed at the result of the last four games in this city. Lowe, perhaps, came in for the greatest censure for his light stick work and disposition to cover second base when the ball was marked for the right field."[31] The criticism of Lowe's fielding was directed at his repeatedly being outwitted on the hit-and-run play, racing to second with the intention of tagging out a would-be base stealer while the Brooklyn batter punched the ball through his vacated position for a hit.

Boston recovered from the Brooklyn defeats. They took two out of three from both New York and Philadelphia, and won the opening game of a western trip to go two games above .500. But an eight-game losing streak followed. Their season remained a long struggle to surpass the break-even mark. As late as September 26, Boston was 64–61, and within striking distance of third place. But the team ended the season as it had started it, losing eleven of its last thirteen decisions, ending up in fourth place at 66–72, a distant 17 games behind first-place Brooklyn.

Spoiled Broth: St. Louis

The Cardinals should have enjoyed the best leadership in the league. Besides Pat Tebeau, their manager, they had two players who were skippers in 1899. Third baseman John McGraw was already being hailed as a great manager for his inspiring leadership of the 1899 Orioles. Right fielder Patsy Donovan had led the Pirates to a 69–58 record in 1899. In addition, catcher Wilbert Robinson had long been hailed as a great handler of pitchers, acting almost as an unofficial pitching coach for Ned Hanlon.

St. Louis (65–75)

Regular Lineup	AVG	OBP	SLG	R	RBI	SB
John McGraw, 3b	.344	.505	.416	84	33	29
Jesse Burkett, lf	.363	.429	.474	88	68	32
Emmet Heidrick, cf	.301	.338	.383	51	45	22
Pat Donovan, rf	.316	.368	.342	78	61	45
or Mike Donlin, cf-rf	.326	.361	.507	40	48	14
Bobby Wallace, ss	.268	.328	.381	70	70	7
Bill Keister, 2b	.300	.347	.398	78	72	32
Dan McGann, 1b	.297	.376	.387	79	58	26
Lou Criger, c	.271	.286	.361	31	38	5
or Wilbert Robinson, c	.248	.291	.281	26	28	7
Leading Pitchers	**W**	**L**	**PCT**	**IP**	**H**	**ERA**
Cy Young	19	19	.500	321.3	337	3.00
Bert Jones	13	19	.406	292.7	334	3.54
Jack Powell	17	16	.515	287.7	325	4.44
Willie Sudhoff	6	8	.429	127	128	2.76

But it appeared to be a case of too many cooks spoiling the broth. The Cardinals never came close to first place. They had a brief hot spell in May, shortly after McGraw and Robinson joined the team, and climbed as high as a tie for second place. Then they went into a season-long slump, spending most of the campaign in sixth or seventh place. They managed to slip into a tie for fifth with Chicago when the season ended because the Orphans played the last few games of the year as if they were in a coma.

McGraw was widely blamed for the Cardinals' poor play. St. Louis fans evidently expected McGraw to transform the team into one that played like the championship Baltimore Orioles teams. But, although McGraw was named team captain when he joined the Cardinals, he had little real control over their performance. The Cardinals were Tebeau's team, and Tebeau's style of play was directly opposite to that of the Orioles. The Orioles stressed aggressiveness and teamwork between batter and baserunner. Tebeau believed in letting the batters wait for their pitch and then try to hit it as hard as they could. At first McGraw tried to impart his approach to his teammates, though being careful to stay within the confines of his authority as team captain. Several times he asked Jesse Burkett to protect the baserunner by offering at the ball or blocking the catcher's view when the runner was trying to steal. Burkett, a veteran who had twice led the league in batting, simply ignored the advice.[32]

By midseason McGraw had apparently lost interest in trying to lead the St. Louis team in any but a perfunctory way. When he missed several games in June after being spiked, he chose to attend the horse races rather than the Cardinals' games. He did the same later in the season when he was out of action with a painful outbreak of boils.[33] As a player, however, he had another sterling season. He was now the best leadoff man in the game, averaging almost a walk a game and owning one of the highest batting averages in the league. His on-base percentage in 1900 was .505. At the beginning of August he was batting over .400, although a late-season slump brought his final average down to .344. He stole 29 bases and scored 84 runs in only 99 games.

A Team of Fighters: Chicago

This was a scrappy team. Unfortunately, too many of its scraps had nothing to do with winning games. In spring training catcher Tim Donahue and third baseman Harry Wolverton traded punches. Donahue had a sarcastic sense of humor that he sometimes aimed at his teammates. In conversations with local reporters, he was effusive in praising the abilities of young Bill Bradley, a rival for Wolverton's position. One of Donahue's wisecracks set off Wolverton, who was worried about losing his job. Wolverton responded by attacking Donahue. A week into the season the Orphans traded Wolverton to Philadelphia.[34]

In May, second baseman Cupid Childs encountered Pittsburgh's Fred Clarke at a train station. He quietly took off his hat and coat, then attacked Clarke. He landed a couple of punches, as did Clarke. The two grabbed each other, fell to the platform and wrestled for a few moments before teammates could separate them. The train station fight was a continuation of a confrontation that had started in that day's game when Clarke slammed into Childs while breaking up a double play.[35]

By midseason Donahue and outfielder Jimmy Ryan were feuding. Ryan was about as tactless as Donahue, but less witty in his remarks. Chicago writers concluded that the only solution to their feud, which had been simmering for several seasons, was to let one of them go.[36] Both were gone from Chicago after the 1900 season. Ironically, they again became teammates briefly for the Washington Senators in 1902.

Chicago (65–75)

Regular Lineup	AVG	OBP	SLG	R	RBI	SB
Jack McCarthy, lf	.294	.329	.354	68	48	22
Cupid Childs, 2b	.241	.323	.286	67	44	15
Sam Mertes, cf-rf–1b	.295	.356	.407	72	60	38
Jimmy Ryan, rf	.277	.329	.393	66	59	19
or Danny Green, cf	.298	.339	.416	63	49	28
John Ganzel, 1b	.275	.316	.394	29	32	5
Bill Bradley, 3b	.282	.330	.399	63	49	14
Barry McCormick, ss–3b	.219	.292	.303	35	48	8
or Bill Clingman, ss	.208	.292	.245	15	11	6
Tim Donahue, c	.236	.313	.292	21	17	8
or Frank Chance, c	.295	.413	.396	26	13	8

Leading Pitchers	W	L	PCT	IP	H	ERA
Jimmy Callahan	13	16	.448	285.3	347	3.82
Clark Griffith	14	13	.519	248	245	3.05
Ned Garvin	10	18	.357	246.3	225	2.41
Jack Taylor	10	17	.370	222.3	226	2.55
Jock Menefee	9	4	.692	117	140	3.85

In September outfielder Sam Mertes, possibly fatigued from his season's work and not wanting to tax his fighting abilities, took on a relatively easy opponent. He scored a one-punch TKO over one of the reporters who covered the team. The fight occurred aboard the team's train. A fellow reporter described Mertes' pugilistic strategy, writing, "He met the reporter in a narrow passageway in the sleeper and cleverly sidestepped, enticing his adversary into the belief that he was politely standing aside to let him pass. Then as the reporter went by Mertes swung his right and the battle was over. The reporter can now give expert testimony as to the effect of a solar plexus blow without interviewing [boxers] Corbett or Ruhlin."[37]

Mertes was the victim of mistreatment, in this case at the hands of a manager trying to find some way to inject offense into a weak batting order. Although he had played second base in the minors, Mertes' fielding skills were better suited for the outfield. Mertes had played for manager Tom Loftus in the minors. Loftus admired his athleticism and thought he might be able to help the team by moving to the infield. When first baseman John Ganzel became sick, Loftus replaced him with Mertes. Sam did well for a few games before his inexperience caught up with him. Shortstop Bill Clingman made two wild throws "and Mertes aggravated each throw," the *Chicago Tribune* reported, "by making froglike dives toward the ball." Mertes' difficulties gave the opposition two unearned runs. To save Mertes from further embarrassment, Loftus sent in Ganzel to complete the game at first base.[38]

A couple of weeks later, Loftus was ready to throw Mertes back into the fire. Shortstop Bill Clingman, normally a good fielder and mediocre hitter, had been suffering through a terrible season in the field while upholding his reputation as an easy out at the plate. Thinking that "good hit, no field" was better than "no hit, no field," Loftus decided to try Mertes at shortstop. After a week in which Mertes made only two errors, mostly because he couldn't manage to get in front of many grounders, Loftus quietly moved him back to the outfield.[39]

Good Idea, Bad Timing: Cincinnati

If Branch Rickey was the father of the modern farm system, the Reds' owner, John T. Brush, might be considered its grandfather. Brush had a well-deserved reputation as a disagreeable cuss, but he was innovative. His hometown was Indianapolis, where he owned a team in the Class A Western League. (Class A was the highest minor league classification at the time.) In the mid–1890s Brush devised a plan to help both his hometown and his National League teams.

During the drafting period that ran for several months each fall, Cincinnati would

Cincinnati owner John T. Brush was smart and innovative, but was a divisive force among National League owners (Library of Congress).

select Indianapolis' best players, as well as a few players from other teams. Later the Reds would sell most of those players back to Indianapolis, retaining a couple for the major league team and disposing of the remainders by selling or releasing them, or by sending them to Indianapolis with a "string attached." The "string" was an agreement whereby Cincinnati could recall the player in midseason. Brush's scheme served two purposes. It offered protection to the Indianapolis team during the draft period; the other teams could not draft Indianapolis' best players because Brush had already claimed them. It also served as a means by which Cincinnati could enable promising young players to gain experience while the Reds maintained control over them, which otherwise would not have been possible under the existing rules. Several other teams soon followed his lead. Some minor league owners saw these arrangements as a threat to their welfare. *The Sporting News* also believed the "farming evil" should be stamped out. It served as a conduit for statements blasting Brush and others who followed the practice. The benefits of the system were enough that it continued despite a vigorous campaign to outlaw it.[40]

Neither Cincinnati nor the other teams that tried it gained much from these nascent farming efforts. Team budgets were so tight that no more than a handful of players were farmed out in any one year. Few players were given more than one season to develop their talents, and the vast majority of farmed players failed to succeed at the major league level.

Most of the new players on the National League rosters continued to come through the two accepted methods of adding players—purchase from a minor league team at a negotiated price or acquisition through the draft at a fixed price. Knowing they would likely lose their top players through the fall draft, minor league owners usually tried to sell them before the end of the minor league season at a price above the draft price. The National League teams would try out their new acquisitions when the major league season began winding down in late August and September. If a player showed promise, he would be invited to join the team the next spring for a longer, more thorough trial.

In preparation for the 1900 season, Brush decided on an aggressive push to bring young talent onto the Cincinnati team. While other teams were ignoring minor league talent at the end of the 1899 season, knowing that many good major league players would become available when league reduction occurred, Brush purchased more than a dozen of the best minor league prospects. In the spring of 1900, when other teams were rounding out their rosters with players cut loose during the reduction, Brush declined to participate in the buying. "The Reds are a strong team," he insisted. "Last fall we purchased the players that were considered the cream of the minor leagues."[41]

Cincinnati (62–77)

Regular Lineup	AVG	OBP	SLG	R	RBI	SB
Jimmy Barrett, cf	.316	.400	.389	114	42	44
Tommy Corcoran, ss	.245	.278	.325	64	54	27
Jake Beckley, 1b	.341	.389	.434	98	94	23
Sam Crawford, rf	.260	.314	.429	68	59	14
or Algie McBride, rf	.275	.320	.374	59	59	12
Charlie Irwin, 3b	.273	.314	.363	59	44	9
Harry Steinfeldt, 2b-3b	.245	.292	.341	57	66	14
or Joe Quinn, 2b*	.272	.323	.312	30	36	11
Heinie Peitz, c	.255	.318	.330	34	34	5
or Mike Kahoe, c	.189	.215	.257	18	9	3
Leading Pitchers	**W**	**L**	**PCT**	**IP**	**H**	**ERA**
Ed Scott	17	20	.459	315	370	3.86
Noodles Hahn	16	20	.444	311.3	306	3.27
Doc Newton	9	15	.375	235.7	255	4.12
Bill Phillips	9	11	.450	207.3	229	4.30
Ted Breitenstein	10	10	.500	192.3	205	3.65

*Includes record with St. Louis

Few observers agreed with Brush's assessment. A Cincinnati reporter thought sixth place was about as high as the team could hope to finish. Others thought that was too optimistic. As it turned out the skeptics were right. The Reds ended up in seventh place, only 1½ games out of last place. But Brush wasn't far wrong. The Reds were only 4½ games out of fourth place.

How good were the players Brush selected? Let's take a look at the careers of some of the players he acquired in the fall of 1899:

Sam Crawford, outfielder–19 years, 2,517 games, .309 batting average, 1,391 runs, 1,525 RBIs, 309 triples (all-time triples leader). Elected to the Baseball Hall of Fame in 1957.

Kid Elberfeld, shortstop—14 years, 1,292 games, .271 batting average. Noted for good defense, good batting average for Deadball Era, terrible temper for any era. Elberfeld was released by the Reds before the 1900 season started, largely because he wasn't impressive at third base and wasn't going to replace the Reds' captain, Tommy Corcoran, at shortstop.

Socks Seybold, outfielder—9 years, 997 games, .294 batting average, batted in middle of order for two pennant-winning Philadelphia Athletics teams. Reds manager Buck Ewing let Seybold sit around for a few weeks before letting him play in the fall of 1899. Seybold, rusty from the lack of work, didn't play well and was sent to Indianapolis for the 1900 season.

Jimmy Barrett, outfielder—10 years, 866 games, .291 batting average. One of the top outfielders in baseball for five years; his career was sidetracked by injury.

Mike Kahoe, catcher—11 years, 410 games, .212 batting average. Was great defensive catcher, couldn't hit. He had been on the Indianapolis farm team for several years by 1899.

Phil Geier, outfielder—5 years, 349 games, .249 batting average.

Danny Shay, infielder—4 years, 231 games, .240 batting average.

Casey Patten, pitcher—8 years, 106 wins, 128 losses, 3.36 ERA. Patten was the ace of the Washington Senators' staff for several years. The Reds farmed him to Kansas City in 1900.

Bill Phillips—7 years, 70 wins, 76 losses, 4.09 ERA. Phillips was one of the players Brush had kept in Indianapolis for several years. He was a regular starter for the Reds through the 1903 season.

Doc Newton, pitcher—8 years, 54 wins, 72 losses, 3.22 ERA. Newton spurned the major leagues for the Pacific Coast League in 1903–04. He twice won 30 games there in what would have been the peak of his career.

Jack Cronin, pitcher—7 years, 43 wins, 58 losses, 3.40 ERA.

Ed Scott, pitcher—2 years, 23 wins, 26 losses, 4.01 ERA. Scott was the workhorse of the Cincinnati staff in 1900, pitching 315 innings and going 17–20. He came down with a sore arm while pitching for Cleveland in 1901, ending his major league career.

Emil Frisk, pitcher/outfielder—2 years, 8 wins, 10 losses as a pitcher; 2 years, 131 games, .261 batting average as an outfielder.

Cincinnati's fans didn't get a chance to fully appreciate the wealth of talent Brush assembled in preparation for the 1900 season. It never had a chance to mature in the Queen City. Limited roster space forced the Reds to dispose of several players, such as Elberfeld, Seybold and Patten, who might have helped them in 1900 had they been given a chance. Others, such as Geier, Shay and Frisk, weren't good enough for the highly talented teams of 1900, though they were good enough to play several years in the majors afterwards, when there were sixteen major league teams rather than only eight.

Eventually trades and American League raids took away all but one of these promising new players. Phillips remained with Cincinnati for several years, but Crawford was the only other member of the group who remained with the Reds past 1901, and he signed with Detroit after the 1902 season. Brush left the Reds in 1902, selling the team midway through the season to become the new owner of the New York Giants.

Polishing the Big Apple's Team

It took a while for the Giants to piece together their 1900 team. Each of the magnates wanted to see an improved team in New York, but not at the expense of his own team. When Giants owner Andrew Freedman encouraged donations, the magnates sent him the best players they didn't want. During spring training spare parts arrived from throughout the league. From the defunct Washington team came Win Mercer, a pretty fair pitcher who wanted to move to third base. Pittsburgh sent over Frank Bowerman, a journeyman catcher who could easily be spared by the talent-rich Pirates. Boston donated two promising youngsters, Charlie Frisbee and Charlie Hickman. Both looked like they could hit, but neither seemed too good at catching the ball. Cincinnati owner John T. Brush, ever the hard-headed businessman (and, by the way, a minority stockholder of the Giants), contributed two solid players in pitcher Pink Hawley and outfielder Kip Selbach. Both men suffered from foot-in-the-mouth disease and had worn out their welcome in Cincinnati.[42]

New York (60–78)

Regular Lineup	AVG	OBP	SLG	R	RBI	SB
Geo. Van Haltren, cf	.315	.371	.398	114	51	45
Kip Selbach, lf	.337	.425	.461	98	68	36
Jack Doyle, 1b	.267	.317	.325	69	66	34
Elmer Smith, rf*	.265	.337	.369	61	52	19
George Davis, ss	.319	.376	.406	69	61	29
or Win Mercer, inf-p	.294	.366	.310	32	27	15
Kid Gleason, 2b	.248	.280	.295	60	29	23
Charlie Hickman, 3b	.313	.359	.482	65	91	10
Frank Bowerman, c	.241	.268	.293	25	42	10
or Mike Grady, c	.219	.331	.283	36	27	9
Leading Pitchers	W	L	PCT	IP	H	ERA
Bill Carrick	19	22	.463	341.7	415	3.53
Pink Hawley	18	18	.500	329.3	377	3.53
Win Mercer	13	17	.433	242.7	303	3.86
Ed Doheny	4	14	.222	133.7	148	5.45

*Includes record with Cincinnati

After manager Buck Ewing sorted things out, he still had holes at third base and right field. He gave Mercer a chance to prove he could play third base. Mercer's .802 fielding average after 19 games proved he needed to go back to the mound. Ewing then turned the position over to Hickman. Hickman was an improvement over Mercer—his fielding average was .842, only about 60 points below an acceptable level in 1900. For a while Hickman's batting prowess matched his fielding ability as he struggled to bat .200. But in July Charlie started slugging the ball into the outer reaches of the Polo Grounds. The fans loved it. Hickman became one of their favorites, and the more they cheered, the better Charlie hit. He put together a 26-game hitting streak. He smacked out the "longest hit of the year" in the New York, Pittsburgh and Boston ballparks. In September he crept up to second in the league in home runs and received the nickname "Home Run Hickman." He ended the season with a .313 batting average and was among the league leaders in triples, home runs and slugging average.[43]

The hole in right field took longer to plug. Frisbee lasted four games. He managed to reach five fly balls in those games, catching two and dropping three. Then two outfielders who couldn't do the job for the Giants in 1899 showed they still couldn't do it in 1900. With no other help in sight, Brush again sent an aid package to the Giants. This one was in the form of Elmer Smith, one of the league's better outfielders for a decade, now a journeyman finishing out his career. Smith was adequate, and thus a big improvement over his predecessors in right field.

When the season began the Giants appeared to have a decent pitching staff. But two of their starters, Cy Seymour and Ed Doheny, couldn't locate home plate. Seymour, a 25-game winner in 1898, walked 54 batters in 53 innings. He was sent to a minor league team in June in hopes of regaining his control there. Doheny walked 6.5 batters per game. He was 4–12 when the Giants loaned him to the American League Chicago White Stockings in late July. The only New York pitcher who pitched well at the beginning of the season was Bill Carrick. Ewing and his successor, George Davis, rewarded Carrick for his good work by trotting him out to the mound as often as possible. Eight times Carrick pitched with two days' rest, and three times with one day off. Twice he pitched two days in a row. By the season's end he had pitched 341⅔ innings, which was still two innings less than the likewise-overworked McGinnity threw for Brooklyn.

Ewing quit as manager on July 13. Shortly afterwards he stated that Davis, his successor, was the leader of a clique that had worked against him.[44] While the team apparently was split into two or three warring cliques, its obvious weaknesses were likely more responsible for the Giants' losses than the men named by Ewing. Those weaknesses had largely been addressed by the time Ewing resigned. Hickman was hitting almost well enough to offset his terrible defense at third, Elmer Smith was an able right fielder, and the pitching stabilized somewhat. Mercer pitched well once he went back to the mound, and Hawley did a complete turnaround. He was 15–7 after June. The improvements didn't transform the Giants into world-beaters, but it did make them competitive with the rest of the league. They had a brief spurt under Davis where they won ten out of fourteen games, then settled into a win one, lose one pattern for the rest of the season.

Big Ed Decided to Bunt

During the 1890s the sacrifice was a key part of each team's offensive strategy. Every team sacrificed much more often than modern teams do, and every player was called upon to sacrifice at least occasionally. Even a team's cleanup hitter would sacrifice a few times each year. But some of the better hitters, the sluggers of the era, did not like to sacrifice and avoided doing so as much as possible. One of those players was Ed Delahanty. Delahanty's reputation as a slugger was such that the term "a Delahanty bunt" referred not to a ball dumped into the infield, but to a line drive reaching the outfield wall.[45] From 1894, the first year such records were kept, through 1899, Delahanty sacrificed between four and six times a year. The 1900 season, however, was different. Delahanty laid down 14 sacrifice bunts that season and beat out several more while attempting to sacrifice.

Delahanty's changed attitude regarding the sacrifice bunt may have grown out of his becoming the Phillies' captain midway through the 1899 season. As captain, Delahanty probably felt a deeper sense of responsibility to the club and the other players. During the last month of that season, the Phillies were battling to win $2,500 in prize money their owner had offered for finishing in second place. Knowing that opposing fielders normally played deeper for him than for other batters, Delahanty decided to alter his approach at the plate. He started slapping the ball over the infield, trying to place the ball for hits rather than slugging it. The strategy worked. He hit .434 over the last 30 games of the season. He finished 1899 with a league-leading .410 average. In 1900 Delahanty returned to his normal style of batting, but resorted to the sacrifice bunt more often than ever before.[46]

Baseball teams did not have advance scouts—or for that matter, any full-time scouts—in 1900. But if advance scouts had existed then, they might have discerned a pattern in Delahanty's sacrifice attempts. As was mentioned above, the Phillies' batting order featured two small, fast men at the top of the order followed by three sluggers—Delahanty, Nap Lajoie, and Elmer Flick.

Leadoff batter Roy Thomas had a .451 on-base percentage in 1900. It was not unusual for him to open a game or an inning by reaching first base. The next batter, Jimmy Slagle, would often sacrifice Thomas to second. But Slagle was very fast and an adept bunter, as well as a good place hitter. He would at times beat out a sacrifice bunt or otherwise reach first base while moving Thomas to second. When these two were on first and second with no one out, Delahanty often chose to give himself up, laying down a bunt in an attempt to move the runners up a base.

Game reports show at least 13 times during the season when Delahanty chose to bunt in that situation. Interestingly, on nine of those occasions, Slagle was safe at first on a sacrifice attempt that preceded Delahanty's sacrifice attempt. On only one of the 13 sacrifice attempts did Delahanty fail to advance the runner. Seven times he was safe at first on his sacrifice attempt (five were hits, two times the game report doesn't specify a hit or error). Five times he was thrown out at first and credited with a sacrifice.

While Earl Weaver and most sabermetricians would groan at the thought of the game's foremost slugger bunting with two men on base and no outs, Delahanty's strategy seemed to work very well. The game reports show the Phillies scoring every time Delahanty tried it. (The game reports didn't usually describe innings in which no runs were scored, so there may have been unreported instances in which Delahanty bunted unsuccessfully in two-on, no-out situations, though it is likely his failure would have drawn a comment.) The strategy resulted in one run being scored four times and two runs scored six times. On three occasions the strategy started innings in which four or more runs were scored.

Nap Lajoie was, of course, a key factor in the strategy's success. Lajoie was noted for being a free swinger. He rarely walked and almost never struck out. He was as formidable a slugger as Del, so outfielders played well back for him. Delahanty could be very confident that Lajoie would put the ball in play and that the speedy Thomas and Slagle would advance on any batted ball not hit directly at an infielder.

Occasionally Delahanty laid down a bunt with the intent of beating it out for a base hit. In early September he had five bunt hits in one week.[47] While he was successful in his bunting, Delahanty did not win any points for style. On one of his sacrifice attempts he was safe because the ball sailed into right field for a single. After witnessing some of Delahanty's bunt attempts, a Pittsburgh reporter commented, "Del bunts as gracefully as a cow waltzing."[48]

Wee Willie Was Big

Willie Keeler came along at the right time. Never before or since have the game's playing conditions and strategies been so suited to his talents. Keeler wasn't big enough to hit the ball very far, but he was talented enough to hit it sharply and consistently. He was one of the fastest runners in baseball, and generally considered the fastest from the batter's box to first base.[49] He rarely struck out, and excelled at "scientific baseball"—what would later be incorporated into such terms as "the fundamentals," "inside baseball," or, more recently, "situational hitting."

Most sources state that Keeler used a small, light bat, but in an interview with a Cincinnati sportswriter, Keeler said that was wrong. "My bat is heavy and of average length," he said, "but I use very little of it with which to hit the ball. I grab the bat almost in the middle and I have never had any occasion for changing my style." Keeler had a habit of hitching up his trousers a couple of times as he approached the batter's box. He crowded the plate and leaned over it. "My eyes are almost over the center of the plate," he told the Cincinnati reporter. "I never swing until I am sure that the ball is over the plate, and then I do it quickly, with a sort of snap motion.... It does not require a long swing nor a big bat to make base hits," Keeler said. "All that is necessary is to meet the ball squarely with the bat, and it will travel fast and far enough. Just swing hard enough to meet the ball before it passes the plate."[50]

Keeler is famous for a statement he probably first made during the 1901 season. While chatting with a group of people that included a reporter from the *Brooklyn Eagle*, Keeler brought out a letter he had received from a fan. The fan asked if Keeler had written a "treatise" on the art of batting. If so, the fan asked if Keeler would please send him information on how to obtain a copy. The fan concluded the letter by stating,

Wee Willie Keeler's batting style was ideal for the strategies of "scientific baseball" (National Baseball Hall of Fame Library, Cooperstown, New York).

"I have always considered you the best batter in the country and from your work this year I am thoroughly satisfied that you are. Hence, wishing to become a batter myself, you can readily see why I wish to obtain information from the country's best batter."

"Wouldn't that make you chesty?" Keeler remarked. "I've already written that treatise and it reads like this: 'Keep your eye clear and hit 'em where they ain't.' That's all."[51]

Many baseball fans, including some writers, seemed to believe that Keeler had the ability to purposely "hit 'em where they ain't," that is, that he could hit the ball pretty much wherever he pleased. They loved it when Keeler had a multi-hit game in which he sprayed the ball around the field.

After one game a writer reported that Keeler had made four hits and missed a fifth only because slow-footed catcher Deacon McGuire was forced at second on a ball Keeler would otherwise have beaten out. "Keeler made his five drives in as many different directions," the writer noted, "and again proved himself the greatest place hitter in the business. The first was a slashing drive to right for a single.... The next was the prettiest kind of a bunt along the third base line which [third baseman] Irwin did not attempt to field. Then Keeler rapped a hot one to [shortstop] Magoon, which he would have beaten easily had McGuire not been at first. Then he pasted the ball into left garden for a three-bagger and finished up with a liner which Magoon stopped with one hand and could not hold. Willie's batting was so clever that the crowd applauded enthusiastically when he came in after making his three-bagger and he was compelled to doff his cap."[52]

Keeler did not claim to be able to hit the ball wherever he chose. "A batter can place a ball in either left or right field, providing the proper ball is pitched to him," Keeler told a reporter. "For instance, if there was a man on first and we were playing the hit-and-run game, and I was at the bat, I watch the pitcher, of course, the shortstop and second base and the baserunner. When he starts for second I get ready to hit. If I see that the second baseman is going to cover the bag, I try to pull the ball into right field, but on the other hand, if I see that the shortstop is covering the bag, I try to send it into left field. However, this is only made possible providing the pitcher sends up the right ball for the purpose. If the second baseman covers the bag and the pitcher sends one over the outside corner, neither I nor any one else could be apt to pull it into right field. Should he send it over the center of the plate or inside corner, I could pull it over.... For place hitting every thing has to be favorable or it can not be done. Even when everything is favorable, the batsman will often pop up a little fly. I tell you there is a whole lot of luck about hitting."[53]

A large percentage of Keeler's hits went to the left side of the diamond. Many of them were infield grounders. One writer estimated that half of Keeler's hits came by beating out bunts.[54] Another referred to the area just behind third base as a favorite spot for Keeler's short fly ball hits. In the mid-nineties Keeler and several other Baltimore Orioles became known for the "Baltimore Chop." They would swing down at a pitch, pounding it into the hard ground in front of home plate. Before the ball came down to the fielder, the fleet Orioles were safe at first. Keeler preferred to think of his infield hits as being more along the line of a Baltimore Chop than a bunt. "Now, the truth is, I bunt as little as any man in the league," he claimed. "I hit the ball hard. My long suit is to chop down on the ball and make it bound high. Any time a ball takes two good bounds on that infield it means a base hit for me. I can beat out two bounds nearly every time."[55]

Keeler's batting style was ideal for the offensive strategies of the time. In the Deadball Era, teams could not expect to win games simply by whacking away at the ball. Game balls were kept in play long after they became battered and discolored. Batters who swung for the fences were likely to see their best shots turned into easy fly ball outs. Run-scoring strategies focused on the baserunner. The batter was expected to work at advancing the runner. Managers stressed the importance of sacrificing, using the hit-and-run, and hitting behind the runner. These tactics were termed "teamwork at bat," and were considered key elements of scientific baseball.

Keeler excelled at those tactics, though the sacrifice was not a favored strategy for Ned Hanlon, his manager in Baltimore and Brooklyn. He was universally acclaimed the best "scientific" hitter in baseball. Since scientific baseball equaled winning baseball in the minds of most contemporary observers, Keeler's value to his team was considered greater than his batting statistics might indicate, though those statistics by themselves were outstanding. Because of the way he played the game, Keeler was considered a "winning ballplayer," a player who could lift his team to victory.

After Napoleon Lajoie put up great batting numbers in 1901 and 1902 and earned the distinction of being the game's best "pure hitter," Keeler's former teammate, Joe Kelley, insisted that Keeler was a more valuable player. "Give me a team of Keelers and I could beat the best ball nine that was ever organized," Kelley said. "There isn't a department of play in which Keeler has not got Lajoie beaten as a winner, and I do not underrate the ability of the Frenchman as a great player, but a team of Keelers would take the flag from a team of Lajoies in a walk.... [Keeler] is the ideal run-getter, and is not weak on any count, either inside or out."[56]

Keeler's professional baseball career started in 1892, when he was 20. He had been playing semi-pro ball in Brooklyn and New Jersey since he was 16. He was signed by the Binghamton Bingos of the Eastern League, one of the better minor leagues of the time. For Binghamton he was a good-hitting, poor-fielding third baseman. Handicapped by being a left-handed thrower, he made errors galore. But he could hit. He led the league with a .373 batting average and scored 109 runs in 93 games. The New York Giants bought his contract at the end of that season. In a short trial, Keeler showed that he could hit big league pitching, batting .321. Although his fielding problems continued, the Giants saw enough potential to bring him back the next spring.

Over the winter the Giants signed a new manager, John Montgomery Ward, who didn't believe a left-handed thrower could ever play third adequately. When the 1893 season opened, Keeler's usual position was on the bench. Ward put him into a few games as a middle infielder and then tried him in center field. Keeler immediately made a couple of costly errors, but Ward told him to keep plugging away. In his third game as an outfielder, Keeler fractured his ankle. He was out for eight weeks. By the time his injury healed, he had been traded to Brooklyn.

In Brooklyn, his hometown, Keeler was given another chance to prove he could play third. He again proved he could not. He also struggled when tried in the outfield. By August he was back in Binghamton. Over the winter he was traded again, this time to Baltimore. His new manager, Ned Hanlon, put Keeler in the outfield and told him to forget about third base. Keeler quickly became the sensation of the Orioles' training camp, and his brilliant play carried over into the new season. In his first full year he became a key figure on one of the greatest teams in baseball history.[57]

The Orioles won the pennant in each of Keeler's first three seasons with them, from 1894 through 1896. They finished second in 1897 and 1898. Keeler and most of the Orioles' players moved to Brooklyn in 1899, and added two more pennants to their string. In each of those years Keeler finished among the league leaders in batting average, hits and runs scored. Entering the 1900 season, his *lowest* batting average as a regular player was the .371 he posted in 1894, his first year with the Orioles. He led the league in batting with a .424 average in 1897 and hit safely in 44 straight games. His 1897 batting average still stands as the best ever by a left-handed batter and his 44-game batting streak remains the National League's longest, having been tied by Pete Rose in 1978. In 1898 his batting average fell to .385, which was still good enough to earn his second straight batting crown. Willie smacked 219 hits in 1894, his first full season, and continued to gather more than 200 each year until 1901.

The enduring image of Keeler with the Orioles is of Willie punching a base hit through the hole vacated by a middle infielder on the hit-and-run. But another picture representative of his talents would be one of him crossing the plate while scoring a run. He finished second in runs scored each year from 1894 to 1897, dropped to fourth in 1898, and led the league in 1899. He scored more runs than any other National League player during those years. Although no one would describe Keeler as a slugger, in the nineties he got plenty of extra-base hits. His speed enabled him to pick up extra bases on flares down the foul lines and he had enough power to drive the ball between the outfielders at times. In the days before the lively ball, power hitters often had more triples than home runs. During the nineties Willie reached double figures in triples every year except 1898. He finished fourth in triples in 1897 and sixth in 1894.

Once he settled in the outfield, Keeler overcame his fielding deficiencies. By the end of the nineties, he was considered the best defensive right fielder in the league. His speed enabled him to cover lots of ground and his arm was among the best in the league. As his high number of runs scored would indicate, Willie was a good baserunner. While he never led the league in stolen bases, he usually ranked high in that category. When fans and writers discussed the best players in the game at the turn of the twentieth century, Willie was normally mentioned as the top right fielder.[58]

Keeler played a key role in the Superbas' drive toward the 1900 National League pennant. Like most of the other Brooklyn players, he got off to a slow start. Through the first quarter of the season he was batting only .284, a decent average for most players but low for him. He picked up his pace in mid–June, getting eight hits in twelve at-bats as Brooklyn swept a three-game series against Cincinnati. In the following series, against the Boston Beaneaters, who were at that point still considered the greatest threat to beat out the Superbas, he picked up nine hits and scored six runs as Brooklyn took four straight games. He added five more hits and scored three more runs in the next three games, during which the Superbas twice beat the Phillies and moved into first place.

Over the rest of June and most of July Keeler hit well but never challenged the league leaders, as his average fluctuated between about .310 and .340. On July 22, he was batting .319. Then he got hot and never really cooled down the rest of the season. From July 23 until the season ended he batted .413, bringing his final batting average up to .362. Among his last 66 games, he went hitless in only three.[59] In the crucial five-game series with the Pirates in early September, Willie was at his best even though all the Superbas could manage was a win, a tie and three losses. He had four hits in a losing effort in the first game. He added two more hits and scored three runs in the second game, a 6–6 tie. In a doubleheader the next day he got two hits in the opener, a 15–7 loss. In the nightcap, a six-inning 6–5 victory, he stroked a hit and scored two runs, including the game-winner. He added another hit in the final game, another loss.

He added a hit or two almost every day over the next month, as the Superbas fought off another challenge by the Pirates. That fall, in looking back at the season, a Pittsburgh writer cited Keeler's great hitting as the key to Brooklyn's championship. "Day after day his stick work was timely and the great factor of his team's success," the writer noted, adding that Willie continued to hit even when his teammates were slumping.[60]

In 1901 the American League declared itself a major league and began offering high salaries to National League players. Keeler resisted the offers for two years, preferring to continue playing in his home city. By 1903, however, the price of loyalty became too expensive. He signed with the New York Highlanders, playing with them in their first year in the American League. He remained with the Highlanders until 1910, when he moved a few blocks away to join the Giants and his old teammate, John McGraw. He played in only 19 games that year, almost all of them as a pinch-hitter or pinch-runner.

Major league batting averages had begun declining steadily after 1894. In 1901 the National League adopted the modern rule that declared foul balls to be strikes until a batter had two strikes. The American League adopted the same rule in 1903. This rule change, combined with other developments in pitching and fielding, caused batting averages to reach all-time lows within a few years. Keeler's batting averages declined accordingly but remained among the highest in his league through 1906. He also remained among the leaders in hits and runs scored during those years. In 1907, at the age of 35, Willie hit only .234. In his last two years with the Highlanders he batted in the .260s, with few walks and very little power. When he retired after the 1910 season, his lifetime batting average was .341, the twelfth-highest ever recorded.

At the time of his retirement Keeler was considered a special player, one of the greatest who had ever lived. In the mid-twenties he was named one of the top 25 players in baseball history.[61] In the mid-thirties, when the Baseball Hall of Fame was organized, he seemed sure to be enshrined with the first group of inductees. In 1936 he ranked third in the first vote for nineteenth century stars, trailing Cap Anson, the long-time manager and first baseman of the Chicago White Stockings, and Buck Ewing, a great catcher for the New York Giants. None of the nineteenth century stars received the required 75 percent of the votes, however. In 1937 Keeler finished tied for fifth (with Eddie Collins) in the voting for modern players, missing the cutoff by 26 votes. He missed the cutoff by 20 votes in 1938, but made the cut in 1939, entering the Hall along with Collins and George Sisler. He was the fourth outfielder elected, following Ty Cobb, Babe Ruth, and Tris Speaker.[62]

In 1942, Billy Evans, an umpire during Keeler's last few years and later a well-respected baseball executive, named Keeler as one of the thirteen best hitters of all-time. He was the only player on Evans' list who had not played in the lively ball era. As the decades passed, however, the number of baseball people who had seen Keeler play dwindled, as did Keeler's standing among the game's luminaries. By the end of the fifties, when *Sport* magazine conducted a poll to name the greatest players of all-time at each position, Keeler received little attention. In *Total Baseball*, Michael Gershman lists the 100 greatest players of all-time. His list includes 26 outfielders, including Sam Thompson and Billy Hamilton, whose careers overlapped Keeler's. Keeler was omitted. In *The New Bill James Historical Baseball Abstract,* Keeler is listed as the thirty-fifth best *right fielder,* below such greats as Rusty Staub, Pedro Guerrero, and Dixie Walker.[63]

It seems you had to see Keeler play to fully appreciate his talents.

Kip's Bad Rep

Kip Selbach was one of the players sent to New York in the 1900 pre-season effort to field a decent team in the league's biggest market. A short, stocky man—he was 5'7" and weighed 190 pounds—he was deceptively fast. Considered one of the league's best defensive left fielders, he had excellent range and could throw far and accurately.

Selbach came into the National League with the Washington Nationals in 1894. He soon became one of the team's most popular players. He hit higher than .300 in each of his five years with the Nationals, scoring more than 100 runs three times. He was a patient, disciplined hitter. He had some power, as well as the ability to hit the ball into right field when needed. He walked 60 to 80 times a year and had as many as 30 to 40 stolen bases. Kip was the kind of solid, well-rounded player who could help a good team win a pennant. Unfortunately for him, most of his career was spent with losing teams that couldn't even dream of winning a pennant.

By the end of the 1898 season, Selbach had grown tired of losing all the time and started complaining about the team's lack of success. At least that is what the Washington owner said in December when he sold Selbach to Cincinnati for $5,000, a premium price in the 1890s. Selbach was happy when he got word of the trade, perhaps too happy. He told a reporter that he was sure he could help the Reds. They were a good team, Selbach said, though they had some players known to be "quitters."[64]

When the 1899 season opened, Selbach was put in center field. He was terrible there, costing the team several games with his fielding misadventures.[65] It was at this time that Selbach's winter comments became public. Not surprisingly, his new teammates did not appreciate the putdown, especially considering the self-righteous Selbach's erratic play in center field. After a few weeks, Selbach was moved back to left field, where he once again played very well. Although Selbach hit .296 with the Reds and led the team with 104 runs scored, Cincinnati reporters considered his transfer to New York in 1900 to be "addition by subtraction."[66]

The animosity the Cincinnati writers felt toward Selbach continued even after he went to New York. One of the Cincinnati writers turned around Selbach's comment about Cincinnati players being "quitters," quoting a similar criticism of Selbach ostensibly voiced by a Brooklyn player. According to the Cincinnati writer, one of the Superbas remarked, "Have you noticed how Al Selbach is hitting the ball this spring?" In response, a teammate said, "Well, that's the old gag. When the season started Selbach fielded desperately, and could not hit a barn. Just as soon as the Giants began to lose he got all his confidence back. Since then he has been hitting and fielding like a star. That's the way with that fellow. So long as there is nothing at stake he is a world-beater, but let his team begin to win and he will fall dead. There are a great many players like Selbach. They are stars with a losing team, but when they get with a winner, they lose their nerve and never make good."[67]

Outside of Cincinnati, the writers generally had a high regard for Selbach's abilities. In August a Pittsburgh reporter wrote, "It is not so long ago someone remarked that Selbach was a good enough man on a poor team, but that he was not up to the standard of first-class players. Well, that may be true to some extent, but the fact remains that the New York left fielder has been one of the most consistent players of the league, and has done good work. Little on the field gets by him, nothing ever drops his way that he fails to get. He has been ready with the stick, and lately has developed the base-stealing habit—quite an all-round record."[68]

Based on his final numbers, Selbach had a good season in 1900. In fact, a pretty good case could be made for the assertion that he was the seventh- or eighth-best player in the National League that season. He finished eighth in batting average (.337), seventh in on-base percentage (.425), and seventh in slugging percentage (.461). On the bases, he racked up 36 stolen bases, the eighth-highest total in the league.

Of course, Selbach put up those numbers with a team that finished in last place. Several more seasons would pass before he would finally get a chance to show what he could do with a winning team. After changing leagues in 1902 and toiling for losing teams in Baltimore and Washington, he played a key role in helping Boston win the 1904 American League pennant.

Intersecting Career Paths: Pink Hawley and Joe McGinnity

On April 21, 1900, Pink Hawley and Joe McGinnity took the mound as the Giants played their home opener against the Superbas. Hawley was beginning his ninth major league season, McGinnity his second. This was the first time the two faced each other in the National League, but they had already opposed each other several times in a spirited rivalry.

Eight years earlier, during the summer of 1892, Hawley was the ace pitcher for a semi-professional team representing Fort Smith, Arkansas. McGinnity filled the same role with the nearby Van Buren Browns. The two teams played many of the same opponents, and both claimed to be the best team around. Van Buren fans claimed that in McGinnity, they had the best pitcher in the Southwest. McGinnity had pitched a two-hit shutout against the top amateur team in St. Louis and a one-hitter against an Arkansas team that had previously won 12 games in a row. Fort Smith fans made the same claim for Hawley, who had fanned 21 batters in a game.

Fort Smith and Van Buren tangled in a series of games in late July and early August, with each team winning the same number of games. Finally, Van Buren issued a challenge: The two teams would play a three-game series for the championship of Arkansas and a purse of $1,000. The showdown between the two teams and their ace pitchers turned out to be a showcase for Hawley. He beat McGinnity, 6–4, in the opening game, giving up only four hits. After Van Buren tied the series the next day, Hawley and Fort Smith cruised through the deciding game, as McGinnity was bombed, 13–2.[69]

Immediately after the deciding game, the 19-year-old Hawley joined the St. Louis Browns. He impressed everyone with his fastball, which was compared to that of Amos Rusie, the Nolan Ryan of the 1890s. The Browns were a terrible team while Hawley pitched for them. In 1892, he won only six games and lost fourteen, but he could be dominant at times. He pitched a pair of two-hitters and two three-hitters that season.[70] The next season was a similarly punishing one for Hawley, who went 5–17, but in 1894 he caught up with the league. He won 19 games, lost 27, and, probably more importantly, showed enough talent to be traded out of St. Louis. He went to Pittsburgh, one of the eight or nine National League franchises of the nineties that were actually serious about putting together a winning team.

While Hawley was establishing himself as one of the top pitchers in baseball, McGinnity was making a less favorable impression. McGinnity's work at Van Buren had led to a contract with Montgomery of the Southern League in 1893. There he won only ten while losing nineteen, but earned a promotion to Kansas City of the Western League for 1894. At the start of that season Kansas City's owner/manager, Jimmy Manning, said he thought McGinnity had the makings of a great pitcher. McGinnity failed to live up to Manning's expectations. He was plagued by wildness and had several games in which he was hit very hard. He was given his release near the end of June. McGinnity's record with Kansas City was 8–10. He gave up 157 hits in 124 innings.[71]

A heavy workload—typical for a star pitcher in the 1890s—probably shortened Pink Hawley's career (Library of Congress).

McGinnity likely was, at least to some extent, a victim of the new rule that moved the pitching distance back five feet, beginning in 1893. All pitchers were hurt by the change, but the ones most affected were those who depended upon breaking pitches, as well as a few who pitched from one side of the previous four-foot-wide box. It took time for the pitchers to recalibrate their breaking pitches to the new distance. Until they could do so, they were forced to rely primarily upon their fastballs and pitch location.[72] Hawley had a great fastball and, once he learned to control it, became one of the game's top pitchers. McGinnity's fastball was not of the same caliber.

At this point in their lives it seemed that fate had smiled on

Hawley, while taking a sterner attitude toward McGinnity. The future would reveal a much more complicated reality.

In the 1890s baseball teams placed a heavy burden on their pitchers. The more success the pitcher enjoyed, the heavier the burden became. In 1892, Hawley's rookie season and the last year at the shorter distance, eleven National League pitchers threw more than 400 innings; 24 exceeded 300 innings pitched. The schedule that year called for 154 games for each team. In 1893, the first year at the new distance, the schedule was reduced to 140 games. That season four pitchers exceeded 400 innings pitched, 18 had more than 300. At least two pitchers pitched more than 400 innings every year through the 1896 season, while several others exceeded 350 innings each year. As might be imagined, these workloads exacted a heavy toll on the pitchers' arms.

As Hawley became more successful on the mound, he was rewarded with both a larger salary and one of the league's most demanding workloads. During his last year in St. Louis, Pink pitched 392 innings. With Pittsburgh in 1895 his workload grew even heavier. The Pirates started off well that year and seemed to have a good chance to win the pennant, even though the team's pitching was somewhat thin. Manager Connie Mack, who was a catcher when teams had only one regular starter or a rotation of two starters, decided Hawley was the young man who could carry the team to the championship. Mack took advantage of off-days to start Hawley as often as possible. When there were no off-days, he started Hawley on short rest. Hawley started 50 of the Pirates' 134 games. Then, to make sure the young man wasn't slacking off, Mack used him in relief in six other games. Hawley won 31 games, lost 22, and saved one. He pitched 444 innings at the age of 22. After the season Mack admitted that Hawley had been overworked, but pointed out that Hawley had taken on the extra work without any complaints.[73]

The heavy workload Hawley endured in 1895 began to take its toll the next year. He labored in the late innings of games. Mack complained that Hawley didn't appear capable of maintaining his effectiveness through nine innings. Chicago manager Cap Anson counted thirteen games lost by Hawley in the last inning.[74] Hawley became a .500 pitcher, going 22–21 in 1896 and 18–18 in 1897. Having reached the major leagues while still little more than a child, Hawley lacked the maturity needed to deal well with adversity. While pitching for St. Louis, he had been accused of sulking when opposing batters got too many hits off his deliveries. In Pittsburgh he added to that a reputation for demanding special treatment. He quarreled with Frank Killen, Pittsburgh's other star pitcher. He accused teammates of rooting for the other team when he pitched. By the middle of the 1897 season, the Pittsburgh team was split into pro–Hawley and pro–Killen factions. At the end of that season Hawley was traded to Cincinnati.[75]

The trade served as a wake-up call to Hawley, albeit for only a short time. He worked hard to get into good condition at the start of the season. Over the years he had added a late-breaking curve and a change-up to his fastball. All of his pitches were working for him when he opened the 1898 season. In his first seven games he allowed a total of eight runs, and he won his first nine games. He was once again overpowering. In one game the Phillies had runners on second and third, with Ed Delahanty and Nap Lajoie coming to the plate. Hawley fanned the two sluggers to end the threat. With Hawley leading the way, the Reds were in first place until the

Joe McGinnity. The "Iron Man" was noted for his underhand curveball, which he called "Old Sal" (National Baseball Hall of Fame Library, Cooperstown, New York).

last week of August. On September 9 they trailed Boston by only one game, then lost eight of their next nine games, falling into third place, where they finished the season. Hawley concluded the season with a 27–11 record, but Cincinnati fans were deeply disappointed by the team's September collapse.[76]

Never afraid to create controversy, Hawley made waves before the 1899 season started by objecting to a temperance clause management had inserted into every Cincinnati contract. The clause prohibited a player from taking even a single drink of an alcoholic beverage during the season. Hawley insisted he would not sign a contract that contained the clause. After receiving a letter from the owner, he eventually signed, evidently agreeing to some form of the temperance clause. When the Reds got off to a slow start in 1899, Hawley again became the focus of criticism. He had difficulty adjusting to a new balk rule, committing several balks that led to runs in close games. In June the Reds suspended him for failing to overcome the habit that led to the balk calls. Later in the season he was accused of losing because he was not in good condition. By season's end Cincinnati's fans and ownership had both soured on Hawley. No one protested when he was given to New York in March of 1900.[77]

While Hawley was living the life of a star pitcher in the National League, McGinnity found work in the mines around his new hometown of Springfield, Illinois, and in a saloon he had opened with a friend. He continued to pitch, earning money playing semi-professional ball with a Springfield team and participating in pickup games whenever he could. He used those games to perfect a new pitch. While pitching with Kansas City, McGinnity had become intrigued by a submarine pitch thrown by Billy Rhines, an opposing pitcher who led the National League in earned run average twice. Rhines' submarine pitch was a straight fastball, with no curve. "I was much taken with the delivery," McGinnity said later, "and thought it could be developed into more effectiveness by using a curve." The new pitch was very difficult to control, McGinnity said. "I kept at it, however, and gradually gained command of the delivery, but it took me five years of practice to get it down fine."[78]

By 1898 McGinnity was ready to try professional baseball again. He secured a position with Peoria in the Western Association, a step below the Western League. He went 10–3 in the half-season the league operated, but gained more attention for a hard slide into third base. The slide broke the leg of the opposing team's third baseman and brought a denunciation of his dirty tactics on the front page of *The Sporting News*. McGinnity wrote a letter to the paper's editor denying he had done anything wrong and expressing sympathy for the injured player. A few weeks later, when McGinnity won a 21-inning marathon against St. Joseph, *The Sporting News* printed a detailed write-up of the game. After the season ended, his contract was purchased by Brooklyn.[79]

For McGinnity the 1899 season offered great opportunities. He went to spring training with the Baltimore half of the Brooklyn-Baltimore syndicate. Since all of the experienced pitchers in the organization had been assigned to Brooklyn, the Orioles' spring training was one big tryout camp for pitchers. McGinnity made a great impression, both during the spring and in the Orioles' early games. After his second start, in which he shut out the Giants, a Baltimore reporter remarked that Orioles manager John McGraw had "found a real jewel, a 'Lulu,' in McGinnity." A week later he pitched a two-hitter against the defending champion Boston Beaneaters, prompting a Boston writer to comment, "This McGinnity must be some kind of twirler."

In midseason *The Sporting News* observed, "McGinnity impresses one favorably, professionally and personally." The paper's reporter said that when McGinnity was complimented for his success, he modestly gave credit to his catcher, Wilbert Robinson. "I rely a great deal on Robbie," McGinnity was quoted as saying. "I don't mean that I am an automaton and incapable of thinking for myself, for I feel sure that now that I have had a chance to study the batters that I could do credit to myself if left to my own resources. I feel safe in saying that there is not a pitcher in the National League who would not be aided greatly by Robbie."[80]

At season's end, McGinnity had won 28 games, lost 16 and saved two. He threw from a variety of arm angles. He had an effective overhand drop (the pitch currently called a "12-to–6 curve"), a sidearm curve, and a fastball that was good enough when mixed in with his other pitches. His best and most discussed pitch was the submarine curve he had developed back in Springfield. He gave it the nickname "Old Sal." In 1899 the batters called it his "raise ball." They tended to swing under it, popping the ball up into the infield or short outfield.

The nickname Baltimore writers often used in referring to McGinnity in 1899 was the "Indian Territory man," a reference to his having lived in the area that later became Oklahoma. In 1900 McGinnity became part-owner, along with his wife's father and brother, of an iron foundry there. It was common at the time to tag a ballplayer with a nickname based on his occupation before he entered baseball. For instance, St. Louis' Jack Powell was the "boilerman," while Chicago's Jack Taylor was a "railroad man." During the offseason McGinnity's connection with the iron foundry became widely known among baseball writers, and before the 1900 season was far gone, he had become the "Iron Man." At that time the term referred to his supposed occupation, but before the season ended it would take on a double meaning, connoting more his pitching endurance than his non-baseball occupation.[81]

The April confrontation that began the 1900 season for McGinnity and Hawley brought little in the way of surprises. Both men pitched well enough, Hawley yielding eight hits and three walks, McGinnity nine hits and five walks. McGinnity had by far the better support and gained the victory, 5–2. The game set the pattern for the first half of 1900—McGinnity won almost all of his games, Hawley lost almost all of his. Down the stretch, as we have described above, when Brooklyn's lead seemed in peril, manager Ned Hanlon put the team's fate in McGinnity's hands. The "Iron Man" saved the pennant for his team and happily pocketed a reward for doing so.

Hawley, meanwhile, sank closer to professional oblivion. After pitching creditably against McGinnity, he was blown out of his next six games, the opposition scoring in double figures in each game. The Giants salvaged a tie in one of those games by scoring ten runs. New York's baseball writers began calling for his release. One wrote, "Hawley has not won a game this season and the announcement that he had been released would not cause surprise or regret.... He has been the softest snap in the National League this season."[82]

Then, as he had done before in his career, he gradually turned things around. His first victory, which didn't come until the last week of May, was a well-pitched game against the Pirates. On June 13 he shut out Chicago, facing only 29 batters. His next start was a 2–1 loss in which one of the runs scored on an error. By July 1 his record was only 3–11, but he was now giving his team a chance to win nearly every game he started. He won four of his next five starts. On August 11, he outdueled Cincinnati's Frank Hahn, 1–0, allowing only three hits, and followed that with another three-hitter the next week against Chicago. Once accused of having "a $10,000 arm and a three-cent head," Hawley was now winning games by pitching intelligently. After a

5–4 victory over Boston, veteran writer Tim Murnane commented, "Hawley pitched a superb game for the visitors, using a fine change of pace and a slow curve that kept the home team on edge to the last."[83]

Over the last three months of the 1900 season, Hawley was one of the top pitchers in the league, putting up a 15–7 record after July 1. That was his last good season. When the American League declared itself a major league in 1901, Hawley jumped to Milwaukee, which was relatively close to his home in Beaver Dam, Wisconsin. Playing for a terrible team, Hawley was ineffective. His most notable feat with Milwaukee came on May 3, when he was knocked out of the box in the second inning by the Chicago White Stockings. The game, Milwaukee's home opener, was the third opening game loss for Pink that season. He had lost previous home openers in Detroit and Cleveland. Pink never quite got into good condition in 1901, and he tended to tire in the late innings of his games. He was released near the end of August, posting a 7–14 record in his last major league season.[84]

Hawley was only 28 years old when he reached the end of his major league career. By contrast, McGinnity, who was almost two years older than Hawley, continued to pitch for many more years. He pitched in the major leagues until 1908 and in minor leagues until 1925. He was 54 years old when he threw his last pitch in professional baseball. A major factor in both his success and his durability was that "underhand raise ball" he developed after his professional career had seemingly come to an end.

A Loud Noise in Brooklyn: Roaring Bill Kennedy

A few months before Pink Hawley began his career in St. Louis, a young man from an Ohio River town in southern Ohio made his debut in Brooklyn. Like Hawley, Bill Kennedy had both a big fastball and an outsized personality. As a rookie in 1892 Kennedy led the National League in strikeouts per nine innings. After that season he no longer ranked among the leaders in strikeouts, either because his fastball lost some of its bite at the longer pitching distance of 60 feet, 6 inches or, more likely, because he learned not to expend too much energy trying for strikeouts.

The 1892 season was split into two halves, with the winner of each half scheduled to meet in a post-season playoff. In the first half Brooklyn finished second, 2½ games behind Boston. Kennedy was used sparingly then, as the team relied upon more experienced starters. He started only one game in the first half, beating Baltimore, 12–10. His next start came in August, when he began pitching regularly in a three-man rotation. He finished the season with a 13–8 win-loss record. In 1893 he became the team's top pitcher and remained the staff ace until the consolidation with Baltimore in 1899. Kennedy was 25–20 in 1893 and 24–20 in 1894. When the Bridegrooms dropped deep into the second division from 1896 through 1898, Kennedy's record fell slightly below .500, but he was still considered one of the better pitchers in the league.[85]

Kennedy quickly became a favorite among the Brooklyn fans. They respected his pitching talent and were amused by newspaper accounts of his antics. Kennedy acquired two commonly mentioned nicknames: "Brickyard," which is usually cited in modern baseball encyclopedias, and "Roaring Bill," which was favored by Brooklyn baseball writers of the time. He was loud, somewhat temperamental, and a bit egotistical. Upon his arrival in Brooklyn he was immediately portrayed as a "rube," a country bumpkin who was somewhat awed and mystified by big city ways. His baseball salary soon enabled him to acquire fine clothes and expensive habits, but the rube image remained with him throughout his playing days.

As a rookie in 1892, Kennedy was reportedly so pleased at the amount of money he received on his first payday that he immediately invested 50 dollars in the most colorful suit he could find. He converted the remainder of his pay into a large wad of one-dollar bills, which he proudly displayed as he went about town. It didn't take enterprising New Yorkers long to relieve him of the conspicuous roll of bills.

Later, during a long period of inactivity, Kennedy disappeared. Team officials soon received a telegram from Cincinnati's manager saying that Kennedy was at his home in Bellaire, Ohio. Brooklyn's manager, John Montgomery Ward, asked for help in getting Kennedy to Cincinnati, where he was to rejoin the team. In Cincinnati Ward asked Kennedy what had happened. "I had too much money," Kennedy replied, adding that he wanted to show his fellow townspeople his newfound wealth. "Everybody came out to see me, except the band, and they all touched me up. About two days after I got home I was cleaned out so badly I had to skirmish around to get a drink."[86]

His teammates loved to play practical jokes on Kennedy. Ed Stein, a teammate for several years, later recalled that Roaring Bill, an avid smoker, was an easy mark for exploding cigars. "Bill has smoked more loaded cigars than any other player in the league," Stein told a reporter as he related one such incident. "Scrappy Bill Joyce took three cigars out of his pocket and juggled them in front of Kennedy's eyes. Then he borrowed the cigar Bill had between his teeth, lighted his own and threw Kennedy's on the sidewalk. Kennedy made a blind snatch to save his smoke, but failed. With an apology for his thoughtlessness, Joyce pulled out one of the two cigars he had left, and a few moments later there occurred one of the greatest illuminations that ever afforded a lot of ballplayers a good laugh."[87]

Another teammate told of a rainy afternoon in Chicago when the Brooklyn players were sitting around a hotel lobby. Many of the players were reading newspapers. Kennedy had never attended school and was illiterate. He was sensitive about his lack of education and tried to cover it up. That afternoon he grabbed one of the newspapers, looked for a picture so he could figure out how to hold the paper right-side-up, and began to "read." After a short while one of the other players came up to Bill and yanked the paper out of his hands. Kennedy lived up to his nickname, roaring until the chandeliers shook. The player gave Kennedy another paper, apologizing for the interruption. Kennedy found a picture, arranged the paper comfortably in his lap and resumed "reading," never realizing he was now holding a German-language newspaper.[88]

The consolidation of the Brooklyn and Baltimore teams came as a wake-up call of sorts to Kennedy. For the first time in years he faced competition for his job, and Manager Hanlon did not take too kindly to a bad habit Kennedy had developed. Roaring Bill didn't always cover first base on a grounder that pulled the first baseman away from the bag. His former managers had scolded him and occasionally levied fines when Kennedy loafed on grounders to first, but they couldn't get him to change his ways. Hanlon, on the other hand, insisted that the game be played according to his standards and impressed upon the players that nobody was irreplaceable. Kennedy got the message. Brooklyn writers noted in spring training that Roaring Bill was now hustling over to cover first on grounders to the right side.

He also seemed to be controlling his temper better. In previous seasons he tended to become angry when his teammates committed errors behind him, yelling at them, rushing his delivery, and losing control of the ball. Under Hanlon he was much more likely to remain calm in such situations.[89]

Kennedy's pitching was a vital part of Brooklyn's successful pennant runs in both 1899 and 1900. Roaring Bill was 22–9 in 1899 and 20–13 in 1900. During both years he hit a rough spot in the middle of the season, starting the rumor mills churning with speculation that he was about to be released. He came back, however, to finish both seasons strongly. Kennedy's slump in 1900, which came in August just as the Pirates were beginning to play well, was especially worrisome to Brooklyn fans, since he had been the only pitcher other than Joe McGinnity who had been able to win consistently.

Roaring Bill's troubles began on July 31, when he took a 17–1 pasting at the hands of the resurgent Pirates. Over the next month he managed only one win, while losing three and tying one. Kennedy started coming out of his slump early in September, when he regained the speed that had been missing from his fastball, although he was still wild. Hanlon gave him a chance to regain his control by using him in relief of his other struggling starters. On September 22, with three weeks left in the season, Kennedy relieved Wild Bill Donovan in a losing effort against the Giants. Hanlon was elated with Kennedy's pitching. Hanlon later cited that New York game as being decisive. "Just as soon as I saw that Kennedy had recovered his form ... I knew that it was all over." Kennedy returned to the pitching rotation after that, winning three of his remaining four starts, his only setback being a well-pitched 2–1 loss to Philadelphia.[90]

In the spring of 1901 Kennedy came down with a sore arm, which severely curtailed his pitching during the next three years. He won only four games over the 1901 and 1902 seasons before closing out his career with a 9–6 record with Pittsburgh in 1903. Kennedy is not normally given much attention in discussions of the great pitchers of the 1890s and early 1900s. But during the years that he pitched, 1892 to 1903, only three pitchers won more games than Roaring Bill. All of them (Cy Young, Kid Nichols, and Clark Griffith) are in the Baseball Hall of Fame. For the years that Kennedy started regularly, from 1892 to 1900, only Young and Nichols had more victories.

Two

1901, National League

The Baseball War's Opening Salvo

The event that most shaped the National League pennant race in 1901 occurred during the offseason. After the 1900 season, Ban Johnson, president of the American League, declared that his league would expand into the East. In October of 1900 the American League voted to put teams in Washington, Baltimore, and Philadelphia. Johnson had hoped to gain the National League owners' consent to these moves, but he was prepared to go ahead with his plans whether he got it or not. He asked for time to discuss the matter at the National League winter meetings in December of 1900. When the owners ignored him, he decided to go on the offensive. In January, the American League's Buffalo franchise was formally shifted to Boston, a move Johnson had delayed, hoping to use it as a bargaining chip with the National League.

Recruitment of players soon proceeded at a rapid pace. The American League announced it would not hire National League players who had already signed a contract for 1901, but would go after players who were bound only by the reserve clause of the contracts they had signed for the 1900 season. This meant that most of the National League players were considered fair game, because few National League players had signed contracts for 1901. A group of investors had tried unsuccessfully to set up a rival major league, to be named the American Association, after the 1899 season. The players knew that either those investors or the American League owners were likely to challenge the National League after the 1900 campaign. Therefore most of them held off on signing new contracts at the end of the season, as was customary.

Johnson's agents were successful. Every National League team lost at least one starting player. Cities with a team in each league were prime targets. The teams in each of those cities—Boston, Philadelphia, and Chicago—lost key players. The former syndicate cities—St. Louis and Brooklyn—also lost some of their best players. The defections to the American League and each team's ability to compensate for its losses were key elements in deciding the 1901 National League pennant race.[1]

1901 National League Standings

Team	W	L	Pct.	GB
Pittsburgh	90	49	.647	—
Philadelphia	83	57	.593	7.5

Brooklyn	79	57	.581	9.5
St. Louis	76	64	.543	14.5
Boston	69	69	.500	20.5
Chicago	53	86	.381	37
New York	52	85	.380	37
Cincinnati	52	87	.374	38

A New Powerhouse: Pittsburgh

The Pirates came through the raids relatively unscathed. They lost only third baseman Jimmy Williams and Harry Smith, a backup catcher who was on the Pirates' reserve list but had not played any games for them in 1900. Another loss was unrelated to the American League raids. First baseman Tom O'Brien had gone on a barnstorming trip to Cuba after the 1900 season. While there he contracted a serious disease. He died in February 1901.

As it turned out, the Pirates' replacement players performed better than those they lost. Tommy Leach took over for Williams at third base. He was probably the top third baseman in the National League in 1901 and became one of the Pirates' best players for the next decade. Kitty Bransfield, a rookie in 1901, took O'Brien's place at first base. He was a much better fielder than O'Brien and hit more consistently in 1901 than O'Brien did the previous year.

Shortly after the season opened, the Pirates made another important change to their roster. They released Rube Waddell. Rube was his usual disruptive self that spring. During spring training he injured his hip in a tag football game organized to give the team some exercise. The injury wasn't serious, but Rube milked it for all the attention he could get. He arranged for two visits from the local doctor and missed three days of practice. On the fourth day, while tending the gate, he noticed some nice-looking young ladies in the stands. He talked manager Fred Clarke into letting him pitch. Although he limped onto the mound when he started pitching, in the heat of competition he forgot about the leg and began charging about the diamond while fielding the ball. The injury had obviously healed and Rube was simply using it as an excuse to avoid practice.[2]

Pittsburgh (90–49)

Regular Lineup	AVG	OBP	SLG	R	RBI	SB
Fred Clarke, lf	.324	.395	.461	118	60	23
Ginger Beaumont, cf	.332	.382	.418	120	72	36
Lefty Davis, rf*	.291	.389	.380	98	40	26
Honus Wagner, ut	.353	.417	.494	101	126	49
Kitty Bransfield, 1b	.295	.335	.398	92	91	23
Claude Ritchey, 2b	.296	.358	.354	66	74	15
Tommy Leach, 3b	.305	.347	.422	64	44	16
Chief Zimmer, c	.220	.292	.275	17	21	6
or Jack O'Connor, c	.193	.238	.257	16	22	2

Bones Ely, ss		.208	.234	.258	18	28	5
Leading Pitchers	**W**	**L**	**PCT**	**IP**	**H**	**ERA**
Deacon Phillippe	22	12	.647	296	274	2.22
Jack Chesbro	21	10	.677	287.7	261	2.38
Jesse Tannehill	18	10	.643	252.3	240	2.18
Sam Leever	14	5	.737	176	182	2.86
Ed Doheny**	8	7	.533	150.2	156	3.23

*Includes record with Brooklyn
**Includes record with New York

The practice time missed due to the injury and later because of rain may have kept Rube from building his arm strength. When the season started he was wild and didn't have his normal overpowering speed. In his first start he pitched well for six innings but blew up in the seventh, when he gave up five runs. Two days later, he disappeared from sight. He had gone to his home, which was near Pittsburgh, without receiving permission. His father brought him back a week later. Clarke started him the next game, but Rube was terrible. In the first inning he gave up four walks and three hits, good for five runs. These two appearances were enough to convince Clarke that Waddell was more trouble than he was worth. The next day the Pirates released Rube to Chicago. According to a later report, the compensation was a cigar.[3]

The Pirates were a good hitting team—they finished second in runs scored—but their strength was their pitching and defense. They had a good defensive player at every position. Pirate fans could plausibly argue that left fielder Fred Clarke, right fielder Honus Wagner, and shortstop Fred Ely were the best fielders in the league at their positions, although Ely was beginning to slow down. By midseason they were also making that argument about third baseman Tommy Leach. Second baseman Claude Ritchey was widely praised as being "steady as a clock,"[4] while pitcher Sam Leever described new first baseman Bransfield as "the most graceful first baseman I have ever seen."[5] Center fielder Ginger Beaumont was very fast and had sure hands. The team's catchers, Chief Zimmer and Jack O'Connor, were experienced veterans.

Everyone agreed the Pirates had the league's top pitching staff. Deacon Phillippe was the staff ace, but Jesse Tannehill and Sam Leever were considered to be almost as good. Tannehill had been the Pirates' top pitcher before the consolidation. At the beginning of the 1901 season, Jack Chesbro had yet to establish himself as one of the league's top pitchers. He was described as an "inner and outer," meaning that he pitched well in some outings but was easy pickings in others.[6] As the season progressed, however, Chesbro demonstrated that he, too, was one of the top pitchers in the league.

Because the other top teams of 1900 were hit harder by the American League raids, the Pirates were universally considered the favorites to win the 1901 pennant. But the pennant race didn't unfold the way people expected. For two months the leaders were New York and Cincinnati, two teams thought to be competitors for the cellar. Open dates and rainouts allowed those two teams to ride good fortune and the arms of two outstanding young pitchers—Christy Mathewson and Noodles Hahn—to the top. Chicago occupied last place, while the other five teams, including Pittsburgh, struggled to remain just above or below the .500 level.

During those two months the Pirates never dropped very far behind, but they weren't able to put together any long winning streaks. They played lots of close games and lost about half of them. In mid–June the Pirates swept a three-game series from New York to move into first place. They stayed there for the rest of the season, except for a couple of hours on July 4, when they lost the first game of a doubleheader to New York. Their victory in the second game put them back in first. Although New York began drifting slowly toward the bottom of the standings, three legitimate contenders—Philadelphia, St. Louis, and Brooklyn—stayed on the Pirates' heels. Until mid–September the Pirates' lead was never more than a few games.

Injuries and inner turmoil kept the team off-balance most of the season. Although the Pirates had ably replaced the players lost to the American League and sickness, the team's depth suffered as a result. When Clarke was injured in May, his replacement was pitcher Jesse Tannehill. Tannehill was a good hitter for a pitcher, and he did not embarrass himself in the outfield, but he was a big drop-off from Clarke. Waddell's release was undoubtedly beneficial for Clarke's peace of mind, but it left the pitching vulnerable when injuries occurred, as they nearly always did in those days of small staffs and heavy workloads.

At the beginning of the season Sam Leever was the Pirates' most effective pitcher. He won his first four starts and was 9–3 on June 19, when he opposed Christy Mathewson and the Giants. While batting in the third inning, he stopped one of Mathewson's fastballs with his pitching arm. After taking off ten days to recover from the blow, he relieved in the fourth inning of a big game against Philadelphia. As was often the case with relievers at that time, he went to the mound without warming up sufficiently. On one of his pitches, he felt something give in his shoulder. Again, in keeping with normal conduct for pitchers in his day, Leever finished the game and got ready for his next start, in which he shut out the Giants in a 12–0 blowout. The arm continued to bother him, though. After resting for a week, he hooked up with the Phillies' Doc White in a pitchers' duel. Leever gave up a two-run single in the fourteenth inning to lose the game, 4–2. Afterward his arm hurt so much he was convinced his career was over. Fortunately, after two months of rest his arm recovered. But he pitched only four more games the rest of the season, all of them after mid–September, when the Pirates had built a relatively safe lead.[7]

Pittsburgh was able to weather Leever's injury largely because Jack Chesbro elevated his game a notch. At the beginning of the season Chesbro's role was one that would today be described as a long reliever-spot starter. He finished both of the games Waddell started for the Pirates, pitching poorly in the first game but well in the second. After Waddell's release, Chesbro and lefthander Lewis "Snake" Wiltse shared Waddell's starting spot, and they took Jesse Tannehill's starts while Tannehill replaced the injured Clarke in left field.

At first Chesbro was inconsistent. He pitched two good games, followed by two bad ones, reinforcing his reputation as an "inner and outer." For a short spell in late May Clarke sent him back to the bullpen. On June 7, Chesbro sparkled in a relief appearance. He replaced Tannehill in the fourth inning of a game in which Pittsburgh trailed Brooklyn, 4–2. He pitched eight scoreless innings, allowing only three hits, as the Pirates rallied to win, 5–4, in 11 innings. From the fifth through the tenth innings, he allowed no hits and only one base on balls, facing just 18 batters in those six innings. That showing put him back in the starting rotation.

For the remainder of the season, Chesbro was the Pirates' most effective pitcher. On June 16, his second start after returning to the rotation, he beat Boston, 1–0, allowing only four hits and striking out nine batters, five of them in a row. In his next start he shut out New York on three hits. He added three more shutouts over the course of the summer, giving him six for the 1901 season and earning a tie for National League leadership in that category. He closed out the season by winning ten of his last twelve games, allowing only 88 hits and 31 runs in those games.[8]

In late July, Manager Clarke made a move that may have won the pennant for the Pirates. Clarke announced that he was going to try a new infield combination, with Honus Wagner replacing light-hitting Fred Ely at shortstop. At first Clarke stated merely that Ely would be rested, but three days later he gave Ely his release. Later it was learned that Ely had been working as an agent for the American League.

Wagner was not eager to play shortstop. He preferred to play third base, a position he had played often before, with Tommy Leach moving over to shortstop. Leach, at Clarke's urging, appealed to Wagner to take over the shortstop position. Leach argued that Wagner could cover more ground, and said the Dutchman could withstand the rigors of the position better than he could, especially since he was just recovering from an illness. Wagner relented.[9]

On July 27 he played his first major league game at shortstop, against the St. Louis Cardinals. St. Louis fans were so impressed with his fielding that they immediately put him in the same class with their own shortstop, Bobby Wallace, which was the highest praise a Cardinals fan could give.

As the Pirates moved around the league, the same assessment came from other observers. A writer for the *Brooklyn Eagle* described Wagner's play as "brilliant," but not surprising, since Wagner had previously shined in several different positions. A Chicago correspondent wrote, "Wagner was the whole thing in the field. He cavorted as clumsily as a cow, but his thick frame was seen all over the diamond. He knocked down bounders as they hopped in all directions." Wagner did not let the pressure of moving to shortstop affect his hitting. While making the transition he hit safely in 23 straight games, the longest consecutive hitting streak of his career.[10]

When the Pirates began their last road trip on September 2, they led the Phillies by 2½ games and the Superbas by 3½ games. They faced a grueling schedule of nine games in five days, playing a doubleheader against Boston on September 2, followed by a single game the next day and three straight doubleheaders against New York. It seemed to be a golden opportunity for their challengers to gain ground.

Instead, the Pirates swept all nine games. In the six games against New York they scored 80 runs on 104 hits. Over the same period the Phillies won five games in a row and lost two games in the standings to the Pirates. From New York, the Pirates went to Philadelphia, where they took two out of three from the Phillies. Mathematically the race was not over, but psychologically the Pirates had delivered a powerful blow. The Phillies were never able to mount another serious challenge as the Pirates won 17 of their last 24 games, clinching the pennant with almost two weeks left to play.

More Ginger: Philadelphia

The Phillies didn't lose as many players to the American League as some of the other National League teams, but the players they lost had key roles on their 1900 team. Their most notable loss was star second baseman Nap Lajoie, who went on to have a tremendous season with the crosstown Philadelphia Athletics. The Phillies also lost three starting pitchers—Chick Fraser, Bill Bernhard, and Wiley Piatt. Fraser was one of the better pitchers in baseball in both 1900 and 1901. Bernhard had the misfortune of being the Phillies' only effective starter early in the 1900 season. He was used so often that he developed a sore arm. He pitched poorly the second half of the 1900 season and was still sub-par in 1901. Piatt, like Bernhard, was a victim of early success. He posted a 24–14 win-loss record with Philadelphia in 1898 and went 23–15 in 1899. He pitched more than 300 innings in both seasons, which likely affected his arm. He was a mediocre pitcher in both 1900 and 1901.

Philadelphia (83–57)

Regular Lineup	AVG	OBP	SLG	R	RBI	SB
Roy Thomas, cf	.309	.437	.334	102	28	27
Harry Wolverton, 3b	.309	.356	.369	42	43	13
Elmer Flick, rf	.333	.399	.500	112	88	30
Ed Delahanty, lf	.354	.427	.528	106	108	29
Ed McFarland, c	.285	.326	.356	33	32	11
Hughie Jennings, 1b	.262	.342	.354	38	39	13
Bill Hallman, 2b	.184	.236	.236	46	38	13
Monte Cross, ss	.197	.281	.236	49	44	24
Leading Pitchers	**W**	**L**	**Pct.**	**IP**	**H**	**ERA**
Red Donahue	20	13	.606	295.3	299	2.59
Bill Duggleby	20	12	.625	284.7	302	2.88
Al Orth	20	12	.625	281.7	250	2.27
Doc White	14	13	.519	236.7	241	3.19
Jack Townsend	9	6	.600	143.7	118	3.45

Lajoie was so much better than any other second baseman in baseball that he was truly irreplaceable. The Phillies did as well as could be expected by signing Bill Hallman, an aging veteran who had slipped back into the minors after the 1898 season. Hallman gave the Phillies solid defense and helped on offense by sacrificing whenever the opportunity arose. He led the league with 29 sacrifices, five more than his closest challenger. Other than that he fell somewhat short of replacing Lajoie. His .184 batting average, for instance, fell .242 short of equaling Lajoie's 1901 figure of .426.

To replace the three pitchers lost to the American League, the Phillies brought in three rookie hurlers: Bill Duggleby, Doc White, and Jack Townsend. All three pitched well. As a result, the Phillies' pitching, relative to the league, was better in 1901 than it had been in 1900.

The American League raid was indirectly responsible for the Phillies' most important acquisition of 1901. At the beginning of the 1901 season, Hughie Jennings remained in law school at Cornell instead of reporting to the Brooklyn Superbas. While at Cornell he promised John McGraw he would join the Orioles if he played baseball in 1901. Meanwhile, in accordance with a previous agreement among American League clubs, the Philadelphia Athletics submitted a claim for Jennings to league president Ban Johnson. When McGraw insisted that Jennings would play for the Orioles, Johnson issued a statement saying the only American League club with a right to sign Jennings was Philadelphia. Caught in the twin crossfire of both inter-league and intra-league warfare, Jennings looked for a safe haven. He talked Ned Hanlon into dealing him to the Phillies.

When Jennings joined Philadelphia on June 22, they were playing their usual lethargic brand of baseball. "One noticeable failing of the Phillies has been the way the players loaf down to first base on infield hits," noted a Pittsburgh writer. "This has always been a fault of the Philadelphia team," he continued, "but it was particularly prominent last week."[11] Jennings immediately changed that mindset. His first game was a ten-inning loss, but it was a loss that had a different feel to it. The game went into extra innings because Jennings, coaching at third base, sent a runner home to score from second base on an infield grounder. "That is something new for the Philadelphia club," a Philadelphia writer exclaimed.[12]

The Phillies won their next six games to move within two games of the league-leading Pirates. Through July and August they stayed close to the lead, never quite catching the Pirates but always remaining within striking distance. Even when the Pirates pulled away from them in September, the Phillies continued to play winning ball.

Fans and writers throughout the league were unanimous in giving Jennings the credit for the Phillies' improved play. "It is safe to say this one player has increased the strength of the Philadelphia team fully 20 percent," one writer said. "Jennings is a hustler, who infuses ginger wherever he may be," said another, "and he has not failed to put new life in the Phillies." "Hughie Jennings was at first base and his presence gingered up the team beautifully," said a Brooklyn reporter. "Half a dozen of his putouts were on bad bounding throws which few first basemen would have stopped. Jennings was never still, encouraging the players at all times, and keeping them up to top-notch speed throughout. Those who wondered why the Phillies have braced up since Jennings joined the team went away satisfied that Hughie was the cause."[13] The Phillies were 24–24 before Jennings joined the team. Under his leadership as team captain they were 59–33.

Upon seeing Jennings' playing statistics, a modern observer might wonder just how much credit Jennings should get for the Phillies' improved play. After all, Hughie batted only .262, with 38 runs scored and 39 RBIs. But he brought great defense to first base, where Ed Delahanty had been mediocre. Delahanty moved to left field, where he was a decent defensive player. Therefore Jennings' bat replaced that of Jimmy Slagle, who was batting .202, with a .277 on-base percentage, and his glove improved a defense that was already pretty good. The Phillies ended up leading the league in fielding percentage. Their solid defense, in turn, increased the effectiveness of a deep pitching staff that finished behind only the Pirates in earned run average. While baseball critics of 1901 almost certainly went overboard in praising Jennings, it appears he justly deserves a lot of credit for the Phillies' improvement.

Please, Please—Not Toward Third: Brooklyn

The Superbas were hit very hard by the American League raids. They lost three key players: Pitcher Joe McGinnity, third baseman Lave Cross, and center fielder Fielder Jones. Also, the great depth of talent resulting from the amalgamation of 1899 was swept away. To fill out his 1901 roster, Hanlon had hoped to be able to choose from pitchers Harry Howell and Joe Yeager, third baseman Doc Casey, first baseman John Anderson, and outfielders Dave Fultz and Tommy Dowd, all of whom were on the Superbas' reserve list for 1901. Instead, they all played regularly for American League teams.

Brooklyn (79–57)

Regular Lineup	AVG	OBP	SLG	R	RBI	SB
Willie Keeler, rf	.339	.369	.420	123	43	23
Jimmy Sheckard, lf	.354	.409	.534	116	104	35
Joe Kelley, 1b	.307	.363	.425	77	65	18
Tom Daly, 2b	.315	.371	.444	88	90	31
Bill Dahlen, ss	.266	.313	.358	69	82	23
Tom McCreery, cf	.290	.355	.433	47	53	13
Charlie Irwin, 3b*	.227	.277	.293	50	45	17
Deacon McGuire, c	.296	.342	.375	28	40	4
or Duke Farrell, c	.296	.320	.384	38	31	7
Leading Pitchers	**W**	**L**	**PCT**	**IP**	**H**	**ERA**
Bill Donovan	25	15	.625	351	324	2.77
Frank Kitson	19	11	.633	280.7	312	2.98
Jim Hughes	17	12	.586	250.7	265	3.27
Doc McJames	5	6	.455	91	104	3.27

*Includes record with Cincinnati

The timing of the raids also played a part in damaging the 1901 Brooklyn team. Although rumors about the American League signings were rampant in February and early March, concrete news did not come until well into March. Hanlon didn't know he had lost Lave Cross until just before spring training. Over the winter Hanlon sold reserve infielder Gene DeMontreville to Boston. That deal obviously would not have been made had Hanlon been able to anticipate his other losses. Hanlon might also have been more aggressive in his dealings with Hughie Jennings, who, as mentioned above, attended law school until June and then forced a trade to Philadelphia.

Hanlon managed to patch up his decimated pitching staff by persuading Jim Hughes and Doc McJames to come out of retirement. Both had been stars with the 1899 Superbas. Additionally, young Bill Donovan, a Hanlon project since 1899, had apparently conquered his wildness. With Bill Kennedy and Frank Kitson returning from the 1900 staff, Hanlon seemed to have a solid group of pitchers going into the season.

To replace center fielder Jones, Hanlon signed Tom McCreery, a Pittsburgh reject. In the mid-1890s McCreery appeared to be a coming star. In 1896, his first full season, he hit .351 and led the league with 21 triples. However, he also led the league with 58 strikeouts, a high number for the nineties. He struck out 73 times the next season. In 1897 he was traded to New York, in 1898 to Pittsburgh. He was a seldom-used substitute for the 1900 Pirates. For Brooklyn, he played solid, and at times spectacular, defense in center field. His batting average in 1901 was .290, but he struck out quite often, a deadly trait for the type of offense Hanlon favored.

Finding a replacement for Cross proved to be difficult. During the first half of the season third base became the Superbas' equivalent of the Little League right fielder who couldn't catch a ball. The Brooklyn players went into each game knowing that any ball hit to third could be the one that would cost them the game. The weakness at the hot corner added extra pressure that must have affected every Superbas' play.

Jimmy Sheckard was Hanlon's first hope at third. Sheckard was a good athlete; he was quick and had shown good hands in the outfield. He had been an infielder in his last minor league season. However, he was switched to the outfield shortly after coming to Brooklyn in 1897 because his fielding at shortstop was not up to major league standards. In his eleven games there for Brooklyn in 1897, he made 19 errors, for a .753 fielding average. Sheckard practiced at third base during spring training of 1901 and played twelve games there for the Superbas once the season started. He made twelve errors in those contests, fielding .721. Hanlon quickly decided to send him back to the outfield.

Next Hanlon tried Frank Gatins, a 30-year-old minor league hopeful. Gatins had been a shortstop in the minors. At third he didn't make many errors, but that was partly because on many routine hits he didn't get close enough to the ball to make a miscue. And his .228 batting average didn't atone for his fielding deficiencies.

Hanlon became so desperate that he even toyed with the idea of trying Willie Keeler at third. Willie, of course, had failed miserably as a third baseman in his first trip to the majors nine years earlier. In early June, when both Gatins and the normal backup third baseman, Joe Kelley, became ill, Hanlon asked for a volunteer to play third. Willie stepped forward.[14] That day he played very well, handling eight chances, all difficult, including an unassisted double play.

Willie's one day of success led to nine days of embarrassment. Hanlon kept him at third for a few days, sent him back to the outfield, then tried him again at third. Over a two-week period he played ten games at third base. He lost one game on a throwing error, made three errors in another game, and generally showed little range. His fielding average at third was .760. Brooklyn fans, who were quite fond of Wee Willie, likely felt grateful when Hanlon abandoned his experiment.

It was mid–July, halfway through the season, before Hanlon finally found an adequate third baseman. He signed Charlie Irwin, a veteran recently released by Cincinnati. Irwin was a good fielder who no longer could hit very well. He batted only .215 for the Superbas, but relieved the anxiety that had previously welled up on any ball hit toward third. When Irwin joined the team on July 17, the Superbas had won 37 and lost 34. They were in fifth place, but trailed Pittsburgh by only 6½ games. Over the remainder of the season they won 59 and lost 32. Like the Phillies, they lost their chance at the pennant when the Pirates blew away the Giants in early September. Three weeks later, the Phillies clinched second place by winning six games in a row while the Superbas were idle.

The Superbas were able to stay competitive largely because of Bill Donovan's emergence as a star pitcher. Before 1901 Donovan had been a long-time "project." He had great stuff, but was the proverbial fastballer who could throw the ball through a brick wall if he could only manage to hit the wall. He debuted in the National League with the Washington Nationals in 1898. In 88 innings that season he allowed 88 hits, a very good ratio for a pitcher laboring for the woebegone Nationals, but he walked 69 batters, an unusually high ratio for that era. Hanlon picked him up in a trade after the 1898 season, and Donovan did most of his pitching in the minors for the next two years. With Hartford in 1900, he gained sufficient control to dominate minor league hitters. At one point he won 15 out of 16 games.[15]

With the 1901 Superbas, Donovan soon fell into a role similar to the one filled by McGinnity the previous year. Early in the season he was the team's only consistently effective pitcher. Hughes was wild at the beginning of the year and missed a couple of starts with a tender arm. McJames, who had not pitched at all while practicing medicine in 1900, was unable to regain the touch on his overhand curve, the pitch that made him successful. Kitson was hit hard and Kennedy came down with a sore arm. Donovan, on the other hand, seemed to pitch better when used often. For Hanlon, who had a reputation for overworking his top pitchers, Donovan's willingness to take the mound was ample reason for using him as often as possible.

By mid–June Hanlon was using him the way a team's ace was often used. Donovan pitched as often as he could, and the rest of the staff fit in around him. Occasionally he was used in relief to save or win a game. Donovan appeared in ten games in June, eleven in July. Over the season he pitched in 33 percent of Brooklyn's 137 games, starting 38 and relieving in seven. Four of his 25 wins came in relief, and he recorded one save.

Addition by Subtraction: St. Louis

The Cardinals lost a lot of good players to the American League in 1901. Whether that was a good thing or a bad thing is open to question, given the debilitating squabbling among the players in 1900. Certainly the Cardinals would have been very happy if Cy Young had not gone to Boston. Catcher Lou Criger, a great defensive catcher, also was missed, and manager Patsy Donovan would probably have welcomed back catcher Wilbert Robinson. On the other hand, few tears were shed over the departure of the other players. Outfielder Mike Donlin was a terrific hitter, a poor fielder, and an undisciplined rascal. Second baseman Bill Keister's terrible fielding more than canceled out his good bat. John McGraw's body came to St. Louis in 1900, but his competitive fire didn't. No one would have wished for a repeat of the turmoil his presence caused in 1900. Three other American Leaguers—Ossee Schreckengost, Charlie Hemphill, and Fritz Buelow—were on the St. Louis reserve list. Only Buelow played for St. Louis in 1900, and he got into only six games. Of those three, only Schreckengost might have played for St. Louis in 1901 had the American League raids not occurred.

St. Louis (76–64)

Regular Lineup	AVG	OBP	SLG	R	RBI	SB
Jesse Burkett, lf	.376	.440	.509	142	75	27
Emmet Heidrick, cf	.339	.366	.470	94	67	32
Dan McGann, 1b	.272	.333	.392	73	56	17
Patsy Donovan, rf	.303	.344	.371	92	73	28
Dick Padden, 2b	.256	.315	.331	71	62	26
Bobby Wallace, ss	.324	.351	.451	69	91	15
Otto Krueger, 3b	.275	.353	.363	77	79	19
Jack Ryan, c	.197	.218	.250	27	31	5
or Art Nichols, c	.244	.290	.308	50	33	14
Leading Pitchers	**W**	**L**	**PCT**	**IP**	**H**	**ERA**
Jack Powell	19	19	.500	338.3	351	3.54
Jack Harper	23	13	.639	308.7	294	3.62
Willie Sudhoff	17	11	.607	276.3	281	3.52
Ed Murphy	10	9	.526	165	201	4.20

With one exception, the Cardinals' replacement players were not impressive. The exception was pitcher Jack Harper, who won 23 games in his first full season in the majors. The other replacement players—catchers Jack Ryan and Pop Schriver, utilityman Art Nichols, second baseman Dick Padden, and third baseman Otto Krueger—struggled to reach the journeyman level. Padden, a slick fielder but mediocre hitter, was the best of the lot.

Let's evaluate the talent flow: a team that finished fifth in 1900, with a 65–75 record, lost a great pitcher who was still at the top of his game, the best leadoff hitter in the league, two of the better catchers in the league, two outstanding hitters who were weak fielders, and several players who could provide team depth. They are replaced by a group of pretty mediocre players. The result was an improvement of 11 games, to 76–64, and involvement in an exciting pennant race into September. How could that be?

Part of the answer is that the 1900 team had an enormous amount of talent that was mostly wasted. That team wasn't focused on winning games. The 1901 team, even after its losses, still had plenty of talent. The outfield of Burkett, Heidrick and Donovan was great both offensively and defensively. The infield was solid defensively, even with Otto Krueger booting 12 percent of his chances at third base. With an average fielder at third, it would have been the league's best.

The Cardinals led the league in runs scored in 1901. The only weak hitters in their lineup were Padden and the catcher, and Padden was adept at moving runners along on the bases. The team had good overall speed and was smart and aggressive on the bases. Leadoff hitter Jesse Burkett had an outstanding season. He scored 142 runs, 19 more than anyone else, and either led the league or finished high in most of the important offensive categories. Emmet Heidrick and Bobby Wallace also had great seasons at bat.

The Cardinals' pitching staff was short on quality pitchers. Manager Donovan, whose career dated to the early nineties, when some teams used only two regular starting pitchers, overcame that problem by going with a three-man pitching rotation for much of the season. The practice was a little tough on the pitchers' arms, but it kept them in the race.

The team's season started to unravel in August, when pitcher Jack Powell marched into the front office and offered to separate Louis Heilbronner's head from the rest of his body. Heilbronner, the team's business manager, declined the offer and quickly retreated into a back office.[16] Without bothering to consult with manager Donovan, Heilbronner had released reserve infielder Pete Childs and signed two minor league players who went on the injured list as soon as they arrived in St. Louis. He decided to make up a game with Boston by scheduling a doubleheader during one of St. Louis's worst hot spells. And he kept the players on edge by instituting petty economies, such as refusing to grant player requests for free passes and questioning Donovan when he gave a player a day off to take care of personal business.[17]

A month after Powell's outburst, first baseman Dan McGann abruptly quit the team. He became angry when Donovan criticized him for the way he handled a play at first base. Donovan didn't think the incident was anything to get upset about, but McGann felt his honor had been challenged. When a reporter asked him if he planned on rejoining the team, he replied, "Not on your daguerreotype. It would make me showing the white feather if I did, and I am a Kentuckian, so I won't. I wish the boys the best luck in the world, but they will have to get along without me."[18] After McGann's departure, the Cardinals lost eight of their next eleven games and the players began focusing on deciding which American League team they wanted to play for in 1902.

Battle Damage: Boston, Chicago, New York and Cincinnati

The American League's raids caught all of the National League teams by surprise. Those who finished in the first division in 1901 either took lighter losses in the raids or were better able to adjust to the losses incurred. A baseball reporter filing a damage report on the second-division teams would write something like the following:

The American League raids left the Beaneaters with a fine pitching staff, a solid defense, and a polite, inoffensive batting order.

Boston (69–69)

Regular Lineup	AVG	OBP	SLG	R	RBI	SB
Jimmy Slagle, rf*	.242	.325	.288	55	27	19
Fred Tenney, 1b	.282	.340	.322	66	22	15
Gene DeMontreville, 2b	.300	.321	.364	83	72	25
Duff Cooley, lf-cf	.258	.302	.338	27	27	5
Billy Hamilton, cf	.287	.404	.356	71	38	20
Bobby Lowe, 3b	.255	.284	.299	47	47	22
Herman Long, ss	.216	.254	.284	54	68	20
Malachi Kittridge, c	.252	.312	.304	24	40	2

Leading Pitchers	W	L	PCT	IP	H	ERA
Kid Nichols	19	16	.543	321	306	3.22
Bill Dinneen	15	18	.455	309.3	295	2.94
Vic Willis	20	17	.541	305.3	262	2.36
Togie Pittinger	13	16	.448	281.3	288	3.01

*Includes record with Philadelphia

Ban Johnson's men took third baseman Jimmy Collins, three of Boston's four outfielders, and both catchers. All played important roles in the new league. Collins was the manager and best player on the rival Boston team. Chick Stahl and Buck Freeman starred on that team. Hugh Duffy managed and played the outfield for Milwaukee, Bill Clarke was captain and primary catcher for Washington, and Billy Sullivan caught for the pennant-winning Chicago White Stockings. Parson Ted Lewis, who had announced his retirement from baseball, returned in May and became one of the Boston American League team's better pitchers.

Manager Frank Selee came close to replacing Collins' glove by moving Bobby Lowe to third base and playing newly acquired Gene DeMontreville at second. The new catchers, Malachi Kittridge and Pat Moran, were improvements over Clarke and almost as good as Sullivan defensively. In keeping with the team's main theme, neither hit very well. Togie Pittinger was an able replacement for Lewis on the mound. Tryouts for the vacant outfield spots began in spring training and were still in progress at dusk on October 5, when the groundskeeper insisted on clearing the field after the Beaneaters' last game.

The 1900 Chicago Orphans didn't seem to be anything special. They never got close to first place, and as the season progressed, Chicago fans became more interested in the new team in town, the American League's White Stockings, who were considered a minor league team that season. So it is somewhat surprising to note all the good players who left the Orphans to play in the American League in 1901.

Clark Griffith had been the Orphans' top pitcher for several years. For the White Stockings in 1901 he was almost as good as Cy Young, who won 31 games that year. Jimmy Callahan twice won 20 games for the Orphans. He had the second-best ERA in the American League in 1901. Bill Bradley was a highly regarded rookie for the Orphans in 1900. The next year he was considered to be one of the top third basemen in the new major league. Sam Mertes finished fourth in RBIs for the White Stockings in 1901, and Jack McCarthy played so well in Cleveland that Griffith named him to a "mythical" American League all-star team. Ned Garvin had the second-best ERA in the National League in 1900. He ranked fourth in strikeouts among American League pitchers in 1901.

The Orphans finished 65–75 in 1900. After their six best players defected to the American League, expectations for the 1901 team weren't high. In spring training some Chicago baseball writers gave the team a new nickname, the Remnants, as in "that which remains after the good stuff has been taken."[19]

Chicago (53–86)

Regular Lineup	AVG	OBP	SLG	R	RBI	SB
Topsy Hartsel, lf	.335	.414	.475	111	54	41

Danny Green, cf	.313	.364	.421	82	61	31
Charlie Dexter, rf–1b	.267	.302	.315	46	66	22
or Frank Chance, rf-c	.278	.376	.361	38	36	27
Jack Doyle, 1b	.232	.263	.277	21	39	8
Cupid Childs, 2b	.258	.359	.297	24	21	3
Fred Raymer, 3b	.233	.257	.272	41	43	18
Barry McCormick, ss	.234	.288	.304	45	32	12
Johnny Kling, c	.273	.301	.320	26	21	8
Leading Pitchers	**W**	**L**	**PCT**	**IP**	**H**	**ERA**
Tom Hughes	10	23	.303	308.3	309	3.24
Jack Taylor	13	19	.406	275.7	341	3.36
Rube Waddell*	14	16	.467	251.3	249	3.01
Mal Eason	8	17	.320	220.7	246	3.59
Jock Menefee	8	12	.400	182.3	201	3.80

*Includes record with Pittsburgh

The Giants had a significant turnover in their roster in 1901, partly because of the American League raids and the internal dissension that wracked the club the previous year. As soon as the 1900 season ended, manager George Davis announced that first baseman Dirty Jack Doyle, second baseman Kid Gleason, and catcher Mike Grady would have to go. Davis said they had formed a clique against him.[20] Gleason and Grady later signed with American League teams, while Doyle went to Chicago in a trade that brought infielder Sammy Strang and first baseman John Ganzel to New York.

American League signings stripped the Giants of the three pitchers who had made the team respectable over the second half of the 1900 season. Win Mercer and Bill Carrick signed with Washington, while Pink Hawley went to Milwaukee. Two other players who played with the Giants in 1900, outfielder Pop Foster and pitcher/outfielder Cy Seymour, also went to the American League, but neither seemed to figure much in the Giants' 1901 plans anyway. Unlike the previous season, none of the other National League clubs rushed in to help the Giants in 1901. The Giants replaced their losses largely by bringing in minor league players. Two of their new pitchers, Roger Denzer and Chauncey Fisher, had been top pitchers for the American League champion Chicago White Stockings in 1900. Signing them would have been a nice coup for the Giants had they performed well. They didn't; both came down with sore arms. Denzer won two games and lost six; Fisher pitched in only one game for the Giants, giving up nine runs in four innings.

New York (52–85)

Regular Lineup	AVG	OBP	SLG	R	RBI	SB
George Van Haltren, cf	.335	.396	.405	82	47	24
Kip Selbach lf	.289	.350	.376	89	56	8
Sammy Strang, 3b	.282	.364	.341	55	34	40
Charlie Hickman, rf	.278	.315	.387	44	62	5
or Algie McBride, rf*	.266	.306	.344	46	47	6
George Davis, ss	.301	.356	.426	69	65	27
John Ganzel, 1b	.215	.256	.262	42	66	6

Ray Nelson, 2b	.200	.262	.215	12	7	3
John Warner, c	.241	.268	.268	19	20	3
or Frank Bowerman, c	.199	.235	.257	20	14	3
Leading Pitchers	**W**	**L**	**PCT**	**IP**	**H**	**ERA**
Dummy Taylor	18	27	.400	353.3	377	3.18
Christy Mathewson	20	17	.541	336	288	2.41
Bill Phyle	7	10	.412	168.7	208	4.27

*Includes record with Cincinnati

The Giants never found an acceptable second baseman, shuffling players in and out of that position all season. The highest number of games any one player had at second base was Ray Nelson's 39. Nine other players were also tried there without success.

This was year two of the Reds' youth movement. Rebuilding that way can be pretty painful, since many young potential stars flame out quickly. For the Reds the pain was made more severe by the American League's aggressiveness. In 1901 the American League took pitcher Ed Scott and outfielder Jimmy Barrett, two of the more successful newcomers of the previous season. Two borderline players, catcher Bob Wood and outfielder Phil Geier, also signed with the new major league.

Scott's loss hurt more on paper than it did on the field. He was the Reds' top pitcher in 1900, but he came down with a sore arm at the beginning of the 1901 season, pitched poorly for Cleveland and was released. Barrett played well for Detroit in 1901 and for several years afterwards. Just as painful to the fans as those losses may have been the performances of several players rejected by the Reds after their 1899 auditions for the 1900 team. Shortstop Kid Elberfeld, outfielder Socks Seybold, and pitcher Casey Patten were all among the American League's best players in 1901.

Cincinnati (52–87)

Regular Lineup	**AVG**	**OBP**	**SLG**	**R**	**RBI**	**SB**
John Dobbs, cf	.274	.338	.345	71	27	19
Dick Harley, lf	.273	.323	.327	69	27	37
Jake Beckley, 1b	.307	.346	.429	78	79	4
Sam Crawford, rf	.330	.378	.524	91	104	13
George Magoon, ss	.252	.331	.324	47	53	15
Harry Steinfeldt, 3b	.249	.303	.380	40	47	10
Bill Fox, 2b	.176	.201	.201	9	7	9
or Heinie Peitz, c–2b	.305	.364	.401	24	24	3
Bill Bergen, c	.179	.199	.234	15	17	2
Leading Pitchers	**W**	**L**	**PCT**	**IP**	**H**	**ERA**
Noodles Hahn	22	19	.537	375.3	370	2.71
Bill Phillips	14	18	.438	281.3	364	4.64
Doc Newton*	10	18	.357	273.3	300	3.62
Archie Stimmel	4	14	.222	153.3	170	4.11

*Includes record with Brooklyn

The Reds' recruiting class of 1901 did not yield any outstanding players. Previously the American League's predecessor, the Western League, and the Eastern League had been the prime recruiting grounds for young players. The American League, of course, kept most of its players in 1901 and signed several of the most promising players from other minor leagues. That left comparatively slim pickings for the National League teams. One of the youngsters the Reds owned very briefly in 1901, however, went on to have a pretty good career. Over the winter the Reds drafted Christy Mathewson from the Giants. They immediately traded him back to New York for Amos Rusie, a great pitcher during the nineties who had not pitched since 1898. It is impossible to know what machinations were behind those dealings. The two owners involved, John T. Brush of Cincinnati and Andrew Freedman of New York, were both fond of backroom maneuvering. It is likely the deal was more about giving Freedman a cover to cut ties with Rusie than it was about Mathewson, who had shown plenty of talent in a brief trial with New York in 1900.

A Fine Utility Player: Honus Wagner

In August of 1898 the owner of Tommy Leach's minor league team told him he had a choice to make. The owner had offers for Leach from two major league teams, Louisville and Washington. He told Tommy he could choose which team he wanted to go to. Tommy, who played third base, didn't know anything about the major league teams, so he asked his manager which team he should choose. The manager told him, "Knowing what I know, I'd say take Louisville. If you go to Washington, they have a man who's a darned good third baseman. His name is Wagner." So Tommy chose to go to Louisville. When he got to Louisville, he saw this big guy at third making plays that seemed impossible. Sitting on the bench, Tommy poked the player next to him and asked the name of the big fellow on third. "Why that's Wagner," was the reply. "He's the best third baseman in the league." Tommy groaned loud enough to be heard by everyone on the bench.

Leach learned later that Washington did have a third baseman named Wagner. That was Al Wagner, the brother of Tommy's new teammate, Honus Wagner. Anyway, it all turned out for the best, Leach later said. He got to play on a team that won four pennants. "And it also turned out," he said, "that while Honus was the best third baseman in the league, he was also the best first baseman, the best second baseman, the best shortstop, and the best outfielder. That was in fielding."[21]

When Louisville purchased Honus Wagner in 1897, manager Fred Clarke stated that one of Wagner's best traits was his ability to play several positions. Over the next several years Clarke took full advantage of that trait. He moved Honus all over the diamond, playing him in every position but left field, which would have been a waste of his great throwing arm; catcher, where he would be exposed to injury; and pitcher, though Honus did mop up in a couple of games. Wagner didn't want to play shortstop and Clarke held off until 1901 before shifting him to that key position. Except for 1900, when Honus played 118 games in right field, he really didn't have a regular position until 1903, when he settled in at shortstop.

Although Honus had played first base and third base in his last two minor league seasons, he began his major league career in center field. Near the end of the 1897

season he was tried at second base. He played a few games there to begin the 1898 campaign, but basically split that season between first and third base. In 1899 he played 75 games at third and 61 in the outfield, while filling in a few games at first and second.

Wagner was moved around partly because Clarke was in the process of building a promising young team at Louisville. Clarke appeared to be using Honus as a sort of wild card to be inserted into whatever position most needed shoring up at a particular time, based not so much on Wagner's play as the performance of other young players on the team. Honus was an "experiment" at second base when the 1898 season opened. He appeared to be mastering his new position during the first couple of weeks, but George Carey, the new slick-fielding first baseman, wasn't able to hit his weight. So Clarke sold Carey and moved Honus to first and tried another youngster, Heinie Smith, at second. By midseason, after Smith had also batted poorly, Clarke shuffled his infield to make room for newly acquired first baseman Harry Davis. Honus went to third base as a part of the changes.[22]

By the end of the 1898 season, Wagner was gaining praise for his play at third base. He remained at third until midway through the 1899 season. According to a Louisville reporter, he was "playing a magnificent game at third base" when Clarke sent Honus to right field to fill in for the injured regular.[23] The new third baseman, the aforementioned Tommy Leach, played so well, however, that Clarke decided to keep him at third. Honus became the new regular right fielder. As had happened the previous season when he moved to third, Honus soon began receiving plaudits for his play in right. In a game against Baltimore, he picked up a ball near the fence and fired it to third to head off the runner. The Orioles marveled at the play. "I'll bet it would take two throws for any other right fielder in the league to have got that ball in," Wilbert Robinson declared. "It was the greatest return from deep field I ever saw."[24]

After the 1899 season a Louisville club official described Wagner as being "at once a utility player and a specialist, his specialty being the outfield, so Fred Clarke believes."[25] That is essentially the role Honus played over the next three seasons. In 1900 he was the regular right fielder, but he played 19 games in the infield while filling in for injured players. In 1901 he started the season in right field, filled in at third for a month while Leach was out with an injury, and then finished the schedule at shortstop. After the 1901 season the Pirates signed Wid Conroy to play shortstop. But in 1902 Wagner did not resume his position in right field, as he would have preferred. He, rather than Conroy, started the season at shortstop, but in the first week of May he moved to the outfield as he began a season-long odyssey replacing injured, suspended, or slumping players in several positions. By the end of the year he had played all three outfield spots, shortstop, first base, and, for one game, second base.

Conroy, who did not play up to expectations with the Pirates, returned to the American League in 1903. Going into spring training that year, Wagner recognized the inevitable and accepted his return to shortstop on a permanent basis.[26]

Opposite: Generally considered the best shortstop ever, Honus Wagner was used as a "super utility player" from 1897 through 1902 (Library of Congress).

There Was Something About Harry: Harry Wolverton

Maybe Harry Wolverton wasn't careful about not crossing paths with black cats or walking under ladders. He seemed to be very unlucky. He was seriously injured in each of his first three seasons in the National League. With Chicago in 1899, his rookie season, he and catcher Art Nichols collided while chasing a foul ball. Wolverton was hit in the head, missing several weeks as a result. In 1901, as a Phillie, he bumped into Boston first baseman Fred Tenney while running out a grounder. He tumbled to the ground, breaking his collarbone and ending his season in mid–August.[27]

He was injured by another collision during the 1900 season. That one happened off the field, while riding a trolley car. He hit a pole. The trolley car didn't hit the pole; Harry did. It seems the trolley car was full when Harry tried to board it. Being a strong, athletic fellow, Harry decided he could stand on the steps and cling to the car

Harry Wolverton encountered some bad luck early in his career (Library of Congress).

while it took him to his stop. While he was riding along, he was struck in the head by one of the poles that stood between the trolley car tracks. Fortunately, the pole was able to score only a glancing blow on Harry's head. He was dazed by it but not seriously injured. He missed only a few games as a result.[28]

Harry was unfortunate in other ways, too. He and Jimmy Williams were considered the best third basemen in minor league baseball in 1898. Harry was purchased by Chicago near the end of that season. He hit well in a one-month tryout that year and had a good year with the bat in 1899. In the field, he showed good range but was somewhat error-prone. After the minor league season ended in 1899, the Orphans picked up another good-looking minor league player, Bill Bradley, who was so impressive at third base that many people said he would be the next great player at that position. The next spring Harry was nervous about losing his job to Bradley. He got into a fight with catcher Tim Donahue, then made a costly error in the season opener. After playing three games, Harry was benched and then sold to Philadelphia.[29]

Harry's season-ending injury in 1901 couldn't have come at a worse time. Rumors of American League signings for 1902 were swirling about, including one that several Phillies had been signed by Washington. Soon after Harry's injury, Ed Delahanty confirmed he was one of the defecting players. A couple of weeks later the Phillies announced they had discovered Wolverton was among the group headed to Washington. Therefore, they said, Harry was immediately suspended without pay for the rest of the season. Harry, who lost about $500, was the only Phillie so punished. The rest of the Philadelphia defectors, including Delahanty, played out the season and were paid in full.[30]

A Rising Star: Jimmy Sheckard

In 1901 it appeared Jimmy Sheckard was on his way to becoming one of baseball's greatest players. He had shown rare ability as a very young player, reaching the National League at the age of 18 and playing well as a regular after that. He had sharpened his skills under two of the top managers of the time, John McGraw and Ned Hanlon. Within a couple of years he had earned a reputation as one of the league's top baserunners and defensive outfielders. Then, in 1901, he improved his hitting, ranking with the top batters in the league and becoming one of the best players in baseball.

Sheckard began his professional career in 1896, playing for three different lower-level minor league teams. In 1897 he was with Brockton, of the New England League, which was then roughly the equivalent of a modern Class AA or High A league. He led the league in batting with a .370 average and in stolen bases with 52. He scored 117 runs in 107 games. During the season the Brockton manager tried to convert him to the infield, but the conversion didn't exactly pan out. In 59 games at shortstop he fielded .853. Only one other shortstop in the league did worse.[31]

Brooklyn bought his contract after Brockton's season ended and brought him in for a tryout. Sheckard showed he could hit, batting .286 with eight extra-base hits in 13 games. He made 19 errors in eleven games at shortstop. That uneven performance was good enough for Brooklyn's manager, who said, "I will hold on to Sheckard because of his batting. He is not a shortstop; I knew that when he came here. But despite his errors he won several games by his stickwork."[32]

Playing in the outfield in 1898, the 19-year-old Sheckard started the season by batting .500 over the first two weeks. In one game he slammed a home run, two triples, and a single. Although his batting average dropped steadily as the season progressed, he remained among the leaders in extra-base hits until he became sick just after midseason. He ended the campaign with a .277 batting average, .349 on-base percentage, and .392 slugging percentage. Those numbers don't seem all that remarkable until they are compared with what other 19-year-olds have done. His batting average was the eleventh-highest ever by a 19-year-old with at least 300 plate appearances. His on-base percentage was the seventh-highest ever. Four of the six players ahead of him in on-base percentage are in the Baseball Hall of Fame, the other two being Tony Conigliaro, who had Hall of Fame talent before being hit in the face by a pitch, and Edgar Renteria, who was a five-time all-star in a 16-year major league career that began when he was either 19 or 20. (Some sources list Renteria as 19 in his rookie year, others list him as 20.)

After the Brooklyn-Baltimore consolidation in 1899, Sheckard found himself in Baltimore playing for McGraw. McGraw stressed the importance of getting on base and running the bases aggressively. Sheckard evidently listened to the master. He reached first 56 times through walks and 18 times by being hit by a pitch, well above his 1898 totals. Once he reached base, he looked for any opening to take an extra one. He dueled McGraw for the league leadership in stolen bases, coming in first when McGraw missed most of the last month of the season. He finished the season with a .295 batting average, 77 stolen bases, and 104 runs scored.

Back in Brooklyn in 1900, Sheckard endeared himself to the home fans with his aggressive base running.[33] He stole 30 bases that season, but it was his ability to take an extra base on a hit to the outfield or even on an infield grounder that the fans loved. He scored 74 runs in only 85 games. He also brought cheers with his play in the outfield. His speed gave him good range and he had one of the best throwing arms in the league.

During his first three years in the National League, Sheckard had shown only average power for an outfielder. In the spring of 1901 he worked at pulling the ball toward the right field fence, which was relatively short in Brooklyn, though it was 42 feet high.[34] His practice paid off with a shower of drives off the fence and a few over it. By season's end he had garnered 29 doubles, 19 triples and 11 home runs. He led the league in triples and slugging percentage and was second in home runs. Sheckard almost always followed Willie Keeler in the batting order, hitting either in the number two or three slot. Keeler hit close to .400 for much of the season before tailing off in the last couple of months. The two gave the Superbas a potent run-scoring combination. Keeler scored 123 times, Sheckard 116. Sheckard drove home 104 runs, trailing only Honus Wagner and Ed Delahanty.

He Doesn't Need the Money: Emmet Heidrick

A scouting report on Emmet Heidrick after the 1901 season: Size: 6' 185 pounds—a big man for his time. Speed: One of fastest runners in league. Throwing Arm: Top

Later a key member of the great Chicago Cubs teams of 1906–10, Jimmy Sheckard displayed impressive ability at a young age (Library of Congress).

notch—good distance, very accurate. Defensive Range: Among best in game—Manager Pat Tebeau compared him with Jimmy McAleer, possibly the top defensive outfielder of the 1890s.[35] Hitting for Average: Sixth-best in league in 1901; lifetime batting average through 1901 is .324. Hitting for Power: Eighth-best in league in 1901; in middle of league before 1901. Other Factors: Father is wealthy man, Emmet doesn't need his baseball salary.[36]

From a purely athletic point of view, a person's social status wouldn't seem to be appropriate for a baseball scouting report. But for Heidrick, it became a part of how fans and teammates viewed his performance. Emmet was injured every summer. It's possible his injuries were related to the intense summer heat in St. Louis. Whatever the reason, when it got hot—in the pennant race and on the diamond—St. Louis players and fans came to expect Emmet to show up on the injured list with a pulled muscle.

Heidrick's injuries were undoubtedly real enough. For instance, when team president Frank Robison accused his players of not taking adequate care of themselves during the 1900 season, Heidrick sent him a doctor's note testifying to the seriousness of his injury.[37] But after a while many St. Louis fans and some of Emmet's teammates began thinking maybe he wasn't tough enough, that he took himself out of the lineup for injuries other players simply played through. At the turn of the twentieth century baseball teams had little depth. The unwritten ballplayers' code required one to keep playing, even with minor injuries, unless his team would not be greatly harmed by his absence. When a regular player was out of the lineup, the drop-off in talent was pretty sharp. The Cardinals' fourth outfielder in 1901 was Art Nichols, their backup catcher, who couldn't come close to replacing Heidrick either in the field or at bat.

In July of 1901 Heidrick missed ten days because of an injury to his side. Before he recovered completely he had to leave the team because of the death of his father. A week after he returned, as the Cardinals were pressing the Pirates for first place, Heidrick smacked an extra-base hit into right-center. Before he reached second, he slowed down, in obvious pain. The visiting players gathered around him, concerned about the injury, but the St. Louis players remained on the bench. After some time Jesse Burkett trotted out to second and talked Heidrick into staying in the game for another inning. Heidrick was back in the starting lineup the next day, but St. Louis newspapers reported the Cardinals players were still fuming. It appears that at least a few players thought the "rich kid" lacked intestinal fortitude.[38]

Heidrick missed 20 to 30 games almost every season. When he played, though, he performed very well. In 1901 most baseball observers would agree that a Brooklyn reporter's assessment of his talent wasn't far off the mark: "For sensational fielding, good hitting, and fast base running, Emmet Heidrick of the St. Louis club ranks at the top of the league. He has such performers as [Billy] Hamilton, [Roy] Thomas, [Danny] Green, and [Ginger] Beaumont beaten a mile, not to speak of our own Tom McCreery."[39]

As league averages plummeted over the next three years, Heidrick's averages fell accordingly, although they remained good in comparison to the league average. His batting average dropped to .289, then to .280, and in 1904 to .273. After that season, at the age of 27, he retired to help run his family's lumber company. Four years later he came out of retirement briefly, but hit only .215 in 26 games.

A Tale of Two Lefties: Lefty Davis

For Lefty Davis, 1901 was both the worst of seasons and the best of seasons. After playing well for four seasons in the highest minor league classification he finally got his chance in the majors. He blew it. He played dreadfully in Brooklyn and was released. But luck was with him. An old teammate helped get him a job with the Pirates. With Pittsburgh he was magnificent, playing a key role as the team beat off three challengers to win the pennant.

Lefty was one of the players who got squeezed out of a major league job by the National League's contraction in 1900. Louisville drafted him after he hit .338 for Minneapolis in 1899, the third-highest average in the Western League. When the Colonels were consolidated with the Pirates, Lefty was sent back to Minneapolis. He had another good season in 1900 and was picked up by the Superbas. An opening was created for him in left field when Jimmy Sheckard was moved to third base. That turned out to be a nightmare, both for Lefty and the Superbas. For two weeks manager Ned Hanlon shuddered whenever a ball was hit down the third base line. If it was a grounder, it was likely Sheckard would butcher it. If it was a fly ball, the chances are Lefty would boot it. Early in May Sheckard went back to the outfield and Lefty went to the bench. Over the next month he played only a few games. Then in June, Hanlon tried Willie Keeler at third and Lefty got another chance. Again he stumbled around in the field. He couldn't catch a ball hit right at him, and he wasn't hitting, either. In mid–June he was given his release. His record: A .209 batting average and .822 fielding average.

Luckily for Lefty, the Pirates' president, Barney Dreyfuss, thought he was a good player who had simply gotten off to a bad start. Dreyfuss was Louisville's president in 1899, when that team drafted Lefty. After the Superbas released Davis, Dreyfuss asked pitcher Deacon Phillippe about him. Phillippe, Lefty's teammate at Minneapolis, urged Dreyfuss to give him a trial. So Dreyfuss signed Lefty. When Honus Wagner filled in at third base during Tommy Leach's illness, Lefty went to right field. This time he did everything right. He scored 28 runs in his first 30 games, hit .319, and fielded 1.000.[40]

When Brooklyn came to Pittsburgh in mid–July, Lefty put on a show for his ex-teammates. In one game he recorded three singles and two walks in five times at bat and had six putouts in right field. Hanlon sat on the bench, wondering if this was the same Lefty Davis he had released a month earlier.

As the season drew to a close Hanlon and Joe Kelley were discussing Lefty's performance with a Cincinnati writer. "There must have been something wrong with Davis while he was with us," Hanlon said. "For some reason or other he could do nothing for us. He did not hit or field, yet he was fast on his feet, and I was convinced that he had it in him."

"Yes, that's right," Kelley said. "We gave him every chance. I'll bet he lost no less than six or eight games for us by dropping fly balls. In Boston he lost us two games in one series in the ninth by dropping flies, and he could not hit a lick for us. Since he joined Pittsburgh," Kelley added, "he has played great ball and hit harder than any man in the league."[41]

For Pittsburgh in 1901, Lefty batted .313, scored 87 runs in 87 games, and fielded .975, a good average for the time. Apparently, Lefty could only play well at the major league level when he was wearing a Pittsburgh uniform. In 1902 he hit .280 in 59 games for the Pirates before a broken leg ended his season prematurely. He signed with the New York Highlanders in 1903 and hit .237, which wasn't good, except when compared with his fielding, which was horrible. When Lefty was released at the end of the season, his manager explained why he got rid of Lefty: "Davis turned out to be the worst fielder I ever saw. He dropped maybe 50 flies and about 150 got away from him through misjudgment." (For the record, Lefty fielded .906 in 1903, making 19 errors in 202 chances.)[42]

The Toast of New York: Christy Mathewson

Christy Mathewson took the baseball world by storm in his first full season with the New York Giants. He helped a bad team stay near the top of the league standings for the first ten weeks of the campaign before it began a free-fall toward a seventh-place finish. He set New York fans buzzing about their team's new "pitching marvel" and became a great drawing card throughout the league. Mathewson's season was so spectacular it might have formed the basis of a dime novel. And to add more drama, he ended the season by battling a sore arm, raising the possibility that New York's new baseball hero could face a tragic end to his budding career.

Matty was not quite ready in July of 1900, when the Giants acquired him from Norfolk of the Virginia State League, where he had compiled a 20–2 record. In five games with the Giants he won none, lost three, and gave up 32 runs in 33 innings. Despite the lackluster record, Matty made a favorable impression. After his first appearance, in which he allowed seven runs in four innings as a reliever, a reporter wrote, "The youngster has lots of speed and gives promise of making his way." Manager George Davis said, "His work in the game Tuesday convinces me that he is a good one, and that he will prove a valuable man for New York." That was after Matty gave up almost two runs per inning pitched. One can only imagine what they might have said if he had pitched well.[43]

When the 1901 season opened, Matty didn't just pitch well; he was spectacular. In his first three games he gave up a total of 10 hits, beating Boston, 5–3, Philadelphia, 3–2, and then Boston again, 2–1. He ran his winning streak to six straight by pitching shutouts in his next three games. He now had two impressive streaks going: Victories and scoreless innings. In his next game he reached victory number seven and built the scoreless innings streak to 39 before Pittsburgh reached him in the ninth inning of a 2–1 win. The winning streak increased to eight straight with a two-hit, 1–0 victory over Cincinnati.

By this time Matty had made a deep impression on those who mattered most—his fellow players. "I do not exaggerate when I say I have never seen the equal of Mathewson as a pitcher," said slugger Ed Delahanty. "He has everything that the best pitcher I have ever known had, and more. He can control curves with more speed than the speed of the straight balls of the speediest of our pitchers. He can command slow balls

Christy Mathewson became a favorite of New York fans with a sparkling rookie season in 1901 (Library of Congress).

better than any man I know."⁴⁴ Brooklyn veteran Tom Daly echoed Delahanty's comment. "Mathewson's pitching has not been a case of a pitcher getting away with something to which he is not entitled," Daly said. "He has everything that you have ever seen a pitcher dish up. Speed, change of pace, cross-fire curves, control, and an easy graceful motion which is very deceptive. He may get trimmed now and then, but, barring accident, he will always be a great pitcher."⁴⁵

Even when he finally lost, in his next game against St. Louis, Mathewson pitched outstanding ball. He lost, 1–0. The winning run scored after a controversial call at third base, when Mathewson fielded a short bounder and tried unsuccessfully to get the runner going to third. Mathewson lost again two days later, pitching four innings of relief in a ten-inning game against St. Louis. He won his next start and then lost four straight outings. On June 30, Matty's record stood at 12–6. The Giants were 27–21, in second place behind the Pirates. The remainder of the season was comparatively rocky, for both Mathewson and his team. The Giants won only 25 games after that. Mathewson fared better, winning eight more and losing 11 to finish the season at 20–17. On July 15, he pitched a no-hitter against St. Louis, beating them, 5–0. He walked four men in the game, and benefited from great fielding plays on three batters.

As expected, the Mathewson of 1901 was not yet the consummate professional on the mound who emerged through time. By the middle of the decade Mathewson had grown into a master of his craft. He could throw with great speed, but learned to save his best fastball for times when he needed it most. Similarly, he used his trademark pitch, the fadeaway (now called a screwball), mostly in clutch situations. And, perhaps above all, he capitalized on pinpoint control. Chief Meyers, his catcher from 1909–1915, claimed Matty had perfect control.⁴⁶

As a Giant rookie in 1901, however, Mathewson dominated with raw ability. He had explosive stuff that he couldn't always control, sometimes to the detriment of opposing players. He hit Jake Beckley in the head with a pitch, knocking Beckley unconscious for 15 minutes. Pirate pitcher Sam Leever was out for nearly two weeks after taking one of Matty's pitches on his throwing arm. Some game reports mention that catchers Aleck Smith and Frank Bowerman were continually jumping around trying to handle his pitches. Smith injured his non-glove hand stopping one of Matty's tosses. "He is a very hard man to catch," Smith told a reporter. "His balls take such sudden shoots that every now and then they land in the catcher's ungloved hand. I had my hand bruised several days ago, but went in again yesterday and had to quit before the game was over. But this fellow is a pitcher. I have never seen his equal. He has everything that is on the calendar."⁴⁷

While it would be inaccurate to say that Matty lacked control, he certainly had not acquired the mastery of his pitches he later achieved. He ranked sixth highest in the league in total number of bases on balls given up, and two-thirds of the league's regular starters walked fewer men than Matty per nine innings pitched. He led the league in wild pitches with 23, four more than anyone else. One of his losses early in the season was a one-run defeat in which an opposing baserunner stole home off his "slow delivery."

To National League owners, the most important aspect of Matty's great 1901 season was his immense popularity with the baseball public. New York fans loved him and fans in other cities turned out in large numbers to see the games he was scheduled to pitch. One magnate ventured the opinion that Matty's popularity had earned the league an extra income of about $100,000.[48] As his success mounted, fans in New York began ending every inning he pitched by loudly applauding his efforts. After the game's last out they would spill onto the field, pursuing him to the clubhouse, some of them waiting until he came out so they could follow him home. In July, while he walked to the bench after being knocked out of the box for the first time all season, the fans stood and applauded him as if he had just won the game.[49]

Matty carried a very heavy workload in 1901. As early as June, some reporters were commenting about the way the Giants were using him. He was pitching about every third game, although rainouts and days off made the Giants' schedule fairly light for most of the first two months. In August Matty began complaining of soreness in his shoulder. On August 30, he pitched normally for the first five innings, then seemed to lose the speed on his fastball. He sat out for the next ten days because of a "cold in his shoulder." On September 9 he pitched a two-hitter to beat St. Louis, 5–1, then was out for another twelve days. He pitched two more games before the season ended. In his last game, on October 5, he came out after seven innings because his shoulder was too sore to finish. Matty's injury was likely a muscle or tendon strain that seemed to respond to rest. During the winter Matty complained of a "tired arm," but the injury had apparently healed when spring training began in 1902.[50]

Rambling Rube

As the 1901 season began, Rube Waddell had not spent a complete season as a major league pitcher, yet he was already one of the most widely discussed players in the game. The enduring image of Rube is that of a harmless screwball. A story often told about Waddell is one in which his roommate, Ossee Schreckengost, refused to sign with the Athletics unless they put a clause in Rube's contract prohibiting him from eating crackers in bed.[51] The story does seem, in fact, to capture the aspect of Rube's character that contemporaries chose to remember late in life. Eating crackers in bed is something only a child would do. And Rube was, indeed, a big man-child.

That is how two former teammates described him in Lawrence S. Ritter's *The Glory of Their Times.* "He was just an overgrown boy," Tommy Leach said while recalling the time when he roomed with Rube. Sam Crawford, Rube's teammate with Grand Rapids in 1899, used almost identical language. "Rube was just a big kid, you know.... You couldn't control him 'cause he was just a big kid himself. Baseball was just a game to Rube."[52]

But the "big kid" analogy does not capture the complexity of Rube's character. Sure, he loved to fish, watch parades, and at times played with children around the ballpark. But he also loved to drink. And he often failed to show up for practices and even games he was scheduled to pitch. At the beginning of Rube's career, baseball management weighed Rube's talent against his childlike approach to the game, along with his unchildlike affinity for the bottle and his irresponsible ways. Several of these men, including the business and field managers at Pittsburgh and Chicago, decided the talent was not worth the trouble of dealing with Rube.

Rube's first major league team was the Louisville Colonels. He appeared in two games for them in 1897, returned to the minors and then rejoined the Colonels the last month of the 1899 season, compiling a 7–2 record. When the Louisville team was dissolved after the 1899 season, Waddell, along with the other top players on the team, was transferred to Pittsburgh. Although he had very little major league experience, Rube was already a celebrity. *The Sporting News* included him in a pictorial supplement issued at the start of the season, explaining that his "personal eccentricities" and his professional achievements had made him one of the most notable figures in the game.

Stories of Rube's eccentricities were beginning to abound. Ed Scott, one of his minor league teammates, recalled the first time he went out with Rube. "Without fully realizing the consequences, I started out with him one night for a walk," Scott said. "He carried a light cane, and before we had gone a block he was whirling it around like a Hindu juggler, and everybody on the promenade was kept sidestepping and feinting until I counted myself out of the parade and escaped."

A similar, and potentially more dangerous, episode occurred after Rube joined the Pirates. In those days, utility players and pitchers who were not expected to pitch that day were often assigned as ticket takers at the turnstiles. One day in Brooklyn Rube drew that assignment. As he stood at the gate, he took tickets with one hand, and in the other he held a frontier-style hatchet. At intervals he would turn quickly, hurling the hatchet into a wooden post. The damaged fence post remained unrepaired for years, a landmark attesting to Waddell's eccentricities.[53]

As might be expected, Rube was somewhat uninhibited on the mound. He liked to taunt the opposing batter. If the batter took a swing at a low pitch, Rube would remind him he was playing baseball, not cricket. If he missed a high pitch, Rube would advise him to get a pole. Once, while pitching in the Polo Grounds, Rube persisted in telling the New York batters they would not get a run off him. When the Giants scored two runs in the eighth inning, the New York fans began to heckle Rube. Undaunted, he turned to the crowd, bowed politely and gave a brief speech in which he said he meant what he had said about pitching a shutout, but circumstances over which he had no control had prevented him from carrying out his plans.[54]

Rube's natural talents were as riveting as his off-beat personality. Leach confessed in *The Glory of Their Times* that he was mesmerized by Waddell's ability. "I used to stand there at third base and watch him throw. I wasn't playing, I was watching! 'How can a man throw that hard?' I used to wonder to myself. He had a terrific curve ball, too, and great control."[55]

With the Pirates, Rube had difficulty turning his great stuff into victories. For the most part he was just pitching in hard luck. He had the lowest earned run average in the National League in 1900, but had only an 8–13 win-loss record, despite pitching for a second-place team. That season Rube earned a reputation for going "ballooning"— the term then used for blowing up under pressure. Whenever men reached base against Rube, opposing teams would ratchet up the noise level, at times standing along the foul lines to get after Rube. The tactics seem to have worked, at least to some extent.

Opposite: **Rube Waddell's eccentricities at times tried the patience of his managers and teammates (National Baseball Hall of Fame Library, Cooperstown, New York).**

While Rube's earned run average was the lowest on the Pirates' staff in 1900, he gave up about .50 more unearned runs per game than the team's other regular starters, an indication that he was less able to overcome his teammates' errors and work out of trouble than the rest of the pitchers.[56]

After he was released to Chicago in 1901, Rube got plenty of practice pitching out of trouble. In Chicago he was reunited with Tom Loftus, a mild-mannered man who had been his manager at Columbus–Grand Rapids in 1899. Rube fared better under patient, laid-back men like Loftus. He began pitching well immediately, winning three of his first four games with Chicago. But the Chicago team was one of the poorer clubs in the league. Even on days when Rube was pitching well, the results could be discouraging. On June 6, Rube pitched reasonably well but was beaten, 14–4. The box score showed he had allowed 16 hits, but, in one writer's opinion, almost half of those were on balls that should have resulted in outs. The team's aging, overweight second baseman had been unable to reach three routine grounders, the left fielder misjudged two easy fly balls, and twice fielders threw to the wrong base. In addition to those plays there were a few more errors of judgment to go along with ten blunders that showed up in the box score as official errors.[57]

Such support would wear on any pitcher. But Rube, of course, was not just any pitcher. He tended to gain strength from success and lose it when his efforts ended in failure. In July he was suspended briefly for not showing up at practices, failing to keep himself in condition, and because he did not "show a disposition to do the right thing." Rube, like an errant child, apologized to Loftus, begged forgiveness, and was reinstated after a couple of days.[58]

Near the end of July Rube had a run-in with one of his teammates. On a day when the temperature in St. Louis was said to be around 113 degrees, Rube decided he didn't want to leave his hotel room. Jack Taylor, a pitcher with a gruff, contentious personality, remarked that Rube was "taking a loaf." Although that is exactly what he was doing, Rube was offended by the remark. He confronted Taylor in the train after the game. A fight was avoided only when other players and the porter separated the two men.[59]

On August 24, Rube failed to show up for a game. The next day he appeared, carrying an affidavit supposedly signed by a train conductor attesting that the train that was to bring Rube back from a fishing trip had been wrecked. Loftus accepted the excuse. Rube then took the mound and beat St. Louis, 5–3, adding two key hits to his performance. A reporter thought the effort justified Rube asking the team for $13.50 to pay the cash-on-delivery charges on an Irish setter puppy that had arrived from St. Louis while Rube was away fishing.[60]

Three days later Rube defeated Cincinnati, 5–4. He then disappeared for the rest of the season. In September he was found pitching for a semi-pro team. Chicago reporters joked that his new contract called for free bait, a silver-mounted fishing reel, and six days of fishing a week—an offer too good to resist.[61]

In addition to landing lots of fish and adding an Irish setter to his family, Rube's year in 1901 included plenty of good performances on the mound. After going 0–2 for Pittsburgh, he won as many as he lost for Chicago, posting a 14–14 record. His team's leaky defense probably took away a few victories in low-hit games and added significantly to his ERA. Rube was among the league leaders only in strikeouts. He ranked fifth in total strikeouts with 172 in 251⅓ innings. In strikeouts per nine innings, he was second to teammate Tom Hughes. Hughes had 6.58 strikeouts per nine innings, Rube had 6.14, and Christy Mathewson followed with 5.92. Rube's 3.01 ERA was tied for fourteenth among the 33 pitchers who pitched at least 140 innings. He ranked twenty-second in runs per nine innings, more a reflection of his team's lack of skill on defense than his own pitching ability.

During the autumn of 1901 Rube joined a group of major league players on a tour of the West Coast. When he left, Jim Hart, the Chicago team president, remarked that Rube would sign to play with the local team in every town on the tour. As for his own team, Hart indicated he would make no effort to sign Rube for 1902. Rube may or may not have been aware of Hart's statements. During the winter he signed to play for Los Angeles in 1902.[62]

Harsher Times

In late August of 1899, while playing in Louisville, John McGraw received a telegram saying his young wife, Minnie, was gravely ill. He rushed home on the next train to Baltimore. While he was on the train, Minnie's physicians performed an operation to remove her appendix, which had ruptured. By the time McGraw arrived home there was little he or the physicians could do but wait and hope Minnie would be able to fight off the infection that remained in her body. Sorrowfully, she did not have the strength. She died three days later. McGraw was devastated by the loss. Baseball games no longer seemed important to him. He stayed away from the team for three weeks, telling a reporter he would be of little use because a lack of sleep had left him physically weak.[63]

Hughie Jennings, McGraw's former teammate and close friend, would have been able to commiserate with him in his grief. Jennings had lost his wife the previous year. Another former teammate, Heinie Reitz, would lose his wife during the 1900 season. The wife of Billy Gilbert, a teammate in Baltimore and New York, would die in 1904. A month after McGraw was called home, a rival player, Elmer Smith, was at his wife's bedside when she died of tuberculosis. Fellow players Duke Farrell, George Decker, and Tommy McCarthy had become widowers in 1897 and 1898. And there were others.[64]

Deadball Era players lived in a world that was in many ways much harsher than today's modern world. A look at the most elemental of considerations, human mortality, may highlight how different the era was. At the turn of the twentieth century, major advances in medicine and health care still lay in the future. Infectious diseases were the leading causes of death. There were still epidemics of yellow fever and smallpox. People died from pneumonia, influenza, typhus, and scarlet fever. Tuberculosis was the most deadly disease, killing three times as many people as cancer. These diseases struck infants and young children especially hard. Women of child-bearing years were also vulnerable. One of every sixteen women died giving birth. In 1900 the average life expectancy at birth was 48.2 years for men and 51.1 for women. A man who reached his twentieth birthday could expect to live to age 62, a woman a year longer.[65]

While it is rare for a modern player to be struck down by sickness while still a young man, at the turn of the twentieth century one or two active or recently retired players died nearly every year. As mentioned above, in 1901 the Pirates lost Tom O'Brien just before the season began. O'Brien succumbed to a disease he contracted while on a trip to Cuba during the autumn of 1900. In September of 1901 pitcher Doc McJames, who had just been released by the Brooklyn Superbas, died as a result of injuries incurred in a carriage accident.[66]

In 1902 Tim Donahue, the Chicago catcher whose sharp tongue had sparked a fight with teammate Harry Wolverton in 1900, asked permission to report late to spring training with his new team, the Washington Senators. Donahue said he had come down with a stomach ailment and needed a little more time to recover. When he reported in late April, Washington baseball reporters were surprised at the state of his health. Donahue was, they said, a sick man who was in no condition to play baseball. In mid-May injuries to the team's other two catchers gave manager Tom Loftus no recourse other than to put Donahue behind the plate. Through sheer grit, Donahue managed to play two games, although he was obviously in great pain. He went home to nurse his illness, and less than a month later he passed away, a victim of Addison's disease.[67] Before the 1902 season ended, another active player died as a result of disease. George Prentiss, a promising young player who pitched briefly for Boston and Baltimore that year, died from typhoid fever. Donahue was 32 when he died; Prentiss was 26.[68]

As in other segments of the population, a relatively high percentage of major league players of this era died at young ages. Of the 185 players who were active in the National League in 1900, four died while in their twenties. Seventeen, or 9.2 percent, failed to see their fortieth birthday. Among those were Rube Waddell, Ed Delahanty, Harry Steinfeldt, and Emmet Heidrick. Thirty-three (17.8 percent) died before reaching the age of 50. Among those who died while still in their forties were Frank Chance, Christy Mathewson, Herman Long, and Wild Bill Donovan. Jake Beckley and Willie Keeler both died within a year after turning fifty.[69]

Although major league players were likely one of the healthiest segments of the population, every season saw players miss playing time because of the diseases that plagued Victorian society. In 1901 the Cincinnati Reds thought they could count on Tommy Corcoran to provide a solid foundation for their infield. He was in the middle of an 18-year major league career that began in 1890 and lasted until 1907. In April he was called home to be with his twin infant sons, who had typhoid fever. While there, Corcoran became ill, nearly died, and didn't return to the team until the end of August. Then he found that he was too weak to play regularly. After trying to play for a month, he sat out the last ten days of the season. A winter's additional rest enabled him to play again in 1902 at close to his normal pace.[70]

Corcoran's brush with death was more serious than the attacks suffered by most major leaguers. But others also fell victim to serious and potentially deadly diseases. Throughout this period reports of players being unable to play because they were sick with malaria were common. During the 1900 and 1901 seasons, at least eight major leaguers, including Corcoran, fell ill with typhoid fever. Wiley Piatt came down with typhoid fever in 1900. Two years later, he contracted smallpox. Piatt was resilient, however. He continued to pitch in the major leagues after both illnesses and lived to be 72 years old.[71]

The effects of childhood diseases, as well as childhood accidents, could be seen among the era's ballplayers. Perhaps the most striking example is the number of ballplayers with speech and hearing problems, considering that professional baseball players comprised only a minute part of the population. It was customary to assign the nickname "Dummy" to such players, making it relatively easy to identify them decades later. Two deaf players, Luther Taylor and William Hoy, both better known by the nickname they shared (which of course was "Dummy"), had long and distinguished careers. Several other deaf players were also active during this era.

George Leitner, who did most of his pitching as a semi-professional on Baltimore's sandlots, was good enough to be picked up by four different major league teams when injuries depleted their pitching staffs. He appeared in only five games and was 0–2 in his major league career, both losses coming with the New York Giants in 1901. Leitner was a relatively small man for a pitcher, standing only 5'7" and weighing 120 pounds. He managed to fool major league hitters for a few innings in each game by using an assortment of breaking pitches thrown with submarine and sidearm deliveries. Eventually, though, the batters seemed to catch on to his style. Leitner figured in a couple of situations that could be the subject of trivia questions. He was one of three deaf players who pitched for the 1901 New York Giants, the others being Taylor and William Deegan. In 1903 Leitner started against another deaf pitcher while pitching for Des Moines in the Western League.[72]

Luther "Dummy" Taylor was one of several deaf players in the early Deadball Era (Library of Congress).

"Dummy" Kihm played first base for Indianapolis and Columbus in the American Association during this time. Although he never played for a major league team, he ranked among the top hitters in the association for a couple of years. The *Washington Post* once commented that Kihm "covers the sack like [Charlie] Comiskey and wallops the leather like [Jesse] Burkett."[73]

Knowledgeable baseball fans are quite familiar with Mordecai "Three-Finger" Brown, the Chicago Cubs' Hall of Fame pitcher. When he was five years old, Brown lost most of the index finger on his right hand while helping his brother run a feed chopper. The other fingers were severely cut, but were sewn up and bandaged by a local doctor. Two weeks later Brown fell while playing with a pet rabbit and broke the remaining fingers on that hand in several places. Brown and his sister re-bandaged the fingers. When Brown's hand healed, he was left with the stump of his index finger, a crooked middle finger, and a little finger that had little sense of touch and could not be completely straightened.[74]

A few other players seem to have had accidents similar to Brown's. Bill Coughlin, a third baseman for the Washington Senators and Detroit Tigers, was missing one finger. A teammate in Washington, Frank Huelsman, was missing parts of two fingers. An item appearing in *The Sporting News* in 1897 noted that three members of the Pawtucket team of the New England League were missing two fingers.[75]

Three

1901, American League

The New Major League

Five of the 1901 American League teams were holdover franchises from the 1900 American League. On those clubs the 1900 players formed the core of the 1901 teams, fortified with players signed away from the National League. They were the Chicago, Milwaukee, Detroit and Cleveland franchises, which remained in those cities, and the Kansas City franchise, which relocated to Washington. New teams were organized in Boston, Philadelphia and Baltimore, combining signees from the National League with some players who had been with American League teams in 1900. All eight teams had a few players from lower-level leagues.

1901 American League Standings

Team	W	L	Pct.	GB
Chicago	83	53	.610	—
Boston	79	57	.581	4
Detroit	74	61	.548	8.5
Philadelphia	74	62	.544	9
Baltimore	68	65	.511	13.5
Washington	61	72	.459	20.5
Cleveland	54	82	.397	29
Milwaukee	48	89	.350	35.5

The American League of the late 1890s (which was then called the Western League) might have had trouble sustaining a claim to major league status. It had a good number of players whose names National League fans would recognize, but would consider has-beens or fringe major league players. The consolidation of 1900 helped to strengthen the American League in two ways. First, it set loose about two dozen players whom fans could recognize as solid major leaguers. While they were not stars, they had played well enough to show they could compete at the game's top level. Milwaukee's John Anderson, for instance, led the league in triples and slugging percentage in 1898. Steve Brodie and Bill Hoffer had been members of the great Baltimore teams of the mid-nineties.

Second, the consolidation allowed the American League to retain young players who were on the verge of graduating to the National League. The annual National League raids on minor league teams didn't happen after the 1899 season, with the exception of John T. Brush's gambit to outwit his fellow magnates. And, as noted, the Reds were able to retain only a few of the players they obtained.

The raid on National League teams over the winter of 1900–01 netted about 40 more former senior circuit players. As a result, the rosters of the American League teams that opened the 1901 season had many names baseball fans knew well.

Almost a dozen of the players who came over from the National League in 1901 were considered stars. Jimmy Collins and Nap Lajoie were universally deemed the best at their positions in 1901, and some observers were saying they were the best ever. Cy Young, who still had 225 victories in his future, was already considered one of the game's all-time greatest pitchers. John McGraw was noted both for his ability to get on base and his ferocious competitive drive. Such players contributed to the feeling that the American League was, indeed, a major league, even if it was not quite the National League's equal.

On the other hand, the vast majority of the ex–National Leaguers who dotted American League rosters in 1901 were considered by knowledgeable fans to be average or below-average players. After all, most of them had been rejected by the National League either in 1900 or before. Also, while there were a lot of good ballplayers in the American League in 1901, their ranks thinned rapidly when it came to manning eight teams.

All the teams had at least one glaring weakness. The further down the standings one looked, the more numerous and glaring the weaknesses became. The 1901 American League somewhat resembled one of the relatively weak modern-day divisions, when a division winner might be only the fourth- or fifth-best team in a 14- or 16-team league. Ernest Lanigan, a well-respected baseball reporter and statistician, estimated in June of 1901 that the National League was about 50 percent better than the American League.[1] Lanigan might have overstated the difference between the two leagues, but the National League was undoubtedly much the stronger of the two leagues in 1901.

The Defending—and New—Champions: Chicago

The White Stockings were the defending American League champions. They had won the 1900 pennant by a comfortable margin, and most of their key players remained with the team in 1901. New manager Clark Griffith inherited a solid core of capable, experienced ballplayers in the spring of 1901. He added to this core five talented ex–National League players, including himself.

Chicago (83–53)

Regular Lineup	AVG	OBP	SLG	R	RBI	SB
Dummy Hoy, cf	.294	.407	.400	112	60	27
Fielder Jones, rf	.311	.412	.365	120	65	38
Sam Mertes, 2b	.277	.347	.396	94	98	46

Frank Isbell, 1b	.257	.311	.329	93	70	52
Fred Hartman, 3b	.309	.355	.431	77	89	31
or Jimmy Burke, 3b-ss	.264	.327	.297	20	21	11
Herm McFarland, lf	.275	.384	.383	83	59	33
Frank Shugart, ss	.251	.301	.345	62	47	12
Billy Sullivan, c	.245	.271	.351	54	56	12
or Joe Sugden, c	.275	.339	.333	21	19	4
Leading Pitchers	**W**	**L**	**PCT**	**IP**	**H**	**ERA**
Roy Patterson	20	15	.571	312.3	345	3.37
Clark Griffith	24	7	.774	266.7	275	2.67
Jimmy Callahan	15	8	.652	215.3	195	2.42
John Katoll	11	10	.524	208	231	2.81

At first glance, except for its pitching staff, the team did not appear to be too impressive. It was filled with players who were essentially National League rejects. First baseman Frank Isbell had spent much of the 1898 season in the National League with the Chicago Orphans. He had proven to be very versatile, but not very successful. Given trials as a pitcher, outfielder and utility infielder, he failed at each position. He was returned to St. Paul (the White Stockings' location in 1898), where he eventually began to concentrate on first base, although through the 1900 season he still pitched occasionally and filled in as a utility player. Isbell was a smart, athletic player who had become an excellent fielding first baseman and a fine baserunner. Unfortunately, he still wasn't much of a hitter. His batting average in 1901 (.257) was the lowest of any regular American League first baseman.[2]

Shortstop Frank Shugart was nearing the end of his career. He first reached the majors in 1890 in the Players' League. Although he struggled somewhat in the field and was mediocre at bat, he stayed in the league until 1896, playing with second-division teams. He dropped back into the minors in 1896 and remained there until 1901, except for 40 games with the Phillies in 1897.[3]

Third baseman Fred Hartman's skills were similar to those of Shugart. He had enjoyed some decent seasons with the bat in the National League. He hit .319 in 49 games with the Pirates in 1894, but couldn't field well enough to stay in the league. He returned in 1897, batting .306 with St. Louis. The next year he was traded to New York, where his fielding woes brought catcalls from the bleachers and a decline in his overall performance. Midway through the 1899 season, he was sent back to the minors. He had batted .275 for the White Stockings in 1900, and played his usual mediocre defense at third, posting an .894 fielding percentage, the third-worst in the league.[4]

The White Stockings' second baseman was an outfielder who played out of position during the 1901 season. The team's second baseman in 1900, Dick Padden, left Chicago in the spring of 1901 to play for the St. Louis Cardinals. The minor leaguer signed to replace Padden soon proved inadequate. Manager Griffith had seen Sam Mertes struggle when tried at first base and shortstop by the Chicago Orphans in 1900, but he must have seen something he liked. He moved Mertes to second base as a stopgap measure. Although Mertes had some difficulty fielding slow grounders, he did well enough that Griffith decided to keep him at the keystone position for the remainder of the season. Mertes played 132 games at second base in 1901, but just one more game there over the remaining five years of his career.[5]

In the outfield the White Stockings had two returnees from the 1900 team and one of the better players signed away from the National League. Left fielder Herm McFarland had played in the National League briefly for Louisville in 1896 and Cincinnati in 1898. He was a regular for the 1900 White Stockings, but was slated to be a reserve outfielder with the 1901 team before Mertes was moved to second base.[6] Center fielder Dummy Hoy was one of the players who lost his major league job due to the contraction of 1900. He had played for Louisville in 1899 but did not have a position when the Louisville and Pittsburgh teams were combined. Hoy sometimes had problems fielding grounders hit into the outfield, but he was an excellent leadoff batter. For the 1900 White Stockings he scored 115 runs, only two fewer than the league leader. The right fielder was Fielder Jones, one of the leading players on the pennant-winning Brooklyn Superbas in 1900.

The team's catchers were Billy Sullivan, who had established himself as one of the best young receivers in the game with Boston in 1900, and Joe Sugden, a capable veteran who got squeezed out of the National League by the 1900 consolidation.

The pitching staff was the White Stockings' primary strength, both in quality and depth. Two of their starters, Griffith and Jimmy Callahan, had been standouts in the National League. Griffith had been the ace of the Chicago Orphans' staff, winning at least 20 games every year from 1894 through 1899. Callahan had gone 20–10 in 1898 and 21–12 in 1899. A third pitcher, Roy Patterson, was 17–8 as a rookie with the 1900 White Stockings. Although two veteran pitchers won more games than he did in 1900, Patterson was considered the ace of the staff by the end of that season. Jack Katoll had been a workhorse for the 1900 White Stockings, posting a 16–14 record. Lefthander Zaza Harvey was 7–14 with Minneapolis, which finished last in the American League in 1900.[7] John Skopec, also a lefthander, was a rookie who had pitched well in the Interstate League in 1900.

These 1901 White Stockings were not "hitless wonders" like the 1906 team, but as baseball families go, they might have been a favorite uncle to that team. They were considered a "lucky" club, but like many good baseball teams, their luck came from doing the little things that win games. In one game they beat Cleveland, 4–2, even though they were held hitless for the first nine innings. They were patient batters, walking 95 times more than any other team. They were excellent baserunners. The top base stealers in the league were Isbell (52), Mertes (46), and Jones (tied for third with 38). They were masters at the hit-and-run game. "It is not hard to figure out why they win games," one reporter explained. "Every man has the hit-and-run game down fine and every little point is taken advantage of to the fullest extent. Hartman is about the slowest man on the team, and even he can get around the bases at a lively gait."[8]

The White Stockings' pitching staff was the best in the league with a 2.98 ERA, despite encountering a variety of misfortunes. Callahan broke a bone in his wrist during spring training and was unable to pitch until mid–June. Skopec was a pleasant early-season surprise, but by the end of May he had lost track of the strike zone. When the team left for an eastern trip in June, Skopec remained in Chicago, practicing each morning in a vain effort to recover the ability to throw strikes. Eventually he was released to a minor league team. Katoll missed almost a month due to a hand injury and a two-week suspension. Griffith missed more than two weeks due to a broken finger when the pennant race was at its hottest. Only Roy Patterson was available throughout the season, and he had a tender arm for the first month.[9]

At the beginning of the 1901 season, American League fans faced the same intriguing uncertainty National League fans had enjoyed at the outset of the 1900 campaign. Fans in each city felt their team was pretty good, but had no idea how good the team needed to be to compete for first place. A Milwaukee oddsmaker made the White Stockings the favorites at 13–5. Baltimore was next at 3–1; Boston, Philadelphia, and Detroit followed at 5–1; and Washington, Milwaukee and Cleveland trailed at 15–1.[10] A glance at the final standings indicates the oddsmaker was a pretty good judge of talent, even if he did overrate John McGraw's Baltimore team.

The White Stockings lived up to the Milwaukee oddsmaker's expectations. They trailed Detroit in the early weeks of the season but never fell very far off the pace. They moved into first place as May drew to a close. Detroit held second until mid–June, but as the season progressed, Boston emerged as the White Stockings' strongest competitor. Boston caught the White Stockings on June 20, the two teams being even in the games-behind column, but Boston holding first by a few percentage points. Four days later the White Stockings reclaimed first. During the next month Boston twice edged ahead of the White Stockings but couldn't hold the lead. On July 17 the White Stockings held a half-game lead over Boston but trailed them by four percentage points. The next day they won and Boston lost, giving the White Stockings the lead both in games and percentage points. The two teams won and lost on the same days for five days before the White Stockings went on a five-game winning streak to put a small ray of daylight between the two teams.

Chicago and Boston battled on until late August when the White Stockings' vaunted "luck" seemed to desert them, partly because of their own misconduct. On August 21, Katoll gave up a bases-loaded triple to fall behind Washington, 4–0, in the fourth inning. His next pitch went past the catcher, hitting the umpire, Haskell, on the shoulder. Haskell waved the runner home from third. Katoll, angry over this and previous decisions by Haskell, picked up the ball and threw it at Haskell, hitting him in the leg. Haskell banished Katoll to the bench and was immediately surrounded by two other Chicago players. In the ensuing argument Shugart punched Haskell in the mouth, drawing blood. He also was ejected from the game. League president Ban Johnson, who had spent the entire season sparring with Griffith, McGraw, and several other ex–National Leaguers over their constant umpire-baiting, immediately suspended both Shugart and Katoll. His statements to reporters implied that Shugart might be banned from playing in the American League again.[11]

Katoll's suspension came at a bad time for the White Stockings. Harvey had just been released to Cleveland and Callahan was out with a stomach ailment. Katoll's absence left the White Stockings with two healthy pitchers—Griffith and Patterson. Griffith lasted into the fourth inning of the next game, when a line drive broke the middle finger on his pitching hand. The White Stockings' lead, already down to a half-game, seemed about to disappear.

Relieving Griffith was Roy Patterson, now the only healthy pitcher on the staff. A Chicago writer had joked that when he won, Patterson was the "St. Croix Wonder," and when he lost he was just plain "Pat."[12] In most of his appearances for the White

Stockings in 1900, Patterson had been a wonder. But against stronger opposition in 1901, all too often he was simply "Pat." He pitched well in his first three games of the season, beating Cleveland, 8–2, losing to Detroit, 3–2, and pitching six innings of strong relief against the Tigers. But on May 5 he lost to Milwaukee, 21–7, giving up 25 hits to the worst team in the league. He followed that performance with several ineffective outings, and then beat Baltimore and Boston, two of the better teams in the league. Through mid-August he continued to be an "in-and-outer." He pitched some good games, but he also had games where he was completely ineffective. On the day before Griffith's injury, Patterson had defeated Baltimore, 6–5, bringing his record to an undistinguished 13–14. The White Stockings trailed Baltimore, 4–2, when Griffith was forced out of the game. Patterson held the Orioles scoreless the rest of the way, as Chicago rallied to win, 6–4.

The White Stockings were facing 22 games over the next 21 days. Callahan came off the injured list to help out in the emergency. Although Griffith hurriedly acquired another former National League pitcher—Wiley Piatt, who had been released recently by the Philadelphia Athletics—and Katoll came off his suspension before the 21 days were over, the task of keeping the team in the pennant race fell mainly upon Patterson and Callahan.

The two pitchers met the challenge, alternating starts over the next week and then teaming with Piatt in doubleheaders on August 31 and September 2. Callahan pitched well, appearing in nine games—three in relief—over those 20 days and going 4–2. Patterson appeared in eight games and pitched magnificently. He won four games in a row, two of them shutouts, in the critical ten days after Griffith's injury. He then added a victory over Boston as the White Stockings swept a four-game series to gain a seven-game lead. His only loss came against Milwaukee on the last day of the marathon stretch. The effort won Patterson the admiration of White Stocking fans, who credited the "St. Croix Wonder" with saving the pennant for their team.[13]

Roy Patterson, the "St. Croix Wonder," played a pivotal role in the Chicago White Stockings' pennant drive in 1901 (National Baseball Hall of Fame Library, Cooperstown, New York).

A Gentleman's Team: Boston

The Boston American League team really had no widely recognized nickname in 1901. They were often called the "Beaneaters," as were their

National League counterparts. Reporters also called them the "Somersites" (after their principal owner, Charles Somers), the "Collinsites" (after their manager, Jimmy Collins), and "Americans" to distinguish them from their National League counterparts. Modern references have come to accept Americans as the most commonly used nickname. Most of the time sources simply referred to this team as "the Bostons."

Boston (79–57)

Regular Lineup	AVG	OBP	SLG	R	RBI	SB
Tommy Dowd, lf	.268	.315	.337	104	52	33
Chick Stahl, cf	.303	.377	.439	105	72	29
Jimmy Collins, 3b	.332	.375	.495	108	94	19
Buck Freeman, 1b	.339	.400	.520	88	114	17
Charlie Hemphill, rf	.261	.312	.332	71	62	11
Freddy Parent, ss	.306	.367	.408	87	59	16
Hobe Ferris, 2b	.250	.290	.350	68	63	13
O. Schreckengost, c	.304	.356	.386	37	38	6
or Lou Criger, c	.231	.270	.276	26	24	7
Leading Pitchers	**W**	**L**	**PCT**	**IP**	**H**	**ERA**
Cy Young	33	10	.767	371.3	324	1.62
Ted Lewis	16	17	.485	316.3	299	3.53
George Winter	16	12	.571	241	234	2.80

Boston had no previous American League team to use as a nucleus for the 1901 team, but five members had played for the Boston National League club in 1900. (They were Collins, Buck Freeman, Chick Stahl, Ted Lewis, and Nig Cuppy.) Cy Young and Lou Criger came from St. Louis. Three players—Tommy Dowd, Ossee Schreckengost, and Charlie Hemphill—had played in the National League in 1899 and in the American League in 1900. As a result, it was, for the most part, a veteran team. Two rookies, Freddy Parent and Hobe Ferris, played key roles in the middle of the infield. Two other rookies were on the pitching staff. Fred Mitchell was used as an extra pitcher, while George Winter, who pitched for Gettysburg College earlier in the year, became a regular starter after being signed in mid–June.

With a couple of changes in the starting lineup and the infusion of more pitching, these players formed the core of teams that were strong contenders for the American League championship in 1901 and 1902 and winners in 1903 and 1904.

The Boston team offered a sharp contrast to the White Stockings, mirroring to some extent the personalities of their managers. Chicago manager Clark Griffith had a somewhat rebellious personality. He had many disagreements with Cap Anson and his other managers while with the Orphans. He was a relatively small man who didn't have a great fastball but developed a habit of cutting the ball with his spikes to gain an edge. He was tenacious in battling both the batters and the umpires. As described above, his White Stockings similarly founded their success on an aggressive style of play. They fought to get on base and then schemed to get around the bases, subordinating the hitter to the baserunner by emphasizing the stolen base, sacrifice and hit-and-run. They pressured not only the other team but also the umpires, drawing several suspensions as a result.

By contrast, Boston manager Jimmy Collins was a quiet and courteous man with a laid-back personality. He had a great deal of natural ability. He was a smooth fielder, a solid hitter, a good but not overly aggressive baserunner. Like their manager, Collins' Boston players knew how to play scientific baseball. They could execute the hit-and-run, and they generally followed the book when it came to sacrificing. But they didn't overdo it. They appreciated the value of a solid line drive hit into the outfield, possibly for extra bases. Only Philadelphia, whose lineup featured Lajoie and two other sluggers, had more extra-base hits than Boston. Neither did Collins emphasize the stolen base—only seventh-place Cleveland and the slow-footed Senators had fewer. When Boston's style of play worked, the critics in the stands cheered. When it failed, the critics complained, as one reporter did after a 4–0 loss: "It was a case of straight-away hitting, without any variety in the way of a little bunting to keep the other fellows guessing, and the result was a defeat without the thought of a little hustling."[14]

As for fighting the umpires, Collins did not believe in doing that. After a losing game in Chicago, in which the White Stockings appeared to have gotten all the close decisions, Collins was asked why he had not protested more vigorously. "It looked as if we had much the worst of it," he replied, "but kicking apparently does no good. All the teams visiting Chicago are complaining of the home umpiring here." Throughout the league Boston had the reputation of being a well-behaved, gentlemanly team.[15]

Offensively, Boston was led by the ex–Beaneaters—Collins, Freeman and Stahl. After Nap Lajoie, who, statistically speaking, was in a league by himself in 1901, the Boston batters topped the American League slugging categories. Excluding Lajoie, Collins had the most extra-base hits and the most total bases on extra-base hits. Freeman had the most home runs and RBIs and the highest slugging percentage (again, excluding Lajoie). In triples—a more significant power category than home runs in 1901—Boston players ranked fourth through seventh in the league. Collins and Stahl each had 16 triples, while Freeman and Ferris had 15 apiece.

Defensively, Boston was able to put excellent fielders in six of the eight non-pitching positions. Hemphill, the right fielder, was a mediocre defender who had trouble picking up grounders. Freeman, moved from the outfield to first base in 1901, was a mediocre glove man on his good days, terrible the rest of the time. The two rookies in the middle of the infield, shortstop Freddy Parent and second baseman Hobe Ferris, who could have been the team's Achilles' heel, proved to be great assets. Their fielding brought praise from writers throughout the league.[16]

On the mound, Boston was one of six American League teams with little pitching depth. For most teams that was a weakness. For Boston, not so much. Lack of pitching depth gave Collins an excuse to pitch Cy Young as often as he could, and in 1901 Young was the league's best pitcher by a wide margin. Young started 41 games in 1901, 30 percent of Boston's games, and he relieved in two others. With a 33–10 win-loss record, 1.62 ERA, five shutouts, 158 strikeouts and only 37 bases on balls in 371⅓ innings pitched, he finished first or second in every important pitching category. He led in wins, ERA, and strikeouts, and tied for first in shutouts. He had the fewest walks per nine innings (0.90) and gave up the fewest hits per nine innings (7.85). Clark Griffith, with a 24–7 record, led him in winning percentage, .774 to .767. Joe McGinnity finished ahead of him in innings pitched with 382.

A Thrilling Start: Detroit

The Tigers finished fourth in the American League in 1900 with a 71–68 record. The team lost its best outfielder, Dick Harley, when he signed with Cincinnati in the spring of 1901. Manager George Stallings added a washed-up veteran second baseman (Kid Gleason), a young outfielder with one year in the National League (Jimmy Barrett), a catcher who split the 1900 season between Denver of the Western League and the bench in St. Louis (Fritz Buelow), and a journeyman American League player who had failed in two trial runs with Louisville in 1897 and 1898 (Doc Nance). Stallings also retained Ed Siever, a minor leaguer who pitched well for the Tigers the last two months of the 1900 season. With his team thus fortified, Stallings, known to be somewhat stubborn and opinionated, told Detroit writers he thought his team would do well in the tougher American League of 1901.

He was right. The Tigers led the league for the first month and stayed on the heels of the top two teams thereafter. Their final 1901 record, in a stronger American League, was five games better than their 1900 record.

Detroit (74–61)

Regular Lineup	AVG	OBP	SLG	R	RBI	SB
Doc Casey, 3b	.283	.335	.357	105	46	34
Ducky Holmes, rf	.294	.347	.406	90	62	35
Jimmy Barrett, cf	.293	.385	.378	110	65	26
Kid Gleason, 2b	.274	.327	.364	82	75	32
Kid Elberfeld, ss	.308	.397	.428	76	76	23
Doc Nance, lf	.280	.355	.373	72	66	9
Pop Dillon, 1b	.288	.324	.391	40	42	14
or Davey Crockett, 1b	.284	.336	.343	10	14	1
Fritz Buelow, c	.225	.269	.316	28	29	2
or Sport McAllister, ut	.301	.344	.386	45	57	17
Leading Pitchers	W	L	PCT	IP	H	ERA
Roscoe Miller	23	13	.639	332	339	2.95
Ed Siever	18	14	.563	288.7	334	3.24
Jack Cronin	13	16	.448	219.7	261	3.89
Joe Yeager	12	11	.522	199.7	209	2.61

Stallings could feel confident about his team because the core players from the 1900 Detroit club were guys who probably would have been playing in the National League in 1901 if it were still a 12-team league. Some had been forced into the minors by the 1900 consolidation, others had been frozen there because of it. First baseman Pop Dillon had played well in an 1899 trial with Pittsburgh. He wasn't able to make the powerful 1900 Pirate team, but was still considered to be a pretty good player. Shortstop Kid Elberfeld, dropped by the Phillies because of an injury and by the Reds because they had veteran players at short and third, was considered one of the most talented infielders in the minor leagues. Third baseman Jimmy Casey had been the regular third baseman for the 1899 pennant-winning Brooklyn Superbas. Catcher/utilityman Sport McAllister had spent parts of four seasons with the Cleveland Spiders.

Right fielder Ducky Holmes was one of several good players on the 1899 Baltimore team who were forced into the minors by the consolidation.

Among the pitchers, Joe Yeager had been a starter for Brooklyn in 1898 and a pitcher/utility player for the 1899 pennant winners. He posted a 20–11 record in 1900 with Detroit. Yeager was on the Brooklyn reserve list when he signed his 1901 contract with Detroit. Jack Cronin had gone 4–4 in short trials with Pittsburgh in 1898 and Cincinnati in 1899. Roscoe Miller would have been given a trial with one of the National League teams in 1901 if the baseball war had not erupted. He had won nineteen games and lost only nine with Detroit in 1900.

More than 10,000 fans turned out for Detroit's opening game against Milwaukee, celebrating the city's return to the major leagues after an absence of thirteen years. The crowd overflowed the stands, bringing about the ground rule that any ball hit into the crowd ringing the outfield would be a double. It was a festive occasion, marred only by the drubbing being absorbed by the home team.

Going into the bottom of the ninth the Tigers seemed hopelessly behind, trailing, 13–4. Casey led off the inning with a double, giving the crowd hope that a last-ditch rally might take some sting out of the impending lopsided defeat. Barrett beat out a slow roller to third and Gleason singled, scoring Casey. The crowd cheered. It looked like a nice little rally was developing—too late, of course, to make any difference, but pleasing just the same. Holmes and Dillon followed with drives into the crowd, generating two more doubles and three more runs. At least now the defeat would be by a more respectable score. Another double made the score 13–9, and Milwaukee's manager brought in relief pitcher Pete Husting to put out the fire.

As often happened in this era, Husting came into the game without throwing any warm-up pitches on the sideline. His first pitch was wild, allowing the runner to reach third. The crowd was excited by now and pressing in toward the infield. Detroit players went out to move the crowd back, unintentionally enabling Husting to throw a few warm-up pitches. Nance grounded to Conroy for the first out. Husting, still a little wild, walked Buelow on four pitches. Frisk singled to left, scoring another run. It was now a 13–10 game.

Casey beat out a bunt, filling the bases, but Barrett fanned. Two outs. Gleason hit a sharp grounder to third that went off third baseman Jimmy Burke's glove for an error, making the score 13–11. Holmes tapped another one towards Burke and beat it out, another run scoring. It was now 13–12, the bases were full, and Pop Dillon was the batter. He'd already hit three drives into the crowd for ground-rule doubles, one earlier in this inning. Could he do it again? Dillon drove the ball far over the left fielder's head, deep into the crowd. The Tigers scored ten runs in the bottom of the ninth to win their first (major league) American League game, 14–13.

The next day the Tigers fell behind early, trailing, 4–1, after four innings and 5–2 after seven. They rallied in the eighth, scoring twice to pull within a run, 5–4. The outlook seemed bleak, however, when the first two batters in the ninth were retired. But Holmes walked and Dillon singled, sending Holmes to third. With Kid Elberfeld, a patient hitter at bat, Dillon stole second. Elberfeld then drilled a fastball deep into left-center for a double, plating two runs and producing another great come-from-behind victory.

In game three, the Tigers fell behind, 8–4, going into the bottom of the fourth.

They rallied but were still behind, 9–8, when they went to bat in the bottom of the eighth. By now the walk-off double act was getting a little old, so the Tigers created a variation. To demonstrate their grasp of "scientific baseball," they went to a "bunting" attack.

Buelow started the inning by tapping one toward short and beating it out. Yeager dropped a bunt along the third base line and beat it out. Casey did the same thing, loading the bases. Barrett slapped one into center field, scoring two runs to take the lead. Gleason resorted to the bunt again but popped it up to the pitcher. After Holmes grounded out short to first for the second out, it became time to start swinging away again. Dillon drove a double to left, scoring two runs. A steal of third, a walk and a single scored another run, as the Tigers pulled off another late-inning victory, 13–9.

In game four the Tigers went back to their slugging script, scoring three runs in the eighth and four in the ninth to win, 12–11. Four straight late-inning come-from-behind victories—not a bad way to start a season.[17]

As the season progressed, the Tigers, like most of the American League teams, found themselves somewhat thin in pitching. Stallings dealt with the problem by relying heavily on Roscoe Miller. From the beginning of June through Labor Day, Stallings shuffled his pitchers in a way that put Miller on a virtual three-man rotation while the other pitchers on the staff worked a slightly less demanding schedule. Off-days gave Miller some rest, but he shouldered a very heavy pitching burden in 1901. He started ten games on two days' rest. Three times he started a game on only one day's rest after pitching complete games, and on two other occasions started a game after pitching three or four innings the previous day. Although he missed most of the first three weeks of the season because of sickness, he finished third in the league with 332 innings pitched.

As if pitching on a three-day rotation wasn't enough, Miller's workload was made even more burdensome because he was involved in five extra-inning games, all of which he completed. One of those games lasted 16 innings and another went 15. After the 16-inning game, he returned to the mound with two days' rest and pitched an 11-inning contest. Miller's only setback in extra innings came in the 15-inning game, which he lost, 2–1, to Cy Young, pitching 12 scoreless innings before giving up the deciding run.

Only 24 years old in 1901, Miller appeared to have a bright future. Such was not to be the case. In four major league seasons he compiled a lifetime record of 39–45. He had losing seasons in 1902 and 1903 before closing out his major league career with a 7–7 record with Pittsburgh in 1904.

Mack Cobbles Together a Winner: Philadelphia

Connie Mack's club was one of the three American League teams that had no 1900 franchise to use as the nucleus for its 1901 roster. As with the Chicago and Boston teams, several of the Athletics' top players came from the team's intra-city rivals. Second baseman Nap Lajoie and pitchers Chick Fraser and Bill Bernhard played for the Phillies in 1900. Though third baseman Lave Cross was signed away from

Brooklyn, he was a long-time favorite of Philadelphia fans, having played there from 1889 through 1897. Pitcher Wiley Piatt was released by the Phillies near the end of the 1900 season, but Philadelphia fans undoubtedly remembered his two 20-win seasons, in 1898 and 1899. To those ex–Phillies, Mack added four top players from 1900 American League teams: Outfielder Socks Seybold and catcher Doc Powers, both of whom played for Indianapolis in 1900, and outfielder Phil Geier and infielder/outfielder Dave Fultz, both from Milwaukee. The American League holdovers were all promising young players who had dropped out of the National League because of the 1900 contraction.

Although Lajoie had one of the finest seasons in baseball history in 1901, and the A's had top players in several other positions, the team Mack put on the field at the beginning of the campaign was not a good one. Fultz did not play well at shortstop, the team's Opening Day first baseman couldn't hit, and both center fielder Geier and Opening Day right fielder Jack Hayden struggled with the bat. Hayden was trying to make the jump from college ball to the major leagues, which few players were able to do with success.

The Athletics were also in dire need of pitchers. In the spring Mack had put together a potentially outstanding pitching staff. In addition to Fraser, Bernhard, and Piatt, he signed veteran Vic Willis and rookie Christy Mathewson. Willis and Mathewson both won 20 games in 1901, but they did so for their previous teams. Both decided against jumping to the American League before spring training started. When the season began, Bernhard still showed the effects of being overworked by the Phillies in 1900 and Piatt was ineffective. Only Fraser pitched well.[18]

Philadelphia (74–62)

Regular Lineup	AVG	OBP	SLG	R	RBI	SB
Dave Fultz, cf	.292	.334	.355	95	52	36
Harry Davis, 1b	.306	.340	.452	92	76	21
Lave Cross, 3b	.328	.358	.465	82	73	23
Nap Lajoie, 2b	.426	.463	.643	145	125	27
Socks Seybold, rf	.334	.397	.503	74	90	15
Matty McIntyre, lf	.276	.346	.341	38	46	11
Doc Powers, c	.251	.292	.341	53	47	10
Joe Dolan, ss	.216	.282	.299	50	38	3
or Bones Ely, ss	.216	.230	.275	11	16	6
Leading Pitchers	**W**	**L**	**PCT**	**IP**	**H**	**ERA**
Chick Fraser	22	16	.579	331	344	3.81
Eddie Plank	17	13	.567	260.7	254	3.31
Bill Bernhard	17	10	.630	257	328	4.52
Snake Wiltse	13	5	.722	166	185	3.58
Wiley Piatt*	9	14	.391	191.7	218	4.13

*Includes record with Chicago

Mack scrambled to find players who could fill the team's weak spots. He moved Fultz into the outfield, where he became an outstanding center fielder, and signed Joe Dolan, another ex–Phillie, to play shortstop. He picked up Harry Davis for first base.

Davis had played for several National League teams during the late nineties but had not been able to hit. Playing for Providence in the Eastern League in 1900, however, he had hit .332, one of the highest averages in the league. He not only hit well for the A's in 1901 but played very well defensively at first base. Seybold became a regular in the outfield and developed into one of the league's premier sluggers.

In July, Mack purchased outfielder Matty McIntyre, sending Hayden to a minor league team. McIntyre was not a great fielder, but he hit well, solidifying the outfield. Dolan, a utility player for the Phillies, was barely adequate at short. In August Mack signed Fred Ely, the ex–Pirate shortstop. Ely couldn't hit, but he was still reliable in the field, which was what the A's needed most. Mack rounded out his pitching staff by adding Eddie Plank, who had pitched for Gettysburg College in 1900, and Lewis "Snake" Wiltse, a veteran minor league lefthander who was released by Pittsburgh in July.

About two-thirds of the season had passed before Mack finally got his team together. The A's were terrible during the first month, losing 17 of their first 26 games. They rose to mediocrity for the next two months, winning about as many games as they lost, and then became the best team in the league in August and September. They won 42 of their last 62 games.

The Athletics' top pitcher was Chick Fraser. During a 13-year major league career, Fraser was a solid, above-average pitcher who spent much of his career toiling for losing teams. As a rookie in 1896, Fraser was the ace of the Louisville staff, a distinction that sounds more imposing than it really was. Fraser was 12–27 for a team that won 38 games and lost 93. Fraser was then a young player on a team that seemed to be in a perpetual rebuilding mode. Both Fraser and the team improved in 1897. Fraser was 15–19 and the team won forty percent of its games, though it still finished in eleventh place. After that season Nick Young, the National League president, described Fraser as one of the top pitchers in the league.[19]

While suffering through a poor season in 1898, Fraser apparently tired of the Sisyphean task of trying to pitch winning games for a bad team. He asked manager Fred Clarke (who was his brother-in-law) to send him to another team. Cleveland took Fraser on a conditional basis in September but returned him after the season ended. He was then traded to Philadelphia.

Fraser's career record at that point was 36–66, but Philadelphia writer Ernest Lanigan was excited about the deal that brought him to the Phillies. "I don't want to rave over a player who has been tried by two clubs and found wanting," Lanigan wrote, "but on account of Fraser's showing against the Philadelphia club, its manager was fully justified in securing him.... Mark my prediction, ye scribes; Fraser will win more than half his games during 1899."[20] Playing for a good team for the first time in his career, Fraser more than fulfilled Lanigan's expectations. He won 21 games while losing only 12. He had another fine season in 1900, going 15–9.

During his first few weeks with the A's in 1901, Fraser might have had nightmares about finding himself back in Louisville pitching for a team that wasn't quite ready for prime time. For a while, any ball hit to shortstop or to Jack Hayden's outfield position had an excellent chance of putting a man on base. The first two men the A's tried at shortstop fielded .818 and .757. Those fielding averages might explain why Connie Mack was content to play Joe Dolan at shortstop until August, despite Dolan's .881 fielding average. Mack started Hayden out in right field, then moved him to left field, but opposing batters were still able to find him. In the 50 games before his exile to the minors, Hayden fielded .841.

Fraser was a good pitcher, but he didn't have the kind of overpowering stuff that completely shuts down opposing batters. As a result, when would-be ground ball outs ended up in left field or bouncing off the stands behind first base and easy fly balls to the outfield became singles or doubles, Fraser wound up losing games. He lost five of his first seven games and didn't get over .500 until mid–July. By then Mack had managed to find a decent player for each of the eight non-pitching positions. Fraser's winning percentage improved along with the team behind him. He won 16 of his last 22 decisions.

Mack's team continued its winning ways in 1902, but unfortunately for Fraser, he did not enjoy the victories. In April 1902, in a series of cases normally associated with his more famous teammate, Nap Lajoie, a Pennsylvania court issued an injunction prohibiting Fraser from playing with any professional baseball team other than the Phillies. Fraser responded to the injunction by returning to the Phillies, who by then were almost as bad as the Louisville teams he played for in the 1890s. For most of the rest of his career, Fraser played for teams that struggled to win forty percent of their games. The next time Fraser played for a team that finished above .500 was in 1907, when he became a part-time starter for the pennant-winning Chicago Cubs. He finished his career with a 175–212 record, which wasn't bad considering the awful teams he played for most of the time.

McGraw's Orioles, Act II

The Orioles were John McGraw's team. He was part-owner, chief promoter, manager and star player. After the Baltimore National League team was consolidated with the Brooklyn franchise in late 1899, McGraw became involved in an effort to set up a rival major league, to be named the American Association. When the effort failed, McGraw announced that he would retire from baseball rather than leave his Baltimore business interests. Although he eventually agreed to play for St. Louis in 1900, he insisted that his contract omit the reserve clause that would have tied him to St. Louis after that season. When the American League decided to challenge the National League, McGraw focused his considerable energy on organizing the Baltimore franchise.[21]

The Orioles featured nine players who had played regularly in the National League in 1900. They included second baseman Jimmy Williams, shortstop Bill Keister, third baseman McGraw, left fielder Mike Donlin, catcher Wilbert Robinson, and pitchers Joe McGinnity, Harry Howell, Jerry Nops, and Jack Dunn. Two others had played part of the 1900 season in the National League. Cy Seymour, who pitched briefly for the Giants in 1900 before being sent to the minors, made a successful comeback with the Orioles as an outfielder. Roger Bresnahan had spent most of 1900 with a semi-professional team but appeared in two games with the Chicago Orphans as a catcher.

Two of the Orioles were ex–National Leaguers who had played in the American League in 1900. They were center fielder Steve Brodie, McGraw's teammate with the

Orioles in 1899, and pitcher Frank Foreman, who was with Buffalo in 1900. Foreman had been a good National League pitcher for a half-decade before he found himself under John T. Brush's control in Cincinnati in the mid–1890s. Brush preferred to use Foreman's talents on his Indianapolis farm team where, incidentally, the salary scale was lower, rather than letting him stay in the National League. Foreman eventually became frustrated with this treatment. In 1900 he refused to sign with Indianapolis, playing instead for Buffalo.[22]

McGraw rounded out his roster with players from the lower minors and semi-professional ball. First baseman Frank Foutz had played with a low-level minor league team in 1900. He lasted only 20 games and was replaced by another 1900 minor leaguer, Burt Hart. Outfielder Jim Jackson had played on the Philadelphia sandlots in 1900.

Baltimore (68–65)

Regular Lineup	AVG	OBP	SLG	R	RBI	SB
John McGraw, 3b	.349	.508	.487	71	28	24
or Jack Dunn, ut	.249	.301	.296	41	36	10
Mike Donlin, lf	.340	.409	.475	107	67	33
Jimmy Williams, 2b	.317	.388	.495	113	96	21
Bill Keister, ss	.328	.365	.482	78	93	24
Cy Seymour, rf	.303	.337	.373	84	77	38
Steve Brodie, cf	.310	.378	.389	41	41	9
or Jim Jackson, cf-lf	.250	.291	.330	42	50	11
Burt Hart, 1b	.311	.383	.374	33	23	7
Roger Bresnahan, c	.268	.323	.369	40	32	10
or Wilbert Robinson, c	.301	.335	.377	32	26	9
Leading Pitchers	W	L	PCT	IP	H	ERA
Joe McGinnity	26	20	.565	382	412	3.56
Harry Howell	14	21	.400	294.7	333	3.67
Frank Foreman	12	6	.667	191.3	225	3.67
Jerry Nops	12	10	.545	176.7	192	4.08

Remembering the 1899 season, when McGraw led a team composed of Brooklyn's castoffs to a strong fourth-place finish, Baltimore fans expected to see the Orioles play smart, "scientific" baseball. To their surprise and McGraw's chagrin, the 1901 Orioles were constantly outwitted by their opponents. Baltimore writers complained that McGraw couldn't get his men to play together. The writers claimed that only three or four of the Orioles could bunt well enough to sacrifice successfully.[23]

As a team the Orioles were poor fielders and their baserunning was awful. A play that was much too representative of the 1901 Orioles' abilities occurred in August. In the fourth inning of a game against Boston, Brodie led off with a single and went to third on another single by Jackson. The next batter, Roger Bresnahan, hit a sharp grounder back to pitcher Ted Lewis. Lewis threw to third baseman Jimmy Collins, trapping Brodie in a rundown between home and third. While Brodie danced back and forth between home and third, the runner on first (Jackson) rounded second and started toward third. The Boston players executed the rundown close enough to third so Jackson couldn't take third base if Brodie were tagged out. After a few tosses between Collins and catcher Ossie Shreckengost, Brodie was tagged out by Schreckengost, who immediately threw to second, where Jackson was tagged for the second out. While this was going on, the batter (Bresnahan) had rounded first and edged forward until he was close to second base. When Schreckengost threw to second to get Jackson, Bresnahan ran back toward first. After tagging out Jackson, the Boston second baseman threw to first in time to get Bresnahan for the third out. It was a "witless play," said a disgusted Baltimore writer. It was enough to "stamp all the Orioles concerned as unsafe to be without a nurse."[24]

While the 1901 Orioles were not able to match McGraw's grasp of scientific baseball, they did show a propensity to imitate his fiery temper on the diamond. Baltimore games were not quiet affairs. The players chattered constantly throughout their games. They tended to challenge any close decision that went against them. Clashes with umpires were a constant feature of their games, two of which were forfeited because the Orioles spun out of control while protesting close calls. Through mid–August umpire Tom Connolly had officiated six Baltimore home games. In five of those six games, the crowd had become so worked up because of arguments over close calls that Connolly needed police protection to exit the park.[25]

Fines and suspensions for bad behavior became almost like badges of honor for the Orioles. McGraw was suspended for five days in mid–May; Donlin for several games in early June. McGinnity was thrown out of two consecutive games in mid–June. At the beginning of August, Hart was suspended for ten days for throwing his glove at an umpire and slapping him in the face. Three weeks into August, McGinnity became enraged at an umpire's decision and spit on him. He was suspended indefinitely and threatened with permanent expulsion from the league. He was reinstated only after he and McGraw visited Ban Johnson and agreed to apologize to the umpire.[26]

Through all of this turmoil the Orioles managed to remain within striking distance of first place until the beginning of September, when injuries and a worn-out pitching staff proved too heavy a burden to overcome.

A Considerable Trick: Washington

The Senators were a baseball cocktail blended by taking a generous portion of owner-manager Jimmy Manning's fifth-place Kansas City Blues, mixing in a strong dose of the last-place New York Giants, and adding a flavoring of several veterans who were no longer wanted by their previous teams. That doesn't sound like a very tasty baseball treat, but then again Washington fans were used to the baseball equivalent of rotgut liquor. They welcomed Manning and the American League to the nation's capital.

Despite their second-division finish in 1900, Manning's Blues had not been a bad team. They gave the Senators five young players who seemed to have a lot of potential. Third baseman Bill Coughlin was a whiz with the glove and outfielder John Farrell was fast, had good hands, and was a decent hitter. Pitchers Dale Gear, Watty Lee, and Casey Patten pitched well in Kansas City. The three other ex–Blues were veterans who had dropped out of the National League. Shortstop Bill Clingman was an above-average defensive player who unaccountably developed a case of dropsy with the 1900 Chicago Orphans. Manning picked him up after the Orphans released him in mid-season. Outfielder Jack O'Brien had played with Washington in 1899. He was a borderline major league player. He batted .282 with middling power and a few stolen bases—not too bad, but not good enough to earn a job in the National League of 1900 after the consolidation wiped out some 16 outfield positions. Outfielder/first baseman Sam Dungan played three years in the National League in the mid–1890s and had a sip of coffee in 1900 with the Chicago Orphans before going to Kansas City. In the National League his hitting had been decent, but not good enough to offset his poor fielding. In the Western/American League, his hitting was so good the fans forgave his fielding gaffes. He was a popular player there during the latter part of the 1890s. In 1900 he led the league with a .337 batting average and was third in slugging with a .433 average.

Washington (61–72)

Regular Lineup	AVG	OBP	SLG	R	RBI	SB
Irv Waldron, cf*	.311	.368	.378	102	52	20
John Farrell, 2b-cf	.272	.336	.386	100	63	25
or Joe Quinn, 2b	.252	.287	.331	33	34	7
Sam Dungan, rf	.320	.368	.415	70	73	9
or Dale Gear, p-rf	.236	.251	.302	17	20	2
Boileryard Clarke, c	.280	.335	.360	58	54	7
Mike Grady, 1b-c	.285	.351	.470	57	56	14
Pop Foster, lf**	.279	.353	.422	69	60	10
Bill Coughlin, 3b	.275	.317	.395	75	68	16
Billy Clingman, ss	.242	.308	.304	66	55	10
Leading Pitchers	**W**	**L**	**PCT**	**IP**	**H**	**ERA**
Bill Carrick	14	22	.389	324	367	3.75
Watty Lee	16	16	.500	262	328	4.40
Casey Patten	18	10	.643	254.3	285	3.93
Win Mercer	9	13	.409	179.7	217	4.56
Dale Gear	4	11	.267	163	199	4.03

*Includes record with Milwaukee
**Includes record with Chicago

Coming from New York were pitchers Bill Carrick and Win Mercer, utilityman Mike Grady, and outfielder Pop Foster, who joined the Senators three weeks into the season. All four were players who could help a team on a good day and hurt it on a bad day, each of which occurred at about the same frequency.

To round out the team Manning signed old-timers Bill Everitt (first base), Joe Quinn (second base) and Boileryard Clarke (catcher). Everitt had been a very good hitter for five years with the Chicago Orphans before coming down with "rheumatism" in his throwing arm. The malady led to his release midway through the 1900 season, and he still suffered from it in the spring of 1901.

Quinn was a "wily veteran" who had been hanging onto a major league job by his fingernails since 1896. He was released by two second-division National League teams in 1900, a warning signal that Manning overlooked when he signed him for the Senators.

Clarke was the best of the three veterans. His career had been spent largely as a backup catcher with the Baltimore Orioles. He suffered from a sore arm throughout the 1900 season. He became available because Boston manager Frank Selee grew tired of watching Clarke throw the ball into center field whenever a runner tried to steal second base.

While Washington fans approached the season with optimism, Manning seemed to realize that his combination of still-too-young and already-too-old players wouldn't hold up under the hot sun of a pennant race. The Senators got off to a good start. They won their first four games, stumbled a bit, swept a four-game series from Boston, and went into Chicago in June with a chance to move past the White Stockings into first place. When the Senators failed to advance, Manning philosophized: "Of course, we would like to win the pennant, but we will not be disappointed not to win it…. In another year we expect to have a team together that will make any of them hustle. It is considerable of a trick to get a new team going."[27]

The trick of fielding a competitive team was made harder by Manning's limited bankroll. He didn't have enough money to compete with the better-financed teams in bigger cities. President Johnson mandated a 16-man roster limit for American League teams in 1901, which wasn't a problem for Manning. He could only afford to keep 14 men on the payroll. Everitt's arm gave out after the first month and Quinn's after two months. To fill their places, Manning moved Dungan from right field to first base and Farrell from center field to second base, thereby creating holes in the outfield. Other injuries soon reduced the number of men available on some days to ten or eleven players, including the entire pitching staff. By mid-season the Senators began to take on a distinctly minor league appearance as pitchers Watty Lee and Dale Gear began sharing the right field position while also taking their turns in the rotation.

Manning was a good baseball man who got the best effort out of the talent he had. The Senators played hard for him but began to sink in the standings as the long season wore them down. On July 4 they were still two games over .500, trailing the first-place White Stockings by only 7½ games. A seven-game losing streak dropped them into fifth place by mid–July, and they fell behind the Athletics into sixth as July came to a close. They remained there for the rest of the season except for a few days in mid–August, eventually establishing themselves as the best of the league's three losing teams. Sadly for Washington fans, the 1901 Senators' .459 winning percentage was the franchise's best until 1912.

Cleveland Still Had the Blues

Like the Senators, the Cleveland Blues were a 1900 American League second-division team. While Manning had a core of good young players that he strengthened by signing a half-dozen players from the National League of 1900, Cleveland manager Jim McAleer decided to build his team around veteran American League players.

Those players all had some National League experience, but most were no longer considered major league material. McAleer signed only three men who played in the National League in 1900. Two of those players—Bill Bradley and Jack McCarthy—played very well for the Blues. The third—Ed Scott—pitched into August with a sore arm before being released.

With the exception of first baseman Candy LaChance and center fielder Ollie Pickering, the holdover American League players all struggled in 1901. By May 17 the Blues' record was 4–17, and all hope of having a successful season was gone. They limped along with a losing record for the rest of the year, rising to sixth place briefly in August, but spent most of the season battling an even more inept Milwaukee team for seventh place.

The Blues' collapse was accelerated by bad luck or foolish valor, depending upon one's perspective. On paper the team's three veteran pitchers appeared to be solid. Bill Hoffer, who once won 31 games for the Baltimore Orioles, had a 16–12 record for the 1900 Blues. Bill Hart, a veteran of seven National League seasons, was 18–15. Scott was Cincinnati's top pitcher in 1900, finishing with a 17–20 record. Because of bad weather during spring training, the three veterans were unable to get into proper condition for the opening of the season. Feeling a sense of responsibility to the team, all three tried to pitch. They were uniformly bad and they all ended up with career-breaking sore arms.[28]

Cleveland (54–82)

Regular Lineup	AVG	OBP	SLG	R	RBI	SB
Ollie Pickering, cf	.309	.383	.377	102	40	36
Jack McCarthy, lf	.321	.382	.402	60	32	9
Jack O'Brien, rf*	.271	.320	.329	59	44	15
or Zaza Harvey, rf	.353	.392	.459	21	24	15
Erve Beck, 2b	.289	.320	.401	78	79	7
Candy LaChance, 1b	.303	.314	.381	81	75	11
Bill Bradley, 3b	.293	.336	.403	95	55	15
Bob Wood, c	.292	.327	.384	45	49	6
Frank Scheibeck, ss	.213	.258	.264	33	38	3
Leading Pitchers	W	L	PCT	IP	H	ERA
Pete Dowling**	12	25	.316	306	340	4.15
Earl Moore	16	14	.533	251.3	234	2.90
Bill Hart	7	11	.389	157.7	180	3.77
Ed Scott	6	6	.500	124.7	149	4.40

*Includes record with Washington
**Includes record with Milwaukee

McAleer started what turned out to be a season-long search for pitchers to replace the three veterans while still using them whenever they were able to pitch. McAleer's most successful find was Earl Moore, a 21-year-old rookie who had been with the team since spring training. Moore's first start came on May 1. He beat Milwaukee, 6–3, holding the Brewers to six hits. In his next start he held Detroit to three hits in the first eight innings before allowing four hits and two runs in the ninth. On

Earl Moore's performance was one of the few bright spots in a dismal season for the 1901 Cleveland Blues (Library of Congress).

May 9, Moore faced the White Stockings, a team noted for maximizing their run-scoring opportunities. Moore retired the White Stockings in order in each of the first three innings.

In the fourth inning Moore walked lead-off batter Dummy Hoy. Fielder Jones followed with a grounder to second baseman Erve Beck, who fumbled the ball, then threw too late to catch Jones at first. Two batters later, with men on first and third, the White Stockings tried a delayed steal. Cleveland catcher Bob Wood threw back to Moore, a decoy throw meant to catch the runner on third straying too far off base. Moore's throw to third was wild, going into the bleachers, giving the White Stockings two runs and tying the score, 2–2. The White Stockings went down in order the next five innings. Moore had pitched a nine-inning no-hitter, but the game was not over. In the tenth the White Stockings picked up two hits, which combined with more shoddy fielding by the Blues brought in two runs for a 4–2 Chicago victory.[29]

Moore and the White Stockings found one another to be tough opponents each time they faced off in 1901. On June 29 Moore took another no-hitter into the eighth inning before weakening. He gave up four hits and four runs in that inning, losing, 4–1. In his last appearance against Chicago, on August 13, Moore pitched into and out of trouble throughout the game, giving up eight bases on balls. The White Stockings were able to get only one hit off him, however. Moore won the game, 4–0, with the aid of a sensational bases-loaded catch by center fielder Pickering.

Moore seemed to be at his best against the top teams. He pitched well in all but one of his six starts against Boston, winning three and losing three. In three of those outings he allowed only five hits. In another Moore and Parson Ted Lewis both pitched two-hitters, with Moore winning a close 1–0 game.

At this stage of his career Moore's best pitch was his fastball. Game summaries, especially early in the season, commented on his fine speed, with one writer comparing him to a younger Cy Young. He threw with a sidearm motion, sometimes dropping down to an underhand delivery.[30] Moore remained one of the top pitchers in the American League through 1905. He pitched only a few games during each of the succeeding three years before resurrecting his career with the Phillies in 1909. His last season was 1914, when he pitched for Buffalo in the Federal League, finishing his career with a 163–154 win-loss record.

McAleer's search for new players was not restricted to the pitcher's mound. He told a Detroit writer in June that he also needed an outfielder or two and a couple of infielders. Throughout the season he brought in a steady stream of young players for tryouts, focusing especially on the shortstop and right field positions. Near the end of the season it appeared he had come up with a young outfielder who might become as successful in the field as Moore had been on the mound. The bright prospect was Zaza Harvey.

Harvey had gained national attention in 1899 while pitching and playing the outfield in the California League. He had gotten off to a slow start that season due to an illness, losing six of his first seven starts as a pitcher. By season's end, though, he was dominating the opposing hitters, at one time winning six consecutive games in which he allowed a total of five runs and 21 hits. As an outfielder he was a very fast runner, played solid defense, and sprayed the ball around for a .350 batting average, the second-best mark in the league.

The Chicago Orphans considered themselves fortunate to be able to draft him for the 1900 season. When Harvey joined the team the next spring, he proved to be an exceptionally quiet youngster who said little to his manager or teammates. Because he injured his arm early in spring training, he had little chance to show what he could do. He appeared in one regular-season game for the Orphans, shutting out the Cincinnati Reds in four innings of relief. In May the Orphans farmed him to the Minneapolis Millers of the American League. With the Millers, a poor team, Harvey was only 7–14 as a pitcher. He also played the outfield, and posted a .301 batting average in 51 games.[31]

In 1901 Charlie Comiskey signed Harvey to pitch for the Chicago White Stockings. Manager Clark Griffith used him sparingly as a spot starter and reliever. Harvey showed some promise but wasn't quite ready for the hot pennant race the White Stockings were engaged in. In August he was loaned to Cleveland with the understanding that he would play the outfield in place of Jack McCarthy, who had suffered a severe knee injury. "Harvey has had the outfield bee buzzing in his head for a season or more, and it apparently interfered with his pitching ambition," commented a Chicago reporter. "He may do Cleveland some good."[32]

Playing regularly for Cleveland, Harvey did lots of good. During his first three weeks with the Blues, he hit .373, made several fine catches in the outfield, dazzled the fans with strong throws from the outfield to home plate, and showed great speed on the bases. He ended up batting .353 for Cleveland, while stealing 15 bases and showing some flashes of power.

Over the winter the Blues acquired Harvey's contract from Chicago. In 1902 Harvey began the season as he had ended 1901. He was batting .348 in early May when he told his manager he needed to take time off to recover from a stomach illness. Harvey said he had been feeling pain for a couple of years and had played through it, but now the discomfort had become so severe he could no longer continue playing. He went to the hot springs in West Baden, Indiana, for treatment. Three weeks later he returned to his home in California, still suffering from the illness. Sixteen months later, responding to a fan's inquiry, the *Cleveland Plain Dealer* reported that Harvey was still too sick to play baseball. He never again played major league baseball, retiring with a lifetime batting average of .332.[33]

Losing Brews Fan Discontent

The Brewers were constructed along the same lines as the Blues, with similarly disappointing results. Nine Brewers were holdovers from the 1900 team, which had finished second, trailing Chicago by only four games. They were joined by only three players who were in the National League in 1900. One of those three was manager Hugh Duffy, who did not expect to play regularly in 1901. The other two were pitchers Pink Hawley and Ned Garvin, who had pitched well enough in 1900 for Brewers fans to have high hopes for them in 1901.

The obvious problem for Duffy in the spring of 1901 was in replacing three key players from the 1900 team. Infielder Dave Fultz had been an offensive sparkplug, catcher Harry Smith anchored the team's defense, and pitcher Rube Waddell had been Rube at his best, a pitcher Duffy was not going to be able to replace.

Second baseman Billy Gilbert had a solid rookie season but could not fill Fultz's place in heart of the batting order. Catcher Billy Maloney hit well, but neither he nor the other Brewers catchers could fill Smith's shoes behind the plate. And on the mound the problem turned out to be much bigger than anyone anticipated. Three of the Brewers' top pitchers of 1900—Bill Reidy, Tully Sparks, and Pete Dowling—possessed stuff that translated into victories in the high minors but not at the major league level. And to complicate matters, neither Hawley nor Garvin pitched well in 1901.

Milwaukee (48–89)

Regular Lineup	AVG	OBP	SLG	R	RBI	SB
George Hogriever, lf	.235	.329	.299	25	16	7
Bill Hallman, rf	.246	.301	.328	70	47	12
John Anderson, 1b	.330	.360	.476	90	99	35
Hugh Duffy, cf	.302	.341	.439	40	45	12
Wid Conroy, ss	.256	.316	.350	74	64	21
Jimmy Burke, 3b	.206	.266	.240	24	26	6
or Bill Friel, 3b	.266	.310	.370	51	35	15
Billy Gilbert, 2b	.270	.320	.327	77	43	19
Billy Maloney, c	.293	.328	.331	42	22	11
Leading Pitchers	**W**	**L**	**PCT**	**IP**	**H**	**ERA**
Bill Reidy	16	20	.444	301.3	364	4.21
Ned Garvin	7	20	.259	257.3	258	3.46
Pete Husting	10	15	.400	217.3	234	4.27
Tully Sparks	7	16	.304	210	228	3.51
Pink Hawley	7	14	.333	182.3	228	4.59

During the opening week of the 1901 season, the Brewers engaged in a series of exciting games that invigorated the fan base. We have already described those games; they were with the Detroit Tigers, and the happy, excited fans were rooting for the Tigers when they came from behind to win their first four games of the season. In Milwaukee, the fans weren't so excited. Their feeling was more a foreboding that a terrible season lay ahead of them. And their apprehension only grew when the Brewers blew their next game, losing once again in the last inning, this time to the heretofore winless Cleveland Blues.

The Brewers rallied briefly, winning ten of their next twenty games to reach a season-high win-loss percentage of .400. Then the losses began to mount again and the fans began to turn against the team. Two players, third baseman Jimmy Burke and right fielder Irv Waldron, became favored targets for critical fans. Neither was a poor ballplayer, but both had weaknesses the fans pounced on.

Burke was a versatile player who could help a major league team in a utility role but struggled whenever he was used as a regular. He had been a popular player with the Brewers in 1900. In 1901, however, he had the misfortune of making errors that lost several early-season games for the Brewers. A group of fans made him a scapegoat and began booing his every move. Burke responded to this additional pressure by booting the ball even more than usual and hitting poorly.[34]

Waldron had also played for the 1900 Brewers. He was a good hitter and a fast runner. He led the Western Association in batting in 1897. During the next three years he was considered one of the top outfielders in the Western/American League. Charlie Comiskey once called him the best outfielder ever to play in the Western League. In 1900 he batted .294, stole 34 bases, and scored 92 runs for the Brewers. Waldron tended to be unsteady in the field and at times used poor judgment on the bases. He had the bad luck to exhibit those weaknesses during a streak when the Brewers won only five of twenty-four games.

In one game he was on first base when Duffy lined a pitch to the right field fence.

Waldron lost sight of the ball. He went toward second, then turned and started back toward first, thinking the ball had been caught. Duffy, rounding first, yelled at him to go forward. Waldron turned and raced around to third but was thrown out. Duffy, who by this time was more than a little upset with the way his men were playing, scolded Waldron while standing on second base and later fined him. A couple of days later a Milwaukee reporter, in the blunt manner of the era, informed his readers, "Around the American League circuit Waldron is considered the most stupid baserunner in the country."[35]

On July 9 the Brewers released Burke and Waldron, a move both players must have welcomed. Burke was immediately signed by the Chicago White Stockings. He proved to be a valuable substitute at shortstop and third base for the White Stockings in the most critical stages of the pennant race. When the White Stockings released Burke in mid–September, he was signed by the Pittsburgh Pirates, playing 14 games for them as the season came to an end. Thus in 1901 Burke had the rare experience of being booted off a last-place team only to be later welcomed as a valuable addition to both major league pennant winners—all in the same season.

Waldron was picked up by the Washington Senators, who were so crippled by injuries they were playing their pitchers in the outfield. Washington fans and writers thought Waldron looked like a pretty good outfielder, especially in comparison with the Senators' pitcher-outfielders. Waldron hit well for the Senators, as he had for the Brewers, finishing his only major league season with an overall .311 batting average. But his reputation for bone-headed playing must have stayed with him. He spent the rest of his career in the minor leagues despite playing well for several years after 1901.

In a Class by Himself: Nap Lajoie

If Willie Keeler was, as one writer proclaimed, the "Prince of Headwork Batters," then Nap Lajoie was the "Archduke of Line-'em-out Hitters." Lajoie was noted both for his tendency to go after any pitch near the strike zone and his ability to smack any ball he could reach.

In 1902 a friend who had managed Lajoie in the minors described Lajoie's batting approach. "Lajoie was always a natural hitter," he said. "When he was with me he could pound the ball safely more times than any other member of the team. And he had so much confidence in his ability as a hitter that he would frequently pick out wide ones to hit at. Often times, he made safe hits on these same wide ones. When he didn't and he would come back to the bench, I'd reprove him for going after the bad ones, but he would laugh and reply, 'I can hit 'em all if they come within reach of my bat.'"[36]

Lajoie hit the ball hard—so hard he literally smashed the ball and damaged fences. Ernest Lanigan, who appreciated scientific baseball but preferred hitters who could slug the ball, recounted two occasions in 1899 when Lajoie accomplished "the hitherto unknown feat of hitting the ball so hard that he broke it." In his typically precise fashion, Lanigan provided the details: "The first time was in this city, May 13, off Colcolough, and the next time at Cincinnati, June 19, off Breitenstein. On both cases he jolted the ball so hard that the rubber inside was broken." A few years later Tim Murnane, in answer to a fan's query, cited another instance when Nap's powerful swing split a ball. "Lajoie broke a ball in two pieces," Murnane wrote, "by hitting it with a bat during an exhibition game in the fall of 1901."

In the spring of 1901, a St. Louis writer noted that pitcher Willie Sudhoff was celebrating Lajoie's departure from the National League, adding in explanation that "Lajoie once knocked a panel out of the fence with one of Bill's benders." Later that season Cleveland writers buzzed about a similar mark Nap left at League Park, attesting to his power. The center field fence at League Park was about 425 feet from home plate. Behind it was a row of green slats, probably put there to prevent non-paying fans from watching the game. The Cleveland newspapermen delighted in showing visiting writers a hole where one of the slats was broken, explaining that it had been created by a gargantuan swat from Lajoie's bat.[37]

Leading the American League by a wide margin in most of the important batting categories, Nap Lajoie seemed "in a class by himself" in 1901 (National Baseball Hall of Fame Library, Cooperstown, New York).

Nap came to the National League at the age of 21 after a brief apprenticeship in the minor leagues. Like many major leaguers of the time, Nap had played on sandlot and semi-professional teams for several years before entering professional baseball. When he joined the Fall River team of the New England League in 1896, he was already a pretty good hitter. The New England League was a Class B league in 1896, two rungs below the National League in organized baseball's hierarchy. The league's pitchers were no mystery to young Lajoie. He hit safely in his first five games, batting .579. Still batting well over .400 in June, he began attracting the attention of National League managers. Fall River was offering Lajoie and Phil Geier, a fine defensive outfielder who was batting over .380, as a package. After several other teams blanched at the $1,500 asking price for the two youngsters, the Phillies decided to take the deal. In 80 games for Fall River, Lajoie hit .429 with 34 doubles, 17 triples, and 15 home runs.

When he joined the Phillies, Lajoie had not settled into a fielding position. In semipro ball Nap had been primarily a catcher. With Fall River he played the outfield. The Phillies put him at first base. Like Honus Wagner, Lajoie was so talented he could play well at any position. A month after Lajoie joined the Phillies, a National League umpire remarked that Nap was one of the finest first basemen he had ever seen and was a natural hitter. In 39 games with the Phillies, Nap hit .326 with a slugging percentage that would have ranked fourth in the league if he had batted enough times to qualify.

Over the next two seasons Nap staked out a reputation, challenged only by teammate Ed Delahanty, as the game's premier slugger. In 1897 he hit .361, the sixth-best batting average in the league, and led the league in total bases and slugging percentage. The next year he batted .324, the eleventh-highest batting average, but led in doubles and RBIs and ranked second in total bases and third in slugging percentage.

Baseball writers praised his ability lavishly. "Money would not buy Lajoie today," a Boston writer claimed. "He strengthens the Phillies, already a great batting aggregation, both at the bat and in the field. He is quick as a flash at putting the ball on a runner, is good at pickups and can catch high thrown balls without leaving the bag that other players would lose. He is doubtless the wonder of the baseball era."[38]

Everything was not coming up roses for Lajoie, however. While he was establishing himself as a great player, he also began acquiring a negative reputation for his off-field conduct. The Phillies of the late 1890s included several players who hit the bottle pretty hard and young Nap probably was influenced by their habits. In August of 1897 he showed up for two games intoxicated. His manager, George Stallings, benched him the first time, but after the game young Nap quarreled with a fan and hit him on the head. The police arrested him and he was fined by both the city and Stallings.

Two weeks later he was again drunk when he arrived at the park. This time Stallings put Lajoie in the game and let him embarrass himself, which the youngster did with all the flair he normally exhibited in rapping out extra-base hits. In the one inning he played, Nap gave his opponents two runs by booting the ball at first base, then cussed out a fan who criticized his play. This second infraction led to a suspension. The Phillies used the two incidents as a justification for limiting his salary. When Nap received his contract for 1898, it contained only a small increase in pay and included a non-drinking clause, fining him $300 if he abused intoxicating liquors during the season.

Lajoie had no more drinking problems on the field, but after the 1899 season he became involved in a barroom fight. These incidents, together with his locker room encounter with Elmer Flick during the 1900 season, led some baseball observers to believe he was a bad influence on a team. After the Flick incident, Boston writer Tim Murnane remarked, "Lajoie has to make about two foolish breaks each season."[39]

On the field Lajoie's stature continued to grow. In 1898 the Phillies moved him to second base. Within a month he had Phillies fans marveling about his speed in turning the double play. By midseason his teammates were claiming he was the greatest second baseman who ever lived.[40] By August similar comments were coming from rival teams. "That big Frenchman is the wonder of the year," Cleveland manager Patsy Tebeau remarked. "When I heard that Stallings had decided to play him at second I thought he was spoiling a star first baseman for the sake of making an indifferent second baseman. But I doff my hat to Stallings. The Frenchman has certainly delivered the goods and I have not been able to detect a weakness in his fielding."[41]

Except for brief spells when he filled in at other positions because of injuries, Lajoie remained at second base for the rest of his career. The position allowed him to showcase his athletic ability better than either first base or the outfield. He was easily the best second baseman of his time, not only on offense, but also defensively. The word used most often to describe his fielding was "graceful." He moved quickly and seemingly without effort in going after hit balls.

Although Lajoie was 6'1" and weighed close to 200 pounds, he was a deceptively fast runner. Before the 1901 season he agreed to race teammate Jack Hayden in a 100-yard dash. Hayden, a track star at the University of Pennsylvania, lost to Lajoie by a foot.[42] Nap's quickness and speed gave him great range. He had very large hands, which enabled him to make running one-hand catches on hits most other players would not have been able to hold.

Lajoie's extraordinary fielding abilities were captured in daily game summaries in much the same way a play-by-play broadcast or post-game video clips would reflect the fielding gems of players from more recent times. A couple of examples follow, in both of which Lajoie is referred to as "Larry," a nickname arising out of a teammate's inability to pronounce Nap's last name.

Against the Philadelphia Athletics on June 11, 1902:

> By all odds the feature of the game was the most remarkable catch ever witnessed at League Park, big Larry being the hero. It occurred in the fatal ninth inning, and happened in this manner. Seybold put up a sky scraping foul close to the scoreboard. Flick, Hickman and Lajoie made a rush for it, the latter having to run nearly 250 feet. No one thought for a minute that any one of the three would get under it and when Flick and Hickman stopped running no one was surprised. One player, however, did not stop running and that one was Lajoie. Just as the ball dropped, out shot his left hand and into it went the ball. Quick as a flash he turned and shot the ball to Gochnauer at second, in an endeavor to catch Lave Cross, who had been occupying first base. The throw was almost perfect, but Cross by a great spurt just beat it out.

"Notes of the Game." Ban Johnson, who witnessed the game: "Lajoie's catch was the most marvelous one that I ever saw. I never saw a man run so fast on a ball field as he did after that ball."[43]

Against the Boston Americans on July 16, 1902:

> Lajoie made a play off Stahl in the ninth that was the limit. With Collins on the base and one out Stahl smashed a sharp grounder about three yards to the right of second base. Lajoie went off like a shot, and by a long reach with his bare hand played a shooting ball to perfection, never slacking his speed until he had crossed second base. There isn't a ballplayer that could duplicate the play, but to this phenomenon it was like drinking cream off the top of a milk can. Larry has all other second basemen, both of the past and present, beaten by 25 percent, and yet he never makes a false move or dreams of the effect his playing has on the grandstand.

... "Baseball Notes." Lajoie is a wonder.[44]

In 1899 and 1900 Nap again finished among the leaders in batting average and slugging percentage. Assessments of his ability became even more lavish. Early in 1901, a Detroit writer reflected a common view when he sought to praise Detroit second baseman Kid Gleason. "Gleason will without doubt prove to be the best second baseman in the league this year," he wrote, "barring Lajoie, who is in a class by himself."[45] Not only was Lajoie universally considered the greatest second baseman of his time, he was deemed the best ever by many baseball observers. When the discussion centered on the best players in the game, he was generally regarded as the top active player. And, although old-timers might disagree, it was not unusual for baseball writers to refer to him as the best ballplayer of all time. And that was before Lajoie completed his 1901 season, one of the finest ever enjoyed by a baseball player.[46]

The Detroit writer quoted in the preceding paragraph made his comment two weeks into the 1901 season and addressed only Lajoie and other American League second basemen. But the comparison would have withstood criticism had it included all American League players for the entire season. Lajoie really was in a class by himself during the 1901 season. He led the league in virtually every important batting category. He was number one in batting average, slugging percentage, doubles, home runs, runs scored and runs batted in. That was impressive, but it just begins to tell the story. Nap didn't just lead the league in most categories, he led the league by a lot. His batting average was .426. The runner-up was Mike Donlin, who batted .340, *eighty-six* points lower. His slugging percentage was .643, *one hundred-twenty-three* points ahead of Buck Freeman's .520. Lajoie was an impatient hitter who walked infrequently. But his .463 on-base percentage was fifty-one points higher than Fielder Jones.' Nap had 42 more hits than anybody else, scored 25 more runs, and drove in 11 more runs.

The degree to which Lajoie dominated the American League in 1901 was not equaled during the Deadball Era, and seldom has been exceeded in baseball history. The 86-point margin by which he led in batting average has never been approached. The closest anyone ever came was in the National League's first season of 1876, when Ross Barnes won by 63 points. In modern major league history the largest margin was Rod Carew's 52-point lead over Lymon Bostock in 1977. Except for the strange 1887 season, when it took four strikes to retire a batter and a walk (five balls) counted as a hit, Lajoie's margin in slugging average was not exceeded until Babe Ruth and the lively ball changed the nature of the game. His winning margin in on-base percentage was exceeded a number of times both before and after the Deadball Era, but not during that era, not even by Ty Cobb.

A Designated Hitter Born Too Soon: Bill Keister

Bill Keister could flat-out hit. He hit higher than .300 in every full season he played in the major leagues, compiling a career batting average of .312. His baserunning? Not so great. He was fast. He stole some bases—20 or 30 every year. But his judgment was poor; he gave up a lot of unnecessary outs while on the bases. His fielding? Ahhh, don't ask.

Poor Bill didn't stay with any team very long. He spent parts of seven seasons in the major leagues, changing teams after each season. The first two stops don't really count. He had brief trials with Baltimore in 1896 and Boston in 1898. He didn't hit well either time, but showed promise. Since he hit higher than .300 in the Class A Eastern League in 1897 and again after Boston let him go in 1898, he continued to attract attention. Brooklyn drafted him after the 1898 season, just before the team merged with the Orioles. The next spring Keister wasn't even considered for the syndicate's varsity team in Brooklyn, but he won a spot with John McGraw's team in Baltimore. There Keister's season followed a pattern that would be repeated almost every year through 1903.

Fans like hitting, so they tended to warm up to Keister early in the season. In 1899 he was batting higher than .300 in limited opportunities through mid–May, and Baltimore fans were happy to see him get a shot at becoming the team's regular shortstop. Even good-fielding shortstops made a bundle of errors in those years, so there was only mild alarm when Keister butchered several grounders and showed little range in his first few games at the position. After a week or so when he settled in and reduced the errors, Baltimore's writers and fans told themselves he wasn't so bad at short. And he got his batting average above .350, something his predecessor, George Magoon, could only have dreamed of doing.

By late June it became apparent that Baltimore's second baseman, John O'Brien, wasn't going to come out of what appeared to be an early-season slump. McGraw benched O'Brien, brought Magoon back into the lineup at shortstop, and switched Keister to second. Keister's range at second was no better than at short, but fewer balls were hit in that direction, which meant McGraw might have felt he would mess up fewer chances. A few weeks later McGraw changed his mind again. He traded Magoon for Gene DeMontreville, put DeMontreville at second, and moved Keister back to shortstop. By then it was obvious that Keister couldn't field either position very well, but it was hard to bench that .300 batting average.[47]

As the season progressed it became apparent that even Keister's batting game had holes in it. He wasn't a very patient hitter. He rarely walked, though McGraw did get him to stand tough on inside pitches so he could get to first base by getting hit. In 563 plate appearances in 1899, Keister walked 16 times and got hit by a pitch 16 times. Keister was not a good bunter. A Baltimore writer said he was one of the worst bunters on the team. In one of his later stops, another writer claimed Keister wasn't good at "scientific baseball."[48]

In 1900 Keister went along with McGraw and Wilbert Robinson to St. Louis. Playing almost exclusively at second base, Keister helped to make Bobby Wallace the busiest shortstop in the National League. On throws from the catcher to second base, Keister was less than skillful. He wasn't sure-handed and he had a tendency to shy away from the baserunner on tags. As a result, Wallace began handling nearly all the throws from the catcher. Opposing teams loved that arrangement. Whenever they wanted to use the hit-and-run play, there was no guessing as to who would cover second base. They just tried to dump the ball toward the shortstop position, confident that Wallace would be on his way to second base, opening up a hole. Wallace, who had a much better throwing arm than Keister, also handled most of the relay throws from the outfield. "About all that Billy has to do," said a St. Louis teammate, "is to take care of batted balls that go between second and first. He don't have to bother about other duties which second basemen are responsible for wholly or in part, and I tell you it helps him, for he is inclined to be erratic and very apt he is to go ballooning."[49]

One season was about all St. Louis could take of Bill's defense. Although he hit .300 in his only campaign with their team, St. Louis writers considered it a plus when McGraw "stole" Keister for his new American League team. Possibly figuring that Keister would do the least damage at shortstop, McGraw put him there for the entire season. McGraw didn't have much choice. Neither he nor second baseman Jimmy Williams was adequate at the position, and utility man Jack Dunn didn't field any better than Keister when he played there. McGraw's tactic, however, was hard on Keister. As the season wore on, poor Bill's misplays increased. Baltimore fans, unhappy with the Orioles' bungling ways, began heckling Keister, especially during his frequent multi-error games. In a close contest on August 18, Keister gave Cleveland a run by making four errors on two ground balls, fumbling each one and then over-throwing first. After his second misadventure (fourth error), he threw down his glove and marched off the field.[50] In September a Baltimore writer commented that Keister seemed to be "all gone." "He gets the 'terrors' now every time he goes on the field and is worse than useless. His case is a most peculiar one," the writer remarked. "It is nothing but timidity, lack of confidence, stage fright."[51]

Toward the end of the 1901 season, Ernest Lanigan was poring over his baseball statistics, as he was wont to do, and noticed a coincidence. In 1900 the St. Louis Cardinals had finished last in the National League in double plays. Lanigan remembered that Bill Keister was assigned much of the blame for the Cardinals' inability to turn two that year. Keister was no longer with the Cardinals in 1901 and they were leading the league in double plays. Meanwhile, Keister's new team, the Orioles, were last in their league in double plays. "Is he a hoodoo?" Lanigan asked.[52]

Was he a hoodoo, or was it his poor fielding? If Lanigan had checked back one more year, to 1899, he would have found that Keister's team, the Orioles, were also last in the league in double plays. Keister moved on to Washington in 1902 and to the Phillies in 1903, his last major league season. Both teams thought it best to play Keister in the outfield, where his poor defense could do less harm. The Senators, however, ran into a string of injuries that forced them to play Keister at second base for 40 games. Keister managed to figure in nine double plays in those 40 games, about one-third the rate of their other second basemen. The result: Keister's team finished last in twin-killings.

At that point it looked like Keister's fielding was the prime factor in his teams' low double play totals. But the next year the Phillies kept Keister out of the infield the entire season. He played 100 games for them, all in the outfield. But even then they couldn't avoid the inevitable. They finished last in double plays, marking the fifth time in Keister's five full major league seasons his team finished last in double plays. Apparently, he was a hoodoo.

Davey Crockett in Detroit

Detroit's baseball writers could see the dog days of summer coming upon them. A killer heat wave was forming in the Midwest. That blast of hot air wouldn't hit Detroit, but the temperature was getting toasty at Bennett Field. The Tigers had dropped back close to .500. Injuries were starting to hurt the team, which had just purchased a couple of questionable youngsters from the minors. It looked like there were going to be some long days at the ol' ballyard.

That was before the writers got a closer look at one of the youngsters. Suddenly, it was like a cool country breeze was gently making its way through the park. Working out at first base was Daniel Crockett, who, of course, everyone called "Davey." Young Crockett was tall, slim, and awkward. He had long arms. He seemed capable of reaching nine feet for errant throws. "He can stretch so far as to seem elastic," said one writer. When Crockett ran the bases, he was a sight to behold. "Davey is probably the most ungainly runner in the baseball business," the writer said. "He wobbles at the knees, doesn't reach out for a stride, but appears to push himself along with his feet."[53] "Crockett runs like a sewing machine," another said, probably meaning there was a lot of up-and-down and around motion but not much forward movement.[54]

When he got into a game, Crockett immediately attracted attention by his method of tagging a runner on a pickoff throw from the pitcher. When pitcher Roscoe Miller fired the ball to first, Crockett was standing with his legs wide apart. Crockett grabbed the throw, but instead of turning to make the tag, he simply reached back between his legs and tagged out the diving runner. The fans laughed but gave Crockett a round of applause as he walked off the field.[55]

It was as a batter that Crockett made his deepest impression. A left-handed hitter, he had a long swing but usually managed to make contact with the pitch. When he hit it, the ball invariably went toward right field. In his first half-dozen games, the ball usually fell safely. He had 12 hits in his first 23 at-bats, for a nice .522 average.

It looked like the Tigers had come up with a good ballplayer, as well as a delightful character. A week later, an errant pitch from Joe McGinnity caught Crockett just above the eye. He reeled back, fell to the ground, and remained there for several minutes in agony. After team captain Kid Gleason checked out the injury, poured some cool water on the bruised area, and gave some words of encouragement to Davey, the youngster finished the game. The next day, in describing the incident in his game summary, the *Detroit Free Press* baseball writer predicted, "Unless he has a cast-iron nerve, the accident is liable to make him timid at the bat and affect his stickwork."[56]

It is difficult to determine whether Crockett was reacting to the beaning or if his luck was simply evening out, but Davey went hitless for several days afterwards. His terrific batting average plunged toward the league average. When that happened, Davey's shortcomings in other phases of the game suddenly became more noticeable. His slowness afoot limited his fielding ability. Ground balls that the injured Frank Dillon would have picked up easily were scooting past Davey into right field. He was slow in tagging runners. His inventive between-the-legs tag on Miller's pickoff throw was the only putout he had been able to make on such attempts. And on a team that relied heavily on smart baserunning to produce runs, Davey's "sewing machine" running speed was a significant impediment.

On August 13, barely a month after Crockett arrived in Detroit, Dillon recovered from his injury and resumed his place as the team's first basemen. Detroit's writers thought Davey would accompany the team on its eastern trip as a utility player. They were saddened to learn, however, that he had been released. His slowness afoot had been his undoing.[57]

Adjusting Successfully: Cy Young

In the spring of 1901 Cy Young appeared to have begun the last phase of a distinguished pitching career. He was beginning his twelfth major league season. He had not pitched poorly in 1900. Official statistics of the time credited him with 20 wins and either 16 or 18 losses. (More recent compilations put his record at 19–19.)

But he missed three weeks in June because of an injury to his side, struggled at times, and did not seem to be as effective as he had been in the past. More importantly, he had just turned 34, at that time a ripe, old age for pitchers. In the three decades of professional baseball that had elapsed up to 1901, few pitchers had pitched beyond that age and those who had continued to pitch after reaching their thirty-fourth birthday did not do particularly well. Before he finalized his deal with Boston in the spring of 1901, Young gave St. Louis a chance to match the Boston offer, which covered three years. The Cardinals refused to go beyond one year. When Young signed with Boston, Stanley Robison, the Cardinals' treasurer, played down the importance of the event, saying that Young probably would not have lasted more than another year in the National League.[58]

Young, of course, lasted much longer than Robison or anyone else expected. He had an exceptional year in 1901. In the next three years he won 32, 28, and 26 games. He continued to pitch at a very high level through 1909, when he went 19–15 with a mediocre team. He finished his career in 1911, at the age of 44, with a career total of 511 wins.

A possible explanation for Young's great year in 1901 might be that the American League was still comparatively weak, having added some ex–National League players to what was still essentially the minor league organization of 1900. But in 1902, when the American League was universally looked upon as the stronger of the two leagues, and for several years afterward, Young continued to be just as dominating. What was the explanation for Young's ability to continue pitching so effectively at an age when his pitching contemporaries were forced to find other lines of work?

Reed Browning, in *Cy Young: A Baseball Life*, points out that Young added a new weapon to his arsenal in 1901. During the 1890s Young had relied primarily upon his overpowering fastball, which had both velocity and movement, and pinpoint control. He mixed in a curve at times but was basically a fastball pitcher. Early in the 1901 season, according to Browning, Young developed an effective change-up, a slow ball with a nasty drop just as it reached the batter.

A couple of years later one of Young's former teammates marveled at Young's expanded pitching repertoire. When he first heard reports of Young's new pitch, Jack O'Connor, who had caught Young at Cleveland and St. Louis, laughed at them. O'Connor told newsmen that Young varied the speed on his fastball and threw the batter off-stride with an "inshoot" at times. But, O'Connor added, "Young's success is due to his speed and stamina—his ability to shoot 'em over for nine or more innings just as fast as the first ball that he delivers—and his control." However, after O'Connor moved to the New York Highlanders in 1903, he admitted he had been wrong. Young had, to O'Connor's surprise, mastered a slow drop ball.[59]

After the 1903 season Joe Kelley, who faced Young in both the National and American leagues, explained how Young had revitalized his career. Kelley claimed the fans in Boston were watching a "new" Cy Young. "The new one used curves, used a slow ball, and occasionally used speed that reminded one of the old Cy Young who had nothing but speed," Kelley said. "By mixing the hot ones and bending ones, he was even more effective than the Cy Young who could only throw fast ones."[60]

There are plenty of newspaper game summaries indicating Young still had a very good fastball when he first moved to the American League. But by 1903, when Kelley made his statement, Young was well along in his conversion from being a power pitcher to one who relied upon breaking pitches, control and occasional speed to win. In 1904 Young threw a perfect game against the hard-hitting Philadelphia A's. Boston writer Tim Murnane praised Young's performance without mentioning his fastball. "It was clean cut, not a real hard chance being offered, and every ball sent up, if not over, was very close to the corner of the plate," Murnane said. "It was a case of wonderful command and a knowledge of every man's weakness. On that day Young had a fine drop ball, and as good curves as I ever saw him use."[61]

In his biography, Browning cited Young's ability to adjust to changing conditions as one of his strong points. Over his career Young adjusted to a longer pitching distance and more confined pitching space, a different shape for home plate, a rule forcing the catcher to stand closer to home plate, and changing rules regarding the bunt and foul balls. Many of these

Cy Young's attention to the details of his craft and to physical conditioning enabled him to extend his career and made him one of the greatest pitchers in baseball history (Library of Congress).

changes benefited the pitcher, at the batter's expense. But in each case, Young was already doing well under the existing rule, and opposing pitchers with less talent than Young might have become more competitive against him if he had not been able to use the new rules to his advantage. One of the last adjustments Young had to make was in his pitching style, as age took away his overpowering fastball. He obviously made that adjustment very well.

Young worked hard at his profession, both on the field and off it. While not a "natural hitter," he hit well enough to avoid being an automatic out. At a time when many pitchers were still lackadaisical about covering first base on grounders to the right side, he always made the effort. He was sure to back up bases when the play called for it, and he was active in fielding his position. He was able to change his pitching style after the move to Boston, not because he suddenly mastered the slow drop ball and other breaking pitches, but because he had been working on them for years. In the late 1890s it became an annual spring ritual for his hometown newspapermen to announce that Young was "practicing on a slow ball." When he finally started relying more on his breaking pitches in games, it was the fruit of years of experimentation with such pitches.[62]

Young's work off the mound was also an important a factor in his longevity. One writer noted that Young was active every minute during pre-game practice. When he spoke to Young about his activities, Young remarked, "I find it an excellent thing for a pitcher to get out every day in uniform and take a little exercise. It helps his wind and keeps him in condition for better work in the box."[63] During the offseason Young stayed active at his farm in Ohio. One of his chores, often mentioned in newspaper accounts, was to split logs with an axe, which strengthened his arm, back and shoulder muscles, and helped maintain his endurance. He also enjoyed hunting during the off-season. When the season approached, he would often go to Hot Springs, Arkansas, for several weeks of exercise and "boiling out" in the springs.[64]

The combination of Young's exceptional ability, his attentiveness to his craft, and his conditioning efforts added up to one of the greatest pitching careers in baseball history. Bill James rated Young as the fourth-best pitcher in baseball annals, behind Walter Johnson, Lefty Grove and Pete Alexander and ahead of Warren Spahn, Tom Seaver, Christy Mathewson, and a few thousand other pitchers. (James' rankings were done when Greg Maddux, Roger Clemens, and Randy Johnson were still in mid-career.)[65] When a pitcher is mentioned as being in a group with the men named above, the specific ranking really isn't important and would be subject to strong criticism regardless of what it might be. These are all great pitchers, and Young ranks with the best of them.

With Young, two features stand out: His tremendous durability and sustained performance at a very high level. In his career Young pitched 7,356⅔ innings. Pud Galvin, who did all his pitching before the pitcher's box was moved back to 60'6", is second at 5,941⅓, with Walter Johnson a close third at 5,914⅔. Phil Niekro is fourth at 5,404⅓ innings pitched. Given the high rankings of Young and Johnson, one might think that this was a category dominated by Deadball Era pitchers. That would be wrong. Five of the top ten innings pitched totals belong to men whose careers started in the 1960s. The difference between Young and anyone else—over 1,400 innings— would be about four seasons for a number one starter during the Deadball Era, about five seasons from the late twenties to the nineties, and about six seasons since the nineties.

All but a small percentage of Young's innings came in seasons when he was among the top pitchers in his league. This is broadly reflected in Young's total of 511 career victories. Johnson is second with 417 career wins (94 behind Young), Alexander and Mathewson are tied for third at 373 (138 behind Young). Young's victory total is so much higher than anyone else's that any discussion of it is quickly recast to focus on related statistics, such as wins-above-team (WAT). But even then Young finishes comfortably ahead of everyone else. (Young's career WAT is 99.7; Johnson is second at 90.0, followed by Alexander at 81.6, Mathewson at 64.9, and Grove at 62.9.)[66]

Young stands out in another, more focused measure of a pitcher's effectiveness— opponents' on-base percentage (OOB). From 1892 through 1908 Young ranked among the top five in his league in opponents' on-base percentage every year but one—1906, when his team finished last by eight games. For his career he was in the top five sixteen times, and finished first eight times. Johnson was in the top five fourteen times, finishing first on six occasions. Mathewson was in the top five eleven times, and finished first six times. Alexander, Kid Nichols, and Spahn also finished in the top five eleven times.

A good case can be made that the Cy Young Award, honoring each league's best pitcher in a season, is named after the right pitcher.

A Logical Decision: Frank DeHaas Robison

Pretend it's March of 1901 and you are Frank DeHaas Robison. Your star pitcher, Cy Young, comes up to you and says something like, "Boss, I have an offer from an American League team. If you match it, I'll keep pitching for you. If not, I'm going with them." You learn the offer is $3,500 per season for three years. (That would be about equal to the top salary any player received in the late 1890s.) Young just turned 34 years old and, while he had experienced a decent season in 1900, he didn't seem to be as good as he had been in the past. What do you do?

With the aid of 100 percent hindsight we know the correct answer. You reach into your desk, grab a pen and a blank contract, and say magnanimously, "Heck, Cy. You've been a good and loyal employee for a long time. Let's make it $3,750 per year for five years. Sign here." Robison had hindsight, but unfortunately for him it stopped with the 1900 season. And everything he would likely have gleaned from checking over past records would have led him to make the decision he made, which was to offer Young a one-year deal, knowing it would likely be turned down. Even today, when at least one 40-year-old veteran takes the mound for some team nearly every year, general managers are cautious about the terms of multi-year contracts with pitchers who have passed their 34th birthday. In 1901, all available data would have screamed, "Don't do it!"

In 1901 pitching was definitely a young man's profession. The National League had just completed its 25th season and the American Association had functioned as a second major league for ten years (1882–1891). Over that time very few pitchers had been able to continue pitching in a major league beyond their 30th birthdays, much less for four more years. In 1876, the National League's inaugural season, only one pitcher was older than 27; Cherokee Fisher was 30. He went 4–20 with Cincinnati, which finished last with a 9–56 record. The next time a National League team had a regular starter over 30 was in 1882, when Bobby Mathews pitched 289 innings for Boston after reaching that age. Mathews remained the oldest regular starter among major league pitchers through the 1886 season, when he was 34. He pitched in seven games the next season, his last in the major leagues. After Mathews retired, the oldest pitcher in the major leagues was Charlie "Old Hoss" Radbourn, who lasted until the age of 36 in 1891. (The 1890 season provided an interruption to Radbourn's reign as the oldest pitcher. That year teams from three major leagues scrounged around the sandlots looking for any potential pitcher. Two relatively old gentlemen—Ed Green, age 40, and Ed Cushman, age 38—pitched regularly in the American Association in 1890, then faded out of sight.) From 1876 to 1900 around 20 pitchers had been able to pitch in the major leagues past their thirtieth birthdays. Only a handful had held on beyond the age of 34, and their records after reaching that age wouldn't have caused Robison to push hard to sign Young in 1901.

Through 1900 only three pitchers had posted winning seasons past the age of

34. Mathews went 13–9 with the Philadelphia Athletics in the American Association in 1886. He pitched only four games after July 1 of that year. In 1887, at the age of 35, he appeared in seven games and posted a 6.67 ERA. Tim Keefe, a Hall of Fame pitcher, closed out his career by going 4–11, 19–16, and 10–7 after reaching the age of 34. His winning percentage was lower than his team's all three of those years, and only the middle year would have been considered worth an above-average salary. Only Charlie Radbourn's record as a relative old-timer might have persuaded Robison to reach for his checkbook in 1901. Radbourn was 20–11 in 1889 at the age of 34. He was a number two starter for Boston that year. The team's top starter, John Clarkson, was 49–19. In 1890 Radbourn jumped to the Players' League, though he still played in Boston. That year he led the Boston Red Stockings to the pennant with a 27–12 record. If Robison were venturesome in handing out salaries, which he wasn't, he might have forked over top dollar to Cy Young for three years in hopes he could match the two years Old Hoss posted at ages 34 and 35. Radbourn's last year wouldn't have helped Young's cause. He bowed out in 1892 at age 36 with an 11–13 record with Cincinnati.

Among Young's true contemporaries—those who started their careers in the early- and mid- nineties—not one pitched at a top level after reaching age 34. Clark Griffith was the best. Pitching for the New York Highlanders as a spot starter and reliever, he put up records of 7–5, 9–6 with three saves, and 2–2 with two saves. Several pitchers who pitched regularly in 1900 were able to pitch effectively in their mid-thirties, most of them, like Griffith, in limited roles. Two would have commanded top-level salaries based on their performances. Joe McGinnity went 21–15, 27–12, and 18–18 for the Giants at ages 34, 35, and 36. The Pirates' Sam Leever was 22–7, 14–9, and 15–7 at those ages. McGinnity lasted one more year after that, going 11–7 with the Giants in 1908 before dropping into the minors, where he was still pitching past the age of 50. Leever and Deacon Phillippe continued pitching fairly well for the Pirates until 1910, when both were 38.

In 1901 when Frank DeHaas Robison refused to pay top dollar to 34-year-old Cy Young for the next three years, he was making an entirely logical decision. Unfortunately for him, he was dealing with the only pitcher in baseball at that time who was a glaring exception to the logic behind the decision.

Four

1902, National League

A Desperate Counterattack

At the turn of the twentieth century, with the War of 1898 still fresh in their minds, baseball reporters sometimes used military analogies in their writings. If a reporter were to do so in describing the baseball war between the American and National leagues on the eve of the 1902 season, an analogy that might come to mind would be that of the Battle of Santiago Bay on July 3, 1898. On that day the Spanish fleet tried to break out of an American blockade. The fleet was destroyed in a four-hour battle in which only one American sailor died. Combined with Commodore Dewey's similarly one-sided defeat of the Spanish at Manila Bay two months earlier, the naval victory had brought the United States to the brink of victory over Spain, though more fighting remained. If a reporter were to use this analogy, the American League would have been likened to the victorious Americans, the National League to the unfortunate Spaniards.

By mid–April of 1902 the American League seemed about to complete a route of the National League in the struggle between the two major leagues. The new league had caught the older league off-guard at the beginning of the 1901 season when it lured away around 40 of its players, including almost a dozen star players. The National League's initial response was led by one of the Philadelphia team owners, Colonel John I. Rogers, a wealthy lawyer.

In April of 1901 Rogers sought an injunction barring three defecting players—Nap Lajoie, Chick Fraser, and Bill Bernhard—from playing with any team other than the Phillies. At the hearing, testimony focused on Lajoie, the most prominent of the defendants. Rogers, who reportedly was infatuated with the sound of his own voice, spoke for nearly two hours before being interrupted by the judge, who asked him to focus on the primary issue being argued, the mutuality of National League contracts. The players' lawyers were arguing that the contracts were so one-sided as to lack mutuality. While a player was bound for an unlimited amount of time by the reserve clause, the club had only to give a ten-day notice to terminate its obligation to the player, a disparity so great as to call into question the legality of the contract. The court pondered the issue for three weeks before siding with the American League.[1] Although the National League appealed the decision, most major league players believed there was no legal impediment to signing with the American League.

During the 1901 season, agents from both leagues tried to take away the other league's players. The National League was laboring under a huge handicap. The players understood that the new league's success was vital to their future well-being. And the American League clearly was succeeding financially. It drew more fans than the National in two of the three cities where each league fielded a team and had good overall attendance.

Reports of clandestine scheming by both leagues formed a backdrop to the second half of the 1901 season. In late July the Pirates released shortstop Fred Ely, stating that the move was made because of Ely's poor hitting. A few days later they admitted Ely had been acting as an American League agent.[2]

About the same time Ban Johnson charged that John McGraw was negotiating with National League magnates. McGraw's aim, according to Johnson, was for Baltimore to join the National League in 1902 as part of a new 12-team league. Johnson said McGraw's agent had approached Jimmy Manning of Washington and George Stallings of Detroit, both of whom were part-owners as well as managers of their teams, with the idea but had been turned down. McGraw, of course, denied the charge, which was not pursued any further.[3]

There were also reports that men working for the National League had offered high salaries to two Detroit players and to Washington pitcher/outfielder Watty Lee. In August word leaked that several Phillies players, including Ed Delahanty, had signed with the American League. In mid–September the Athletics' Lave Cross announced he had signed with the A's for 1902. Cross explained that he had asked Connie Mack to let him sign right away so National League agents would stop annoying him.[4]

As the season drew to a close, teams of both leagues began announcing their successes in re-signing their players for 1902. Reporters were naturally more interested in the players who had not re-signed with the same team. Over the next few months, as an increasing number of signings became public, a clear pattern emerged: lots of players were moving to new teams, and the movement was overwhelmingly in one direction—from the National League to the American.

By the time the teams gathered to begin the 1902 season, at least 33 players had left their 1901 National League teams to join the new league. Nine players left American League teams to play in the National League, seemingly a good thing for the older league. A closer look at the players who jumped to the National League, however, reveals how badly it lost out to the American League in the competition for players.

Only two of the nine players who crossed over to the National League could be considered losses to their former teams. They were Harry Smith, an alternate catcher who probably would have been retained by Connie Mack if he had decided to stay in Philadelphia rather than going to Pittsburgh, and Wid Conroy, also signed by the Pirates, who probably would have played third base for the Browns if he had gone to St. Louis with other ex–Milwaukee players. The other seven players were men who likely would have lost their starting jobs to ex–National Leaguers in 1902. They changed leagues in an effort to continue playing regularly or simply to remain in the major leagues.

Once again, as in 1901, Pittsburgh benefited from the American League raids. The Pirates strengthened their team by adding Smith, who bolstered an aging catching corps, and Conroy, who replaced Fred Ely at shortstop. (Honus Wagner had strongly voiced his desire to return to the outfield.) They also retained Jimmy Burke, whom they had picked up after Charlie Comiskey released him in September of 1901. Not one Pirate had followed Ely to the American League during the offseason.

The two teams hit hardest by the raids were Philadelphia, which had finished second in 1901, and St. Louis, which had finished a disappointing fourth. The Phillies lost nine players, including such stars as Delahanty, Elmer Flick, Ed McFarland, and Al Orth, while the Cardinals lost their best eight players. The Chicago team, derisively nicknamed "the Remnants" in 1901 because the American League took almost all of its top players before that season, lost the best of the remnants. Brooklyn, the third-place finisher in 1901, lost three good players—Joe Kelley, Tom Daly and Jim McGuire. The remaining four National League teams had few good players to lose, but the American League raiders picked over their bones carefully and made off with at least one useful player from each team.

In mid-winter Boston writer Tim Murnane noted the National League's steady loss of its star players and concluded, "Looking at baseball purely from a playing standpoint, the American League has its rival beat to a pulp."

A week before the season opened, Murnane, like all the other baseball writers, picked Pittsburgh to win the National League pennant easily. Nevertheless, Murnane thought the Opening Day games would be closely contested, except in St. Louis where the Cardinals were to open against the Pirates. "So complete has been the raid of the American League that the teams will be pretty closely matched," he said, referring to the six also-rans who would be playing each other. But Murnane was not exactly enthusiastic about the projected caliber of play. "It is not like the old times and the old clubs," he said. "The players are not the pick of the profession, as they should be, but a grand all-round mixup of good and bad players—mostly bad, when compared with the best in baseball."[5]

Shortly after Murnane made his comment, battlefield conditions in the baseball war changed enough that the comparison with the War of 1898 would have become somewhat off-target. Unlike the Spaniards, who quickly negotiated a peace agreement after losing every important battle in the spring of 1898, the National League owners launched a spirited counter-offensive.

By the spring of 1902 the situation was dire enough that the National League owners realized they needed to set aside their longstanding intra-league hostilities and adopt a unified counter-strategy. They pledged to contribute to a $100,000 war fund to tempt American Leaguers back to their league.

On April 21, 1902, they received good news. Their appeal of the Lajoie case had been upheld by the Pennsylvania State Supreme Court. Citing the decision, they demanded that all the ex–National League players return immediately to their former teams. After taking a couple of days to gather their wits, the American League responded with a legal opinion stating that, since the decision was issued by a state court, it applied only in the state of Pennsylvania. Therefore, the American League claimed, only ex–Phillies players were affected, and only when they were playing in Pennsylvania. The National League's position was further undermined two weeks later by a Missouri state court decision denying injunctions against the St. Louis Browns players who had jumped to the American League. The Missouri court based its decision on the same line of reasoning used in 1901 by the lower Pennsylvania court—the National League's contracts lacked mutuality.[6]

Only a few players changed teams as a result of the legal wrangling. Chick Fraser and Bill Duggleby, both pitchers who had left the Phillies to sign with the Athletics, jumped back to the Phillies. (Fraser, of course, was one of the three players named in the injunction.) Jimmy Sheckard, who had signed with Baltimore in 1901 but jumped back to the Superbas before the season started, had again signed with the Orioles for the 1902 season. After receiving news of the Pennsylvania State Supreme Court's decision, he jumped back to the Superbas for the second year in a row. The other two players besides Fraser who were named in the injunction, Nap Lajoie and Bill Bernhard, were inactive for several weeks before signing with the Cleveland Blues. Elmer Flick, another former Phillie signed by Mack, also decided to play for Cleveland, arriving there about three weeks before Lajoie and Bernhard.

In July the American League was rocked by another crisis. McGraw, after being suspended indefinitely for cursing an umpire, lashed out in anger against American League president Ban Johnson. McGraw claimed he was losing money in Baltimore because of Johnson's unfair treatment of him and his team. He went to New York where he met with Andrew Freedman, the president of the Giants.

On July 7, he announced that after several weeks of intermittent discussions he had come to an agreement with Freedman to manage the Giants. He was to be paid "as much money as any ballplayer ever drew," and was to have "practically unlimited funds" to sign players for his team. McGraw pledged that he would not "draw on the Baltimore team" because "that would not be right." The next day he arranged to sell his shares in the Orioles and departed for New York.[7]

True to his word, McGraw did not recruit his former players. It was Freedman who, a week later, bought enough stock in the Orioles to claim majority ownership. Freedman granted releases to several Orioles players so they could sign with National League teams. Four of them—Joe McGinnity, Dan McGann, Roger Bresnahan, and Jack Cronin—followed McGraw to New York. Joe Kelley and Cy Seymour went to Cincinnati.

Left with only a few players, the Orioles forfeited their game scheduled for July 17. Acting under a league rule giving him authority to take control of any franchise unable to field a team, Johnson stepped in, issued a call for help from other American League teams, and put together a team in time to play the Orioles' next game. The Orioles finished out the schedule with a ragtag team composed of a few holdovers, several transplanted fringe major league players, some minor league pickups, and a few semi-pro graduates.

Meanwhile, agents from both leagues competed against each other for players, promising bonuses and high salaries for 1903 and beyond. During the summer of 1902 fans witnessed an exciting pennant race in the American League, a triumphal march to the National League championship by the Pirates, and a confusing, self-destructive competition for players that drove salaries to a level neither league could have imagined two years earlier nor was willing or able to sustain for very long.

1902 National League Standings

Team	W	L	Pct.	GB
Pittsburgh	103	36	.741	—
Brooklyn	75	63	.543	27.5

Boston	73	64	.533	29
Cincinnati	70	70	.500	33.5
Chicago	68	69	.496	34
St. Louis	56	78	.418	44.5
Philadelphia	56	81	.409	46
New York	48	88	.353	53.5

Like Men Among Boys: Pittsburgh

To understand the Pirates' 1902 performance, it might be instructive to keep in mind Nap Lajoie's 1901 season. Lajoie was arguably the top hitter in baseball going into the 1901 campaign, certainly one of the top two or three. In 1901 he moved into an expansion league—one with maybe ten genuine stars, twenty above-average players, forty or fifty guys who undeniably had major league abilities, and forty or fifty players who were fringe major leaguers by the standards of the 1890s. The National League of 1902 had about the same distribution of skills as the American League of 1901, except that it had about double the number of star players.

In 1901 Lajoie tore apart American League pitching, putting up some phenomenal numbers. The 1902 Pirates, with the same core as the 1900 team but toughened by the experience of two pennant races and strengthened by the addition of players who gave them much greater depth, tore apart the National League in 1902, finishing 27½ games ahead of the second-place Superbas. No team has ever matched that feat, the 1998 New York Yankees coming the closest by finishing 22 games ahead of the Boston Red Sox, who had the second-best record in the American League that season.

The 1902 Pirates had a terrific pitching staff and top players in every position except possibly one. The Pirates arguably had the best player in the league at four positions: Left field (Fred Clarke), center field (Ginger Beaumont), second base (Claude Ritchey), and third base (Tommy Leach). And that was not counting the man generally considered to be the best player in the National League, Honus Wagner. In 1902 Clarke continued using Wagner as a "super-utility" player. Although Honus had established himself as the top shortstop in baseball the previous year, Clarke played him there in only 44 games in 1902. He played 32 games at first base, 30 in right field, 20 in left field, 11 in center field, and one at second base. On days when Wagner was playing but not filling in for one of the four players just named, the Pirates fielded a team with five players who would now be called "all-stars"—and that is without counting their starting pitchers, all of whom posted outstanding records.

Although maybe not "all-stars," the Pirates' other starters were all good players. The catching combination of Chief Zimmer and Jack O'Connor, both savvy veterans who hit pretty well, was second only to Chicago's combination of Johnny Kling and Frank Chance. Kitty Bransfield was probably the third-best first baseman in the league, behind Fred Tenney and Jake Beckley. Before he broke his ankle on July 11, Lefty Davis was the third- or fourth-best right fielder. Shortstop Wid Conroy did not have a great season in 1902, batting only .244, but he was a solid ballplayer. He was considered one of the American League's better shortstops in 1901and was a regular in the major leagues for eleven seasons.

Pittsburgh (103–36)

Regular Lineup	AVG	OBP	SLG	R	RBI	SB
Fred Clarke, lf	.316	.401	.449	103	53	29
or Lefty Davis, rf	.280	.377	.336	52	20	19
Ginger Beaumont, cf	.357	.404	.418	100	67	33
Tommy Leach, 3b	.278	.341	.426	97	85	25
Honus Wagner, ut	.330	.394	.463	105	91	42
Kitty Bransfield, 1b	.305	.336	.395	49	69	23
Claude Ritchey, 2b	.277	.370	.328	54	55	10
Wid Conroy, ss	.244	.299	.312	55	47	10
Harry Smith, c	.189	.211	.222	14	12	4
or Jack O'Connor, c	.294	.306	.341	13	28	2
or Chief Zimmer, c	.268	.338	.324	13	17	4
Leading Pitchers	**W**	**L**	**PCT.**	**IP**	**H**	**ERA**
Jack Chesbro	28	6	.824	286.3	242	2.17
Deacon Phillippe	20	9	.690	272	265	2.05
Jesse Tannehill	20	6	.769	231	203	1.95
Sam Leever	15	7	.682	222	203	2.39
Ed Doheny	16	4	.800	188.3	161	2.53

The Pirates' pitching staff featured the same quartet that pitched so well the previous two years. They were four of the top pitchers of the era—Deacon Phillippe, Jesse Tannehill, Jack Chesbro, and Sam Leever. Consistent with owner Barney Dreyfuss' theme of adding strength to strength, midway through the 1901 season the Pirates picked up Ed Doheny. For several seasons with the Giants Doheny had been an erratic pitcher. He was difficult to hit when he got the ball over the plate, but he hadn't been able to do that with any consistency. After the Pirates picked him up in 1901, he gained better control of his pitches. He went 6–2 with the Pirates in 1901, posting a 2.00 ERA in eleven games. In 1902 he continued to pitch just as well. At a time when other teams in baseball struggled to find three effective pitchers, the Pirates had five, six if Ed Poole is counted. Poole, a holdover from 1901, started the season with the Pirates. Through July 4, he had appeared in only one game before Clarke gave him his release. Poole then signed with Cincinnati, where he went 12–4 over the second half of the season.

The Pirates wasted no time in establishing their dominance in 1902. They won their first five games, lost two, then put together winning streaks of ten, four, six, and five games, losing only one game each time before starting the next winning streak. By May 30, when the Cubs beat them in the second game of a doubleheader, their record was 30–6, and the pennant race was as good as over. Over that span the Pirates outscored their opponents 223 to 100. They outhit the opposition by .297 to .230. Six of the Pirates' regulars were batting higher than .300. Beaumont led the league in batting with a .378 average, Leach led in extra-base hits, and Davis led in runs scored, with 37 runs in 36 games.[8] In the first five games he pitched, Jesse Tannehill lost one, by a 4–2 score, and won four, by scores of 10–2, 18–6, 11–2, and 9–3. On May 30, Tannehill's record stood at 7–2, as did Chesbro's. Phillippe was 6–2, while Doheny and Leever were still undefeated, at 6–0 and 4–0, respectively.

After their blazing start the Pirates slowed down somewhat, but not much. When June ended, the Pirates' record was 41–12. Their .774 win-loss percentage was the highest through June 30 since 1886, when the Detroit Wolverines finished that month at 35–8, for a percentage of .814.[9] In the closing days of the season, Dreyfuss pushed his team to shoot for 103 wins, which would break the existing record of 102, set by the Boston Beaneaters in 1892 and tied by the Beaneaters 1898. In both of those years the schedule called for 152 games, thirteen more than the Pirates played in 1902. The Pirates reached Dreyfuss' goal, but only by playing their last game on a soggy field and beating a Cincinnati team that turned the game into a farce by playing men out of position and starting the game with weak-throwing first baseman Jake Beckley on the mound.[10]

Although overall the season was a great one for the Pirates, it also had some sad moments. On July 11 Lefty Davis headed for second base on a steal attempt. Seeing the opposing shortstop straddling the bag, Lefty decided at the last second to alter his slide to avoid spiking him. As a result, he caught his spikes in the ground, breaking an ankle. The injury ended his season. At the time Lefty was leading the National League with 20 stolen bases and had scored 52 runs in 59 games. Later, tempted by a large contract offer, Lefty decided to jump to the American League.

In August the Pirates released veteran catcher Jack O'Connor because, Dreyfuss said, O'Connor was recruiting players for Ban Johnson.[11] Unlike Bones Ely, who was released in 1901 for acting as an American League agent, O'Connor seems to have been quite successful. Six Pirates, including three star players (Chesbro, Tannehill, and Leach), signed with the American League.

After learning they had committed to the American League, Dreyfuss met with Chesbro and Tannehill at their hotel. He asked them how much money it would take to get them to sign with Pittsburgh for 1903. They each asked for a two-year contract totaling $17,000. Dreyfuss let out a low whistle and asked for some time to think the matter over. He retreated to the hotel bar for a shot or two of confidence builder. When he returned he said, "Boys, the Pittsburgh club is not owned by Andrew Carnegie." He made a counter-offer. "I'll give each of you $11,000 for two years, and if this isn't satisfactory, you may jump to the Johnson crowd if you see fit." Both men declined Dreyfuss' offer.[12]

Hanlon's Projects: Brooklyn

The baseball war between the American and National leagues was clearly a painful experience for Ned Hanlon. Hanlon prided himself on treating his players well. He treated them with dignity, refusing to impose strict rules on their off-field behavior, encouraging them by offering small prizes, such as a hat or suit of clothes for taking off excess weight or making a clutch play, and paying them well by his standards. Of course, his pay standards were those of the 1890s, not the high-salaried wartime years. When top players such as Lave Cross, Joe Kelley, and Deacon McGuire left Brooklyn for higher pay in the American League, Hanlon took their defections personally. As the inter-league conflict continued, and more Brooklyn players jumped to the new league, he became somewhat bitter.

Brooklyn (75–63)

Regular Lineup	AVG	OBP	SLG	R	RBI	SB
Jimmy Sheckard, lf	.265	.349	.372	86	37	23
Willie Keeler, rf	.333	.365	.386	86	38	19
Cozy Dolan, cf	.280	.324	.336	72	54	24
Tom McCreery, 1b	.244	.295	.309	49	57	16
Bill Dahlen, ss	.264	.329	.353	67	74	20
Tim Flood, 2b	.218	.268	.277	43	51	8
Charlie Irwin, 3b	.273	.346	.317	59	43	13
Hughie Hearne, c	.281	.336	.325	22	28	3
or Duke Farrell, c	.242	.281	.277	14	24	6
Leading Pitchers	**W**	**L**	**PCT**	**IP**	**H**	**ERA**
Wild Bill Donovan	17	15	.531	297.7	250	2.78
Frank Kitson	19	13	.594	268.7	256	2.84
Doc Newton	15	14	.517	264.3	208	2.42
Jim Hughes	15	10	.600	245	223	2.87

Hanlon's joy came from successes on the diamond—not just winning games, which he of course enjoyed, but in developing players. He felt deep satisfaction when one of his men learned a technique or developed a playing strategy that made him a better player. He liked working with young players in spring training and at morning practices during the season. Brooklyn reporter Abe Yager said Hanlon's desire to help such youngsters was "nothing less than a passion."[13] The 1902 season gave Hanlon plenty of opportunities to indulge that passion. Just about anywhere he looked on his team, he could see a project, some nearly completed, several still needing lots of work.

One of the Superbas' strengths was the team's pitching staff, which featured three of Hanlon's more successful projects. The staff's ace was "Wild Bill" Donovan. As previously noted, Hanlon nurtured Donovan for two years, working to help him gain control of his outstanding fastball and overhand curve. Donovan put it all together in 1901, becoming one of the top pitchers in baseball.

Frank Kitson had come to Hanlon's Baltimore Orioles during the summer of 1897. Pitching for a terrible team at Burlington of the Class B Western Association, Kitson had put up some good numbers, including one game in which he fanned 11 batters. Hanlon purchased Kitson on the recommendation of a hometown acquaintance for $500, hoping he could be of some help in the 1897 pennant race.

When Kitson arrived, Hanlon was mortified to discover that he was still a raw, unpolished minor leaguer who had no idea how to attack major league hitters. Upset over being duped in the transaction, Hanlon decided he would do whatever he could to salvage something from the deal. He had Kitson work out every day, teaching him all he knew about pitching.

The next spring he kept Kitson on the Oriole roster as an extra pitcher. A month into the season he gave Kitson a trial, starting him against the Pirates, a .500 team at the time. Kitson pitched a shutout, earning another start. That turned out to be a disaster. Kitson allowed 20 runs in a game that was mercifully called after seven innings. Hanlon worked with Kitson for another month before farming him out to an Eastern League team. When Kitson returned in September, Hanlon gave him several starts, and Kitson finished the season with an 8–5 record. In 1899 he pitched for the Baltimore half of the Brooklyn/Baltimore syndicate, winning 22 and losing 16. The next season he became a regular starter for the Superbas.[14]

Until he came under Hanlon's wing, Doc Newton was a perennial prospect who was slowly morphing into a suspect. He was purchased by the Louisville Colonels in 1897 but quickly made a poor impression with his new team. His pitching seemed to be all right. He had "terrific speed," and a good drop ball. Manager Fred Clarke liked that part of Newton's makeup. But when the Colonels offered Newton a contract for $1,000 for the 1898 season, Newton demanded $1,800, saying he was the best young pitcher coming into the National League. Clarke decided he didn't like that part of Newton's makeup. "Newton has too good an opinion of himself to be of any use to us," Clarke told a reporter. "Had he been reasonable we would have found a place for him here, but as it is he will have to go back to minor society.... We do not intend to pay star salaries for raw material."[15]

Newton resurfaced again in 1899 as part of John T. Brush's scheme to rebuild the Cincinnati Reds with the top players in the minor leagues. Pitching for Brush's minor league farm team at Indianapolis, Newton put up a 17–7 record and threw a no-hitter. Once again, Newton wrangled with his team over his salary, but this time he had enough sense to accept the club's offer.[16]

In 1900, his rookie season, Newton showed good stuff but not good results, going 9–15. The only category he came close to leading was bases on balls. He ranked as the third-wildest pitcher in the league. The 1901 season brought more of the same, with even worse results. He cut down his walks somewhat, but made up for that by averaging close to one fielding error a game. Newton pitched some good games but managed to lose most of those. And he pitched a lot of bad games.

His Cincinnati teammates couldn't understand why he struggled so much. "Newton is by far the hardest man to catch of the Reds' pitchers," said catcher Bill Bergen. "His delivery is a peculiar one and his balls take such unexpected shoots that it keeps a catcher guessing. There is nothing in the way of deceivers that Newton has not got in his repertoire of foolers, and I can't understand for the life of me how it is that he is hit hard now and then."[17] Newton had a 4–13 record when the Reds decided they weren't going to wait any longer for him to put his game together. They released him on July 13.

Hanlon snapped up Newton right away. Newton gave up seven runs in five innings in his first game for the Superbas, but Hanlon said he was confident Newton could become a winning pitcher. He just needed to make a couple of adjustments, Hanlon said. Hanlon and veteran catcher Duke Farrell worked with Newton to get more bite on his curveball and they helped him find a more effective motion on his crossfire delivery.[18]

Newton's next two starts came in the second games of doubleheaders played almost two weeks apart. Newton split those two games, losing to the Phillies, 4–3, and beating the Beaneaters, 8–5. Satisfied with Newton's progress, Hanlon inserted him into the rotation for the rest of the season. Newton won five of his next six games, holding the opposition to two or fewer runs in each of the five games he won. Although he lost his last two games, Newton's final 1901 record with the Superbas was 6–5 with a 2.83 ERA. By correcting a couple of flaws in Newton's delivery, Hanlon had found another quality starter for 1902.

To go with his three successful "projects," Hanlon had Jim Hughes, who was a success from the day he first threw a pitch in the National League but wasn't quite sure he wanted to pitch in the senior circuit. Hughes is unknown now to all but the most ardent fans of baseball history, but if he had been able to sustain the pace he set in his first two years, Roger Clemens would now have a shelf full of trophies labeled: "Jim Hughes Award, Best Pitcher xxxx." In his first major league game Hughes pitched a two-hit shutout. Being a smart fellow, he learned from his two mistakes in that game. The next time out he threw a no-hitter against the Boston Beaneaters. He ended his rookie season with a 23–12 record. In 1899 he improved to a fabulous 28–6.

In the spring of 1900 Hughes announced that he was going to open a saloon in Sacramento and pitch in the California League, which played its games mostly on weekends. Hughes' arrangement with local Sacramento merchants, which netted him about $1,800 and saved him the expense associated with spending six months in the East, was probably a gambit to ply more money out of the Superbas. But Hanlon had six top-notch pitchers to choose from that spring and let Hughes stay on the West Coast.[19] Both Hughes and Hanlon were more willing to compromise in 1901. Hughes returned to Brooklyn, and while he was still a good pitcher after that, he wasn't quite able to regain his previous form.

While Hanlon had several more-or-less finished projects to send to the mound in 1902, he had plenty of new projects among the position players. Replacing the three defecting veterans—Joe Kelley, who had spent most of 1901 at first base, second baseman Tom Daly, and catcher Deacon McGuire—proved to be a season-long problem for Hanlon. To replace Kelley, Hanlon moved Tom McCreery from the outfield to first base, but McCreery had trouble mastering the position. Cozy Dolan, who replaced McCreery in center field, was not a good fielder in that position and had yet to master the batting tactics Hanlon liked to use. Daly's replacement was second baseman Tim Flood, who had been purchased from Sacramento of the California League. Flood played very well defensively but couldn't hit. In place of McGuire, Hanlon tried Hughie Hearne, a recruit from Troy of the Class B New York State League. Hearne was a gritty player, but not a polished catcher.

The Superbas played most of their games on the road during the first month of the season. Hanlon watched McCreery botch a number of plays at first base, especially on bunts to the right side. Dolan muffed several fly balls, Flood struggled to hit, and Hearne staggered around behind the plate trying to locate foul pop-ups. The team returned from its first western trip a half-game out of last place with a 12–19 record.

Hanlon vowed there would be a vast improvement in the team's play now that he could iron out some of the players' deficiencies during morning practices. Every morning he sent his weaker hitters down to a corner of the field. Each one picked out a strong-armed youth from the group of onlookers and spent an hour working on his weaknesses, especially in the bunting game. Hanlon was so persistent in doing this that the players began teasing each other about it. If a Brooklyn batter looked bad in an at-bat during a game, when he returned to the bench he would hear his teammates shouting, "Down to the corner of the lot for you."[20]

Hanlon's morning practices may have brought instant improvement, or it might have been mostly a coincidence, but the Superbas went on a winning streak as soon as they returned home. They won twelve of their next thirteen games and moved steadily upward in the standings. When they went to Pittsburgh for a Fourth of July doubleheader, they were in second place, still a long way behind the Pirates, but at least theoretically still a challenger for the pennant.

Then reality hit, as both Tannehill and Chesbro pitched shutouts, beating the Superbas, 3–0 and 4–0, respectively. After those losses, Hanlon set his sights on second place as the only practical goal for his team. For fans who could get excited about a race for second place, the remainder of the season featured a close three-way contest between Brooklyn, Chicago, and Boston, with the Superbas nosing out the Beaneaters the last week of the season.

End of the Road for a Star: Boston

The link with the great Boston teams of the 1890s was badly frayed by the time the 1902 season opened. Billy Hamilton, Bobby Lowe and Kid Nichols left over the winter, Hamilton to retirement, Lowe to the Chicago Cubs, and Nichols to Kansas City as a manager/pitcher. Bill Dinneen, one of the National League's better pitchers, jumped to the Boston Americans. Perhaps more importantly in the long run, manager Frank Selee left the team. Selee had been the team's manager since 1890, leading the Beaneaters to five pennants in twelve years. He was a good evaluator of young players and a patient man—just the type of manager needed to rebuild the team.

Only three members of the 1902 team knew the joy of winning a pennant in Boston: Shortstop Herman Long, a key member of all five pennant winners; Fred Tenney, who played for the 1897 and 1898 champions; and Vic Willis, a member of the 1898 team. Tenney and Willis were to remain with the Beaneaters for several more seasons. For Long, the 1902 campaign would be a struggle and his last in Boston.

Boston (73–64)

Regular Lineup	AVG	OBP	SLG	R	RBI	SB
Billy Lush, cf	.223	.346	.262	68	19	30
Fred Tenney, 1b	.315	.409	.376	88	30	21
Duff Cooley, lf	.296	.339	.372	73	58	27
Pat Carney, rf	.270	.339	.330	75	65	27
Ed Gremminger, 3b	.257	.314	.347	55	65	7
Gene DeMontreville, 2b	.260	.278	.314	51	53	23
Herman Long, ss	.231	.284	.270	40	44	24
Malachi Kittridge, c	.235	.304	.286	18	30	4
or Pat Moran, c	.239	.303	.311	22	24	6

Leading Pitchers	W	L	PCT	IP	H	ERA
Vic Willis	27	20	.574	410	372	2.20
Togie Pittinger	27	16	.628	389.3	360	2.52
Mal Eason	9	11	.450	206.3	237	2.75
John Malarkey	8	10	.444	170.3	158	2.59

During the 1890s, no discussion of the game's top shortstops could be considered complete if it omitted Long's name. He was a spectacular defensive player. He continually made sensational catches and pickups, sometimes improvising as the play developed. A rival player described a catch Long made in 1892:

> With a man on first, the next batter hit a savage grounder over second well out of [Long's] reach. Long made a fine attempt, but seeing he couldn't reach the ball he went up in the air and threw out his left foot. The ball struck the toe of his shoe and bounded high over Long's head. Fairly turning in the air, Long nabbed the ball in his left hand and got the ball to Joe Quinn [at second base] in time to head off the runner there. All this was done while Long was moving at top speed. Of all the great plays I've ever seen at short, this was the greatest.[21]

Long's passionate, all-out play had its downside. He made scores of errors every season, many of them on bad throws. Until the last few years of his career, Long's fielding averages tended to be relatively low. By the end of the 1890s, however, he had managed to reduce the number of errors. His fielding averages for the last few years of his career put him among the league's leaders.

During the first half of his major league career, which began in 1889, Long was a good hitter and baserunner. He had good power, knocking more than 40 extra-base hits almost every year during the 1890s. He scored more than 100 runs eight times. He batted at the top of the order for the 1891–93 champions and in the middle of the order for the 1897–98 pennant winners. His hitting began to decline near the end of the decade, dropping from .322 in 1897 to .265 in both 1898 and 1899, and to .261 in 1900.

In 1900 Long led the league in home runs, thanks in part to the very short left field fence at the South End Grounds, the Beaneaters' home field. With his dazzling defense, he was still one of the top shortstops in the game, if not quite the best any longer. But the 1900 season was to be his last good one. When the National League adopted the modern foul-strike rule in 1901, Long's hitting fell off sharply. His batting average dropped to .216. He brought it up slightly in 1902, to .231, but with very little power.

Long moved to the American League in 1903, but the new foul-strike rule followed him there, and so did his hitting woes. He hit only .213 that year, playing for New York and Detroit. He played only one game in the major leagues in 1904, finishing his career as a player-manager in the minor leagues over the next three seasons.[22]

When the Baseball Hall of Fame was established in Cooperstown, two separate elections were held to select the first group of inductees. One election was for players active after 1900; members of the Baseball Writers Association of America (BBWAA) voted for those players. Another election, to be voted on by 78 "veteran baseball men," was for players active before 1900. Long was one of five shortstops nominated on ballots for the pre–1900 group. When the votes were counted, Long received the most votes of any of the shortstops and finished eighth in the voting. The voting was so spread out among the veteran players, however, that none of them received the 75 percent required for selection. Long received a token vote in the next four elections, all voted on by members of the BBWAA. By 1945, when the Hall got around to forming another committee to select old-timers, Long's supporters were no longer around. He received one vote that year and none thereafter.[23]

Refreshing Changes: Cincinnati

This would have been year three of the Reds' rebuilding plan, but John T. Brush had bigger fish to fry. During the offseason of 1901–02 he had tried to interest Ban Johnson in a plan that would include a transfer of the Cincinnati team to the American League.[24] That failing, he became the leader of the National League's counter-attack in the baseball war. Before the season ended, he would sell his interest in the Reds and become the principal owner of the New York Giants.

With Brush otherwise preoccupied, the Reds had the quietest offseason of any major league team. They lost outfielder Dick Harley to Detroit, a move that brought yawns from the fans of both teams. To replace Harley the Reds signed Dummy Hoy, who had been released by the White Stockings. They also added second baseman Erve Beck, who wasn't even good enough to stick with the hapless Cleveland Blues. Obviously, neither of those signings stirred great excitement among Cincinnati fans.

As a sign of how badly the National League had fared in the off-season contest for players, the comparative lack of any player movement involving the Reds caused writers to forecast that they would be one of the league's top teams in 1902. Remember, the Reds finished last in 1901. If shortstop Tommy Corcoran had not missed most of the 1901 season due to a bout with typhoid fever, the Reds might have finished as high as sixth, since the Remnants and Giants were only a game ahead of them. But the 1901 Reds were weak at second base, lacked at least two adequate starting pitchers, and had only three legitimate stars—outfielder Sam Crawford, first baseman Jake Beckley, and pitcher Noodles Hahn. So when the 1902 version of that team floundered around for the first three months of the season, it should not have been a big surprise.

Cincinnati (70–70)

Regular Lineup	AVG	OBP	SLG	R	RBI	SB
Dummy Hoy, cf	.290	.389	.380	48	20	11
or Mike Donlin, lf	.287	.333	.378	30	9	9
John Dobbs, lf*	.299	.350	.356	70	51	10
Jake Beckley, 1b	.330	.377	.427	82	69	15
Sam Crawford, rf	.333	.386	.461	92	78	16
or Cy Seymour, cf	.340	.378	.414	27	37	8
Erve Beck, 2b	.305	.319	.406	19	20	2
or George Magoon, 2b	.272	.344	.352	29	23	7
or Heinie Peitz, c–2b	.315	.369	.406	54	60	7

Tommy Corcoran, ss	.253	.268	.301	54	54	20
Harry Steinfeldt, 3b	.278	.316	.355	53	49	12
Bill Bergen, c	.180	.214	.224	19	36	2
Leading Pitchers	**W**	**L**	**PCT**	**IP**	**H**	**ERA**
Noodles Hahn	23	12	.657	321	282	1.77
Bill Phillips	16	16	.500	269	267	2.51
Henry Thielman	9	15	.375	211	201	3.24
Ed Poole	12	4	.750	138	129	2.15

*Includes record with Chicago

The real surprise was the one that came in July, when John McGraw, with lots of help from Andrew Freedman and Brush, blew up the Baltimore team and led a half-dozen players back to the National League. The Reds got two of those—player/manager Joe Kelley and outfielder Cy Seymour—and a month later another ex–Baltimore star, outfielder Mike Donlin, joined the team. At about the same time, Barney Dreyfuss delivered another present, pitcher Ed Poole. The changes transformed the team. When Seymour joined the Reds on July 18, they were in seventh place with a 30–41 record. Through the remainder of the season they went 40–29, moving up to fourth place.

Although the turnaround was dramatic, the differences between the before–Kelley and the after–Kelley Reds were not that great. Kelley, Seymour and Donlin were better players than the men they replaced, as was Poole, but not by such a drastic margin. The biggest change was in the amount of energy the Reds put into playing and their approach to the game after Kelley arrived.

For years the Reds had been known as a plodding team that played strictly by the book. "In the old days the Cincinnati team was always easy for Hanlon's bunch, for the reason that we knew exactly what a batsman would do whenever he faced the pitcher," Kelley explained. "It was a case of sacrifice with a man on first base and nobody out or hitting out after one man had been retired. Every game was played along the same lines, with the result that our pitchers and fielders knew exactly what to do, and the Reds, season after season, were comparatively easy for us."[25]

Under Kelley's management the Reds tried to do the unexpected. He favored the hit-and-run over the bunt with a man on first and no outs. At times he bunted when the situation called for hitting away. Kelley's tactics didn't always work, but the change was refreshing for the players, as well as the fans, who looked forward to the 1903 season with high expectations.[26]

New Nickname, New Manager, New Players: Chicago

In the spring of 1902 Sy Sanborn, the *Chicago Tribune's* baseball writer, started to write a story on the Remnants when he realized there weren't really enough remnants left from the 1900 team to merit the continued use of that term. Only four of the 1902 players—catcher Frank Chance, utilityman Charlie Dexter, and pitchers Jack Taylor and Jock Menefee—had played a meaningful number of games for the 1900 team. Since a large percentage of the team's players were youngsters, Sanborn suggested a return to the nickname in use during Cap Anson's later years, the Colts. Sanborn used that moniker in 1902, but other writers preferred the term "Cubs," which soon became the team's widely accepted nickname.[27]

Chicago (68–69)

Regular Lineup	AVG	OBP	SLG	R	RBI	SB
Jimmy Slagle, lf	.315	.387	.357	64	28	40
Davy Jones, cf-rf	.305	.399	.379	41	14	12
Frank Chance, 1b-c	.287	.396	.371	39	31	27
or Charlie Dexter, 3b–1b*	.239	.303	.294	64	44	29
John Dobbs, cf	.302	.352	.353	31	35	3
or Bunk Congalton, rf	.223	.253	.257	14	24	3
or Dusty Miller, rf	.246	.299	.278	17	13	10
Joe Tinker, ss	.261	.298	.332	55	54	27
Bobby Lowe, 2b	.246	.270	.286	41	31	16
Johnny Kling, c	.285	.330	.343	49	57	24
Germany Schaefer, 3b	.196	.250	.223	32	14	12
Leading Pitchers	**W**	**L**	**PCT**	**IP**	**H**	**ERA**
Jack Taylor	23	11	.676	324.7	271	1.33
Pop Williams	11	16	.407	254.3	259	2.51
Jock Menefee	12	10	.545	197.3	201	2.42
Carl Lundgren	9	9	.500	160	158	1.97

*Includes record with Boston

Former Remnants who jumped to the America League included outfielders Topsy Hartsel (Philadelphia) and Danny Green (Chicago White Stockings), infielder Barry McCormick (St. Louis), and pitcher Tom Hughes (Baltimore). The Remnants/Cubs released Fred Raymer, who signed with the minor league team in Los Angeles, and Jack Doyle, who signed with the quasi-minor league team then masquerading as the New York Giants.

Rube Waddell remained on the Remnants' reserve list. But during the winter, while touring with a team of major league players, Rube became enamored with life on the West Coast. He signed a contract to play with the California League's Los Angeles team in 1902. And also with the league's San Francisco team. And with the Oakland team. Reportedly, the three teams rolled dice to determine who got Waddell, with Los Angeles winning. The Los Angeles owner was soon to learn that signing a contract with Rube was in fact a roll of the dice.[28]

The Cubs' most important addition over the winter of 1901–02 wasn't a player. The team hired a new manager, Frank Selee, the former Boston skipper. After twelve years Selee and the Boston owners had grown tired of each other. Although no manager, not even Ned Hanlon, had been more successful than Selee, the Boston owners had paid him a relatively modest salary and allowed him only a limited budget for signing minor league players who might strengthen the team. When he learned he was to be replaced as Boston manager, Selee's response was that he thought the change was probably good for both sides.[29] The Cubs hired him within a month of his release.

The Cubs' plan for 1902 was to rebuild the team by bringing in young players. Selee stuck to that plan with a vengeance. Entering the season only one position player from the 1901 team—catcher Johnny Kling—was guaranteed a starting position. Two former Boston players, second baseman Bobby Lowe and outfielder Jimmy Slagle, were added to provide a measure of stability to the club. Rookie Joe Tinker became the regular shortstop early in the season. In the other four positions, players came and went as the season progressed. The pitching staff was similarly unsettled. Selee started the season with seven pitchers, about two more than most teams carried after mid–June. Three of them were slow in rounding into condition because of arm problems, but Selee was determined to learn whether they were of major league caliber. "Seven pitchers are too many to carry," he said, "but until they are all tried we can't tell who will be let go." After a pause, he added, "The same thing applies to the whole team in a measure."[30]

As a steady stream of players flowed through his lineups during the course of the season, Selee gradually found several "keepers." The first was Tinker, who had played third base for Portland of the Pacific Northwest League in 1901. Selee thought he would make a good shortstop. Tinker was not an instant success at his new position. At first he played the position too far in, leading to unnecessary errors and making it difficult to get to balls he should have fielded. The pressure of learning a new position also affected his hitting. Selee told Tinker to play a few steps closer to the outfield and gave him a few days off to make the adjustment. When he returned to the lineup, Tinker began making plays that drew applause around the league.[31]

At the beginning of the season Selee seems to have viewed Frank Chance primarily as a backup catcher and utility player. Selee built his teams around a sound defense, which was not Chance's strong point. Although Chance was a good catcher, Kling was better, and Chance seemed unable to avoid injuries when he caught. Chance had not been impressive in the outfield when Loftus tried him in right field in 1901. Although Chance was the best offensive player on the 1902 team, he logged lots of bench time through July, when Selee decided to give him a try at first base. Selee's first choice for the position, Hal O'Hagan, was a brilliant fielder who couldn't hit major league pitching. After O'Hagan flopped, Selee put Charlie Dexter there for three weeks while he searched the minor leagues for a replacement. Only when the replacement was injured shortly after joining the team did Selee turn to Chance. While big Frank didn't threaten Fred Tenney's title as the game's best-fielding first baseman, he didn't embarrass himself. Selee, meanwhile, saw a way to get Chance's potent bat into the lineup each day.

Selee's outfield recruits proved to be almost as disappointing as O'Hagan and for the same reason—they couldn't hit. Developments in the baseball war, however, gave Selee the chance to pick up two pretty good outfielders. The first opportunity arose when the St. Louis Browns came to Chicago to play the White Stockings.

The Browns' right fielder, Davy Jones, was very fast and a great judge of fly balls. Jim Hart, the Cubs' president, thought Jones rightfully belonged to the Cubs. Hart had purchased Jones' contract from Rockford of the Three-I League near the end of the 1901 season. After the sale Jones was told to report to Chicago, but he never showed up. Instead, after receiving a better offer from Milwaukee, he joined the Brewers, who moved to St. Louis over the winter. When the Browns visited Chicago in May, Hart decided to try to score one for the National League in the inter-league struggle.

After the Browns' first game against the White Stockings, Jones received a phone call from Hart, asking him to drop in for a conversation. Jones decided to find out what Hart had in mind. In the course of a short chat, Hart noted that quite a number of players had gone over to the American League, adding that he'd like to get some of them to come back to the National League. He asked Jones what it would take for him to sign with the Cubs. "What have you got to offer?" Jones responded. Hart offered a big raise plus a sizeable bonus. To emphasize his offer, he piled a stack of bills in front of Jones.

Sixty years later, while describing the meeting to Lawrence Ritter, Jones said, "Well, what could I do? I was playing for $2,400, and here was a 50 percent raise plus $500 in cold cash stacked up right in front of me." Jones seemed to be a little embarrassed by his youthful contract jumping as he continued explaining his move to Ritter. "And after all, I wasn't even twenty-two years old yet. Besides everybody was jumping all over the lot in those days: Sam Crawford, Larry Lajoie, Clark Griffith, Willie Keeler, Cy Young, Jack Chesbro, Ed Delahanty. You name him, he was jumping from one league to the other. So I signed."[32]

In July another outfielder became available, this time as a result of Joe Kelley and Cy Seymour jumping to Cincinnati. With a sudden surplus of outfielders, the Reds released Johnny Dobbs, a good fielding slap-hitter who had somewhat of a weak arm. Ordinarily being released in July would be a tough break for a baseball player. In 1902 it meant an opportunity for a mid-season raise in pay and possibly a multi-year contract. Dobbs listened to competing offers from several teams and chose the Cubs. Neither Jones nor Dobbs was a great player, but together with Slagle they gave the Cubs a solid defensive outfield and speed on the bases.

In September a shortstop from the Troy team of the New York State League, Johnny Evers, joined the Cubs. Because Bobby Lowe was nicked up and needed some time off, Selee put Evers at second base for a few games. Evers played well enough to stay in the lineup, at either second base or shortstop, for the rest of the season. On September 14, the Cubs' future Hall of Fame trio combined for the first Tinker-to-Evers-to-Chance double play.[33]

On the mound Jack Taylor had an outstanding year, but Selee's spring recruits did not include any strong building blocks for the future. Pop Williams pitched decently in 1902 but came down with a sore arm the next year and did not last in the majors. Bob Rhoads hung on with St. Louis and Cleveland as an extra starter for a few years before learning to throw a spitball and becoming a winning pitcher. Selee's best addition to his pitching staff came in June when he signed Carl Lundgren off the University of Illinois campus. Lundgren pitched well in 1902 and remained an effective starter for the Cubs until 1909.

Why Rebuilding Is Difficult: St. Louis

It was as if Ban Johnson had sent a moving van to League Park on the last day of the 1901 season, loaded up players, equipment, paperwork, and other miscellaneous items, and shipped it all across town to his new American League facility. That didn't happen, of course, but it might have seemed that way to St. Louis fans. Eight of the 1901 Cardinals jumped to the American League in 1902, seven of them playing for the Browns. Dan McGann, who liked to do things his way, made the longer jump to Baltimore so he could play for John McGraw.

St. Louis (56–78)

Regular Lineup	AVG	OBP	SLG	R	RBI	SB
John Farrell, 2b	.250	.308	.290	68	25	9
Homer Smoot, cf	.311	.350	.380	58	48	20
George Barclay, lf	.300	.345	.350	79	53	30
Patsy Donovan, rf	.315	.363	.355	70	35	34
Otto Krueger, ss	.266	.313	.315	55	46	14
Roy Brashear, 1b	.276	.333	.314	36	40	9
or Art Nichols, 1b-c	.267	.333	.327	36	31	18
Fred Hartman, 3b	.216	.251	.255	30	52	14
Jack Ryan, c	.180	.195	.225	23	14	2
or Jack O'Neill, c	.141	.214	.156	13	12	2
Leading Pitchers	**W**	**L**	**PCT**	**IP**	**H**	**ERA**
Mike O'Neill	16	15	.516	288.3	297	2.90
Stan Yerkes	12	21	.364	272.7	341	3.66
Ed Murphy	10	6	.625	164	187	3.02
Bob Wicker	5	12	.294	152.3	159	3.19

The American League took away three-fourths of the Cardinals' infield, two-thirds of their outfield, and three-fourths of their starting rotation. When a dazed Patsy Donovan looked around at what was left, he saw a third baseman who could hit some but couldn't catch a ball if it were lobbed underhanded to him (Otto Krueger), a catcher who was good behind the plate but couldn't hit (Jack Ryan), another catcher who could hit a little but couldn't throw (Art Nichols), a pretty good pitcher who usually had a sore arm (Ed Murphy), and a bunch of untried young pitchers. The only really good player Donovan had left was himself.

Donovan began piecing together his 1902 team by signing third baseman Fred Hartman and second baseman John Farrell. It could be said that he took them away from the American League, but it would be more accurate to say that the American League let them go. Chicago no longer had a role for Hartman to fill. In explaining why he signed with St. Louis, Farrell cited financial reasons, but elaborated by saying, "Besides, I feel I will get more of a chance with St. Louis next year than I would at Washington, for the Cardinal team is rather shy of men while Washington has a big bunch signed, if the stories from the East are true."[34]

Considering how many teams—especially National League teams—were mining the minor leagues for talent at the time, Donovan did a good job of selecting young players to fill out his lineup. Two of his young outfielders, Homer Smoot and George Barclay, batted over .300 as rookies in 1902. Pitcher Mike O'Neill had a fine season and Bob Wicker, another pitcher, was overpowering when he wasn't battling a sore arm. Catcher Jack O'Neill—Mike's brother—was such a good defensive catcher that he stayed in the league for five years even though he hit higher than .200 in only two of those years.

The difficulty of rebuilding almost from scratch at the major league level is revealed by the fate of two of Donovan's best young players. Barclay seemed to be destined for a great career. He was one of the Eastern League's top players in 1901, hitting for a good average with some power and stealing 44 bases. His speed earned him the nickname "Deerfoot."[35]

He made the transition to the National League with little difficulty. On April 24 he was the Cardinals' star in a ten-inning, 9–8 win over Cincinnati. Besides getting four hits in five times at bat, he scored a run by stealing home and later went from first to third on a bunt. Two days later he won a game with a two-run home run in the eighth inning. In June he repeated the game-winning home run feat, this time beating Boston in the ninth inning. He ended the season with a .300 batting average and led the Cardinals in both runs scored and RBIs. His 30 stolen bases were the second most among the Cardinals and sixth highest in the league. Barclay was only 26 years old and seemed to have a bright future ahead of him.

During spring training in 1903 Barclay became sick. He missed some games early in the season but continued playing. In June he went to the hospital for treatment of a disease that was diagnosed as malaria. He returned to the field after a short stay but played somewhat sluggishly. His average hovered in the .230s. He had few stolen bases and covered little ground in the outfield. In August the Robisons, who had a bent for ham-handed treatment of their players, told Barclay he should take some time off to recuperate—without pay, of course.

Barclay ended the 1903 season with a .248 average. He stole only 12 bases that season. The next year he managed only a .200 average with the Cardinals and .226 with the Boston Beaneaters, who purchased his contract in September. His downward trajectory continued in 1905, when he hit .176 in 29 games for the Beaneaters before being released. Barclay died in 1909 at the age of 32.[36]

Like Barclay, Mike O'Neill seemed to be a future star. O'Neill was purchased by the Cardinals after the 1901 minor league season and given several trial starts. He pitched very well. In his first appearance, he gave up only one run in four innings of relief against Brooklyn. His first start was an 11-inning, 4–3 loss to Kid Nichols. He followed that by throwing a two-hit shutout against the hard-hitting Phillies. His 1901 big league tryout ended with a 1.32 ERA in five games.

O'Neill's 1902 debut was delayed by a sore arm coming out of spring training, in retrospect a bad omen. He appeared in only three games until June. He had little of his normal speed in those games, and was ineffective. On June 5, however, he shut out Boston, 3–0. He allowed only seven hits and, according to a Boston writer, "was quite speedy for a left-hander." That game was the first of four straight wins and the beginning of a spell when he won seven of nine decisions. During this time Mike and his brother, Jack, became known as the "famous O'Neill battery."[37]

In mid–July, while O'Neill was pitching with renewed pop on his fastball, other Cardinals pitchers were coming down with sore arms. For several days O'Neill and Stan Yerkes were the only healthy men on the pitching staff, and for about two months they pitched in what was essentially a three-man rotation. Over that time the tender-armed O'Neill started eleven games on two days' rest, two games on one day's rest, pitched in relief twice after pitching a complete game the day before, and started seven games with at least three days' rest. Considering the caliber of support behind him, O'Neill's 16–15 win-loss record and 2.90 ERA stamped him as a star.

Unfortunately, O'Neill did not live up to the high expectations foreshadowed by his rookie season. The heavy workload from mid–July to mid–September of 1902 may have been a factor in his decline, although other pitchers survived similar workloads. The 288 innings O'Neill pitched in 1902 weren't that many by Deadball Era standards, but he packed them into a relatively short span and was only 24 years old at the time. For whatever reason, in 1903 O'Neill was not the same pitcher. He was hit hard in all but a few of his games. In August he became so sick he had to be hospitalized. Like Barclay, his disease was diagnosed as malaria, although the timing and severity of O'Neill's sickness seemed to differ from Barclay's.[38] His record for 1903 was 4–13, with a 3.79 ERA. O'Neill was better in 1904, going 10–14 with a 2.09 ERA for a much-improved Cardinals team.

After the 1904 season O'Neill announced that he had used his baseball earnings to build a house and open a grocery store. He had just gotten married and didn't believe that the life of a baseball player fit well with marriage. Therefore, he was retiring. *The Sporting News* correspondent who reported O'Neill's retirement did so with a figurative shrug of the shoulders, saying O'Neill "showed well in many games last year, but it is safe to say he would not regain his 1902 form if he remained in the profession."[39]

Like many professional athletes who retire at a young age, O'Neill later changed his mind. He returned to the game in 1906 and continued to play until he turned 40 in 1917, but he played only nine more major league games, all as an outfielder for the Cincinnati Reds in 1907. Besides Jack, two of Mike's other brothers played in the major leagues. Jim was a utility infielder for the Senators in the twenties, while Steve caught for 17 years, mostly with Cleveland, and managed four different major league teams between 1935 and 1954, winning the World Series with Detroit in 1945.

Seventy-Five Percent Good: Philadelphia

During the winter the Phillies suffered about the same amount of damage from the American League raids as the Cardinals. They might have been hit a little harder since they lost one more player. Three Phillies moved across town to the Athletics (outfielder Elmer Flick, shortstop Monte Cross, and pitcher Bill Duggleby), four skipped over to the nation's capital (outfielder Ed Delahanty, third baseman Harry Wolverton, and pitchers Al Orth and Jack Townsend). Catcher Ed McFarland went to the White Stockings and pitcher Red Donahue joined the Browns. The Phillies replaced their departed stars with other stars—Eastern League stars, Western League stars, California League stars. After the Pennsylvania State Supreme Court ruling, Duggleby jumped back to the Phillies, as did Chick Fraser, who had joined the Athletics in 1901. Wolverton returned to the Phillies in late July, not because of the court injunction or any other development in the baseball war, but because he wasn't happy in Washington.

Philadelphia (56–81)

Regular Lineup	AVG	OBP	SLG	R	RBI	SB
Roy Thomas, cf	.286	.414	.322	89	24	17
George Browne, lf*	.286	.326	.342	71	40	24
Shad Barry, rf	.287	.343	.363	65	58	14
Klondike Douglass, 1b	.233	.274	.277	37	37	6
or Hughie Jennings, 1b	.272	.330	.355	32	32	8
Red Dooin, c	.231	.262	.270	20	35	8
or Fred Jacklitsch, c	.202	.278	.237	8	8	2
Rudy Hulswitt, ss	.272	.314	.322	59	38	12
Bill Hallman, 3b	.248	.287	.311	14	35	9
Pete Childs, 2b	.194	.256	.206	25	25	6

Leading Pitchers	W	L	PCT	IP	H	ERA
Doc White	14	20	.412	306	277	2.53
Bill Duggleby	12	16	.429	258.7	282	3.38
Ham Iburg	11	18	.379	236	286	3.89
Chick Fraser	13	14	.481	224	238	3.42

*Includes record with New York

As Yogi Berra may have said (possibly in one of his commercials), baseball is 75 percent pitching; the other half is batting and fielding. If that is the case, the 1902 Phillies were 75 percent of the way toward having a pretty good team. The other half did them in. Once Fraser and Duggleby returned, the Phillies had a good starting rotation. Doc White and Fraser both pitched in the majors for thirteen years, each winning close to two hundred games. Duggleby was one of the Phillies' better pitchers for six years. All three pitched well in 1902.

The fourth starter, Ham Iburg, pitched only one year in the majors, but that was mostly because he preferred to pitch on the West Coast. With the Phillies he was noted for being the "junkiest" of junkball pitchers.

Upon seeing him pitch for the first time, Brooklyn writer Abe Yager wrote: "Iburg delivers the ball from every conceivable angle, and, after he reaches his limit, the spectator is led to believe that he will next stand on his head and perform the same evolutions."[40] After Iburg held the Giants to five hits while striking out eight batters, veteran Jack Doyle remarked, "That fellow is a bird. Why he will fool 'em all the first time any team goes up against that little soap bubble he hands up. What is the most remarkable thing about his work is that he can get a quick, sharp curve to the spongy delivery."[41] Like most junkball artists, Iburg tended to give up more hits in the later innings after the batters had a chance to see his pitches a few times, but he continued to pitch effectively throughout the season.

Behind this solid starting rotation was a team that looked like a classic cellar-dweller—a roster full of guys who could field but not hit or who could hit but not field, with some substitutes who could do neither.

The most solid regular player was center fielder Roy Thomas. He was a pesky hitter who had tried the patience of Cincinnati's pitchers in 1900 by fouling the ball off numerous times and paid for it by taking a punch in the mouth and fastballs to the ribs and "fleshy part of the anatomy."

Thomas claimed he might have been violating the rule by intentionally fouling off pitches in 1900 but was no longer doing so because of the foul-strike rule.[42] That may have been true, though intentional fouls were no longer illegal, they were just strikes. What didn't change was that Thomas was still walking all the time. In the nine years between 1899 and 1907 he led the National League in bases on balls seven times, finishing second and third in the other two years. He twice led the league in on-base percentage and finished among the leaders in the other years over that time frame.

In 1902 Thomas led the league with 107 walks and an on-base percentage of .414. Not that it mattered much, since his teammates too often left him stranded on base. Tim Murnane of the *Boston Globe* expressed his sympathy for Thomas' plight. "When it comes to effectiveness, Roy Thomas is out of his element this season," Murnane wrote. "What a lovely time Roy had when Del (Ed Delahanty) and Larry (Lajoie) were on hand to drive him home. The Phillies were hitters in those days."[43]

The Fourth Estate Gets Its Chance: New York

From the press box or the stands it sometimes appears easy to spot errors in the way a team is managed. In our time, when baseball's playing strategy is largely limited to late-inning situations and pitching changes, most second-guessing is about player acquisition rather than on-field developments. In the early 1900s, however, it was common for reporters to second-guess a manager's strategy, especially regarding the sacrifice and hit-and-run plays. Since the reporter had the second guess rather than the responsibility for the actual decision, he could appear authoritative and much smarter than the lunkhead whose failure to call for a sacrifice had lost the previous day's game. In 1902, one of the experts from the fourth estate was given the opportunity to show the lunkheads how a team should be managed. Following their disappointing 1901 season, the Giants fired George Davis (or at least made no effort to prevent him from jumping to the White Stockings). In his place they hired Horace Fogel, a Philadelphia sportswriter.

The Giants didn't give Fogel an easy task. He had to take over a team that finished a game out of last place and then lost four starting position players and its second-best pitcher. The American League had signed left fielder Kip Selbach (Baltimore), infielder Sammy Strang (Chicago), catcher Jack Warner (Boston), and batter-still-looking-for-a-position Charlie Hickman (Boston). Pitcher Dummy Taylor signed with Cleveland but jumped back to the Giants in May of 1902 after appearing in only four games with the Blues.

New York (48–88)

Regular Lineup	AVG	OBP	SLG	R	RBI	SB
George Browne, lf	.319	.355	.407	30	14	13
Jack Dunn, rf-ss–3b	.211	.256	.249	26	14	13
or John McGraw, ss	.234	.401	.234	13	5	7
or Roger Bresnahan, of-c	.287	.352	.388	16	22	6

Dan McGann, 1b	.300	.356	.383	25	21	12
Steve Brodie, cf	.281	.327	.332	37	42	11
or Jack Doyle, 1b	.301	.340	.387	21	19	12
or Jim Jones, lf	.237	.275	.289	16	19	7
or George Yeager, c	.204	.277	.241	6	9	1
Billy Lauder, 3b	.237	.252	.288	41	44	19
Heinie Smith, 2b	.252	.278	.297	46	33	32
Joe Bean, ss	.222	.247	.244	13	5	9
Frank Bowerman, c	.253	.279	.324	38	26	12
Leading Pitchers	**W**	**L**	**PCT**	**IP**	**H**	**ERA**
Christy Mathewson	14	17	.452	276.7	241	2.11
Dummy Taylor	7	15	.318	200.7	194	2.29
Roy Evans	8	13	.381	176	186	3.17
Joe McGinnity	8	8	.500	153	122	2.06
Tully Sparks	4	10	.286	115	123	3.76
Jack Cronin	5	6	.455	114	105	2.45
Roscoe Miller	1	8	.111	72.7	77	4.58

Fogel didn't exactly break new ground in finding replacements. He picked up a couple of minor leaguers from the usual sources, the Eastern League and the California League, and took in several discards from other National League teams. He also eventually ended up with three ex–Baltimore players that John McGraw didn't want. Considering McGraw's actions during the 1901 and 1902 seasons, it is tempting to see some sort of backstage maneuvering in the Baltimore-to-New York player movements, but it is more likely that it was just a coincidence. The three players—utilityman Jack Dunn and outfielders Jim Jackson and Steve Brodie—were trying to hang on to jobs in the major leagues and the Giants needed all the help they could get.

For the first month of the season Fogel seemed to have a magic touch. In mid–May his team of rejects, has-beens, and never-will-bes were fighting the Cubs for second place. Of course, in baseball it is not unusual for bad teams to have short periods of success before reality eventually catches up with them. Reality caught up with Fogel's Giants in a big way. After going 15–10, the Giants lost eleven games in a row. Their sinking ship righted itself for ten days, then began taking on a torrent of water. Losing streaks of five and thirteen games followed in short order. By July 6 their record stood at 20–42 and Fogel was long gone as their manager.

It would be easy to feel sorry for Fogel. After all, he was put in an almost impossible situation. But why would he compound his problems by picking a fight with his best player?

Christy Mathewson ended the 1901 season with a sore arm and nursed it over the winter. When he started the 1902 season by shutting out the Phillies on a three-hitter and holding the Beaneaters down to five hits, concerns about possible arm problems lessened. But after Matty pitched in Chicago in an early May game, his arm began bothering him. Six days later he still couldn't raise his arm above his shoulder.[44] Still, he volunteered to pitch against the Cardinals despite the pain. It took a while for him to loosen up. He allowed three runs to the Cardinals in both the first and second innings but won the game, 10–7.

Three days later, when Fogel started him against Cincinnati, Matty "seemed a bit scary about using his speed." He tried to get by using off-speed pitches. He gave up only six hits, but lost, 6–1, largely because his teammates made six errors behind him. The next day Fogel accused Matty of not putting forth his best efforts. "He seems to be laboring under the impression that the reputation he established last season will carry him through the remainder of his career, whether he pitches winning ball or not, but in this he is greatly mistaken," Fogel said. Fogel threatened to suspend Matty without pay unless he "took a decided brace in his work."[45]

When Matty learned of Fogel's statement, he confronted the manager. The two men yelled at each other, with Matty ending the confrontation by demanding his release.[46] Matty's teammates, some of whom weren't very fond of him, rallied to his defense. Team captain Jack Doyle asserted that no one could reasonably accuse Matty of not doing his best to win. "His heart is in the game and with his team," Doyle said. "I know and so does Fogel, that Mathewson pitched for us in St. Louis when it pained him every time he raised his arm above his head. That shows the metal of which he is made."[47]

Fogel remained the Giants' manager for about two more weeks after the incident. Matty's other pain, the one in his arm, stayed with him until the end of June. Overall, the season was a rocky one for Matty. He appeared in the fewest games of his career until 1915, when he was no longer an effective pitcher. Even though he tied for the league lead in shutouts and had an ERA of 2.11, he had his only losing season until 1915. When the painful 1902 season neared its end, he decided to leave the Giants, signing with the St. Louis Browns. (Then again, maybe he decided to stay in New York. He also signed with the Giants.)

The Giants' season and, in fact, the team's future, changed in July when John McGraw teamed with Andrew Freedman and John T. Brush to battle McGraw's former partners in the American League. "I have severed all connection with the American League and have shaken the dust of Baltimore from my feet as far as my business interests are concerned," McGraw announced upon his arrival. "I am not talking pennant this year, that being out of the question," he said, "but I shall gather together a string of players who will pull the team out of last place, and next season I expect to be in the running from flagfall to finish.... My orders are to spend money and to stop at nothing."[48] McGraw didn't make good on his first promise, the Giants finishing in the cellar, 7½ games behind the Phillies. But he did fulfill his promise of remaking the team into a pennant contender and, in the course of doing so, obeyed the order to spend money and stop at nothing.

McGraw began changing the Giants almost immediately. Besides the four players he brought over from Baltimore, he signed pitcher Roscoe Miller from Detroit and picked up outfielder George Browne, who had been released from the Phillies. McGraw left the team frequently over the next couple of months, disappearing on recruiting trips. He wasn't interested in recruiting minor leaguers; he was after some of the American League's best players.

He signed some players whose contracts ended with the 1902 season, including infielder Billy Gilbert (Baltimore), outfielder Sam Mertes (Chicago White Stockings), and catcher Jack Warner (Boston Americans). He also signed some players who already had signed with other teams for 1903, such as Mathewson, shortstop George

Davis (Chicago White Stockings), shortstop Kid Elberfeld (Detroit), and outfielders Ed Delahanty (Washington) and Dave Fultz (Philadelphia Athletics). McGraw wasn't the only person who didn't let an existing contract interfere with signing a player. It would take a peace conference to sort out the tangle of double contract signings and an inter-league crisis to stop McGraw and Brush from trying to grab Davis.

A Fielding Wonder: Fred Tenney

Boston first baseman Fred Tenney made catches that "seemed utterly impossible" (Library of Congress).

Defensively, Fred Tenney was the gold standard for first basemen during this part of the Deadball Era. When a first baseman made a difficult one-hand catch or stretched a long way to grab a ball, he was said to have made the play "a la Tenney." A good fielding young first baseman would be called "a future Tenney."

During pre-game infield practice, Tenney often put on a show for the fans. In describing Tenney's routine, one writer said he "made back-handed, one-handed and bare-handed catches that gave the impression the ball was under a spell."[49] Tenney played the game with the same flair, as can be seen in the summary of a 3–1 Boston win over Cincinnati. The writer attributed Boston's victory to Tenney's artful play at first base. "Not one, but a dozen sensational catches he made of what looked like wild throws. He nailed them first with one hand, then with the other, until the fans became accustomed, and seeing that he was a hindrance to the Reds' success, ceased to applaud his efforts.... His playing yesterday was nothing short of marvelous. He made catches that seemed utterly impossible."[50]

Tenney joined the Beaneaters in 1894, literally coming straight from the Brown University campus, where he had been the college team's catcher. At one o'clock on the morning of June 16, as Tenney and other Brown seniors were well along in their senior dinner celebrations, Tenney received a phone call from Frank Selee. Both Beaneaters catchers were injured and Selee needed a catcher right away. He asked Tenney to catch for Boston that afternoon. Tenney eagerly agreed. He managed to get to bed by four o'clock, awoke early enough to catch a train to Boston, and made his major league debut that afternoon. Although Tenney broke a finger in the fifth inning, he finished the game, performing well enough to be offered a contract for the remainder of the season.[51]

Tenney, who threw left-handed, was not quite good enough for the major leagues as a catcher. He had trouble throwing accurately to second base. Selee sent him to the minors for parts of both the 1895 and 1896 seasons and played him in the outfield more often than behind the plate. Tenney's hitting kept him in the National League. He hit .395 in 27 games in his first season, dropped to .272 in 1895, then hit .336 in 1896.

Tenney started the 1897 season in right field, but after a few games Selee decided to try him at first base. The man Tenney replaced, Tommy Tucker, was a good fielder who was popular with Boston fans. For a while, whenever Tenney made an error, the fans responded with the chant, "Tuck, Tuck," a call to bring Tucker back to first base. By the end of June, however, Tenney was being praised as Tucker's equal in the field.[52]

Before the season ended, Tenney was gaining recognition was an exceptionally talented fielder. In July Earl Wagner, the owner of the Washington Senators, cited Tenney's play as one reason the Beaneaters would likely win the 1897 pennant, saying, "That chap is the greatest first baseman I ever saw—bar none."[53] Wagner's opinion soon became the accepted wisdom throughout baseball.

Tenney was noted for originating the 3–6–3 double play. While it seems unlikely that no other first baseman ever made the play before, Tenney was the first to do it consistently and as a planned maneuver. Tenney said the idea for the play came up after second baseman Bobby Lowe was barely able to get a batter at first on a slow, high-bounding grounder on which a baserunner moved up to second. Tenney told Lowe that he could have gotten a force out at second if he had taken the ball. Lowe agreed to allow Tenney to make the play on a similar hit. Tenney said he made the first 3–6–3 double play shortly after that in a game against Cincinnati. "The batter hit the ball over first," Tenney recalled. "I grabbed it and threw to [Herman] Long, then hurried to the bag and took Long's throw for a double play. It seemed that you could have heard a pin drop for ten seconds, and then the crowd just let out a roar. It had seen something new."[54]

During the 1890s the bunt and hit-and-run plays were increasingly emphasized by National League managers. Tenney's move to first base was part of a trend in which fewer first basemen fit the prevailing mold of the relatively immobile slugger, such as Dan Brouthers or Cap Anson, and more were smaller, agile men like Tenney. During the 1898 season, veteran writer Henry Chadwick described the change. "The modern first baseman is of medium size, and is as agile as a cat," Chadwick said. "The first baseman now skates up and down the line, hands grounders to the pitcher, backs up as the shortstop has ever been supposed to do, and mixes with the play at every considerable turn." To make his point more clearly, Chadwick noted that "Fred Tenney has been seen to plunge into the thickest of a complicated play and turn up behind third base when the smoke had cleared."[55]

As a batter Tenney and many of his contemporary first basemen hit more like little Willie Keeler than big Dan Brouthers. Although he batted left-handed, Tenney frequently tried to slap the ball along the left field foul line. He was said to be the best scientific hitter on the Boston team.[56] He usually batted second because he could handle the bat well, and often ranked among the league leaders in sacrifices. Tenney hit higher than .300 seven times in a career that lasted 17 years. As his batting average dropped as part of a widespread decline in hitting during the early 1900s, Tenney began working harder to get on base by drawing walks. He finished among the top ten in walks six times in the seven-year period from 1902 to 1908.

A Wee Bit of a Slugger: Tommy Leach

You could say that Tommy Leach and Hack Wilson had a number of things in common. Both stood about 5'6", both played center field for the Chicago Cubs (Leach moved to the outfield in mid-career and played three seasons with the Cubs), both led the National League in home runs, and both finished in the top ten in total bases and slugging percentage several times.

Of course, in reality Leach and Wilson were very different, both in build and as players. Wilson was a squat 190-pound slugger who had some speed; Leach was a small, fast runner who was able to get the ball past the outfielders and leg out quite a few extra-base hits.

From a statistical viewpoint, however, Wee Tommy looked very much like a Deadball Era slugger. He led the National League in home runs in 1902 and finished in the top ten five other years. Now, he never hit many home runs—he twice got as high as seven in a season—but he legged out quite a few triples and racked up a lot of extra bases. His 22 triples led the National League in 1902 and he was in the top ten five other seasons. Six times he finished in the top ten in total bases. Despite the incontrovertible statistical truth of the assertion that Leach was a slugger, if we could go back in time and make that assertion to a baseball fan of the era, we would probably be met with a chuckle, and perhaps an incredulous roll of the eyes.

For Wee Tommy, the 1902 season got off to a sour start and then turned very sweet. On April 16 he got his first look at his new uniform. It made his blood boil. All through the previous season he had been forced to put tucks in his baseball trousers to make them fit and had worn garters on his arms to keep his sleeves from falling down over his hands. His complaints brought a promise that his 1902 uniform would be the right size. Yet here he had just been handed a uniform that seemed to be made for Bill Lange, the 6', 200-pound former Colts outfielder. "Wonder if these fellows think I'm the Sultan of Turkey," Leach screamed. "I've got trousers two feet wide and they will make me look like a clown. Somebody will tell me soon that they will shrink in the washing."[57]

The next day Leach flew around the bases in his baggy uniform to score the only run of the game, as the Pirates won their season opener, 1–0. Tommy had three hits, including a triple. He scored one run as the Pirates blew out the Cardinals in game two and had a home run, triple, and three runs scored in another blowout in game three. In the eighth inning of game four, with the score tied, 3–3, he led off with a single. Chief Zimmer then tapped a pitch to the right side of the infield. The first baseman fielded the ball and flipped to first, getting Zimmer. Meanwhile, Wee Tommy kept going, sliding into third safely. He scored the winning run on a fly to the outfield.

Leach scored a run in each of the next four games, although two of them turned out to be the Pirates' only losses in their first seventeen games. In his first eight games, Leach had ten hits, four of which were triples, and scored ten runs.

For Leach and the 1902 Pirates, the good times just continued to roll on. Tommy reached ten triples for the season by June 26. On August 13 in Boston he hit a three-run home run over the short left field fence against Vic Willis. The next day he hit two more over the fence, and added a double and a single in five times up. In his next game, against Philadelphia, he stole home on the Phillies' slow-ball artist, Ham Iburg. Throughout the season Leach fielded his position with flair. He excelled at charging bunts and making the pickup and throw to first in one smooth motion. He had great range on foul fly balls down the left field line, getting off to a fast start and displaying his great speed.[58]

Leach's career hit a rough spot in the middle of the decade. His batting average fell to .257 in both 1904 and 1905, with a concomitant loss of power. In the field he started making an increasing number of throwing errors. The Pirates' first baseman, Kitty Bransfield, complained that Tommy's throws were very difficult to catch. They came at him like spitballs, Bransfield said, taking a sharp, unpredictable break just as they approached first.[59] In midseason of 1905 Leach collided with Jake Beckley, suffering two broken ribs. The injury further hampered his throwing and eventually led to his move to the outfield.[60]

The Future King of Sluggers: Sam Crawford

When John T. Brush decided to rebuild the Cincinnati Reds by signing the best young minor league players, he asked W. T. Watkins to scout the minors for him. He told Watkins, "Don't stop until you have found me another Lajoie." One day Watkins stopped in Chatham, Ontario, to check out the local team. A young outfielder, Sam Crawford, caught Watkins' eye. "He struck me as being a corker," Watkins later said. Crawford was sold to Grand Rapids before Watkins could negotiate a deal for him. So Watkins hustled over to Grand Rapids and quickly arranged to buy the youngster. He then sent a short wire to Brush: "I have your man."[61]

Crawford was 19 years old when he came to Cincinnati late in the 1899 season. He was still in his first season of professional baseball. His career had consisted of 43 games with Chatham in the lower-level Canadian League, where he hit .370, and 60 games at Grand Rapids in the Class A Western League, where he hit .333.

After joining the Reds, Crawford continued to hit as if he were in just another minor league. In 31 games he hit .307 with three doubles, seven triples, and one home run. Ed Grillo, the baseball writer of the *Cincinnati Commercial Tribune*, echoed Watkins when he wrote, "I feel Mr. Brush has captured one prize, at least, in his dragnet. Sam Crawford looks to me like a full-fledged star, though still a bit crude." Crawford was a fast runner, Grillo said, and he seemed to have good instincts when going after fly balls. But, most importantly, the youngster could hit. "It is not a case of swing with might and main with him," Grillo wrote, "yet he puts lots of force behind his bat and the ball fairly burns the air when he meets it."[62]

When the 1900 season began, Crawford was the Reds' fourth outfielder. During the first week he started a game-winning rally with a pinch-hit single and got two hits as a late-inning replacement. On April 28 he started his first game, contributing two hits to a 7–4 victory over the Pirates. The next day he went 3-for-5 and threw out a runner at the plate. He played regularly for a while after that, but his inexperience soon showed itself. He made a few baserunning blunders and misjudged several fly balls. Another rookie, center fielder Jimmy Barrett, made similar mistakes. When the Reds fell to last place, the two young outfielders received much of the criticism for the team's poor record. While asserting that the two were talented youngsters who would someday be good players, Grillo wrote, "Crawford and Barrett have been playing dopey ball." He blamed their poor fielding for the loss of three games over a period of five days. "They seemed to be unable to start after the ball and in each instance failed to reach [it] when a more experienced man would have been sitting under it."[63]

Crawford spent some time on the bench in May and June, working on his game during morning practices. When he began playing regularly again, his fielding showed marked improvement. In August Ned Hanlon noticed the change. "If ever there was a player in the National League who picked up quicker than this man Crawford, of the Cincinnatis, someone wants to point him out," Hanlon said. "When he first came here he was a rough, uncouth sort of a fielder, who never seemed to know exactly where the ball was going to land, or whether he would get it when it did land. In the last few games in which Brooklyn has played against the Cincinnatis he has been going after the ball as sharply as any outfielder in the league, and he will be making base hits when some of these other ballplayers are out of the business."[64]

Crawford's upbringing and the strong personality it engendered probably helped him to get through this rough spell and others he encountered in the future. Crawford grew up in the small Nebraska town of Wahoo. When he was seventeen, he and several other teenagers from the town formed a baseball team. They borrowed a lumber wagon from the father of a team member and traveled through other towns in the region.

When they arrived in a new place, one of the boys, who played a cornet, would gain attention by playing the instrument loudly in the center of the town. After a crowd gathered to see what all the fuss was about, the boys would challenge the town team to a ball game. During the game the Wahoo team would pass a hat for donations. The proceeds would be used to buy provisions—round steak bought at twelve pounds for a dollar was the usual fare, supplemented by apples requisitioned from nearby orchards. The boys usually slept outside at night, sometimes finding shelter in an unlocked barn or at a fairgrounds. The barnstorming trip lasted three or four weeks and led to an offer for Crawford to play semi-professional ball. From there he found his way to Chatham and, eventually, to Cincinnati.[65]

Such experiences gave Crawford a sense of self-assurance. Cincinnati teammate Ed Scott told of Crawford's reaction as a rookie at Grand Rapids when Scott tried to intimidate him. Scott faced Crawford while pitching for Indianapolis a few days after Crawford came to Grand Rapids. As soon as Crawford stepped into the batter's box, Scott shouted in to his catcher, Mike Kahoe, saying he would take care of this rookie. "I don't believe, Mike, that this fellow could hit it if I'd let him have it in his hand." According to Scott, Crawford glared at him and yelled, "Look here, you long-legged, hungry-looking stiff, don't you know that the man who told you that you could pitch has been sent to an asylum? Now, just put one over here and I'll put wings on it for you." Crawford then lined the next pitch to left field, the outfielder just managing to grab the ball before it hit the fence.[66] While Scott's story is probably apocryphal, or at best highly embellished, it likely represents young Crawford's level of self-confidence. At the least, Grillo thought it reflected Crawford's character closely enough to include it in his newspaper column.

On Cincinnati's first eastern trip in 1900, Crawford couldn't get the ball to drop for base hits. "I should have fattened my batting average on our trip," he said. "I saw nothing that fooled me, yet I was unable to land on the ball and get it safe very often." Thinking back over his previous year's play, Sam remembered, "I had just such a streak as that one week last season, and I was wearing my hair as long then as it is now. I went to see the barber and had it cut, and the very next day I started to crack them out." The next day, after failing to connect with the ball in morning practice, Sam stopped by the hotel barber shop for a haircut. That afternoon he picked up two singles and two doubles against two of the Phillies' best pitchers.[67]

Crawford finished his first full season in the highly competitive National League of 1900 with a .260 batting average. He displayed his power by hitting 15 triples and seven home runs, both good enough to rank sixth in the league. Back in Wahoo over the winter he started visiting a nearby gymnasium regularly in preparation for the 1901 season. Years later, as a veteran ballplayer, Crawford said he was convinced that, for men with the ability to play at a high level, "the whole secret to success in baseball, as I see it, is wrapped up in that one word, condition."

As a result of his workouts, when Crawford reported for spring training he was lighter than the year before, but stronger.[68] He got off to a strong start with the bat. In the Reds' fourth game, which was played in Chicago, he drove one of Jack Taylor's pitches off the scoreboard in deep right field for a long home run. He had four hits in that game, adding a triple and two singles to his home run, and accounted for seven of the Reds' runs in a 9–2 win. A few days later, in St. Louis, he hit a "mighty drive into the right field seats." In mid–June he hit "the longest drive of the year" into deep right-center field in Cincinnati, rounding third base before the Phillies' Elmer Flick was able to pick up the ball. He repeated the feat against the Phillies five weeks later, again legging out a long home run on which Flick had no play at the plate.[69] By the end of the 1901 season, Crawford, still only 21 years old, was being included in discussions of baseball's top power hitters. He ended the season leading the league with 16 home runs, five more than runner-up Jimmy Sheckard. He finished third in triples (16), slugging percentage (.524), and RBIs (104).

In the fall of 1901 the Cincinnati ballpark was destroyed by fire. To replace it Brush built an elegant new park using concrete and steel architecture. The new park had a significant impact upon Crawford's hitting. The distances to center and right-center fields were from 20 to 50 feet closer than they had been. To a modern baseball fan, shorter fences automatically mean more extra-base hits. But that wasn't necessarily the case in the Deadball Era. Many of Crawford's home runs in 1901 were on hard-hit balls that got past the outfielders and kept rolling while Sam dashed around the bases. Twelve of his sixteen home runs in 1901 were inside-the-park hits. In the new park those balls bounced off the fence, enabling the outfielders to retrieve the ball and return it to the infield more quickly.⁷⁰ In 1902 Sam hit only three home runs while getting 22 triples, an increase of six. He hit about the same number of doubles in each season (20 in 1901, 18 in 1902).

Overall, Crawford enjoyed another fine season with the bat in 1902. He led the league in triples and total bases and was second in batting average (.333) and slugging percentage (.461). Off the field, the 1902 season was somewhat chaotic for Sam. He was a prime target for American League agents. Sometime during the year, probably in August, he signed an agreement to play with Detroit in 1903, receiving a $1,000 signing bonus as part of the agreement. Later that month August Herrmann, the leader of a group that had just purchased the Cincinnati team from Brush, called each of the Reds into his office to negotiate new contracts. Several Reds signed 1903 contracts while in Herrmann's office. Crawford refused to sign, saying he needed more time to think about it.

Herrmann persisted, at one point hinting that Crawford would be prohibited from going on a swing through the East with the team and suspended without pay unless he told Herrmann what his plans were for 1903. Herrmann's actions irked Crawford, who told the press, "I said before that I wanted time to answer, but since they seem to want to force me, I will say that I will do nothing until the end of the present season, come what may. I refuse to say anything, even though it prevents me from taking the Eastern trip." A few days later Crawford signed to play with Cincinnati in 1903, returning the $1,000 cash advance to the Tigers.⁷¹ The next January, in the peace agreement between the two warring leagues, Crawford was awarded to the Tigers. Crawford played with the Tigers from 1903 through 1917.

In 1916 *Baseball Magazine* focused its February issue on Crawford, "The King of Sluggers." Asserting that only two of Crawford's contemporaries, Nap Lajoie and Honus Wagner, had enjoyed more brilliant careers, F. C. Lane, the magazine's editor, said, "In Sam Crawford the game beholds the greatest mauler of a baseball who ever trod the basepaths." Lane conceded that other men, "by reason of fleetness of foot and this alone," had

In 1916 the editor of *Baseball Magazine* asserted that Sam Crawford was "the King of Sluggers" (National Baseball Hall of Fame Library, Cooperstown, New York).

achieved higher batting averages than Sam but claimed "no other player, past or present, has ever hit at the same consistently weighty average as the famed athlete of Wahoo, Nebraska." Lane described Crawford as a natural hitter, able to bat .300 from the first day he put on a uniform. "He is the typical slugger," Lane said, "who stands erect in the face of the best the pitcher can give him and whales away with the full sweep of his enormous shoulders."[72]

Crawford was an outstanding player whose record probably is not truly appreciated even though he was elected to the Baseball Hall of Fame in 1957. Two of baseball's all-time greats are largely responsible for that. One was Ty Cobb, Crawford's teammate from 1905 until the end of Crawford's career. Crawford was a great player; Cobb was the greatest player of the Deadball Era. Although Crawford had great batting numbers while with Detroit, he seldom ranked first in the most noticed categories, even on his own team. Cobb was almost always first, both on the Tigers and in the league. Still, in his own time Crawford was widely recognized as one of baseball's foremost power hitters.

After Crawford retired, Babe Ruth (and the lively ball) changed the definition of a power hitter. While Crawford played, power hitters racked up lots of doubles and triples, with a few home runs added in. Ruth hit homers by the dozens. Other sluggers soon followed his example, and home runs became the measure of a power hitter. Triples, in Crawford's time an important element in a hitter's power output, became more associated with smaller, fast-running players than with power hitters. A modern fan, upon learning that Crawford holds the all-time record for triples with 309, is more likely to conjure up the image of a sinewy speedster than of a broad-shouldered, muscular athlete like Sam Crawford.

When he was making the case for Crawford's title as "The King of Sluggers," Lane talked mostly in generalities, emphasizing the number of hits, runs scored and stolen bases attained in a season. A look at modern record books, which include a wider array of statistics, indicates more clearly just how great Crawford was. He was among the league leaders almost every year in at least a half-dozen categories—often in eight or ten. During his 18-year career (not counting the month he played in 1899), Crawford finished in the top five in his league as follows:

Batting Average	7 times
On-Base Percentage	4 times
Slugging Percentage	11 times
OPS (On-Base Plus Slugging)	10 times
Hits	11 times
Doubles	6 times
Triples	11 times
Home Runs	6 times
Total Bases	12 times
Runs Scored	4 times
Runs Batted In	12 times

Sam Crawford was not just one of the better players of his time; he is one of the better players in the Baseball Hall of Fame.

Setting the Standard: Bill Bergen

The low-average 1960s and 1970s gave us Mario Mendoza and the "Mendoza Line." The even-more-punchless Deadball Era gave us Bill Bergen. During the period when Mendoza played, most Sunday newspapers carried listings of major league batting averages. Many newspapers conserved space by not listing averages below .200. That was often the level of Mendoza's batting average, thus linking his name to the .200 cutoff point.[73] Bergen outdid (or, maybe, under-performed) Mendoza by regularly posting batting averages far below .200. He gained a measure of notoriety by owning the lowest lifetime average of any long-term regular player in baseball history.

Bergen's lifetime batting average was .170. But the low average was only part of Bill's legacy. He had very little power, and no self-respecting pitcher was going to put him on base by walking him. So his lifetime slugging percentage and his lifetime on-base percentage were commensurately low. He "slugged" at a .201 rate and got on base at a .194 rate. Those marks are also the standards for batting futility.[74]

Bergen was such a good defensive catcher that within weeks after his debut with Cincinnati in 1901 he was being hailed as one of the best catchers who ever played. An opinion expressed by veteran catcher Duke Farrell was shared by many: "He [Bergen] is undoubtedly the greatest throwing catcher I have ever seen." Farrell explained that Bergen's greatest strength was "his ability to throw from any position in any direction. He can stand behind the bat, and, without moving his feet an inch, shoot the ball to first, second or third with the same motion."[75]

Bill told a Cincinnati reporter that he spent years practicing his quick release. "When I first started out to play ball I would wind up my arm, take a step and swing before throwing and, though I had a strong arm and could throw speedily, I seldom got my man," Bill said. The lack of success in nabbing baserunners led Bergen to streamline his throwing motion. "I learned to make those snap throws gradually," he explained. "When I was warming up a pitcher I would try to get the ball out of the mitt and my arm in a throwing position just as quickly as possible. I guess I practiced this for hours every day."[76]

In addition to throwing quickly and accurately, Bergen was also accomplished in his receiving skills. "Bergen catches and makes the most difficult plays without an effort," the Cincinnati reporter said. "He does not jump about, take a hop, skip and a jump, and thereby earn the applause of the stands, as do some of the youngsters who make a favorable impression in the league. His work is finished, and when he makes a play, no matter how difficult it may be, it seems to have been easy from the stands."

Another reporter claimed Bergen had a "sixth sense" for judging the location of foul flies. "He acts differently on foul flies than any other backstop in the business," this reporter said. "If the ball is hit so that it goes straight back toward the grandstand or up in the air and far enough to drop on the roof of the stand, Bergen merely turns around and watches the sphere go out of sight. But when it goes up in the air within reaching distance, he is all animation.... He never misses anything within reach and seldom goes after anything out of reach."[77]

As he had analyzed and worked on improving his throwing motion, Bergen had thought about his batting weaknesses. "I know, too, that I have a fault at the bat, because

I step away," he said shortly after joining the Reds. "But I am trying hard to break myself of this, and I believe that I will some day be able to face a pitcher and swing at the ball without stepping backward. I do it now unconsciously."[78] That habit—pulling away from the ball as it approached the plate—may explain another batting mark Bergen holds. In more than three thousand plate appearances, he was never hit by a pitch.

As woeful as it may appear, the 1902 season was one of Bergen's more successful seasons at bat. His 36 RBIs were a career high, and the 19 runs scored only two fewer than his career high. He walked 14 times, the most in his career. In late August he may have had the hottest streak of his career.

On August 17 his eighth-inning double drove in the tying run in a game the Reds won, 2–1. Two days later he singled to right field in the bottom of the ninth, driving in two runs to bring the Reds an 8–7 victory. In the first game of a doubleheader the next day, he drove in four runs to spark a 10–4 win, then had three hits in a 15–1 triumph. But remember, this is Bill Bergen. In describing this batting streak the *Cincinnati Commercial Tribune* reporter explained, "In every case with Bergen it is the same ball that does the work, a hit that looks like a fluke, but which invariably goes safe. It lands just over the first baseman's head, and yet out of reach of the right fielder. He has hit at least five balls in this very spot when two men were on bases and two out."[79]

In 1903 Bergen batted a career-high .227. His comparative success apparently came because early in the season he briefly corrected his unconscious habit of stepping back and away from the plate. But in July a reporter wrote, "Billy Bergen seems to have fallen into his old habit of pulling away from the plate again. For a while Bergen was standing up and stepping into the ball, with the result that he was hitting very well, but of late he seems to have forgotten this and is stepping away."[80]

Over the rest of his career, which lasted through the 1911 season, Bergen never again hit higher than .190. He twice hit .159, hit .139 with three extra-base hits in 346 at-bats, and bottomed out at .132.

"Noodles": Frank Hahn

It was at Crosley Field in Cincinnati during World War II. The old man, a meat inspector for the government, came into the locker room. He put on an old uniform and began working out, as was his custom. He didn't say much, just went about his business. After he had worked out a little, he helped organize batting practice. The players didn't know much about him. He had a funny nickname—"Noodles." People said he used to pitch for the Reds a long time ago. The Reds' manager, Bill McKechnie, whose baseball career stretched back nearly forty years, treated him with some deference.

One day Steve Mesner, a young third baseman for the Reds, ran across a yellowed newspaper clipping about a Cincinnati pitcher who had struck out 16 batters in a game one season and thrown a no-hitter the next. The pitcher's name was Frank "Noodles" Hahn. Mesner immediately thought about the old man. After all, there couldn't be too many people with the nickname Noodles.

He searched out Lee Allen, a club employee who knew a lot about old-time baseball. "Could this be that old fellow who works out with us?" he asked Allen, who confirmed that it was, in fact, the old man. "Well, what do you know?" Mesner said, his voice showing a new-found respect for the old fellow. Later, in writing about the incident, Allen explained that Hahn wasn't one of those ex-ballplayers who talk constantly about the "good old days." If Mesner hadn't run across the newspaper clipping, the Reds' players would never have known what a fine pitcher Noodles had been in his day.[81]

Noodles' formal name was Frank Hahn, and he had pitched for the Reds some forty years before Mesner discovered the newspaper clipping about his pitching exploits. Hahn said he acquired his nickname as a small child. One of his neighbors was an elderly gentleman who had little money. Hahn's grandmother would often prepare food for the elderly man, and little Frank would be given the task of taking it to him.

Frank "Noodles" Hahn was the National League's top left-handed pitcher at the turn of the twentieth century (National Baseball Hall of Fame Library, Cooperstown, New York).

Noodle soup was one of the man's favorite dishes, and Frank was often seen carrying it to him. "My brothers started kidding about the noodle soup," Hahn later confided to a reporter. "Finally they dropped the soup and used to call me 'Noodles.' It was not long until everybody else called me by that name. And it has been 'Noodles' ever since." (Note: This story, related to a reporter in 1899, is one of several versions Hahn told over the years.)[82]

Noodles gained considerable local attention when, as a 15-year-old pitching for a Nashville amateur team, he shut out the Class B Nashville Volunteers in an exhibition game, holding them to three hits. He was signed by one of the Volunteers' rivals the next season, pitching for them in 1895 and part of 1896. He quit midway through the 1896 season, reportedly because even after he developed a sore arm his manager still insisted that he pitch two days in a row.[83]

He had pitched well enough during that half-season, however, to be claimed by two Class A Western League teams for the 1897 campaign. He ended up pitching for the Detroit Tigers. Although still only 18, he became one of the better pitchers in the league, going 17–16 with a team that finished a few games over .500. A Detroit reporter praised his work, saying he had improved greatly over the second half of the season and was a "comer of the first water." "He has an unlimited amount of nerve and confidence in his own ability," the reporter said, while comparing Hahn favorably to

Ted Breitenstein, who at the time was considered the best left-handed pitcher in baseball.[84]

Hahn was purchased by the Cincinnati Reds after the 1897 season. He probably had not read the Detroit reporter's assessment of his abilities, but the next spring he did his best to live up to it—at least to the part about having unlimited nerve and confidence. The Reds offered him a salary of $1,500, a pretty good figure for an unproven rookie. Hahn sent the proposed contract back to the Reds, saying he would not sign for less than $1,800. Cincinnati's management tried to reason with Hahn, who seemed to be displaying an alternate reason for acquiring the nickname "Noodles." But Hahn wouldn't budge from his figure.

When the season opened, Hahn found himself back in Detroit, signed to a contract calling for $800 and now under the impression he would never get another chance to pitch in the big league. His hopes crushed, young Noodles sought relief at night spots around the Western League. His new lifestyle added inches to his waistline and subtracted miles from his fastball. He had a 12–19 record in late August when the Tigers gave him his release.

In commenting about the team's decision, a reporter said of Hahn, "Unfortunately his star arm is attached below a very amateurial and unprogressive head, and only reformation and hard work can restore him to usefulness upon the mound." Charlie Comiskey, the owner of the St. Paul Saints, signed Noodles but released him after one bad game. "Why, he was twenty or thirty pounds overweight," Comiskey said.[85]

About this time Noodles was due for a break and he got one. Fortunately for him, the team he had treated so arrogantly the previous spring was owned by John T. Brush, and not a less-calculating owner. John T. hated to part with a dollar unnecessarily, and he undoubtedly approved of the decision to teach the stubborn young Hahn a lesson by dispatching him to the minors. But John T. was not going to let one of the other National League owners end up with a young man who could throw a baseball as fast and accurately as Hahn. So through all of Hahn's travails and travels during the 1898 season, John T. held a firm grip on the "string" the Reds had attached to Noodles' contract.

When the spring of 1899 arrived, Brush's team sent the young man a contract. It was for $300 less than the previous year's offer and had a temperance clause that could subtract another $300 from his salary if he indulged in alcoholic beverages. Noodles was elated over receiving the contract offer. He signed it immediately and began working out so he could report to spring training in good condition.[86]

During spring training in 1899, Noodles showed the talent that had attracted the Reds two years earlier. He pitched so well in two exhibition games that the Cincinnati players were calling him the best prospect in years. When the season opened, he pitched infrequently. Manager Buck Ewing had a staff of seven pitchers, and he tried to keep all of them busy enough to stay in reasonable pitching condition. He used Noodles sporadically, primarily against teams with several left-handed batters. Through the end of May, Noodles had started only five games.

On June 23, after he had gone almost two weeks without pitching, Noodles beat the Orioles, 8–3. After one day's rest, Ewing started him again. Noodles pitched well again, beating the Orioles, 4–3, but he made an even deeper impression with his hustle. In the ninth inning, with one out and men on first and second, an Oriole batter hit a grounder to first baseman Farmer Vaughn, who fielded the ball well off of the base. Vaughn threw to the shortstop, Harry Steinfeldt, for the force out but had no chance to cover the bag for the return throw. Noodles, however, had headed toward first as soon as the ball was hit. He raced as fast as he could, reaching the base just in time to catch the throw from Steinfeldt for the game-ending double play. Reds fans howled with delight, and celebrated by flipping their seat cushions onto the playing field.[87]

After his showing against the Orioles, Noodles stayed in the regular rotation for the rest of the year. Umpire Hank O'Day worked one of Hahn's games early in July. "Noodles Hahn is one of the best youngsters I ever umpired behind," he said afterwards. "He has great speed and wonderful command, and his curve ball has a quick break that makes it very hard to meet squarely. He is going to be a success or I miss my guess badly."[88]

By the end of the season Noodles had pretty much fulfilled O'Day's prediction. He finished the season with a 23–8 record, by far the best on the Reds' pitching staff. His 2.68 ERA was the fourth-best in the league, he allowed the third-fewest hits per nine innings, and he had the second-lowest combination of hits and walks allowed per nine innings. His 145 strikeouts led the league. In short, as a rookie he was already one of the best pitchers in the National League.

The success Hahn enjoyed in his rookie season was partly responsible for a slow start in his sophomore year. Since he had clearly been the Reds' best pitcher in 1899, Noodles thought he should be paid accordingly. He asked for the National League's salary limit, $2,400. Reds management thought $2,100 was a more fitting salary for a second-year pitcher. Hahn got the salary he wanted, but had to hold out until early April to get it.

Although he had worked out on his own during the holdout, he wasn't ready to pitch when the season opened. Of course, that didn't mean he wasn't sent to the mound; it just meant the results weren't very pleasing. He started the Reds' third game, beating Chicago, 7–6, despite allowing eight bases on balls. He won ugly again in his second game, beating Pittsburgh, 12–11. He pitched well enough in his third outing, losing, 4–3, but then came a 20–11 shellacking by the Pirates. Noodles lasted three innings in that game, allowing eight runs. After that the losses started piling up. He didn't pitch all that poorly but had a couple of bad innings in almost every game. By the second week of June he had lost nine games in a row, and his record stood at 2–9.

By that time Noodles had rebuilt the strength in his arm and regained command of his pitches. He began a six-game winning streak. In the game that broke the streak, he held Brooklyn to one hit in the first six innings before losing, 4–3, in 13 innings.

On July 12 he threw a no-hitter against Philadelphia, the most potent batting team in the league. He struck out eight Phillies, getting sluggers Ed Delahanty and Elmer Flick twice each. After the game the Phillies were effusive in their praise of the young lefthander. "I have heard it argued that there is no such thing as a jump ball, but anyone who doubted the existence of that sort of fooler should have batted against Hahn today," said Monte Cross. "His fast ball—and they were all fast—jumped no less than two inches just before it reached the plate.... All our players noticed it, and commented on it when they were on the bench. We stood up there and we would see the ball coming. It looked like a cinch that our bats would at least hit it, but we would miss it half a foot. The ball would jump right over the bat."[89]

Noodles followed up the no-hitter with a shutout against St. Louis on an extremely hot, humid day. He allowed nine hits but seemed to toy with the Cardinals. A reporter said Hahn didn't exert himself until the Cardinals put a runner on base. At that point, the reporter said, "Noodles would begin to work, and the next three batsmen were pie for him. He did this in almost every inning."[90]

On the face of it, Hahn's record in 1900 didn't seem all that great. He won 16 games while losing 20. His 3.27 ERA was only the thirteenth-best in the league. But despite his early-season struggles, only five other pitchers allowed fewer hits per game, and he had the ninth-lowest total of hits-plus-walks allowed per game. He led the league in strikeouts for the second year in a row with 132 and in shutouts with four. By the end of the season he was generally considered the best left-handed pitcher in the game.[91]

In 1901 Noodles added a sharp-breaking overhand drop to his repertoire, which previously had featured an overpowering fastball and a curve that moved only a few inches but broke just before reaching the plate. Like all other National League pitchers, he benefited greatly from a potent new weapon—the new foul-strike rule. The combination of a new pitch and foul balls becoming strikes led to a big increase in his strikeout totals.

On May 22 he completely dominated the Boston Beaneaters, striking out 16 batters. Many of his strikeouts came off the new drop pitch. According to a Boston reporter, the Beaneater batters often went after pitches that ended up hitting home plate.[92] Noodles had led the league in 1899 with 145 strikeouts and in 1900 with 132. In 1901 he fanned 239 to again lead the league. Noodles' 16 strikeouts against the Beaneaters set a single-game record that lasted until 1933, when Dizzy Dean struck out 17. Christy Mathewson exceeded Noodles' season record of 239 strikeouts in 1903, but Hahn's 1901 total remained among the top five in National League history until the late fifties.

Noodles' win-loss record in 1901 was only 22–19, but he was pitching for a terrible team. The Reds finished in last place with a 52–87 record. Noodles won 42 percent of his team's victories, a modern record that lasted until Steve Carlton recorded 46 percent of the Phillies' wins in 1972.[93] Hahn was one of the better pitchers in the league at keeping batters off the bases, but with ground balls dribbling through the Reds' makeshift infield all season long, he did not rank as high as he had in previous seasons. The categories in which he most excelled were the ones that came through enduring a punishing work schedule. At the age of 22, Hahn started 42 games, finished 41 of them, and pitched 375⅓ innings. Four of his complete games went extra innings, one each of 11, 12, 13, and 14 innings.

After Noodles lost a game on June 2, in which he had no speed on his pitches, a Cincinnati writer reported that Noodles was suffering "a slight lameness in his arm,"[94] and would not be worked for several days. Several turned out to be six days. On June 8 he beat Christy Mathewson and the Giants, 6–4. During the game he threw hard when he had to but tried to get by with off-speed pitches when he could. After getting two days of rest he started again but lasted only one inning, giving up three runs. Once again he could not put any speed behind his pitches. Despite these warning signs, his manager sent him back to the mound the next day. This time Noodles pitched 12 innings in a game that ended in a 6–6 tie. His next start came after he had three days' rest, and he continued to pitch regularly over the remainder of the season.

After the season ended, Noodles told a reporter he was not yet ready to sign another contract with the Reds. First he wanted to see if Reds management was going to make a real effort to improve the team. "I pitched forty games for the Reds this year," Noodles said, "but that is like pitching eighty for a good team. I am no different from any other player, and cannot last forever, and I do not want to go through another season like the past one.... It was a case of pitching at top speed at all times, and I think another such campaign would tell on me."[95]

Noodles had no way of knowing it at the time but his statement was much too prescient. He had three more good seasons. In 1902 he went 23–12 and his 1.77 ERA was the second-lowest in the National League. The next year he was 22–12, with a 2.52 ERA, seventh-best in the league. In 1904 he had a losing record but still pitched well, going 16–18 with a 2.06 ERA, fifth-best in the league. He began each of those seasons nursing a sore arm out of spring training and in each of those seasons the soreness took a little longer to work out. Over those three seasons he gradually lost his fastball, changing from a power pitcher who blew away opposing batters almost at will to one who pitched according to the situation, relying on his fielders much more than before and saving his best stuff for clutch situations. One reflection of his change in approach was that his strikeout totals declined from 239 in 1901 to 142 in 1902, 127 in 1903, and 98 in 1904.

In August of 1903, after having managed Noodles for a little over a year, Joe Kelley told a reporter, "Hahn should be worked only one game a week, and that game is as good as won if we can give him any kind of support. He is really a great pitcher. He is always steady and does his work without much exertion. But I don't believe that it is good policy to work him more than once a week."[96]

In July of 1904 Cincinnati writer J. Ed Grillo lamented, "Frank Hahn is not the pitcher he was a year or so ago. The once great lefthander is going the way of all southpaws after a few years of service, and now belongs in the class which has seen its best days. He no longer possesses that fast ball with its deceptive shoot which was almost impossible to hit. He lacks the steam, and is now only relying on his head to win games for him."[97]

Comments similar to those of Kelley and Grillo have been made with some frequency throughout baseball history, but they are almost always made in reference to an aging veteran nearing the end of a long career. In 1904, when Grillo noted that he no longer had any speed, Hahn was an "old man" of 25. In 1905 the sore arm that first bothered him in 1902 didn't go away as the season progressed. He pitched infrequently and not too effectively. He had a 5–3 record when the Reds released him in August. The New York Highlanders signed him in the spring of 1906 but let him go after six games. His once-bright career was over at the age of 27.

Five

1902, American League

For the second year in a row American League fans faced the delightful uncertainty of knowing the hometown team had gotten significantly better over the winter but would be facing opposition that had also improved considerably. Every American League team had benefited from the off-season flow of National League players to the new major league. The first-division teams of 1901 had addressed their weaknesses; most of the second-division teams had reloaded with many new players. Only the Detroit Tigers, tied up by ownership issues over the winter, were entering the 1902 season with pretty much the same lineup—and even they had added three veteran players. Baseball writers generally cited the White Stockings (in 1902 already often called the White Sox) as the favorites to win the pennant but mentioned as many as five of the eight teams as possible winners. Everyone agreed the American League was now much the stronger of the two leagues and looked forward to an exciting season.

1902 American League Standings

Team	W	L	Pct.	GB
Philadelphia	83	53	.610	—
St. Louis	78	58	.574	5
Boston	77	60	.562	6.5
Chicago	74	60	.552	8
Cleveland	69	67	.507	14
Washington	61	75	.449	22
Detroit	52	83	.385	30.5
Baltimore	50	88	.362	34

Mixed Luck and Rube Waddell: Philadelphia

Over the last two months of the 1901 season, the A's were the best team in the league. The team's relative weaknesses were at shortstop and the outfield. And, of course, like every 1901 American League team, they needed more pitching. Connie Mack filled those holes while weakening his crosstown rivals by stealing three more of the Phillies' top players: Shortstop Monte Cross, right fielder Elmer Flick, and pitcher

Bill Duggleby. He also signed Topsy Hartsel, the Chicago Remnants' left fielder. Entering the season he had a batting order with speed, power, and the ability to play scientific baseball, a solid defense, and pretty good depth in the pitching staff.

Philadelphia (83–53)

Regular Lineup	AVG	OBP	SLG	R	RBI	SB
Topsy Hartsel, lf	.283	.383	.391	109	58	47
Dave Fultz, cf	.302	.381	.368	109	49	44
Harry Davis, 1b	.307	.343	.444	89	92	28
Lave Cross, 3b	.342	.374	.440	90	108	25
Socks Seybold, rf	.316	.375	.506	91	97	6
Danny Murphy, 2b	.313	.351	.416	48	48	12
Monte Cross, ss	.231	.289	.302	72	59	17
Ossee Schreckengost, c*	.327	.345	.402	50	52	5
or Doc Powers, c	.264	.312	.325	35	39	3
or Luis Castro, 2b	.245	.265	.336	18	15	2
Leading Pitchers	W	L	PCT	IP	H	ERA
Eddie Plank	20	15	.571	300	319	3.30
Rube Waddell	24	7	.774	276.3	224	2.05
Pete Husting**	14	6	.700	212	255	3.99
Snake Wiltse	8	8	.500	138	182	5.15

*Includes record with Cleveland
**Includes record with Boston

Once the season began, Mack had much more luck than he would have desired—lots of bad luck and some good luck, too. The bad luck began just as the season opened, when the Pennsylvania State Supreme Court overturned the lower court's ruling in the Lajoie case. The decision cost the A's five players: Lajoie, Flick, Duggleby, and pitchers Chick Fraser and Bill Bernhard, who had signed with the A's in 1901. Technically, Monte Cross was also affected by the decision. Although Cross continued to play for the A's, the Phillies took no action against him. Mack's recruiting had given the A's enough outfield depth so that Flick's loss was not too damaging, but the team now had a gaping hole at second base and little pitching.

Despite the loss of Lajoie and Flick, the A's still possessed a potent attack, which became even better as the season progressed. Leadoff man Topsy Hartsel was a patient batter with speed and baserunning smarts. Number two hitter Dave Fultz was an expert bunter and another fast, aggressive baserunner. They tied for the league lead in runs scored in 1902, each plating 109. Fultz led in sacrifices with 35. Lave Cross and Harry Davis, the third- and fourth-place batters, were adept at the hit-and-run game and both had good power. Davis led the league with 43 doubles; Cross had 39 doubles and drove in 108 runs. Socks Seybold, who followed them, led the league in home runs with 16, the most home runs hit in the American League in a season until 1919, when Babe Ruth smashed 29. Seybold drove home 97 runs.

It took Mack nearly half the season to find an adequate replacement for Lajoie. But when Danny Murphy joined the team on July 7, he gave the team another good bat. Plugged into the sixth spot in the batting order, he hit .313. He scored 48 runs and drove in 48 runs, a pace that over a full schedule would have yielded 88 runs scored and 88 RBIs. In the 79 games he played, catcher Ossee Schreckengost gave the A's another productive bat, hitting .324 with good power. Shortstop Monte Cross was the only regular who was not a good hitter, and he had one of his better years. While his batting average was only .231, he had a number of clutch hits and moved runners along with 22 sacrifices.[1] The A's led the league in scoring with 775 runs, 100 more than any of the other contending teams. (The eighth-place Orioles were second with 715 runs; the sixth-place Senators were third with 707.)

Despite their ability to produce runs, the A's would not have finished high in the pennant race if Connie Mack had not been able to eventually put together a decent pitching staff. Mack's bad luck began to change when the call went out to other American League teams for help. Several teams promised players; the only one that actually sent any was Boston, which turned over Fred Mitchell and Pete Husting, two pitchers from the back end of its pitching staff.

Mitchell had been an extra pitcher for Boston in 1901, going 6–6 in 17 games. He wasn't quite that good for the A's in 1902, winning five and losing eight. He didn't pitch his first game for the A's until June 9, but after that he gave the team serviceable pitching when the only real alternative was someone from the semi-pro lots.

Husting had pitched briefly for Mack in 1900 with Class A Milwaukee, winning four of his five decisions. He had a 10–15 record for the American League Brewers in 1901. He wasn't a great pitcher for the A's. He was wild in many of his starts, and he gave up his share of hits. The only thing he did really well was win the games he pitched. The A's were 4–4 when he pitched his first game for them on May 3. A month later they led the league with a 20–12 record. At that point Husting was 8–0, the rest of the staff 12–12.

Through the first third of June, Husting, Eddie Plank and Snake Wiltse formed a somewhat-shaky three-man pitching staff. Strangely, the weak link of that trio was Plank, who was by far the best pitcher of the three except for the first six weeks of the 1902 season. During that time he won only three of his eleven decisions. Wiltse won seven of his first nine starts, largely because the A's averaged seven runs a game when he started. He won only one game after that, and was dispatched to Baltimore after John McGraw tore apart his team.

Pitching every third game proved too much for Husting's arm. In mid–June Mack told reporters Husting had "a lame arm from too much pitching."[2] A little thing like a sore arm, however, didn't prevent Husting from taking his regular turn. On June 19 he beat St. Louis, 6–3, to bring his record to 9–2, and three days later he pitched well in a six-inning relief effort. Then he seemed to hit a wall.

Over the next month he was hit hard in every appearance, covering six starts and two relief efforts. In late July Mack decided to give him some time off. When he came back two weeks later he pitched well for a while, winning his first four games. On August 20, after beating St. Louis, his record with the A's was 14–3. That was his last major league win. He was effective in his next two starts but lost both of them. In September he started five times, making it past the first inning only once. Due to Mack's quick hook and good relief pitching, the A's won all five games. The staggering finish brought an end to Husting's baseball career. Having acquired a law degree in college, he retired from professional baseball to practice law after the 1902 season.[3]

By the end of June Plank had recovered from his early-season slump and was winning again. But the A's pitching problems were dragging the team down toward the .500 mark. One day, as he was giving his lineup card to umpire John Sheridan, Mack made a comment about his team's pitching woes. Sheridan said he had heard Rube Waddell was pitching great ball out in Los Angeles, and suggested that Mack try to get him. The California League was outside organized baseball, and its players were considered fair game for teams within organized baseball, not that many baseball people paid much attention to such niceties during the 1902 season. Mack decided to go after Waddell and succeeded in getting him—twice.

In mid-June Mack sent Rube a cable asking him to join the A's. Rube asked for $100 and transportation, so Mack sent the money and a railroad ticket. As Rube was about to board the train for the trip east, his teammates intercepted him at the train station. They told Rube they needed him and asked him to stay in Los Angeles. Rube was overcome by emotion and agreed to do so.

Mack soon learned about Rube's change of mind but was unfazed. He knew Rube's mind could easily be changed again. He sent another cable, and Rube again agreed to play for the A's. This time Mack sent two Pinkerton agents, armed with a $200 advance for Rube, to escort the lefthander. The two agents got Rube as far east as Dodge City, Kansas. There Rube encountered Young Corbett, a boxer who was about to fight Terry McGovern for the featherweight championship. Rube insisted on watching the fight. Afterwards, he became part of Corbett's entourage. Mack, who was in St. Louis with the A's at that time, received a cable from the agents, telling him that Waddell had gone with Corbett to Kansas City, and if Mack wanted him, he would have to come there and escort him the rest of the way. Mack rushed to Kansas City. There he managed to get Rube aboard a train headed for Baltimore, where the A's were headed for a series with the Orioles.[4]

Three months of playing in the California League had put Rube at the top of his game. His win-loss record with Los Angeles was only 11–8, but he held opposition batters to 6.7 hits per game and struck out over seven batters per game. In addition to pitching, he played about 30 games in the outfield, where he hit .283 and made several spectacular catches.[5] Rube pitched his first game for the A's on June 26, losing to the Orioles, 7–3. The loss dropped the team's record to 26–25, good enough for fourth place, six games behind the league-leading White Sox, but only 2½ games ahead of the seventh-place Senators.

After that loss, Rube won his next nine decisions. His first win was a two-hitter against the Orioles. He faced only 27 batters in that game, the two baserunners being thrown out on the bases. He fanned 13 batters, five of them on three pitches. The Orioles managed to hit only two balls out of the infield, both routine flies in the eighth inning. His third win was a 17-inning marathon, a 4–2 victory over Boston. Rube seemingly grew stronger as that game progressed, striking out 16 batters, shutting Boston out over the last 11 innings, and punctuating his performance by turning cartwheels at the end of each inning. Rube's next three wins all came on two days' rest—another win over Boston and two against Chicago, teams the A's had to beat. On July 21 and 22 Rube picked up victories number seven and eight in successive relief appearances against Cleveland. On July 26 he beat St. Louis, 3–1, for his ninth win, which brought the Athletics within one game of the White Sox.

Rube and the A's then encountered a brief slump. The A's dropped eight of their next ten games, with Rube losing three times and pitching a ten-inning tie game. The slump dropped them to fourth place, but still they trailed the White Sox by only 4½ games. At this point Lady Luck gave the A's a big smile. A quirk in the American League schedule gave the A's nine straight games against the Tigers, who had begun fighting themselves harder than the opposition.

The A's lost the first of those nine games, but won the next eight. Husting started the streak with a 9–1 win. Rube followed that with a 13-inning game in which he allowed only four hits and scored the only run after hitting a triple in the last inning. Two days later Rube pitched a two-hitter in the first game of a doubleheader, winning, 8–0. Husting almost matched him in the second game with a four-hit, 9–0 win. After the eight straight wins against Detroit, the Athletics tacked on two more victories against Chicago.

By this time the A's had moved into first place in a four-way battle with Chicago, Boston, and St. Louis. The Browns cut the A's lead to a half-game on September 1 by sweeping a four-game series between the two teams. On the way to Detroit, the A's narrowly escaped disaster when their train collided with a heavy freight train. Both trains suffered significant damage, but no passengers were injured. The A's arrived in Detroit six hours late, worn out from their perilous trip. The situation seemed bad for the A's, but it was just right for Rube, who was eager to come to the rescue. He beat the Tigers, 5–1, allowing only six hits and fanning seven. He rested one day, then announced he would shut out the Tigers in the last game of the series and beat Cleveland all three games of the next series.[6]

Rube fell somewhat short of his prediction. He pitched six innings of the last game against Detroit, a 13–4 blowout, but won only two games against Cleveland. Wilson pitched the other game and lost. But Rube was excited about the pennant race and Mack was willing to let him lead the way to victory.

After the Cleveland series, the A's returned to Philadelphia. When Mitchell struggled in the morning game of the doubleheader opening the homestand, Mack sent Rube to the mound in the third inning. Rube gave up only one run over the last seven innings as the A's rallied to win, 9–5. In the afternoon game Rube relieved Husting in the eighth inning and again the A's fought back to win, 5–4. Rube's twin victories enabled the A's to hold on to a lead of two games over the Browns. Boston was a half-game further back. Over a nine-day span Rube had appeared in six games, winning them all. During that time Plank added a win, rookie Highball Wilson took a loss, and the A's had put a little daylight between themselves and the rest of the league.

The next day, September 11, the A's won two more games against the Orioles while both St. Louis and Boston lost, building the A's lead to 3½ games over St. Louis, four games over Boston, and six over Chicago. With two weeks left in the season the A's had 15 games remaining, seven against Boston, five against the seventh-place Senators, and three against the ragtag Orioles. Besides its games against the A's, Boston still had seven games left against the Orioles, plus two against the Senators, while the Browns had a much more difficult schedule, playing 13 of its last 16 games against Cleveland and Chicago, both tough opponents.

For the A's the key to the race would be the two Boston series. Rube pitched the first of those games, but lost to Cy Young, 5–4. Rain and a Sunday day off gave Rube two days of rest. He came back on Monday in a rematch against Young and won the second game of a doubleheader, 9–2. Plank took the first game, 6–4. Meanwhile, in the West, St. Louis split a four-game series with Cleveland to drop four games behind. Boston trailed by five, with Chicago a half-game behind them.

The A's maintained the pressure by sweeping the Senators in a three-game series. The Browns matched them by taking three from the Tigers, but were starting to run out of games to play. Boston took three of four from Baltimore, but fell another half-game behind. With the pennant in sight, the A's once again turned to Waddell. He beat Young one more time in the opener of a four-game series against Boston. Plank won the second game, eliminating Boston from the race. Boston took the third game, but Rube came back to win the finale, 5–3. The Browns again split a four-game series with Cleveland. They trailed by five games and had only a slim mathematical chance left. Over the next two days the Browns looked out their hotel rooms in Chicago as rain poured down on their pennant hopes while the A's pounded the Orioles for three wins to clinch the pennant.

Dashed Hopes: St. Louis

History tells us the Milwaukee American League franchise moved to St. Louis for the 1902 season. But fans who watched the Browns take the field to start that season knew the team was built around players who were the heart of the 1901 St. Louis Cardinals. Left fielder Jesse Burkett had been the Cardinals' top hitter; Jack Powell, Jack Harper, and Willie Sudhoff had been the team's top pitchers; and shortstop Bobby Wallace, second baseman Dick Padden, and center fielder Emmet Heidrick had provided great defense up the middle. The only former Brewers regular who played an important role with the Browns was first baseman John Anderson. Davy Jones, who played briefly for the Brewers at the end of the 1901 season, won the right field job coming out of spring training, but he jumped to the Cubs 15 games into the 1902 season.

St. Louis (78–58)

Regular Lineup	AVG	OBP	SLG	R	RBI	SB
Jesse Burkett, lf	.306	.390	.418	97	52	23
Charlie Hemphill, rf*	.308	.369	.418	81	69	27
or Bill Friel, rf-cf–2b	.240	.283	.311	26	20	4
Emmet Heidrick, cf	.289	.339	.396	75	56	17
John Anderson, 1b	.284	.316	.385	60	85	15
Bobby Wallace, ss	.285	.350	.393	71	63	18
Barry McCormick, 3b	.246	.304	.308	55	51	10
Dick Padden, 2b	.264	.327	.349	54	40	11
Joe Sugden, c	.250	.330	.305	25	15	2
or Mike Kahoe, c	.244	.270	.340	21	28	4
Leading Pitchers	W	L	PCT	IP	H	ERA
Jack Powell	22	17	.564	328.3	320	3.21

Red Donahue	22	11	.667	316.3	322	2.76
Jack Harper	15	11	.577	222.3	224	4.13
Willie Sudhoff	12	12	.500	220	213	2.86

*Includes record with Cleveland

Manager Jimmy McAleer rounded out his team by signing third baseman Barry McCormick from the Cubs and acquiring catcher Joe Sugden from the White Stockings. For depth he retained catchers Billy Maloney and Jiggs Donahue and utilityman Bill Friel from the Brewers. His most important addition other than the ex–Cardinal players was pitcher Red Donahue, the Phillies' top pitcher in 1901. Bill Reidy, who led the Brewers in wins in 1901, was kept as an extra pitcher for the Browns.

The team that McAleer put together over the winter turned out to be the third-best in Browns history. Its .574 winning percentage in 1902 was exceeded only by the 1922 team that finished one game behind the Yankees with a .604 percentage (93–61), and the 1944 pennant-winning Browns, who had a .578 percentage (89–65).

In pre-season assessments of the pennant race, the Browns were mentioned along with roughly half the league as having a chance to beat out the favored White Stockings. Writers who thought the Browns might win the pennant emphasized the team's strong pitching and outstanding infield defense; those who doubted they would win it pointed to the team's relatively weak hitting. Both groups of writers were right. The Browns stayed close to first place throughout the year because of their deep pitching and solid defense; they failed to win because they just couldn't push enough runs across the plate, finishing seventh in the league in runs scored.

The 1902 Browns were a game bunch of players. They stayed close to the leaders—first the White Stockings, then the A's—deep into September. They played to the maximum of their ability. They failed to win simply because the necessary depth of talent wasn't there.

In retrospect, there is a touch of sadness associated with their failure. The core of the 1902 Browns—their most senior and most talented players—had begun their careers with the Cleveland Spiders, a team that began each season in the mid- and late-nineties with high expectations, only to fall far short of the leaders. When most of the Cleveland players were transferred to St. Louis in 1899 the unreasonably high expectations followed them, as did the disappointing results. The 1902 season was the closest the remaining ex–Spiders came to ending the annual frustration of high hopes linked to inferior results. Three of them—Jesse Burkett, Bobby Wallace, and Jack Powell—contributed solid performances that led the team to the brink of victory, but also fell short at critical times.

For most players, Burkett's 1902 batting numbers would have been considered a good season. Jesse hit .306, had an on-base percentage of .390 (seventh in the league), and scored 97 runs (also seventh in the league). He reached first base more often than any other batter. For Burkett, those numbers were okay, but nothing special. After all, he had hit .376 in 1901, and that was under the new foul-strike rule, which the American League had not yet adopted. At the 60'6" pitching distance, Jesse's lowest batting average before 1902 had been .341. Jesse was 33 years old during the 1902 season, and he had begun to lose some running speed. Some bunts that had previously gone for base hits were now close outs at first base.[7]

Burkett's decline in performance wasn't completely due to advancing age. He also suffered because of illness and injury. He became sick early in June but refused to come out of the lineup. Feeling that even playing at a sub-par level he was still better than any Browns substitute, he continued to play. After a few games a St. Louis reporter gave credit to Burkett for his desire to stay in the lineup, but offered the opinion that Jesse had not been of much help. In mid–July Burkett made a diving catch with the bases loaded, saving a 4–3 victory over Baltimore. He injured his shoulder making the catch. He continued to play despite the injury, but for the remainder of the season was unable to throw with his normal distance and accuracy.[8]

For Wallace, who was at the height of his Hall of Fame career, the 1902 season featured a recurring series of spectacular plays at shortstop. On June 10, he had 19 chances against Boston, the most ever handled by a shortstop in a nine-inning game. Eleven of his chances were assists, six were putouts, and two were errors. He started three double plays by making difficult catches and charged in to make a great scoop and throw to get the runner at the plate on a bases-loaded infield chopper. Despite his efforts, the Browns lost the game, 5–4.[9]

At bat Wallace had one of his better seasons in every way except producing runs. He hit .285 with 32 doubles, nine triples and one home run—pretty good power for the Deadball Era. He had some memorable games with the bat, such as when he drove in all of his team's runs in a 3–2 win over Detroit and when he tripled and scored the only run in a 1–0 win over the A's.[10] He batted fifth on a team that had only five decent hitters, and he followed two batters who hit for good averages but had little patience and thus gave up a relatively high number of outs. After Bobby came the easy-out brigade—three regulars with low averages and little power, followed by the pitcher. The result for Wallace was a lot of frustrating at-bats in which he hit at his normal level but saw too many innings end without runs being scored. In 1901 Wallace had scored 69 runs and driven in 91 while batting sixth for the Cardinals. In 1902, batting one spot higher for the Browns but with men making lots of outs around him, he managed to score 71 runs but drove in only 63.

Powell's determination to do all he could to bring a pennant to St. Louis was shown by a vow he made before the 1902 season began. Powell was, as they would say in that era, a drinking man. A former teammate said of him, "When Powell is winning he considers it his duty to 'celebrate' his success, and when he's losing he indulges in intoxicants to stop the bad streak."[11] Before the 1902 season he promised himself (and McAleer) he would not drink until the season was over. According to McAleer, he kept the pledge.[12] Perhaps because his body took some time to adjust to the lack of internal lubricant, Powell began the season with a sore arm. He lost his first start to Detroit, displaying little speed and lacking control. His arm came around well enough, however, to enable him to pitch shutouts in his next two starts.

Powell had a smooth pitching motion, seemingly throwing the ball with little effort. He was a tough competitor on the mound, battling each batter to the wire, especially with men on base. His managers loved both characteristics, regularly calling upon him to start on short rest during times when the pitching staff was hurting.

During the first week of June McAleer used Powell in five of seven games, starting him three times and bringing him in for short relief stints twice. Beginning in late July McAleer began shuffling his starters, with Powell starting every third game. When the season ended, Powell had appeared in seven more games than any other Browns pitcher and had started five more contests. McAleer used him much more often than the other Browns pitchers against the other first-division teams, 21 of his 39 decisions coming against those three teams. Powell was 5–3 against Philadelphia, 2–5 against Boston, and 3–3 against Chicago. He was 12–6 against the rest of the league.[13]

Misplaced Charity: Boston

Manager Jimmy Collins made several changes to his team during the 1901–02 offseason. He added catcher John Warner and outfielder Charlie Hickman from the New York Giants. Collins thought Warner was a better defensive catcher than Ossee Schreckengost. He traded Schreckengost to Cleveland for Candy LaChance, a good defensive first baseman. The acquisition of LaChance enabled him to move Buck Freeman back into right field, where Freeman was more comfortable, if not much more effective. Hickman replaced left fielder Tommy Dowd, who became a player-manager for Jamestown in the New York State League.

It seemed to be *de rigueur* for an American League team to snatch at least one player from its crosstown National League rival. Collins met that obligation by taking Bill Dinneen away from the Beaneaters. Dinneen replaced Ted Lewis, who retired. Collins gave his team more depth by signing Pete Husting, a regular starter for Milwaukee in 1901, and adding outfielder Patsy Dougherty and utility infielder Harry Gleason, both of whom played in the minors in 1901.

Boston (77–60)

Regular Lineup	AVG	OBP	SLG	R	RBI	SB
Patsy Dougherty, lf	.342	.407	.397	77	34	20
Jimmy Collins, 3b	.322	.360	.459	71	61	18
or Harry Gleason, ut	.225	.265	.313	30	25	6
Chick Stahl, cf	.323	.375	.421	92	58	24
Buck Freeman, rf	.309	.352	.502	75	121	17
Freddy Parent, ss	.275	.309	.374	91	62	16
Candy LaChance, 1b	.279	.309	.351	60	56	8
Hobe Ferris, 2b	.244	.276	.381	57	63	11
Lou Criger, c	.256	.324	.361	32	28	7
or John Warner, c	.234	.286	.320	19	12	0
Leading Pitchers	**W**	**L**	**PCT**	**IP**	**H**	**ERA**
Cy Young	32	11	.744	384.7	350	2.15
Bill Dinneen	21	21	.500	371.3	348	2.93
George Winter	11	9	.550	168.3	149	2.99
Tully Sparks	7	9	.438	142.7	151	3.47

When Collins decided upon the musical chairs routine that gave him a defensive outfield of Hickman, Freeman, and Chick Stahl, he likely envisioned a steady procession of drives off the bats of those three sluggers into the opponents' outfield. He probably saw balls flying over the opposing fielders' heads or bouncing past them to the fence while Boston baserunners hustled around the bases, scoring a flock of runs. He got some of that. By the end of May Freeman was among the league leaders in long hits with nine doubles, six triples and two home runs; Hickman added ten more extra-base hits, while Stahl scored almost a run a game. But Collins probably didn't envision images of his own outfielders misplaying a spate of hits. He got that, too, with Hickman playing a steady stream of ground balls into extra bases while failing to reach routine flies, and Freeman struggling to catch any liner coming at him below the waist.[14]

With his porous outfield defense threatening to offset his team's other relative strengths, in late May Collins decided to bench Hickman. Charlie's replacement was Patsy Dougherty, an ordinary fielder but an excellent leadoff hitter and a fast runner. He replaced Fred Parent at the top of the batting order, enabling the young shortstop to bat lower in the lineup, where he could be free to whale away at the ball, which was his natural style. Dougherty hit .400 and scored 15 runs in his first 19 games. He quickly became very popular with the Boston fans. Hickman, an expensive man to be riding the bench, was soon sold to Cleveland.

With Dougherty stabilizing the outfield defense and improving the offense, Collins had a solid team. Boston's fatal weakness, it turned out, arose from its response for the call to help the Athletics after the Lajoie decision. As mentioned above, Collins responded by sending the A's Fred Mitchell and Pete Husting. At the time they were turned over to the A's, Mitchell and Husting were both considered expendable. But their departure left Collins with three veteran pitchers backed up only by three unproven youngsters.

Collins established a three-man rotation, probably planning to give at least one of the youngsters more regular work as time passed, but none of the young pitchers panned out. Collins rarely used any of them, even in relief. Through the first half of the season his rotation was Cy Young, George Winter, and Bill Dinneen, with little variation. In mid–July Winter was hospitalized with a serious illness, variously described as appendicitis or typhoid fever. To replace Winter, Collins signed Tully Sparks, who had been released by the Giants, and acquired Tom Hughes from the Orioles. Neither pitched well enough to win half his starts, and Collins continued to use Young and Dinneen as two-thirds of a rotation, starting either Sparks or Hughes when the other rotation spot came up.

Boston stayed close to first place all season long, principally because Cy Young had another great season. Young was 35 years old in 1902, but he was more than a match for the best hitters in the game. His repertoire varied from an underhand raise ball, to slow curves and an overhand drop curve ball, to a high fastball that still was one of the best in baseball. In several of his victories, newspaper game summaries attributed his effectiveness to the great speed of his pitches. In late September, after he had already pitched more than 370 innings, a reporter commented: "So fast was Cy that the right field bleachers were fairly peppered with foul balls all afternoon."[15]

Young won his first three starts in 1902. His fourth start was a disaster. He allowed six runs in the only inning he pitched. Collins started him again the next day, and big Cy threw a four-hitter. His next loss came five weeks later, on June 11, after his winning streak had reached ten in a row. At that point Boston was in third place with a record of 22–17. Young was 13–1 then, the rest of the pitching staff combined for a 9–16 record. That pattern held true to some extent through the rest of the season. By July 11, Young was 18–3, the rest of the staff 19–27; on August 14, he was 26–7, while the others totaled 27–37. Largely because Bill Dinneen went 15–5 after July 16, the gap narrowed to 32–11 for Young and 45–49 for everyone else by the end of the season. Young's pitching enabled Boston to stay close to first throughout the season, but he didn't get enough help to lift the team into the lead.

During his time in St. Louis Young heard a lot about being an "old man" as a pitcher. He had started to put on weight and sported a bit of a pot belly. References to his "aldermanic proportions" became relatively common. By 1902, however, comments about his age and weight began appearing in a quite different context. After Young beat the Browns, 7–1, holding them to five hits, a St. Louis reporter commented, "Cy has a bow window on his front and walks as if he carried weight for age." But, for Young, that didn't seem to be much of a handicap, the reporter noted. "If his six feet two of height is well burdened with adipose tissue, none of it is on his arm. That member works freely and accurately and nearly shut out the St. Louis team yesterday."[16] His age now became sort of a badge of honor, as reporters began referring to him as the G. O. M.—that is, the Grand Old Man.[17]

Comiskey's Machine Sputters

Despite having won two straight American League pennants, Charlie Comiskey understood he had to strengthen his team if he wanted to compete for another in 1902. He replaced three-fourths of his infield, signing Tom Daly, arguably the National League's best second baseman in 1901, and George Davis, arguably the older league's best shortstop in 1901. For third base, he picked up Sammy Strang, a promising young infielder who had spent 1901 with the Giants. To supplement Billy Sullivan, one of the American League's best catchers in 1901, he added Ed McFarland, one of the National League's top receivers with Philadelphia in 1901. From his intra-city rivals, the Remnants, he plucked outfielder Danny Green, another young player who seemed destined for stardom. To fortify his pitching staff he signed Ned Garvin, a regular starter for Milwaukee who led the American League in strikeouts per game in 1901 and had posted good earned run averages in the National League the two years prior to that.

Chicago (74–60)

Regular Lineup	AVG	OBP	SLG	R	RBI	SB
Sammy Strang, 3b	.295	.387	.364	108	46	38
Fielder Jones, cf	.321	.390	.370	98	54	33
Danny Green, rf	.312	.388	.391	77	62	35
George Davis, ss	.299	.386	.402	76	93	31
Sam Mertes, lf	.282	.334	.362	60	79	46
Frank Isbell, 1b	.252	.276	.318	62	59	38
Tom Daly, 2b	.225	.303	.288	57	54	19
Billy Sullivan, c	.243	.268	.323	36	26	11

or Ed McFarland, c	.228	.291	.293	29	25	8
Leading Pitchers	**W**	**L**	**PCT**	**IP**	**H**	**ERA**
Jimmy Callahan	16	14	.533	282.3	287	3.60
Roy Patterson	19	14	.576	268	262	3.06
Wiley Piatt	12	12	.500	246	263	3.51
Clark Griffith	15	9	.625	213	247	4.18
Ned Garvin	10	10	.500	175.3	169	2.21

On paper the White Stockings looked like winners—they were nearly a unanimous pre-season favorite among baseball reporters. In his analysis of the team, Chicago reporter Sy Sanborn said there was no question about the individual abilities of the players. The question, he thought, was whether they would be able to work together with a "machine-like unity, which is the only way teamwork can be developed."

During the spring, Sanborn said, they had been able to adapt very well to their teammates' styles, their work being smooth and accurate, especially around second base where the two veterans, Davis and Daly, "worked together with the certainty of a well-regulated timepiece."[18] When the White Stockings crushed Detroit, 12–2, on Opening Day, Sanborn remarked, "As inning after inning slipped away the fans began to realize something of the real strength of the machine which Comiskey has put together for them. There was a clean-cut, offhand method in the way they went about everything, which is the hallmark of confidence, experience and ability."[19]

The first month of the pennant race was a scramble involving just about all the teams except Cleveland, which had not yet been fortified with the enjoined ex-A's players. In June the White Stockings took over first place and seemed about to pull away from the field. Tim Murnane of the *Boston Globe* was, like Sanborn, impressed with the White Stockings' knowledge of scientific baseball. Murnane thought the White Stockings compared well with the Pirates, who had already run away with the National League race. "Griffith makes a fine leader," Murnane wrote the first week of June, "and with such brainy fellows as [Jimmy] Callahan, [Fielder] Jones, Daly, and Davis, and Comiskey as counselors, the Chicago crowd will be a tough one to beat."[20]

The White Stockings built their lead to five games during June, while their pursuers took turns beating each other up. Late in the month the baseball editor of the *Philadelphia Public Ledger* joined the group of writers predicting a runaway victory for the White Stockings. "For the past fortnight Chicago has played championship ball in every department of the game, and now has a good lead. The champions are as good an all round team as there is in the younger organization, with unquestionably the strongest pitching staff," he wrote. "It would seem that they will make the pennant fight in the American League pretty nearly as much of a procession as in the National League."[21]

But the anticipated Chicago victory procession didn't materialize. Comiskey's baseball machine had already started slipping a few cogs. It seems his wily veterans had not only learned the ins and outs of scientific baseball over the years, but also the whereabouts of some of the league's more accommodating late-night watering holes.

In May, Callahan came stumbling back to his Cleveland hotel at four o'clock in the morning. He encountered a bellboy, who evidently committed the transgression of having dark-colored skin. Callahan attacked him, beating and kicking him, until the police arrived. Callahan was arrested and hauled off to court.[22] Ed McFarland and Wily Piatt were more discreet in their evening activities but reportedly also imbibed a bit too freely.[23] In late August, Ned Garvin, who was never overly discreet, became involved in an argument in one of his favorite taverns. Before the disagreement could be settled, Garvin had fought with a policeman, shot the barkeeper, and fled the scene of the crime. When he sobered up he surrendered to the police. Comiskey gave him his release immediately following the incident.[24]

Even more damaging than the players' boozing was the bad luck the team endured in the area of injuries. During spring training McFarland came down with a sore arm that hampered his play for the rest of his career. He had been tough on base stealers while he caught for the Phillies; for the White Stockings he was an easy mark. Manager and star pitcher Clark Griffith had begun suffering stomach pains during the winter. As the season progressed the pain became much worse, eventually being diagnosed as a bad case of gallstones. He missed several weeks and pitched most of the season in discomfort. Callahan hurt a finger in midseason. Although he continued to pitch without missing much time, he became relatively ineffective. After entering July with a 10–2 record, he went only 6–12 over the remainder of the season. He did manage to end the year on a high note, throwing a no-hitter on September 20 to become the first pitcher in American League history to do so.[25]

Roy Patterson, the "St. Croix Wonder" who had been the hero of the 1901 season, followed about the same pattern as he had in 1901. He began the season by losing four of his first five decisions, was an "in-and-outer" until the end of August, and then finished the campaign by winning his last five decisions. But unlike 1901, when his late-season victories were the key to a strong White Stocking finish, in 1902 they were just part of the team's ho-hum fadeout to fourth place.

A Team Transformed: Cleveland

With the Blues it was a case of "if at first you don't succeed, try, try again." Their initial efforts to build a team for 1902 were not real successful. While most of the American League teams focused on the National League in their quest to improve during the 1901–02 offseason, the Blues looked elsewhere—to the Western Association, a Class A league that was attempting to replace the Western/American League in the minor league hierarchy. The Blues signed eight players from the Western Association, as well as two from the Eastern League. The only player they picked up from the National League was pitcher Dummy Taylor, who came from New York and jumped back to the Giants after making four starts for the Blues in 1902.

The influx of minor league players didn't impress too many baseball writers, who generally picked the Blues to be the upside-down champions—that is, to finish last. When the season began the Blues did their darndest to live down to the predictions. Their young pitchers threw shutouts in four of the team's first twenty-one games. That was about the only way they could win. In the other 17 games, the team went 2–15.

Obviously needing some help, the Blues began to sign players released by other teams. Their first significant addition was Elmer Flick, who had become a free agent as a result of the Lajoie decision. Flick, a native of Bedford, Ohio, was considered one of the best outfielders in baseball. He decided to sign with the Blues so he could play near his home. Ten days later the Blues signed Harry Bay, who had been released by Cincinnati. Bay had hit only .210 in 1901 for the Reds, but he was the fastest runner in baseball. For a team as bad as the Blues, he was worth a look. In Cleveland he looked pretty good. He bunted and slapped the ball for 21 hits in his first 39 at-bats, a .539 average, and showed great range in the outfield.[26]

Cleveland (69–67)

Regular Lineup	AVG	OBP	SLG	R	RBI	SB
Harry Bay, cf	.290	.343	.334	71	23	22
or Ollie Pickering, cf	.256	.306	.317	46	26	22
Bill Bradley, 3b	.340	.375	.515	104	77	11
Nap Lajoie, 2b*	.378	.419	.565	81	65	20
Charlie Hickman, 1b**	.361	.387	.539	74	110	9
Elmer Flick, rf*	.297	.377	.408	85	64	24
Jack McCarthy, lf	.284	.329	.398	45	41	12
John Gochnauer, ss	.185	.247	.237	45	37	7
Harry Bemis, c	.312	.366	.404	42	29	3
or Bob Wood, c	.295	.375	.380	23	40	1
Leading Pitchers	**W**	**L**	**PCT**	**IP**	**H**	**ERA**
Earl Moore	17	17	.500	293	304	2.95
Addie Joss	17	13	.567	269.3	225	2.77
Clarence Wright	7	11	.389	148	150	3.95
Bill Bernhard*	18	5	.783	226	176	2.15

*Includes record with Philadelphia
**Includes record with Boston

The Blues' next move was to enter the bidding war for two of the other players freed by the Lajoie decision—pitcher Bill Bernhard and Lajoie himself. The Phillies had begun negotiations with Lajoie as soon as the decision was announced, but Colonel Rogers, the Phillies' owner, characteristically over-estimated his leverage. He offered Lajoie $3,000, virtually the same amount Lajoie had received in 1900, before the baseball war broke out. Lajoie, who was guaranteed $5,000 under his contract with the Athletics even if he didn't play a game, naturally refused Rogers' offer. After Detroit tried unsuccessfully to come to terms with Lajoie, Blues owner Charles Somers began discussions with him. Somers was a wealthy man and was willing to spend liberally to promote his baseball interests. He signed both Lajoie and Bernhard to multi-year contracts at significantly higher salaries than their previous deals.[27]

Shortly after Lajoie's signing, the Blues picked up Charlie Hickman, who had just been released by Boston. Hickman was one of the top sluggers in the game. He added a valuable bat to the lineup. In the field, of course, his value was very much on the negative side of the ledger. The Blues told Charlie to stand near first base when the other team was batting, figuring he could do the least harm there.

When Lajoie made his debut in Cleveland on June 4, the Blues were buried deeply in last place with a 12–24 record. But the team had been transformed, figuratively speaking, from a bunch of 98-pound batting weaklings to a group of muscular sluggers. By Deadball Era standards Flick, Lajoie and Hickman were long-ball hitters, as was third baseman Bill Bradley. With the speedy Bay at the top of the batting order and Jack McCarthy, a good situational hitter, following the four sluggers, the Blues were now a formidable presence on offense. Bernhard joined Earl Moore and rookie Addie Joss to give the team three top-notch pitchers.

The Blues immediately showed off their newfound muscle. They took two games out of three from Boston and three out of four from Baltimore. They began a slow but steady climb up the league standings, reaching fifth place in mid–August. They were unable to close the gap that separated them from the four pennant contenders, but managed to finish two games over .500. By September they were being mentioned prominently as a team to watch in 1903.

Somers got a good return on his mid-season investments, both on the field and at the gate. In batting average his sluggers ranked first (Lajoie, .378), third (Hickman, .361) and sixth (Bradley, .340); in slugging percentage they ranked second (Lajoie, .565), third (Hickman, .539) and fourth (Bradley, .515). Hickman and Bradley tied for second in home runs with eleven each. Hickman was second in RBIs; Bradley was fourth in runs scored. Lajoie hit with his usual power, driving in and scoring runs at a high rate, though he missed too many games to finish among the leaders. The lone pitcher acquired in the mid-season deals, Bill Bernhard, more than fulfilled expectations. He went 17–5 with the Blues after winning his only game with the A's. He led the league in win-loss percentage, allowed the fewest hits per game, and held opposing batters to the lowest on-base percentage.

Lajoie was the top drawing card in baseball in 1902. At that time an attendance of 3,000 was considered a good turnout. Lajoie's first game with the Blues was designated as "Lajoie Day." Although it was played on a Wednesday, 9,827 fans crowded in to see him. They continued to turn out in good numbers throughout the season. In 1901 the Blues played before less than 2,000 fans per game. In 1902 attendance rose to over 4,200 per game.

The Blues drew well on the road, too, with Lajoie serving as the main attraction. On his first trip to Washington 4,000 fans paid to see him, cheering his every move. In Boston Lajoie's former New England neighbors flocked to the Huntington Avenue Grounds to see him play. Three games in late August drew almost 20,000 fans. Altogether, the ten Cleveland games in Boston drew over 55,000. Most baseball observers agreed with the baseball writer who, after checking out the Cleveland attendance numbers, concluded that "Lajoie and Bernhard have paid their own salaries, and left Somers quite a bunch of 'velvet.'"[28]

Not as Good as Advertised: Washington

At first glance it seemed the Senators made some pretty good moves in signing players for the 1902 season. If they had existed in our modern baseball world, the 1902 Senators would have held press conferences to announce that they had added the best pure hitter in baseball (Ed Delahanty), another batter with a lifetime average higher than .300 (Bill Keister), a good third baseman (Harry Wolverton), one of the better fielding shortstops in baseball (Fred Ely), a first baseman who rivaled Fred Tenney in his fielding skills (George Carey), and two of the National League's better pitchers of 1901 (Al Orth and Jack Townsend). Modern baseball fans, able to draw upon the experience of almost four decades of free agency, know that when the players take the field the next spring, reality tends to differ from the rosy descriptions heard at such press conferences. That was the case with too many of the 1902 Senators.

Washington (61–75)

Regular Lineup	AVG	OBP	SLG	R	RBI	SB
Jimmy Ryan, cf	.320	.384	.448	92	44	10
Jack Doyle, 2b	.247	.311	.317	52	20	6
or Harry Wolverton, 3b	.249	.292	.317	35	23	8
Ed Delahanty, lf	.376	.453	.590	103	93	16
Bill Keister, rf–2b	.300	.329	.462	82	90	27
Bill Coughlin, 3b	.301	.348	.414	84	71	29
or Watty Lee, rf-p	.256	.319	.366	61	45	8
Scoops Carey, 1b	.314	.350	.440	46	60	3
Bones Ely, ss	.262	.301	.310	39	62	3
Boileryard Clarke, c	.268	.330	.381	31	40	1
or Lew Drill, c*	.262	.347	.354	35	29	5
Leading Pitchers	**W**	**L**	**PCT**	**IP**	**H**	**ERA**
Al Orth	19	18	.514	324	367	3.97
Casey Patten	17	16	.515	299.7	331	4.05
Bill Carrick	11	17	.393	257.7	344	4.86
Jack Townsend	8	16	.333	220.3	233	4.45
Watty Lee	5	7	.417	98	118	5.05

*Includes record with Baltimore

Delahanty was still a great hitter. Near the end of the 1902 season Boston writer Tim Murnane wrote, "I consider Delahanty the most finished and best batter the game has ever produced. Lajoie, while he is a successful batsman, doesn't pick them out like Del, and many of his hits are lucky stabs and jabs. Delahanty for me all the time is the greatest of the great."[29] Delahanty led the league in slugging percentage in 1902, as well as on-base percentage. His batting average was .376, two points behind Lajoie's .378. The American League recognized Lajoie as the batting champion at the time; some modern references list Delahanty as the leader because Lajoie did not have a sufficient number of plate appearances.

Unfortunately, the Delahanty of 1902 was becoming an aging ballplayer. He had turned 34 the previous autumn, an advanced age for ballplayers of that era. He had put on weight and lost much of his speed. He was addicted to racetrack gambling and had begun the alcohol abuse that would soon lead to his premature death.[30] There were days when Del just didn't feel like playing ball and it showed in his performance. In mid–July of 1902, when big Ed ridiculed the inept play of his former Phillies team, a baseball writer responded, "Any criticism made by Delahanty may be in order, but if he could have heard a few made relative to the manner in which he played the outfield for Philadelphia in the latter part of the season of 1901 both his ears would have burned like incandescent lights."[31] Game reports show that Delahanty had days in 1902 when he wasn't exactly bubbling over with enthusiasm. He was sometimes slow in getting to balls hit his way and he didn't move around the basepaths with a lot of speed. But that big bat largely excused his other shortcomings.

The Senators likely knew what they were getting when they signed Keister. After all, John McGraw let him go without asking for any compensation. But if there was any lingering doubt about his fielding deficiencies, poor Bill removed them on the first day of spring training. He got to the park early that day and went straight to right field to prepare for the season. He quickly demonstrated that he was in mid-season form. He settled under the first fly ball hit to him, reached up for it, and booted it, injuring his little finger in the process.[32] His 1902 season was typical—filled with misjudged and dropped fly balls, poor baserunning, and some pretty good hitting. After the season ended the Senators passed him on to the Phillies.

In retrospect the Senators' acquisition of Harry Wolverton doesn't seem to make much sense. Wolverton was a good defensive infielder, but their 1901 third baseman, Bill Coughlin, was better. Wolverton could only play third base, so the Senators moved Coughlin to second base. Coughlin was a brilliant fielder who was able to make fine catches and throws while playing second, but plays around the bag were not second nature to him. He and shortstop Fred Ely constantly got mixed up on who was to cover the bag on throws. When Ely was injured in June, Coughlin moved to shortstop, where he made some great plays but again had difficulty with the mental part of the position.[33]

Meanwhile, Wolverton never seemed to settle in with the Senators. Harry couldn't seem to stop worrying about the implications of the Lajoie decision. He was slow in fielding bunts while he played for the Senators and couldn't get going at the plate. Washington baseball writers noted that there just wasn't any spark to his play. In July he complained of sickness and asked manager Tom Loftus for some time off. Loftus agreed, so Harry headed for the Jersey shore to rest and reflect on his troubles. After a few days Loftus received a telegram. It stated, "Have decided to rejoin the Philadelphia National League club. If there are any financial differences let me know. Harry Wolverton." Somewhat miffed at Harry's abrupt departure, Loftus responded, "Washington people are tickled to death. Tom Loftus." After a few days Loftus cooled down and said that Wolverton was a good guy who had just found himself in a bad situation.[34]

His work for the Phillies in 1901 seemed to indicate that Jack Townsend would be one of baseball's better pitchers. He played a key role in the pennant stretch drive and batters had not been able to hit his pitches very well. He had given up the fewest hits per game of any National League pitcher. There were some signs, however, that Townsend still had a ways to go to prove himself. He had pitched only 144 innings in 1901—not enough to establish a good track record. And he tended towards wildness, averaging four walks per game and sometimes approaching double figures in bases on balls in a game.

With the Senators, Townsend displayed both traits. He could be very hard to hit at times. His fastball was quick and seemed to have late movement. In June catcher Bill Clarke had to take the next day off after the battering his hands took from catching

Townsend's pitches.[35] When Jack Doyle came to the Senators in July he was impressed with Townsend's stuff. Doyle noted that Kid Nichols had built a successful career around a fastball with a "jump" on it. "Townsend has the same kind of a free-arm delivery that the Kid had," Doyle said," and there is no reason why he shouldn't make as great a pitcher."[36]

But with the Senators Townsend never gained consistent control of his pitches. He had a number of games in which he would be unhittable for a few innings, then would lose his touch, getting behind in the count early, walking batters, and giving up hits by the bunches. He was never able to conquer that weakness. His mediocre 8–16 record in 1902 was his best in four seasons with the Senators and another with Cleveland.

A Team Too Fiery: Detroit

Two American League teams self-destructed in 1902—the Orioles and the Tigers. As one would expect from any team closely associated with John McGraw, the Orioles' destruction came with plenty of fireworks, featuring inter-league intrigue, public charges and countercharges between McGraw and Ban Johnson, movement of star players, takeover of the team by the American League, and eventually the use of the franchise to create an American League team in New York City. The Tigers' self-destruction was more subtle, more like a smoldering fire from within, one that consumed the 1902 team but left the basic structure of the franchise intact for future rebuilding.

The 1901 Detroit team had been a feisty outfit. It managed to finish third more because of the competitive fire within its top players than due to the raw talent they possessed. Their leading players were fierce competitors who played the game to the hilt, winning because they did the little things that pay off in the long run. They relied on the sacrifice, hit-and-run, and aggressive baserunning to create runs. They weren't an easy group to get along with, for either opponents or teammates. Their keystone combination featured two adult "kids" who were noted for their prickly personalities. Shortstop Kid Elberfeld became known as the "Tobasco Kid" because of a hot temper that led to numerous run-ins with umpires and league officials. Second baseman Kid Gleason had a "don't mess with me" approach to life. Outfielder Ducky Holmes had created a sensation a few years earlier when he used an anti–Semitic slur while expressing his dislike of New York Giants owner Andrew Freedman. Catcher Fritz Buelow entered the 1902 season nursing resentment over the disparity between his salary and that paid to Jim McGuire to get him to jump his Brooklyn contract. Pitcher Roscoe Miller and outfielder Jimmy Barrett had testy personalities.

These players were the leaders of the 1902 team. Over the winter the team had brought in McGuire and Cincinnati outfielder Dick Harley from the National League. Pitcher Win Mercer moved over from Washington. Young George Mullin was signed out of Fort Wayne of the Western Association. These additions helped some, but the core of the 1901 team was being asked to compete in the much-tougher American League of 1902.

Detroit (52–83)

Regular Lineup	AVG	OBP	SLG	R	RBI	SB
Jimmy Barrett, cf	.303	.397	.387	93	44	24
Dick Harley, lf	.281	.345	.344	59	44	20
Doc Casey, 3b	.273	.338	.352	69	55	22
Kid Elberfeld, ss	.260	.348	.326	70	64	19
Ducky Holmes, rf	.257	.319	.337	50	33	16
Pop Dillon, 1b*	.208	.261	.264	22	22	2
or Erve Beck 1b	.296	.313	.358	23	22	3
or Sport McAllister, ut*	.204	.230	.254	19	33	1
Kid Gleason, 2b	.247	.292	.297	42	38	17
or Joe Yeager, ut, p	.242	.282	.360	17	23	0
Deacon McGuire, c	.227	.300	.323	27	23	0
or Fritz Buelow, c	.223	.256	.290	23	29	3
Leading Pitchers	**W**	**L**	**PCT**	**IP**	**H**	**ERA**
Win Mercer	15	18	.455	281.7	282	3.04
George Mullin	13	16	.448	260	282	3.67
Ed Siever	8	11	.421	188.3	166	1.91
Roscoe Miller	6	12	.333	148.7	158	3.69
Joe Yeager	6	12	.333	140	171	4.82

*Includes record with Baltimore

The overmatched Tigers managed to compete for the first few weeks of the 1902 pennant race, but it was a struggle. The scientific baseball tactics that worked in 1901 were much less effective against the improved infields of 1902. By mid–June the team had decided to back off of the bunting game somewhat. Sometime later, after the team seemed to switch back, sacrificing three times in a game, Detroit writer Joe Jackson asked Elberfeld about the team's strategy. "The reason we have not been bunting is because we went bad doing it," Elberfeld explained. "When we found we all went wrong and could not lay them down right we quit until we got out of that rut."[37]

Poor bunting wasn't the Tigers' only problem on offense. A week after Elberfeld admitted the Tigers weren't bunting well, sportswriter Jackson bemoaned the poor luck the team was having with the hit-and-run game. The tactic twice killed potential rallies in a recent contest, Jackson said, when batters smashed line drives directly to waiting outfielders who doubled up baserunners who had already neared second base when the ball was hit. "Detroit has devoted itself to the hit-and-run play, which when it works is the money," Jackson said. "When it doesn't work," he continued, "it gives a team a very foolish appearance."[38] The Tigers appeared particularly foolish when one looked at the team's runs scored column. They were running a poor last in that category.

In late June the Tigers hit a rough spell in which they dropped several games below .500. At about that time Mercer received an offer to play and manage in the California League at a higher salary than the Tigers were paying him. He couldn't decide whether to accept the offer or remain loyal to the Tigers, sharing his anguish with Detroit sportswriters and, through them, with the city's fans. Mercer cleaned out his locker and announced he would depart for the West Coast from Chicago when the team played its next series there. When the big day arrived, Mercer said he had changed his mind and would remain with the Tigers.[39]

Shortly after the Mercer drama ended, the Tigers began a streak that would result in ten losses over eleven games. Midway through that streak, Mercer asked out of a game after throwing four pitches that resulted in two base hits. He claimed he had strained a tendon in his arm. Miller came into the game after throwing only a few warmup pitches and gave up five runs before getting out of the inning. After the game several Tigers angrily criticized Mercer, claiming he just wanted to avoid taking a beating. (Mercer took his regular turn a week later.) Manager Frank Dwyer kept the players in the locker room while he delivered a lecture. Detroit newspapers reported that some of the players were accusing others of not giving their best efforts.[40]

A few days later Miller took a 9–2 beating at the hands of the Senators. In the first inning of the game the Tigers made six hits but scored only two runs because of baserunning gaffes. In his game summary Joe Jackson reported that several of the Senators reached base on hits that might have been outs had the Detroit fielders tried harder to reach the ball. After the game Miller confronted a teammate, saying he was "sulking" and not trying to win. A couple of days later Miller left the team, signing to play the rest of the year and 1903 with the New York Giants.[41]

The Giants' new manager, John McGraw, was also talking with Elberfeld. A month later McGraw waved a document before a group of New York reporters, saying it was a two-year contract with Elberfeld. Back in Detroit, the Tobasco Kid denied he had signed any such document. "I was foolish to talk to McGraw at all," he said. "I talked with McGraw because I was a little discouraged at the way things were breaking against the team and against myself. The outlook wasn't very bright and it had its effect on me. But I am no jumper."[42]

While Elberfeld seemed able to move past the discouraging atmosphere surrounding the team, other Tigers could not. Team captain Doc Casey became upset when Detroit management asked him to agree to go to Baltimore in exchange for Jimmy Williams. Casey had just refused offers from the National League while the team was in the East. He refused to go to Baltimore but announced he would now accept offers to play in another city in 1903. At the end of August Ducky Holmes abruptly left the team without permission. He told reporters he had an offer to play for his hometown Des Moines team that would bring more money than he was getting from the Tigers.[43]

In addition to the discontent among its veteran players, other developments contributed toward a circus-like atmosphere surrounding the team. When Ban Johnson asked American League teams to help out the besieged Baltimore club, most of them looked toward the end of the bench to see if they had a non-productive reserve they could spare. The Tigers sent their regular first baseman, starting left fielder, and top utility player before taking back two of the three because the team couldn't function without them.

Miller's departure had left the team short on pitchers. The team was carrying only four regular starters plus Joe Yeager, who served as both a fifth starter and a utility player. Yeager's arm wasn't yet strong enough for regular work. It became sore after a couple of starts. The Tigers then went with a three-man rotation of Mercer, George Mullin, and Ed Siever. Sportswriter Jackson remarked that the three were pitching well. "If it could be assured that no arms would go bad," Jackson said, "the team could well afford to trust to the men that it has until Yeager gets back to afford relief to the trio."[44]

Of course, sore arms tended to be a problem with three-man rotations. On August 11, Siever became hooked up in a tight pitchers' duel with Rube Waddell. As the game progressed, his arm became weaker and weaker. By the ninth inning he appeared to be doing little more than lobbing the ball over the plate. The A's began smashing the ball hard that inning but still couldn't push a run across the plate until the thirteenth inning. Siever had torn a muscle in his shoulder. He told manager Dwyer about the injury but was asked to finish the game. Afterwards, Siever gamely tried to pitch two more times in 1902, making it into the third inning before coming out of both games. He was sent home at the beginning of September in hopes that a winter of rest would bring his arm around.[45]

Siever's spot in the rotation was taken by Arch McCarthy, a recruit from an independent team in Tecumseh, Michigan. McCarthy started eight games and relieved in two for the Tigers in 1902, the only season he pitched in the major leagues. Five other recruits pitched for the Tigers before the season ended, one of them taking leave from his semi-professional team in St. Louis for the occasion. In September the Tigers had cameo appearances from three semi-professional position players, and gave a lengthy tryout to another. During the season they had used Yeager and McAllister in a wide variety of roles, with Yeager pitching and playing five different fielding positions, while McAllister played every position except pitcher and center field. As the season drew to an end Jackson decried the constant shuffling of players. "Count each man for each time he has played any position, and Detroit has had forty-five performers," Jackson wrote. "With so much shifting, so frequent changes, teamwork can hardly be looked for, either at bat or in the field."[46]

Orioles and Patriots

John McGraw seemed to do a pretty good job of recruiting over the winter of 1901–02. He plugged a hole at first base by bringing in Dan McGann from the St. Louis Cardinals. He picked up smooth-fielding Billy Gilbert from Milwaukee to replace the error-prone Bill Keister. He brought in a new outfield consisting of top-ranked players: Joe Kelley and Jimmy Sheckard from Brooklyn and Kip Selbach from New York. And he strengthened his pitching staff by signing Tom Hughes, a young pitcher with great stuff who had pitched well for the Chicago Remnants in 1901. These stars would help offset the Orioles' only significant loss. Mike Donlin was spending the season of 1902 in jail, the result of a drunken escapade in which he had attacked an actress as she emerged from a theater, beating her severely.

Baltimore Orioles (31–41—thru July 18)

Regular Lineup	AVG	OBP	SLG	R	RBI	SB
Joe Kelley, cf	.311	.405	.464	50	34	12
Kip Selbach, lf*	.320	.393	.427	86	60	22

Jimmy Williams, 2b*	.313	.361	.500	83	83	14
Dan McGann, 1b	.316	.378	.420	40	42	17
Cy Seymour, rf	.268	.317	.386	38	41	12
Roger Bresnahan, 3b-c	.272	.337	.409	30	34	12
Billy Gilbert, ss*	.245	.327	.299	74	38	38
Wilbert Robinson, c*	.293	.321	.391	38	57	11
Leading Pitchers	**W**	**L**	**PCT**	**IP**	**H**	**ERA**
Harry Howell*	9	15	.375	199	243	4.12
Joe McGinnity	13	10	.565	198.7	219	3.44
Long Tom Hughes**	10	8	.556	157.7	171	3.71

*Season total
**Includes record with Boston

But the new season didn't go well for McGraw. After the Lajoie decision, Sheckard once again jumped back to Brooklyn. McGraw was thrown out of the season opener in Boston, and a couple of weeks later was fined and suspended for five days after a run-in with umpire Jack Sheridan. On May 24 he was severely spiked in the knee that had been injured the previous season. Infection set in, forcing him out of the lineup for a month. His Orioles, despite an injection of veteran players well acquainted with the elements of scientific baseball, were inconsistent. They played well at times, but all too often they found themselves outwitted by their opponents. They struggled to play .500 ball. On June 8, as the Orioles began a swing through the western cities, Hughes strained a muscle in his shoulder, a serious injury that would sideline him for much of the season.

McGraw, still recuperating from his knee injury, had not made the western trip with the Orioles. He remained in Baltimore, stewing over his franchise's future and his own. He was convinced that Ban Johnson intended to get rid of him as part of a plan to move the Baltimore franchise to New York. On June 18 McGraw went to New York, where he met with Andrew Freedman. He agreed to become the Giants' manager at a generous salary, and he and Freedman agreed upon a plan to disrupt and possibly destroy the American League. On June 28, back in the Orioles' lineup, McGraw and Kelley became involved in a strenuous argument with umpire Tom Connally. Both were ejected from the game and later suspended by Johnson.

McGraw used the suspension as a justification for severing his ties with the Orioles. The team continued to play for two weeks while McGraw's melodrama drew headlines, although the distraction took its toll after a few days. The team McGraw put together had lost its last six games when Freedman took it over. The forfeited game of July 18 brought the streak to seven, dropped the team's record to 31–41 and began a wild ride over the last three months of the season, marked by constant arrivals and departures of players and games that sometimes rose to the highest standards of professional play but often fell to almost amateurish levels.[47]

When the new Baltimore team reached Chicago on August 1, Charlie Comiskey prepared a warm welcome and a new nickname—the "Patriots." He organized a celebration with banners flying in praise of the holdover Orioles, who had remained loyal to their league and franchise. Then, of course, his players went onto the field and beat the stuffing out of the newly christened Patriots.[48]

Baltimore Patriots (19–47—after July 18)

Regular Lineup	AVG	OBP	SLG	R	RBI	SB
Herm McFarland, cf**	.309	.402	.457	59	40	11
Kip Selbach, lf*	.320	.393	.427	86	60	22
Jimmy Williams, 3b-2b*	.313	.361	.500	83	83	14
Tom Jones, 1b	.283	.292	.384	22	14	1
Harry Howell, inf-of*	.268	.312	.395	42	42	7
Harry Arndt, rf***	.254	.355	.339	41	28	9
Billy Gilbert, ss*	.245	.327	.299	74	38	38
Wilbert Robinson, c*	.293	.321	.391	38	57	11
Or Aleck Smith, c	.234	.275	.255	10	21	5
Leading Pitchers	**W**	**L**	**PCT**	**IP**	**H**	**ERA**
Snake Wiltse	7	11	.389	164	215	5.10
Charlie Shields****	4	11	.267	142.3	201	4.80
Jack Katoll	5	10	.333	123	175	4.02
Ike Butler	1	10	.091	116.3	168	5.34
Crese Heismann	0	3	.000	16	20	8.44

*Season total
**Includes record with Chicago
***Includes record with Detroit
****Does not include 3–0 record with St. Louis

Comiskey's nickname didn't quite catch on, but he had a point. The reconstituted Orioles did resemble a rag-tag group of militiamen fighting better-trained and more-skilled professionals. Therefore, it is only fitting that some from their ranks be recognized with "Badges of Honor."

For **Excellence Amid Chaos**—to **Jimmy Williams**. As a rookie in 1899 Williams hit .354 and led the National League with 27 triples. After a mediocre year with Pittsburgh in 1900, Williams once again emerged as a power hitter for the Orioles in 1901. He led the American League in triples that year, with 21, and ranked fourth in slugging percentage. In 1902, though abandoned by his most talented teammates, he continued to exert his best efforts, even when hope for victory seemed futile. Once again Williams led the league with 21 triples. He finished seventh in slugging with an excellent .500 mark.

For **Extreme Versatility**—to **Harry Howell**. Howell was a confident youngster. He was a decent, though not great, pitcher who could hit some, though not a lot. Harry thought he could play just about any position on a ball field if he were given a little practice time. When most of the Orioles' regulars hied off to New York and parts west, Harry planted himself in the infield during morning workouts, assuring new manager Wilbert Robinson he could do a good job wherever Robby needed him.[49] Well, Robby needed players just about everywhere, so he played Harry just about everywhere. Harry didn't catch, but he played every other position. He was pretty good at second base, acceptable under the circumstances in the outfield and first base, not so good at third base and shortstop. He hit .268, with some pop in his bat. After 1902 he went back to pitching, where he had a pretty good 13-year career.

For **Environmental Adaptability**—to **Kip Selbach**. Selbach was a good outfielder. He had good speed, especially for a short, stocky man, was sure-handed, and had a veteran presence about him. If a ball was catchable, Ol' Kip could be depended upon to catch it. But these were the Patriots; they played a different brand of ball than that. So on August 19 Selbach adjusted. That day the Browns sent five fly balls in his direction. He misjudged one but managed to get under it before he let it slip through his hands. He judged four of them perfectly and held on to half of those. Knowing that his teammates often made errors by the half-dozen, Kip tried to do that, too. He booted two ground balls that came his way, but had to be satisfied with a mere five errors on the day.[50]

For **Fan Favorite**—to **Harry Arndt**. Harry had just been anointed Detroit's regular left fielder before the Orioles issued a call for help. Before that, earlier in the 1902 season, he was the "Lajoie of the Michigan State League," where his specialty, according to reports, was hitting doubles and triples. Since the Michigan State League was roughly a half-step above semi-pro ball, being the league's equivalent of Nap Lajoie didn't exactly bring instant baseball immortality. But, befitting someone designated the "Lajoie" of any league, Harry punctuated his arrival in Baltimore by belting out a few clutch hits. Oriole fans—at least the ones who still cared—took him under their wing, so to speak. Harry was one of those fielders who tended to juxtapose sensational catches of difficult chances alongside rank muffs of easy opportunities. He remained a favorite even after a writer pointed out that Harry's "method of catching a fly is to stick his hands up in the air as far as possible toward the ball, something on the order in which a girl catches. It looks awkward, and may account for the two easy ones which he has dropped." After sullying Harry's reputation with that comment, the writer attempted to rehabilitate it. "On overhead catches requiring long runs he is sensational," he wrote, "and has done enough of that work to more than make up for his errors."[51]

For **Run Magnet**—to **Lewis "Snake" Wiltse**. Wiltse started the 1902 season with the Philadelphia Athletics. The A's backed Wiltse with one of the best defenses in the league and scored a bushel of runs for him. Wiltse was 8–8 when he left the A's, a pretty good record considering his 5.15 ERA. Much of his success was due to the A's ability to score lots of runs while he was on the mound. With the Patriots, Wiltse was 7–11. The Baltimore defense was laughable in comparison to that of the A's, but Wiltse's ERA with the Patriots was 5.10, virtually the same as when he pitched for the A's. The Patriots were an inconsistent outfit, but when Wiltse was on the mound, they came close to matching the A's in run-scoring proclivity. In 12 of Wiltse's 19 mound appearances, the Patriots scored at least five runs. Four times they scored in double figures for Wiltse. His wins included scores of 15–5, 21–6, and 15–1. He lost one game by a 17–11 score.

Chutzpah Award—to **Crese Heismann**. Heismann started the season with Cincinnati. He appeared in five games for the Reds and seemed to do all right. He won two, lost one, and had a decent ERA. But the Reds let him go. He appeared in two games for the Toledo Mud Hens of the American Association, but lost both of them. Then he went back to pitching semi-pro ball in the Cincinnati area, still believing he could succeed at the major league level if only he had the chance. After McGraw broke up the Orioles and the American League began gathering players from hither and yon, Heismann saw his opportunity. He wrote a letter to Robinson, asking for a trial at no cost to the Patriots.⁵² Robinson signed him. He pitched his first game for the Patriots in St. Louis on August 29, losing, 7–1, allowing only seven hits but walking six batters. Robinson gave him another start in Cleveland a few days later but yanked him after Heismann gave up hits to the first three batters he faced. The next day Robby trotted Heismann out to the mound again. Heismann lasted the entire game this time, but again lost, by a 7–5 score, allowing ten hits and walking six more batters. Robby then gave the youngster his release. It is not known whether Heismann reimbursed the Patriots for his expenses. From 1904 through 1907 he pitched at the Class C and D minor league levels, roughly the equivalent of Class A ball today.

August Batting Explosion Medal—Team Award. In two consecutive games in August the Patriots were almost unstoppable at bat. On August 23 they beat up on the White Stockings' Wiley Piatt and Roy Patterson, rapping out 20 hits, drawing five walks, and taking a hit-by-pitch. They scored 14 runs. Wiltse was the featured star of the day with a grand slam home run. The Patriots took the next day off to rest up (it was a Sunday), then tore into the White Stockings again on Monday. In that game they pounded Clark Griffith and Dummy Leitner for 21 runs on 25 hits. Jimmy Williams went 6-for-6 in this game, with a double, a triple, and four RBIs. Probably embarrassed by having displayed their hitting muscles so brazenly, the Patriots returned to their softer, more modest ways after that. They were shut out in their next two games.

A Golden Glove: Jimmy Collins

For Jimmy Collins the distance between mediocrity and baseball immortality was about 950 miles, the distance between Boston and Louisville.

Collins grew up in Buffalo, New York. In 1893 he played the infield for his hometown's Eastern League team, but he was primarily an outfielder in 1894. The Boston Beaneaters purchased his contract after the 1894 season. He began the 1895 campaign as a candidate for the Beaneaters' right field position, competing against Jimmy Bannon, a pretty good hitter who couldn't field very well but was a favorite of the Boston fans. Collins came out a poor second in that competition. He got off to a slow start at bat, and became a target for criticism by the boo-birds in the stands and even by some of his teammates. On May 19, after playing only eleven games for the Beaneaters, he was sent to Louisville. The arrangement with the Colonels stipulated that they could have Collins for $500 but the Beaneaters had the right to re-purchase him at any time before May 1, 1896.

Playing regularly in the outfield for the Colonels, Collins began hitting better than he did in Boston. Nevertheless, he was still just another so-so player on a last-place team. On May 31 that changed. That day the Colonels' third baseman, Walt Preston, had a terrible time. The Baltimore Orioles were bunting against him and he couldn't handle those pesky little dump balls. He had made four errors midway through the game when Louisville manager John McCloskey decided he had to come out. McCloskey told Collins to try his hand at third.

One of the Orioles later recalled the occasion for a newspaper reporter. According to his account, as Collins assumed the new position, Hughie Jennings gave him a friendly pat on the back and told him the Orioles—who were, after all, just a congenial bunch of guys—wouldn't take unfair advantage of him. They wouldn't bunt again during that game. Supposedly, Collins replied, "That's all right, Hughie, bunt 'em down to me and I'll show you something." Having been challenged, the Orioles proceeded to drop bunts toward third. First McGraw bunted. Collins threw him out. Then Keeler bunted. Collins threw him out, too. Two more bunts. Two more outs, Collins to the first baseman. Then the Orioles quit bunting. They knew this guy was special.[53]

That's a good story. But, like some other yarns spun by the old Orioles, it's not quite true. The box score shows Collins with one assist that day, so he couldn't have thrown out four Orioles in a row. And after that game he went back to the outfield for two weeks while the Colonels played a minor league recruit at third. The new recruit wasn't a good fielder and he hit worse than he defended. On June 13 Collins was put back in at third, where he did some great work over the rest of the season.

While the old Orioles' yarn isn't *really* the truth, it *should* be. It captures the truth better than the actual facts do. Collins was truly an instant sensation as a fielder at third base. It just takes more than one game to be recognized as a great fielder. Perhaps the breakthrough for Collins came against his former teammates, the Beaneaters. In a 16-inning game against Boston on July 11, Collins handled twelve chances without an error, having nine putouts and three assists. In *The Sporting News* the next week, the Louisville correspondent wrote, "Collins has been putting up a brilliant game at third base and in the Boston games his work surpassed that of [Bill] Nash, the acknowledged king of third basemen. He is so popular with the fans in this city that the other day he was cheered when he made an error, which is quite unusual here."[54]

Collins' reputation as an outstanding third baseman started to spread. He was mentioned in *The Sporting News* column entitled "Caught on the Fly," which consisted of a collection of short notes about baseball matters. One item recounted Collins' play at third against Boston, ending with the comment, "In trying Collins at that bag, manager McCloskey seems to have uncorked a jewel of an infielder." Another item noted Collins's work at bat: "Collins, who was released by Boston because he could not hit the ball, is beginning to hit the ball hard. Since joining the Colonels he has been turned into a third baseman and leads the league in that position."[55]

Back in Boston, the Beaneaters' management saw Collins' emergence as a fine third baseman as an opportunity to solve another problem. During the 1895 season the Boston team was torn by dissension, with outfielder Tommy McCarthy leading one faction and Nash the other. Manager Frank Selee was determined to get rid of both players. The first step in doing so was to exercise the team's option to re-purchase Collins. Selee did that at the end of August. In November he traded Nash to Philadelphia and sold McCarthy to Brooklyn. When the Nash trade was announced, a writer explained why the Beaneaters were willing to part with him. "Boston will miss Nash," he wrote, "but his services, it is claimed, can easily be dispensed with as young Collins, who became a star third baseman while with Louisville, will take his place."[56]

Collins rejoined his old team in the spring of 1896. By the end of spring training, his teammates and Boston's baseball writers were enthralled with his play. Shortstop Herman Long praised him, saying, "I think he is the greatest third baseman in the business." Newspaperman Tim Murnane went even further: "To my way of thinking

Collins will prove the greatest third baseman who ever wore a Boston uniform, and that's saying considerable."[57] Such high expectations carried a high risk for disappointment. While Collins played well enough in 1896, his season was marred by two serious injuries, the first taking him out of the lineup for seven weeks and the second for a month. He appeared in only 84 games, batting .296 with some power. He led National League third basemen in chances per game, handling 4.7 per outing while the next best mark was 4.2 per game. His .909 fielding average ranked fifth.

In 1897 Collins lived up to his fans' high expectations. He hit .346, with 28 doubles, 13 triples and six home runs, scored 103 runs and drove in 132. His RBI total was second best in the league, his slugging percentage tenth best. Once again he handled more chances per game than any other third baseman. That season the Beaneaters and Orioles battled for the pennant down to the last week of the season. The Beaneaters led by .006 when the two teams met with only six games remaining.

While the Beaneaters were taking infield practice before the first game, a bad-hop grounder hit Collins in the eye. Within a few minutes the eye had swollen shut. The Beaneaters bathed the eye in cold water and tried to keep the lids open by applying a substance called "sticking plaster." Collins was able to squint through the swelling and see well enough to play. The Orioles knew about his injury and tested him by bunting a few times, but abandoned the tactic after Collins made the play each time. The Beaneaters won the game but lost the next day, setting up a crucial meeting in the last game of the series. More than 25,000 fans crowded into the park and onto the field to see that game. The Beaneaters slugged their way to a 19–10 win, taking advantage of ground rules awarding a double to any ball hit into the crowd. Collins had three doubles and a single, including two doubles in a nine-run seventh inning. The Beaneaters went on to beat Brooklyn in their next two games to clinch the pennant.[58]

His strong 1897 season established Collins as the best third baseman in the National League. His good hitting seemed to serve as a validation of his remarkable fielding ability, somewhat like the voting for modern Gold Glove awards. Praise came not only from teammates and the press corps but also from opposing players.

Washington pitcher Win Mercer said, "Jimmy Collins, of the Boston team, hasn't a weakness that I know of as a fielding third baseman. He can take a running dive for a bunt that is dropped into his territory, nail the ball with one hand and cut off the runner at first. And he can plow up the speedy bounders on a run, or collect flies on a forward or backward run and hold the ball and touch his man on a steal from second to third."[59] Patsy Donovan said, "It is fairly impossible to bunt with Collins. I used to drop the ball only eight or nine feet into the diamond, and he would throw me out, a feat that no other third baseman in the country could accomplish off me."[60]

Boston reporters generally viewed Collins as not just the best active third baseman but the best in the game's history. One wrote, "Collins is recognized as not only the premier third baseman of the country but the best player on that bag that ever lived." That view gained currency among baseball followers over the next few years. In 1899 the editor of *The Sporting News* answered a question from a reader by stating, "Many experts consider Collins the best third baseman the game ever knew."[61] After a while, whenever someone wanted to tout the abilities of an outstanding third baseman, he would necessarily begin by drawing a comparison with Collins, who became the gold standard for third basemen much as teammate Fred Tenney was for first basemen.

Although his fame is based on his fielding ability, Collins was also one of the better hitters in baseball for nearly a decade. He hit better than .300 five times and was in the top ten in his league in slugging percentage five times. In 1898 he led the National League with 15 home runs, a high total for the era. Eleven of those were popped over the short left field wall in Boston.

Although he had the ability to bunt and hit-and-run, he preferred swinging away at the ball. Under Beaneaters manager Frank Selee, Collins started out in the sixth or seventh spot in the batting order, then moved up to fourth or fifth beginning with the 1898 season. Those were the positions in the lineup where the hitter would be least constrained by scientific baseball strategies. He would be expected to hit away in an effort to drive in baserunners or, with the bases empty, just try to hit the ball hard. As manager of the Boston American League team, Collins sometimes batted in the third

For decades Jimmy Collins was considered either the best or second-best third baseman in baseball history (Library of Congress).

or fourth spot, but often put himself in the number two spot in the order, where the sacrifice or hit-and-run plays were more often called for. However, even batting second, Collins would often hit away rather than sacrifice. Boston sportswriters frequently criticized him for that strategy, and as batting averages declined, Collins tended to employ scientific baseball strategies more frequently.

Collins' fame as a great third baseman long outlived the Deadball Era. In 1924 he was named in *Baseball Magazine* as one of the top 25 players of all time. E. B. Hanna, the author of the article, wrote, "There has been but one Jimmy Collins—graceful, fast, easy, deft; a first-class hitter, sure and quick fielder to the right or left, a thrower whose work stood out even in a position where fine throwers have been numerous."[62] A decade later, when voting began for the Baseball Hall of Fame, Collins received serious consideration but never came close to being elected. There always seemed to be about a dozen other stars rated ahead of him. And considering that the voters were busy weighing the relative merits of Ty Cobb, Babe Ruth, Tris Speaker, Cy Young, Christy Mathewson, and possibly the voter's childhood baseball idol, it is easy to understand why Collins might have been overlooked. In the 1939 election, even Rogers Hornsby failed to get enough votes to be selected. Collins gained entrance to the Hall in 1945, when he was one of ten old-timers selected by a special committee.

As late as 1958, Collins was still generally considered either the best or second-best third baseman of all time, more or less sharing the honor with Pie Traynor. That year *Sport* magazine conducted a poll to name the top player in each position for the two major leagues. Collins was selected as the best third baseman in American League history, Traynor as the best in the National League. With the advent of power-hitting third basemen, such as Eddie Mathews and Mike Schmidt, and a generally greater emphasis on longevity in evaluating the careers of top players, Collins' place among the game's third basemen has fallen dramatically. In his 2001 historical baseball abstract, Bill James rated Collins as the seventeenth-best third baseman in baseball history.[63]

"Scoops": George Carey

The "feel good" story of 1902 was the success enjoyed by George "Scoops" Carey. The long-time minor league star showed not only that he belonged in the major leagues, but that he could be one of the best first basemen in baseball.

Carey was 31 years old in 1902. He had started playing professional baseball ten years earlier, with the Altoona Mountaineers of the Class B Pennsylvania State League. He made his major league debut with Baltimore in 1895, playing 123 games at first base as the Orioles won the second of their three straight pennants. Carey was a whiz with the glove for the Orioles. By May of 1895 he was being touted as another great discovery uncovered by the astute Ned Hanlon. "George Carey is one of the greatest finds of the year," claimed one sportswriter. "He has saved several Orioles from errors by his great pickups of badly thrown balls." Another said, "Hughie Jennings is a great shortstop, but take that mittened marvel, Carey, off of first base and Hughie would harvest a lot of wild throws every day." The Baltimore infielders said Carey was so good that when they picked up a tough grounder, they just threw in the general direction of first base, confident that Carey would catch anything close to the bag.[64]

Carey led National League first basemen in fielding that year, making only eleven errors for a fielding average of .987. But with the bat he was at the other end of the rankings. He hit .261, which would be mediocre for a first baseman in almost any baseball season. But 1895 wasn't just any season. The National League as a whole, including pitchers, hit .296 that year. Eight first basemen hit better than .300. Only one first baseman in the entire league ranked below Carey with the bat, and that was a guy who doubled as a catcher. A month after the 1895 season ended, the astute Hanlon started to look for another first baseman. He sold Carey's contract to Syracuse of the Class A Eastern League, and Scoops began an odyssey that would take him to seven different cities over the next six seasons.

Carey's defensive skills had made a deep impression on the other National League teams. During the recruiting season he continually showed up on their radar screens— or at least he would have if radar had been invented then. In 1897 he hit .351 for

Reading of the Class B Atlantic League, the fourth-best mark in the league. The Louisville Colonels thought that was good enough to warrant another major league trial. They drafted Scoops and put him on first to start the 1898 season. Unfortunately, the Colonels got off to a slow start, losing nine of their first twelve games. Carey's anemic .188 batting average wasn't helping the team very much. His spot at first base was given to a young man named Honus Wagner, who appeared to be a better hitter than Scoops. Carey was shipped off to Minneapolis of the Western League.

Carey had a couple of good years at Minneapolis. He hit .336 for the Millers in 1899, and the next spring, after he had moved on to Buffalo, a Chicago newspaper reported that the Colts were trying to get him. The deal didn't go through, however, and Carey spent that year and the next with the Bisons. He hit only .271 in 1900, and was passed up when the American League teams went looking for players to bolster their newly declared status as a major league. In 1901, he improved to .315, and the Senators decided to take a chance on him for 1902.

Carey's performance in the minor leagues only strengthened his reputation as a great fielder. In 1899 *The Sporting News* ran a short biographical sketch of him in which it said Scoops "is conceded to be the best fielding first baseman in the profession."[65] When describing Chicago's negotiations for Carey in 1900, the *Chicago Tribune* reporter explained, "Carey will be remembered for his connection with the Baltimore and other National League clubs several years ago. He is a remarkable fielder, but until recently he has been considered a weak batter."[66] At times reporters would describe fancy one-handed catches at first base by calling them "George Carey plays." While managing Cleveland, Jim McAleer once reproved a young first baseman for attempting a one-hand catch. "Too much Carey there," McAleer shouted, and instructed the youngster to use two hands when catching the ball.[67]

During spring training of 1902, Scoops was a center of attention. "From the stand Carey appears to be about seven feet tall, with arms that extend nearly to his knees," a reporter wrote. "As a matter of fact, he is something over 72 inches. His hands have a faculty of scooping up almost anything that comes his direction, and it was the prediction yesterday that his ability to cut three or four feet off the flight of a ball from third or short would stop many a hit and save many an error to the man unfortunate enough to throw low to first."[68] Once the season started, Carey drew attention with his characteristic "split," which enabled him to reach far for throws. And he played 29 games and accepted 305 chances before he made his first error.

Perhaps best of all, however, was Carey's batting. After a slow start he began hitting the ball hard and it started dropping in for base hits. By June he was batting .328, and speculation about his ability to hit major league pitching died down. In July his average dropped to .276, but he brought it up slowly. In September he had a hot streak, rapping out 25 hits in 58 at-bats, a .431 pace that helped raise his average to its final level of .314. As the season drew to a close, baseball writers from each American League city selected an all-star team. Carey received the vote of the Baltimore writer as the best first baseman in the league.[69] Harry Davis received five of the eight votes to finish well ahead of Carey in the voting. But for a man who had spent all but a couple weeks over the previous six years in the minors, even that one vote was a reason to feel a great sense of satisfaction.

If 1902 was the season when things came together for Carey, 1903 was the season they fell apart again. Scoops had spent all those years in the minors because his game had holes in it. While he had great hands at first base, he was not particularly agile. And he was a very slow baserunner playing in an era when speed was important. In the spring of 1903 manager Tom Loftus, frustrated by his team's lack of speed, joked to reporters that they should organize a footrace featuring lead-footed catcher Bill Clarke, overweight Ed Delahanty, and Carey. He suggested that two other players, who were at the time disabled with leg injuries, could be added to the race to increase the interest.[70]

Carey started the season with his customary batting slump, and near the end of June his nose was fractured on an unexpected throw. He was batting only .202 on July 23 when Loftus told him to take the train over to Baltimore, where the Buffalo team was playing the minor league Orioles, and see if he could trade himself back to the Bisons.[71] Carey ended up playing for both Buffalo and Nashville before the season ended. He continued playing in the minor leagues until 1909, when he was 38, but never again played for a major league team.

An All-American Guy: Dave Fultz

Dave Fultz represented the finest aspects of American society during the Victorian Era. When the Boy Scouts of America were formed in 1910, they could have pointed to Fultz as a model for youngsters to imitate. Fultz didn't smoke, didn't drink, and some claim he didn't curse. He honored the Sabbath by refusing to play professional sports on Sundays. Fultz was an American blueblood, born into a prominent Virginia family. His mother's great-grandfather, John Morton, was a Colonial leader, having served in the Continental Congress and signed the Declaration of Independence. His father's ancestry included a captain in the Revolutionary Army. His grandfather was a prominent Virginia judge and his father was an officer in the Confederate Army.

In addition to all that, Fultz was one heck of an athlete. At Brown University he ran track and was captain of both the football and baseball teams. He made Walter Camp's College All-American teams as a halfback in 1896 and 1897. The Brown University baseball teams he captained won the national championship in 1896 and the Eastern championship in 1897. The 1897 team also defeated the Western champion in a three-game series.

Fultz was 5'11" and weighed 170 pounds, which made him a relatively big man for his time. He was a very fast runner. But probably his greatest attribute in sports was his indomitable spirit. While playing for Brown he dislocated his shoulder. Feeling he could not let his teammates down, he had his arm strapped to his side in a manner that allowed the use of his forearm. He played several games that way. At times he also played using a heavy knee brace to protect his often-injured knees. A teammate later said of Fultz, "He was absolutely conscientious, fearless, and a good leader."[72]

When Fultz graduated from Brown in 1898, several National League teams tried to sign him. Harry Pulliam, the president of the Louisville Colonels, visited Fultz in Providence. The two men agreed upon terms, but Fultz did not sign while with Pul-

Dave Fultz was an All-American football player before playing major league baseball. He later became a prominent lawyer (Library of Congress).

liam. He wanted to obtain his mother's consent, Fultz told Pulliam. Meanwhile, Fultz's teammate, Billy Lauder, signed with the Philadelphia Phillies. Fultz then sent a telegram to Pulliam, saying he would not sign with Louisville, that he would only play with the same team as his good friend Lauder. The two Brown products joined the Phillies in July.[73]

Philadelphia fans were eager to see Fultz and Lauder play. College baseball and football were popular sports in the 1890s, and the two Brown University stars were well known among eastern sports fans. Both youngsters played well, though they were not yet polished players. Phillies fans, hungry for any display of scientific baseball from their team, were especially happy when Fultz began dropping down bunts and sprinting to first, often beating out the throw for a hit. A Philadelphia writer commented, "Fultz is a clever bunter, and can give the other Philadelphia players lessons in the art of sacrificing." In September Fultz received permission from Philadelphia management to leave the team early so he could coach the football team at the University of Missouri.[74]

Fultz had played second base for Brown. The Phillies' second baseman was Nap Lajoie, which meant Fultz had no chance of winning a regular job at that position with the Phillies. He played only two games for them in 1899 before drawing his release. He soon caught on with the Baltimore Orioles, spending a half-season under John McGraw's tutelage. McGraw's emphasis on aggressive baserunning fit in well with Fultz's football mentality. Fultz played 57 games for the Orioles, splitting his time between the outfield and third base. He hit .295 with only five extra-base hits in 210 at-bats, an indication that the bunt remained a major component of his game.

After the 1899 season Fultz made arrangements to play football again, this time as a halfback for the Duquesne Country and Athletic Club. The season turned out to be a rough one, as he sustained a serious injury to one of his knees. He recovered in time for the baseball season. As part of the National League consolidation, his contract was sold to Milwaukee, where he played second base and shortstop for Connie Mack.

The fall of 1900 brought another return to football, this time with another team from the Pittsburgh area, the Homestead Library Athletic Club. There Fultz was joined by a number of other former Ivy League football standouts. The Homestead team played in a professional league in which teams were to be composed of players who had exhausted their college eligibility. Fultz played two seasons for the Homestead team, then turned to coaching for several football seasons after that. He remained active in football as a referee until he was in his fifties.[75]

Fultz followed Mack to Philadelphia for the 1901 season. He began the season as an infielder, but his fielding deficiencies at both second base and shortstop contributed to the team's poor start. Mack had holes in the outfield as well as the infield, so he soon moved Fultz to center field, where he could use his speed to great advantage. Fultz developed into an outstanding outfielder. Where he really stood out, however, was on the basepaths.

The former All-American halfback was always looking for an opening that would allow him to take an extra base. In July of 1901 a Detroit writer said, "Fultz is about the headiest player on Connie Mack's team. He is a fast and daring baserunner and has scored more runs for his team than any other player."[76] The Detroit writer seemed to overlook Nap Lajoie, who was in the middle of a super season in which he eventually scored 145 runs, but Fultz did lead the rest of the A's in runs scored. He hit .292 and tallied 95 runs.

The 1902 season was even better for Fultz. He followed Topsy Hartsel in the batting order. Topsy seemed to always be on base, which enabled Fultz to capitalize on his bunting ability and to pick up hits using the hit-and-run. He and Hartsel both continually challenged opposing fielders with their aggressive baserunning. After one game a Cleveland writer saluted the two speedsters. "On the bases the locals were clearly outclassed, Davy Fultz of football fame and Topsy Hartsel purloining six bases between them," he wrote. "Not satisfied with twice stealing second base, the ex-collegian [Fultz] purloined third also and ended up by stealing home while Moore was delivering the ball to the batter."[77]

Against Detroit's Arch McCarthy, a semi-pro graduate who had not yet learned to hold runners close to the base, Fultz rapped out a single, then stole second, third and home. He did that in the second inning, but with the A's holding a good lead, was content to steal only one other base in the game.[78] Fultz and Hartsel tied for the league lead in runs scored in 1902 with 109. Fultz led the league in sacrifices with 35 and finished third in stolen bases with 44.

With the bidding for star players reaching a fever pitch during the summer of 1902, Fultz found his services in great demand. When Charlie Ebbets offered him a two-year contract at $5,600 each year to play for the Superbas in 1903, Fultz told

Mack he would sign with Ebbets unless Mack matched the offer. Connie had a lot of admiration for Fultz's competitive drive and his understanding of the game. But his admiration didn't reach $11,200. So Fultz left the A's and ended up playing for the new American League team in New York at about $6,000 per year.[79]

Mack's judgment about Fultz proved to be correct. The injuries he had suffered on the gridiron began to affect his play on the diamond in 1903. He played in only 79 games in 1903 and 97 in 1904, batting .224 and .274, respectively. He scored a meager 39 runs each of those two seasons. He came back to play almost the entire season in 1905, but the campaign and his career came to an end on September 30 after he collided with shortstop Kid Elberfeld, suffering a broken jaw and other injuries that kept him hospitalized for a week.

Welcome to the Big Leagues, Mr. Joss

In late October of 1901 Rube Waddell was invited to come up to Wisconsin to pitch in a semi-pro matchup between Kenosha and Racine. Both teams claimed to be Wisconsin's best. Rube was promised a good wad of cash by Kenosha's backers and he enjoyed the chance to show off against inferior competition. On the day of the game, Rube hopped off the train and made his way to the local ballpark. After his Kenosha teammates went down in order in the top of the first, Rube gave the locals a look at his overpowering fastball, striking out the side.

In the top of the second inning Rube came to the plate with two men on base. Once again, he gave a lesson on how the big leaguers do things. He picked out an outside fastball and lined it to the fence. Rube legged out a triple while driving in two runners to give his team a 2–0 lead. Rube's next demonstration of big league baseball didn't go so well. He tried to steal home but was tagged out easily by the waiting catcher.

Rube's show continued for two more innings. The Racine batters couldn't do much with his major league stuff. The heart of the Racine batting order struck out in the second inning and the bottom three whiffed their way through the third. In the fourth Racine scored on a walk, two stolen bases, and a sacrifice fly. In the fifth a single, two more stolen bases, and an error allowed Racine to tie the score. Rube grew tired as the game progressed and Racine pushed two more runs across.

Meanwhile, the Racine pitcher was steadily mowing down the Kenosha batters. In the ninth inning, trailing, 4–2, Kenosha picked up two singles with two men out. Once again Rube came to the plate with men on base. This time, however, the outcome was different. The Racine pitcher, a tall lanky kid, reached back for a little extra. He fired three pitches past Rube and walked off the mound the victor over one of the most famous (though at that time not yet very successful) pitchers in the country.[80]

The Racine pitcher was Addie Joss and his matchup with Rube became an event of great local pride over the next several decades. As Rube was for Kenosha, Joss was something of a ringer for the Racine team, though he was a native of the area and had been recruited earlier in the fall. He had just completed his second professional baseball season, going 25–18 for Toledo in the Class A Western Association. Joss's semi-pro matchup with Rube didn't cause any big waves outside of the local area, but his record with Toledo brought major league agents buzzing around him. He quickly discovered that playing baseball was a relatively straightforward task compared to dealing with the machinations of baseball moguls.

In September Brooklyn president Charlie Ebbets had completed a sweep through the Western Association, talking with several of the league's best players. When he returned to Brooklyn he announced the signing of six players, including Joss. Addie denied he had signed with Brooklyn, but the Superbas continued to claim him throughout the offseason.

During the winter Charles Strobel, owner of the Toledo team, visited Joss at his home in Juneau, Wisconsin. Strobel gave Joss a $150 advance for 1902 but did not obtain the young pitcher's signature on a contract. Like Ebbets, Strobel announced that Joss would be playing for his team in 1902. Before spring training started, Cleveland manager Bill Armour made the trek to Juneau. Armour managed to get Joss's signature to a 1902 contract, and shortly afterward Joss reported to New Orleans for spring training with the Blues.

Joss pitched well during the spring and was on his way to Cleveland with the team when he received an unpleasant surprise. Strobel had filed a lawsuit charging Joss with obtaining money under false pretenses, a felony that could lead to imprisonment. It seems that Joss had agreed to sign with Cleveland on the condition that

Addie Joss, pictured here near the end of his career, had the lowest opponents' on-base percentage in modern baseball history (Library of Congress).

the Blues pay Strobel a fair price for his release. The Blues agreed, even though at that stage of the baseball war neither major league was bothering to purchase player releases from minor league teams. Strobel responded to Joss's attempt to act honorably by insisting the Blues pay him double the price Joss had named. The Blues refused to pay it and Joss, angry at Strobel's negotiation ploy, decided he would play with Cleveland anyway. By the end of spring training, Joss had returned $100 of his advance to Strobel but still owed him the remaining $50. The Blues hired a good lawyer for him, and a jury found him innocent of the charges. To ensure that Strobel would not pursue the matter further, the Blues promised to send him a player when they reduced their roster later in the season.[81]

It didn't take long for Joss to prove that he was worth all the effort it took to get him under contract. His first appearance was against the St. Louis Browns. He started the game by retiring the first three Browns on two grounders and a strikeout, then he picked up the pace a little. In the second inning he fanned John Anderson, Bobby Wallace, and Dick Padden on ten pitches. He went five innings without allowing a hit. Jesse Burkett led off the sixth inning with a low liner to right field. Zaza Harvey raced in after the ball and scooped it up just as it reached the ground. The umpire ruled that Harvey had trapped the ball and gave Burkett a hit, the only one the Browns were able to record in the game.[82]

Joss's second game was against Chicago. The White Stockings were a more resourceful team than the Browns. When they saw they weren't going to get many hits off Joss, they started working the count and bunting. They were able to manufacture four runs on six hits, five walks, and some aggressive baserunning. It was enough to hand Joss his first loss, 4–0.

From Chicago the Blues moved on to Detroit, where Joss introduced himself to the Tigers by limiting them to two hits, both coming in the ninth inning. A Cleveland writer described the event. "There was nothing to the game but Joss," he wrote. "For eight consecutive innings he retired the Tigers without even the semblance of a hit and in that time but three balls, all easy flies to the outfield, went out of the diamond. Joss forced the Tigers to hit at him, he having no less than eight assists in the first eight innings and also made Gleason hit an easy one to him for the third out in the last inning, when any old kind of hit would have won the game for Detroit."[83]

Since Joss was now pitching in the major leagues, such domination could not continue indefinitely. There were days during the 1902 season and afterwards when the hitters had their way with him. But on most days Joss was a tough challenge for opposing batters. He was a big guy—6'3" and 185 pounds, with a body that seemed to be mostly arms and legs—and he had a deceptive delivery. As he wound up, he would turn toward second base, completely hiding the ball from the batter, and then he would swing back toward the plate, releasing the ball with a sidearm motion.[84] He threw hard and the batter had little time to pick up the ball before it was on top of him. While he had an outstanding fastball, his best pitch was probably a wicked drop ball that batters continually pounded into the ground. When Joss was in form, Cleveland's infielders were kept busy and the first baseman recorded a lot of putouts.

In 1902 Joss had the second-most low-hit games in the league. Cy Young had eleven games in which he held the opposition to five or fewer hits. Joss had nine, including four two-hitters and the one-hitter he pitched in his big league debut.[85]

Joss allowed the third-lowest number of hits per game in the league, allowing 7.52. Waddell gave up only 7.30 per game, while Bill Bernhard led the league in that category by giving up only 7.01. Joss had the most shutouts with five, and his earned run average was the seventh-best in the league.

In terms of overall effectiveness, the 1902 season was a typical one for Joss. Because his 1910 season was cut short by an elbow injury and he died before he had a chance to pitch in 1911, he pitched only eight full seasons in the major leagues. In every one of those years he finished in the top five in opponents' on-base percentage and the top seven in earned run average. He had the lowest career on-base percentage of any pitcher in modern baseball history (.260) and the second-lowest career earned run average (1.89). Only Ed Walsh's 1.82 was lower.

Possibly because he won only 160 games in his career (with 97 losses), Joss received relatively light support in the early Baseball Hall of Fame elections. His highest level of support in voting by the baseball writers was 14.2 percent in 1942. Strictly speaking, he did not meet the mandatory criterion of having pitched at least ten seasons in the major leagues. In 1978, however, the Veterans' Committee ruled that Joss was qualified because he started the 1911 season on Cleveland's roster, even though he did not pitch that year. Having made that determination, which was supported by the Hall's board of directors, the Committee then voted Joss into the Baseball Hall of Fame.[86]

Six

1903, National League

Stumbling Toward Peace

In the fall of 1902 National League owners were entering their third year of baseball war. The war had been costly for them in terms of both dollars and prestige. Most of them were weary of the fight and worried about the rapid escalation of player salaries. When the owners gathered for their annual meeting in December, St. Louis owner Frank DeHaas Robison suggested the league form a committee to negotiate an end to the conflict. Although the dominant personality among the owners, John T. Brush, was eager to continue the fight, the majority supported Robison's motion. As a result of their discussions, a group of owners approached Ban Johnson, the American League president who was in New York at the time, to ask if the rival league was willing to enter into negotiations. Johnson told the owners his league would welcome such discussions.[1]

The peace negotiations took place in January. In real wars the peace terms usually reflect what happened on the battlefields. That was the case in this baseball war. During the conflict the American League had grabbed most of the top players and had outdrawn the National League in the cities where the two leagues competed directly against each other. It was firmly established as the equal, if not the superior, of the National League in terms of playing talent and financial stability. When the terms of the peace treaty were announced, most baseball people concluded that the American League had prevailed. One writer quipped, "Seriously, if the National League got anything out of the peace agreement, except peace and Tommy Leach, it is not visible to the naked eye."[2]

No offense meant towards Wee Tommy, but it is quite likely the National League owners were much happier about having peace than they were about recovering Leach. Peace meant restoration of the reserve clause that gave them control over their players and, indirectly, over the players' salaries. They craved peace so much they were not only willing to concede to the American League territorial rights in the four National League cities already shared by the two leagues, but also recognized the new league's right to put a team in New York City. The peace negotiators representing the two leagues agreed upon these key peace terms fairly quickly on the first day they met. They had a more difficult time agreeing upon which teams would end up with the fifteen or so disputed players.

Cincinnati owner Garry Herrmann played a key role in bringing about the peace agreement that ended the war between the National and American leagues (Library of Congress).

The two sides began discussing settlement of the disputed contracts near the end of the first day they met. Henry Killilea, an American League negotiator, asserted his league would never consent to the loss of Ed Delahanty or George Davis, denouncing the tactics used by Brush and McGraw in getting the two players to sign with New York. Killilea's self-righteous words angered the National League negotiators, who gave examples of dirty tactics employed by American League agents over the previous two years. At that point Cincinnati owner Garry Herrmann interrupted his colleagues.

He said he had a social engagement he needed to attend, and suggested that the negotiators think the matter over and try to start over in a calmer mood the next morning.

When the men came together the next day, both sides had concluded they had too much to lose if they let the peace agreement fall by the wayside because of a few players who sought to fill their own pockets by playing the teams off against each other. Herrmann set an example for the other owners by announcing he would forego his claim to Sam Crawford, thereby letting him go to the Tigers. "If we cannot parcel these rascally players among our teams in a way that will suit both leagues, it would be better to put them all on the ineligible list than to quarrel over them," he said.[3]

The negotiators then proceeded to "parcel" the remaining disputed players. They could not agree upon a system that would produce a result they could all live with, so they discussed each case individually. The general guideline that drove their decisions seemed to be that each league sought to protect its New York franchise without being too unfair to the other teams.

The results of the negotiations were released to the press in the form of eight articles of agreement and a roster of players assigned to each team. Reporters then went over the rosters and told their readers who ended up with the disputed players, which numbered from 14 to 16, depending upon the reporter. Most reporters agreed the American League came off better in this part of the agreement, as it had in other key decisions.

About half of the disputed players were claimed by the New York Giants. Both during and after the 1902 season John McGraw had kept himself busy identifying potential jumpers and tempting them with fat contracts. He didn't seem to care whether they were covered by existing contractual commitments. Of course, McGraw was by no means the only baseball executive who displayed that attitude.

The committee protected the Giants' interests by letting them keep Christy Mathewson and Frank Bowerman, who had signed with the St. Louis Browns in May before later agreeing to contracts with the Giants. They also awarded Sam Mertes to the Giants. (Mertes was also claimed by the Chicago White Stockings.) Three other players—George Davis (Chicago), Ed Delahanty (Washington), and Kid Elberfeld (Detroit)—all of whom were covered by two-year contracts extending through 1903 when McGraw signed them, were awarded to their original teams. Dave Fultz, who was a free agent, had listened to McGraw's entreaties and then signed a contract with the New York Highlanders. McGraw claimed him, but Fultz denied having signed any agreement with the Giants. The peace negotiators awarded him to the Highlanders. McGraw also claimed Boston catcher John Warner. The negotiators didn't seem to know whether there was any substance to McGraw's claim, so they awarded him to the Giants on the condition that they produce an agreement dated prior to the peace conference.[4]

Given the fact that most of these players were already committed to other teams when they signed with the Giants, most neutral observers would conclude that the peace negotiators had tried to deal fairly with the Giants, and possibly had favored them somewhat. But Giants president John T. Brush was enraged by the peace agreement. Upon hearing of the agreement's terms, Brush responded, "The report seems incomplete. There surely must be more than I have read. There should be some account of the National League Committee losing their pocketbooks to the Committee from the American League."[5] He was, of course, upset by the territorial concession allowing an American League team in New York, as well as the allocation of players. Within a few days he obtained a preliminary court injunction prohibiting the league from enforcing the peace agreement.

Although Brush usually had his way with his fellow owners, he found them unwilling to follow his lead when they met to consider ratifying the peace agreement. On the contrary, the owners seemed to have united in opposition to Brush. One of the first items of business was a letter from Philadelphia owner John I. Rogers protesting the New York club's claim to Delahanty. Rogers insisted Brush had violated an agreement of the previous September by signing Delahanty. He threatened to sue Brush over the matter.

Next the owners dealt with statements Brush had made to the press after the peace agreement was made public. Brush had criticized the negotiators for "working behind closed doors." In response to this criticism, Chicago president Jim Hart made a motion to open the meeting to the press. "Quick as a flash both the New York and Brooklyn representatives were on their feet protesting," reported one writer. "Ebbets upset a chair in his anxiety to prevent the press from being admitted, while John T. gave his forelock an extra curl and looked as forlorn as possible." Hart then withdrew his motion.

Later one of the Cincinnati owners offered a resolution requiring the New York club to put up a large bond to insure the National League against damage as a result of Brush's legal move. That resolution passed by a 6–1 vote, with Brooklyn opposing and New York abstaining. The owners ended the conference, which lasted two days, by ratifying the peace agreement, voting 6–2 on five articles of the agreement and 6–0 on the other three, with Brooklyn and New York either in opposition or abstaining.[6]

After the National League's ratification of the agreement, baseball followers voiced their satisfaction with the end of the baseball war. But the fighting had not quite ended. The agreement required players to return any advance payments they had received from teams whose contracts were not recognized in the peace agreement. Two players, George Davis and Ed Delahanty, had received large advances from the Giants. Neither player wanted to return the money, and both wanted to play for the Giants, who had offered much more money than they were to receive from the teams they played for in 1902. Delahanty, who had lost heavily betting on horse races during the offseason, eventually agreed to report to Washington, his debt to the Giants paid by the Senators on the understanding that it would be taken out of his pay over the next two years.[7] Davis, however, refused to report to the White Stockings, as required in the peace agreement.

Davis' contract with the Giants allowed him to be paid even if he did not play any games for the team. He went to spring training with the Giants, but did not play for them when the season began. Upon the advice of his lawyer, he stopped by the Polo Grounds each day to fulfill the legal requirement of offering his services to the Giants. Reportedly, he spent most of his afternoons at the race track. He had been advanced $2,750 of his $4,000 salary, but by early May his bankroll seemed to be getting thin. He contacted Charlie Comiskey, who sent him some money and arranged for transportation to Chicago. Davis changed his mind, however, probably at the behest of Brush or McGraw. He remained in New York.[8]

In June the Detroit Tigers suspended shortstop Kid Elberfeld for lackadaisical playing. They announced that Elberfeld would never again play for the team, and then traded him to the New York Highlanders. The Elberfeld trade was the excuse Brush had been looking for, both to activate Davis and to rekindle the war between the two major leagues.

On June 18 Brush sent a letter to National League president Harry Pulliam, claiming the Elberfeld deal violated the peace agreement. "Elberfeld was under contract with the [New York] National League club for the year of 1903," Brush wrote. "He could have been enjoined from playing elsewhere, and it certainly is most unfair and subversive of the spirit of the 'peace agreement' that he should now be permitted to strengthen a rival club in this city." Brush concluded his letter by asking Pulliam to retaliate by allowing Davis to play for the Giants.[9] Pulliam thought the matter over for a week before giving Brush permission to activate Davis. Then he sent a letter to Ban Johnson notifying him of his decision.

Johnson first learned about Pulliam's decision from newspaper reporters. He rebutted Pulliam's claim that the Elberfeld deal was a violation of the agreement. But, in an uncharacteristically mild manner, he said he would rely upon the National League peace negotiators—Herrmann, Hart, and Robison—to compel Brush to live up to the agreement. "I wired Mr. Herrmann today," he said, "that I should look to him as chairman of the peace committee to act."

Herrmann, angered by Pulliam's action, told reporters, "The idea of Pulliam, an employee of eight club owners, doing as he has done without consultation with his employers is ridiculous, and the Cincinnati club will not give his action its endorsement." He sent Pulliam a letter admonishing him for not consulting with the other owners and denying that the Elberfeld trade was improper. He reminded Pulliam that several National League clubs, including New York, had sent players to Philadelphia in an effort to strengthen the Phillies, even though the American League also had a franchise in that city.[10]

Hart and Robison, the other two members of the National League Peace Committee, also strongly rebuked Pulliam and said the Elberfeld trade was legitimate. But there must have been some sort of freak weather system impeding communications between the midwest and the eastern parts of the country, because the other four National League owners voiced strong support for Brush and Pulliam.

Pittsburgh owner Barney Dreyfuss, who was with his team at the Polo Grounds, told reporters, "Mr. Pulliam did right in declaring Davis eligible to play with New York. Davis signed a contract to play here [in New York] this season and New York can rightfully claim him. Herrmann had better be careful or his club will lose its standing in the National League." James Potter, who had just become the principal owner of the Phillies, said, "We have a President and I shall support him. I consider him fully capable of filling the position he occupies and think he has made an admirable and just decision in answer to the New York club's claim."[11]

Johnson's mood darkened somewhat after learning of the seemingly predominant support for Brush among the National League's owners. "If the American League is forced into another war," he declared, "I am here to say that there will be no peace until the National League has been completely annihilated."

He responded to Pulliam's letter with one in which he defended Detroit's right to trade Elberfeld. He said the American League had acted completely within its rights under the agreement while Brush, on the other hand, had sought to undermine it by trying to prevent the American League from buying land for a park in Manhattan and by playing Davis. Johnson concluded his letter by telling Pulliam he would not attend a scheduled meeting to discuss a new national agreement between the two major leagues and the minor leagues until he knew whether the National League would respect the peace agreement the two leagues had already signed.[12]

As the nation prepared to set off fireworks as part of its Fourth of July celebrations, it appeared likely the national pastime was again plunging toward war. Before Davis could play in Chicago against the Cubs, Charlie Comiskey obtained an injunction from an Illinois court prohibiting him from playing with anyone other than the White Stockings. And John McGraw continued to talk trash about Johnson and the American League, at one point saying he was waiting for the signal for the fight to start so he could secure three or four players from the Athletics.[13]

Sy Sanborn of the *Chicago Tribune* concluded that "the support Brush is getting from the Boston, Philadelphia and Brooklyn magnates can be explained only on the supposition that these magnates desire a renewal of war for the purpose of picking off some of the American League's stars to bolster their weak aggregations." Tim Murnane of the *Boston Globe* lamented, "Just when everything looked peaceful in baseball along comes the irresistible John T. Brush and starts more trouble. Strange that it should be this individual that has started every good-sized trouble in major league ball for the last 14 years, and is now in a position to keep the thing going as long as he lives."[14]

Meanwhile, George Davis, the man at the center of the controversy, had played four games for the Giants and returned to his daily routine of stopping at the Polo Grounds on the way to one of the New York area's race tracks. An officer of the court found him at the Brighton Beach track on July 15, where he served a second injunction against Davis, this one issued by a federal court. Davis played no more games over the remainder of the season. He finished the season with a batting average of .267, getting four hits in 15 at-bats and committing a costly error that contributed to a Giants loss.[15]

The National League scheduled a meeting for July 20 to take an official stand on the issue. Newspaper reporters did not know what to expect from the meeting, but many thought Brush would carry the day. Behind the scenes, however, Brush was beginning to lose support among his colleagues. Dreyfuss and Ebbets had taken the opportunity to talk to their league's peace negotiators and were beginning to modify their view of the situation. When the National League owners came together, Brush found himself standing alone in his desire to repudiate the peace agreement. The owners voted 7–1 to prohibit the Giants from playing Davis in any more games.[16] Six weeks later the two major leagues concluded their negotiations with the minor leagues, establishing a new National Agreement.

Peace once again descended upon the baseball world, except perhaps on the small part of Manhattan occupied by the offices of the New York National League baseball club.

1903 National League Standings

Team	W	L	Pct.	GB
Pittsburgh	91	49	.650	—
New York	84	55	.604	6.5

Chicago	82	56	.594	8
Cincinnati	74	65	.532	16.5
Brooklyn	70	66	.515	19
Boston	58	80	.420	32
Philadelphia	49	86	.363	39.5
St. Louis	43	94	.314	46.5

Still Good Enough: Pittsburgh

The Pirates were weakened by the American League raid of the preceding August. Seven players signed American League contracts at that time. Two of them, Tommy Leach and Harry Smith, later changed their minds and signed with the Pirates. They were among the disputed players awarded to their National League teams by the peace negotiators. Another Pirate—rookie Jimmy Sebring, who had played 19 games at the end of the 1902 season—evidently signed 1903 contracts with both Pittsburgh and Detroit. He was also awarded to the Pirates. Five members of the 1902 team moved over to the American League in 1903, all of them playing for the New York Highlanders. They included pitchers Jack Chesbro and Jesse Tannehill, shortstop Wid Conroy, outfielder Lefty Davis, and the man who served as the American League's agent in Pittsburgh, catcher Jack O'Connor. The Pirates also lost 41-year-old catcher Chief Zimmer, who became the Philadelphia Phillies' manager.For most pennant-winning teams, the loss of two 20-game winners, plus the team's starting shortstop, right fielder, and catcher, would pretty much doom any chances for a second straight pennant. But the 1902 Pirates were so much better than the rest of the National League that those losses just brought them back to the level of the other top teams in the league. Pre-season forecasts of the pennant race almost unanimously picked the Pirates to win again, with Cincinnati generally seen as their toughest opponent and Brooklyn picked as a contender, primarily because the baseball writers believed Ned Hanlon could find a way to win no matter how bad his team looked on paper.

While the 1903 Pirates were still a formidable team, they now had little margin for error. Their 1902 staff of five very good pitchers was reduced to three top pitchers and a collection of hopefuls. Manager Fred Clarke picked up some pretty good prospects, but unfortunately they matured as major league pitchers after the 1903 season. Rookie pitchers Kaiser Wilhelm, Cy Falkenberg, and Jack Pfiester all went on to become decent major league pitchers, but for the Pirates in 1903 they combined for only six wins while losing eleven games. Ultimately, Clarke was forced to round out his staff by signing Roaring Bill Kennedy, who endured an injury-riddled season but pitched well when he took the mound. Lefty Davis was replaced by Sebring, who proved to be a solid player in his first full major league season. O'Connor's place was taken by another rookie, Ed Phelps, who shared the catching duties with Harry Smith. Phelps hit well and was an adequate defensive catcher; Smith excelled on defense but was almost helpless at bat.

The loss of one of the Pirates to the American League played a part in maximizing the team's overall strength. With Wid Conroy no longer on the team, Honus Wagner had little choice but to accept a move to shortstop. In February he wrote a letter to Barney Dreyfuss saying he didn't like playing shortstop and claiming it affected his hitting.[17] Dreyfuss ignored Wagner's complaint, as did manager Fred Clarke.

Pittsburgh (91–49)

Regular Lineup	AVG	OBP	SLG	R	RBI	SB
Ginger Beaumont, cf	.341	.390	.444	137	68	23
Fred Clarke, lf	.351	.414	.532	88	70	21
Tommy Leach, 3b	.298	.352	.438	97	87	22
Honus Wagner, ss	.355	.414	.518	97	101	46
Kitty Bransfield, 1b	.265	.314	.350	69	57	13
Claude Ritchey, 2b	.287	.360	.381	66	59	15
Jimmy Sebring, rf	.277	.325	.383	71	64	20
or Otto Krueger, ut	.246	.323	.344	42	28	5
Ed Phelps, c	.282	.338	.352	32	31	2
or Harry Smith, c	.175	.222	.208	15	19	2
Leading Pitchers	W	L	PCT	IP	H	ERA
Deacon Phillippe	25	9	.735	289.3	269	2.43
Sam Leever	25	7	.781	284.3	255	2.06
Ed Doheny	16	8	.667	222.7	209	3.19
Bill Kennedy	9	6	.600	125.3	130	3.45

Wagner became the Pirates' regular shortstop and would remain at that position through the 1916 season, when he was 42 years old. As a shortstop Honus gave the Pirates a great advantage over the rest of the league. He was at least as good as any other shortstop on defense—and probably was better—and he outhit all of the other shortstops by a wide margin. In 1903 Wagner led the league in batting with a .355 average, was second in slugging percentage with .518, and had the eighth-best on-base percentage at .414. As a right fielder Wagner would have ranked with the best hitters playing the outfield—his OPS (on-base plus slugging percentage) was .932, just slightly below the numbers put up by Clarke, Mike Donlin, and Roger Bresnahan (whose primary position in 1903 was center field). But as a shortstop his OPS was more than 200 points above that of the second-best shortstop. For the next decade the Pirates started every season with a decided roster advantage over the opposition because Wagner hit far better than any other shortstop in the game. That was one reason they were able to contend every year over that time span.

The Pirates' other core players continued to perform at very high levels. Clarke finished second to Wagner in batting average and led the league in slugging percentage with a .532 mark. Center fielder Ginger Beaumont led the league with 137 runs scored, 27 more than the next player. Ritchey played his usual solid game at second base while hitting better than any other second baseman. Little Tommy Leach once again had the statistical profile of a slugger, ranking second in home runs, third in triples, and fourth in runs batted in. Sam Leever and Deacon Phillippe each won 25 games, while finishing first and fourth in earned run average.

When the season started the Pirates quickly found themselves looking up in the standings at the two teams who were to dominate the league, along with the Pirates, over the next decade. The Giants and Cubs both got off to hot starts. By mid–May they were battling each other for the lead, both winning almost 70 percent of their games, with the Pirates close behind in third place. The Pirates played well but lost several games because Clarke needed to find a fourth pitcher to complement the three holdover starters. Falkenberg, Wilhelm, and young Bucky Veil all struggled in their appearances, while Kennedy pitched well. Kennedy beat St. Louis on a five-hitter in his first appearance and followed that by holding the Cubs to six hits. He eventually settled into the rotation as the number four starter, although he missed most of June with an injury.

Near the end of May the Pirates started to get hot. They won the last game of a series against Boston and swept a three-game series with Cincinnati. On June 1, Ed Doheny lost the opening game of a series against the Giants, 10–2. The next day Phillippe shut out the Giants, 7–0. Sam Leever followed with another shutout, by a 5–0 score. Then Boston was whitewashed three straight games, by Wilhelm, Doheny, and Phillippe.

After the Boston series, the local Painter, Decorators, and Paperhangers' Union figured the Pirate pitchers had used up their good paint brushes whitewashing the Giants and Beaneaters, so before the next game, which was against Philadelphia, they presented the team with a new brush. Figuratively speaking, Leever used it for the Pirates' sixth straight shutout, winning a close 2–0 game from the Phillies.[18] The Pirate pitchers must have run out of paint in the next game, though. The Phillies pushed across a run in the fourth inning to end the shutout streak at six games and 56 consecutive innings.

The absence of another shutout, however, did not foreshadow the end of the Pirates' winning streak. They beat the Phillies, 7–3, in the game in which the shutout streak ended and beat the Phillies again the next day, 7–4. Phillippe and Leever then pitched two more shutouts in a row, making it eight in ten games. The Pirates ran their winning streak up to fifteen games in a row before losing the second game of a doubleheader to the Phillies on June 25.

By then they had taken over first place, although they still led the Giants and Cubs by only 2½ and three games, respectively. Still, there seemed little doubt at this stage of the season that the Pirates would be difficult to beat. While the Pirates were in the middle of their winning streak, Ned Hanlon remarked to a Cincinnati reporter, "It looks as if several teams had a chance to beat Pittsburgh out, but Pittsburgh is by far the best team in the league. Yes it is the best team in the country. It is well-balanced to start with, and there is a star at every position, all working together." Hanlon admired the team's talent, but also the character of its players. "I will tell you what makes it a great team," he told the reporter. "All those players take good care of themselves. They don't celebrate if they win games, but just go along in that steady way, always attending to business. It is a truly wonderful ball team when you stop to study it. It ought to win the pennant, but something may occur to beat the team out of it."[19]

Through July and August the Pirates built up their lead, which reached ten games early in September. By then the advantage was large enough that the pennant was almost assured. But the "something" Hanlon warned about did occur during the season's last month. A rash of injuries and illness affected many of the team's key players. Ritchey and Wagner both came down with sore arms in early September. They continued to play through their injuries, but neither could play at his normal level. Clarke wrenched a knee running the bases and missed several games. Otto Krueger, the team's utility player, was hit on the head by a pitch and ordered not to play baseball for the rest of the season. Roaring Bill Kennedy seemed to run out of gas in September, and in the last week of the season Sam Leever came down with a sore arm.

The saddest development was the mental illness that struck Ed Doheny. By mid-season Doheny had become convinced he was being followed by detectives. He complained about them to Clarke, who assured him no one was after him. On July 28, while he and Clarke were playing a game of pool, Doheny said he was going to give the detectives the slip and go home. After he finished playing pool he said goodbye to Clarke and several other players and boarded a train for his home in Massachusetts. He returned to the team in mid–August and pitched a few games before once again becoming sick during the third week in September. This time it was necessary for Doheny's brother to come to Pittsburgh to escort him home. Doheny was hospitalized in a mental institution, where he became progressively worse. In mid–October he attacked a male nurse with a cast-iron stove leg, knocking him unconscious. He never recovered from his illness, dying at the Massachusetts State Asylum in 1916.[20]

The Pirates finished the season 6½ games ahead of the Giants in the standings. But by then they were a beat-up group of players ill-suited to compete in what was to become celebrated as the first modern World Series.

A Successful "Con" Job: New York

The Giants started the 1903 season with a somewhat better team than the one that finished the 1902 season, but not one considered very powerful by the country's baseball writers. With his importation of the ex–Orioles in July of 1902 and the signing of Mertes, Warner, and Baltimore second baseman Billy Gilbert for the 1903 season, McGraw had remade the team. It was now solid defensively but still didn't have much punch offensively. On the mound the Giants had two great pitchers in Mathewson and Joe McGinnity and a pretty good pitcher in Dummy Taylor. The team's other two pitchers—Roscoe Miller and Jack Cronin—had been inconsistent in 1902 and would prove so again in 1903. Most pre-season forecasts had the Giants pegged for fourth or fifth place.

What most of the writers had missed was McGraw's effect upon a team. Like their manager, the 1903 Giants weren't the most talented team around, but they were fighters—most of the time figuratively, sometimes literally. As a player, McGraw's game had been to scrap his way to first, either by fouling off pitches until he could coax a walk, by letting an inside pitch hit him, or by poking the ball past the fielders for a hit. McGraw would then run the bases aggressively, stealing bases and using the hit-and-run play liberally.

New York (84–55)

Regular Lineup	AVG	OBP	SLG	R	RBI	SB
George Browne, rf	.313	.364	.372	105	45	27

or George Van Haltren, cf	.257	.327	.286	42	28	14
Roger Bresnahan, cf	.350	.443	.493	87	55	34
Dan McGann, 1b	.270	.331	.357	75	50	36
Sam Mertes, lf	.280	.360	.437	100	104	45
Charlie Babb, ss	.248	.350	.321	68	46	22
Billy Lauder, 3b	.281	.307	.314	52	53	19
or Jack Dunn, ss–3b-2b	.241	.291	.307	35	37	12
Billy Gilbert, 2b	.252	.348	.281	62	40	37
John Warner, c	.284	.322	.347	38	34	5
Frank Bowerman, c	.276	.306	.338	22	31	5
Leading Pitchers	**W**	**L**	**PCT**	**IP**	**H**	**ERA**
Joe McGinnity	31	20	.608	434	391	2.43
Christy Mathewson	30	13	.698	366.3	321	2.26
Dummy Taylor	13	13	.500	244.7	306	4.23
Jack Cronin	6	4	.600	115.7	130	3.81

His players weren't as good at that strategy as McGraw had been, but most of them employed it to the best of their abilities. For instance, the Giants' keystone combination—Gilbert and Charlie Babb—were mediocre with the bat but willing to sacrifice their bodies to reach base. Gilbert led the league in times hit-by-pitch, taking 22 pitches for the team; Babb ranked second with 20. Dan McGann was tied for third with 12, while catcher Jack Warner, who had only 309 plate appearances, was hit nine times. Roger Bresnahan and Sam Mertes were among the leaders in walks, each coaxing 61 bases on balls, while seven Giants stole at least 20 bases. No Giants player came close to the 67 stolen bases racked up by Frank Chance and Jimmy Sheckard, but the fifth- through eighth-highest stolen base totals were held by McGraw's men.

Their spirited play, together with great pitching by McGinnity and Mathewson, enabled the Giants to get off to a great start. Their record was 30–13 and they were in first place when they arrived in St. Louis in early June. "The Giants owe their position in the race to their hustling," observed a *Sporting News* writer. He compared the Giants to the Pirates and concluded that the Pittsburgh team excelled them at virtually every position. "McGraw has as good a catching department as Clarke, and a pair of pitchers who would be acquisitions to any staff," he wrote. "But a two-pitcher team without strength in other departments has no license to make the record the Giants have. Success stimulated them and they have conned themselves into believing that they can beat any team they meet and they do it."[21]

The Sporting News writer predicted the Giants would drop in the standings, as did many other observers. The Giants cooled off somewhat and soon fell behind the Pirates, but the predicted descent toward fifth place didn't happen, largely because of the way McGraw used his two superstar pitchers. McGinnity and Mathewson were two thoroughbreds who could carry his team to victory most of the time they pitched, and McGraw rode them as hard as he could. Including ties, the Giants played 142 games in 1903. McGraw started his two star pitchers in 90 of them and used them in relief ten times. McGinnity appeared in 55 games, starting 48 and relieving in seven others. His 434 innings pitched were the most of any major league pitcher since 1895. Mathewson started 42 games and relieved in three. He pitched 366⅓ innings, the second-highest total in the league. Between them, McGinnity and Mathewson won 61 games and lost 33, for a win-loss percentage of .649. The rest of the Giants' staff went 23–22, just barely over .500.

McGinnity began the 1903 season with one of the best games of his career, a one-hitter against Brooklyn. He appeared in six of the Giants' first ten games, winning four, saving one and pitching the last two innings of an 11-inning tie. In June, after McGinnity had pitched an 11-inning shutout against the Reds, Cincinnati sportswriter J. Ed Grillo commented that McGinnity seemed to be throwing faster than at any time since 1900.[22] McGinnity's strength was not great speed, of course, but the variety of his pitches and the effectiveness of his underhand rise. But a little extra speed on his fastball would have made him even tougher to hit.

McGinnity's twentieth victory came on August 1, when he won the first game of a doubleheader against Boston. He held the Beaneaters to six hits in that game and won easily by a 4–1 score. Between games he told McGraw he wanted to pitch the second game as well. McGraw probably needed little persuasion before agreeing to send McGinnity to the mound again. The Iron Man pitched another six-hitter, winning, 5–2.

McGinnity's next start came a week later, in the opening game of another doubleheader, this time against Brooklyn. He was scheduled to pitch only that game, but a comment by Ned Hanlon before the contest changed his mind. While Hanlon was congratulating McGinnity for winning both games the preceding week, he made a remark implying the Iron Man had been lucky in doing so. McGinnity told Hanlon he could do it again. Hanlon laughed and dared him to try it. Hanlon's dare was enough for both McGinnity and McGraw, who always resented the fame Hanlon had gained as the manager of the Orioles.

After beating the Superbas, 6–1, in the first game, McGinnity was greeted with loud applause from some 30,000 New York fans when he walked out to the mound to pitch the second game. For a while it seemed that Hanlon would win his dare. The Superbas scored two runs in the fourth inning on three hits and a walk and added another in the next inning thanks to two errors by second baseman Gilbert. Going into the bottom of the ninth inning, the Giants trailed, 3–2, with the bottom of their batting order coming up. Utilityman Jack Dunn led off with a single and Gilbert followed with a safe drive to center. Warner bunted and was safe on a bad throw by Brooklyn's third baseman. Dunn scored the tying run on the play. George Van Haltren, batting for McGinnity, topped a ball down the first base line, and Gilbert raced home with the winning run before a play could be made.[23]

It may have been the strain of pitching doubleheaders two weeks in a row or the workload associated with a long season, but McGinnity lost his next five starts after the Brooklyn doubleheader. His next win came almost three weeks later, against Philadelphia on August 27. Four days after that, with his team playing its sixth doubleheader over a twelve-day stretch, McGinnity again volunteered for "double duty." The opposition this time was Philadelphia, and McGinnity had a relatively easy time in both games.

He allowed five hits in winning the opener, 4–1. He appeared to be even stronger in the second game, allowing only six hits and striking out nine Phillies, a very high total for him. The following day the *New York Sun* celebrated his feat in the overwrought style of the day: "That he is unexcelled and unapproachable as a self-repeating pitcher was shown by Joe McGinnity at the Polo Grounds yesterday. For the third time this year, the man with the galvanized whip and fatigueless physique pitched two games in one afternoon and won them both. First Boston succumbed to the Iron Man's double-up trick, then Brooklyn and now Philadelphia." The *New York Times* noted that the two contests together required only three hours and three minutes to complete and remarked, "At the end McGinnity showed no sign of fatigue—in fact, he seemed fresh enough to tackle the visitors for a third contest if that were necessary."[24]

Mathewson, who was 23 years old in 1903, pitched even better than McGinnity. With a decent team behind him, Matty was very difficult to beat. He was wild and ineffective on Opening Day, allowing nine hits, five walks and throwing two wild pitches while losing to the Superbas, 9–7. He came back to throw a three-hitter against the same team four days later, beginning a streak of four straight wins. After a 4–1 loss to Cincinnati in which he allowed only one hit over the first eight innings while striking out 13 Reds, he started a nine-game winning streak, to bring his record to 13–2 on June 13. He reached the twenty victory mark on August 10 in the midst of an eight-game winning streak. The last game of that streak, an 8–1 victory over Chicago, came on August 24 and gave him an overall record of 25–9. It took another four weeks for him to record his thirtieth win.

Matty led the league in strikeouts for the first time in 1903, fanning 267 batters, the highest total of his career. No National League pitcher pitching at the 60'6" distance had more strikeouts in a season until 1963. National League pitchers as a whole struck out 3.43 batters per nine innings in 1903; Matty averaged 6.56 per nine innings. Over a five-game stretch in early August he averaged 9.6 strikeouts a game.

Eight of Matty's victories were especially important because they came against Pittsburgh. He was the only Giants pitcher who had any success when opposing the Pirates. The Giants and Pirates played each other 17 times through the end of August. At that point the series stood Pirates nine games, Mathewson eight. The two teams met again in the last three games of the season, after the Pirates had clinched the pennant. The Giants won two of those three games, with Mathewson sitting out all three.

Selee Builds a Contender: Chicago

While McGraw was rebuilding the Giants in his characteristic way—chesty, in-your-face signings of big-name stars already under contract to other teams, public announcements of contracts never finalized, defiance of the peace agreement's terms—Frank Selee was rebuilding the Cubs in his own way by following accepted rules quietly, signing solid but unspectacular veterans to provide stability for promising younger players, and keeping to his long-range plan of building around defense and pitching.

When the peace negotiators decided the fate of the disputed players, McGraw's signings were at the center of the discussions. Selee and the Cubs weren't a concern; he had not signed any players who were already under contract with another team for 1903. Selee signed two players away from the American League—third baseman

Doc Casey and outfielder Dick Harley. Casey filled a big hole at third base for the Cubs. He was adequate on defense and a decent hitter but not special in anything except maybe character. He had attended dental school during the offseason for several years, obtaining his degree just before the 1903 campaign began.[25]

Harley, Selee's other "steal" from the American League, was a good defensive outfielder who was savvy about scientific baseball, but not much of a hitter. Harley came into the National League with the lowly St. Louis Browns of 1897 and remained with them in 1898. Each season after that through 1903 he changed teams, dropping to the minor leagues in 1900 as a result of the consolidation, then scrambling to find a spot on a major league team in each of the next three years. True to form, he lasted only one season with the Cubs.

Selee's search for pitchers, which had not been very successful in 1902, bore fruit in 1903. He added two new pitchers who each won 20 games, giving the Cubs one of the better pitching staffs in the league. Jake Weimer came from Kansas City of the Western League, where he had been one of the league's top pitchers for two years. Bob Wicker was obtained in a trade with the St. Louis Cardinals just after the season opened. Over the course of the season Selee used five pitchers regularly, although not always in a fixed rotation. Weimer, Wicker, and veteran Jack Taylor combined for a record similar to that posted by the Giants' Joe McGinnity and Christy Mathewson. The three Cubs won 61 games and lost 31, slightly better than the combined 61–33 record of the two New York stars.

Chicago (82–56)

Regular Lineup	AVG	OBP	SLG	R	RBI	SB
Jimmy Slagle, lf	.298	.393	.357	104	44	33
Doc Casey, 3b	.290	.324	.329	56	40	11
Frank Chance, 1b	.327	.439	.440	83	81	67
Davy Jones, cf	.282	.352	.336	64	62	15
Joe Tinker, ss	.291	.345	.380	67	70	27
Dick Harley, rf	.231	.328	.259	72	33	27
Johnny Evers, 2b	.293	.325	.381	70	52	25
or Bobby Lowe, 2b	.267	.319	.371	14	15	5
Johnny Kling, c	.297	.330	.428	67	68	23
Leading Pitchers	**W**	**L**	**PCT.**	**IP**	**H**	**ERA**
Jack Taylor	21	14	.600	312.3	277	2.45
Jake Weimer	20	8	.714	282	241	2.30
Bob Wicker*	20	9	.690	252	240	2.96
Carl Lundgren	11	9	.550	193	191	2.94
Jock Menefee	8	10	.444	147	157	3.01

*Includes record with St. Louis

Casey, Harley and the 1902 holdovers gave the Cubs a sound defense. The Cubs were outstanding defensively up the middle. Catcher Johnny Kling, shortstop Joe Tinker, second baseman Johnny Evers and center fielder Davy Jones were all among the league's best fielders at their positions. Left fielder Jimmy Slagle was also a very good fielder. At the beginning of the 1903 season Frank Chance was still learning to play first base. He led National League first basemen in errors in 1903, but improved as the season progressed. By the end of the season he was considered a good defensive first baseman.

When Chance signed with Chicago in 1898, many baseball people predicted he would soon become a star. Chance had hit well over the years, especially for a catcher. But his frequent injuries behind the plate and failure to settle in at any other position had caused most observers to begin thinking of him as a capable, though very fragile, utility player. That changed during the 1903 season. On June 30, after complimenting Chance's play at first base, Tim Murnane of the *Boston Globe* remarked, "Chance of the Chicago NL team has developed into a great first baseman." A few weeks later a Philadelphia writer made a similar comment.

In August, after watching Chance play several more games against the Beaneaters, Murnane became even more effusive in his praise: "Chance is perhaps today the most valuable man playing first base. He is no grandstand player, but is a winner." More important than the opinion of baseball writers was Selee's opinion. In November he told a Boston writer that Cincinnati had offered to trade two of its top players—Cy Seymour and Jake Beckley—for Chance. "Selee put up quite a howl when the deal was broached to him," the writer reported. "He claims that Frank Chance is one of the best all-around players in the business and one of the most valuable men playing in the game nowadays."[26]

In 1903 Chance excelled in the statistical categories normally associated with a first baseman. He hit well over .300 (.327), had a good slugging percentage for the Deadball Era (.440), and ranked third in the league in on-base percentage (.439). But his greatest value offensively was in an area not usually associated with a first baseman. He was a very aggressive baserunner, always looking to take an extra base while he was on the basepaths. In 1903 he tied for the National League lead in steals with 67.

Chance's competitive drive contributed to his injury problems. He refused to give in to pitchers who pitched him inside. He finished among the leaders in being hit by a pitch in ten of the eleven years between 1900 and 1910, including four years in which he played 88 or fewer games. In 1900 he was hit by a pitch 15 times in only 187 plate appearances. He was beaned several times. By the end of the decade he suffered constant headaches and hearing loss.

Chance's all-out style set the tone for his team. Like the Giants, the Cubs drew praise for the energy they brought to each game. In late May, Boston writer Tim Murnane wrote, "One of the cleverest teams I have seen at work this season is Frank Selee's Chicagos. Here is a team of light, fast fellows, resembling very much the old St. Louis Browns. The men are willing to take all kinds of chances on the bases.... The outfield is speedy and fine ground coverers and in Tinker and Evers the club has two very fast men. Selee has a knack of getting good work out of young players, and it need surprise no one to see this team playing fine ball right through the season."[27]

Murnane's assessment came as the Cubs ended a stretch in which they won 16 of 17 games and moved into first place for a short period of time. The Cubs battled the Giants for first place until the end of June, when the Pirates blew past both teams. The Cubs and Giants stayed close to each other in the standings throughout the season, usually with the Giants a couple of games ahead and the Pirates maintaining a comfortable but not insurmountable lead over both teams.

After the 1903 season closed, the Cubs and White Sox met in a long intra-city series that ended in a 7–7 tie and dark feelings by Cubs president Jim Hart that Jack Taylor had not tried his best in the series. In December Taylor was traded to St. Louis in a deal that brought Mordecai "Three-Finger" Brown to Chicago. With that trade Selee had brought together the players who would be the heart of the Cubs team for the next decade—Tinker, Evers, Chance, Kling, and Brown.

Costly Altruism: Cincinnati

Garry Herrmann, the Reds' president, was appropriately praised for his role in bringing the baseball war to an end. Herrmann played a key role in both negotiating the peace agreement and in blunting Brush's effort to renew the fighting. But Herrmann's first inclination after he became a club owner was not to make peace, but to fight harder. He signed all his own players to contracts and went after several American League stars. Although he offered high salaries and favorable contract terms, he was, with one exception, unsuccessful in persuading any of the American Leaguers to forsake the new league. The comments made by the players during these negotiations may have convinced Herrmann that making peace was his league's only viable option.

Cincinnati sportswriter J. Ed Grillo acted as Herrmann's agent during the negotiations with several players. He quickly came to realize that the National League was at a tremendous disadvantage in dealing with the players. Typically, when meeting with a player, Grillo and Cincinnati manager Joe Kelley tried to focus on the boost in pay the player would receive and the good things that would come out of his signing with the Reds.

The player was always happy to hear about an increase in pay, Grillo later said, but then would begin ruminating out loud about such topics as how much salaries had increased once the American League came upon the major league scene and therefore how important it was to the players to ensure that the new league succeeded; how the National League owners had slashed salaries after the old American Association collapsed; how, after his 1900 team had failed to contend, Frank DeHaas Robison had publicly accused his players of being drunkards and ruffians; how New York owner Andrew Freedman had repeatedly abused players and umpires; how John T. Brush had worked to ensure that the players' salaries were kept low; and how Boston's three owners did everything possible to pinch pennies. "Why should any player want to go back to the National League?" one of the players had asked Grillo. "When the National League had the field to itself, in only a few instances were the players treated with consideration." The player told Grillo, "I don't know the men who own the Cincinnati club now, but I am told that they are good sportsmen and are all right in every way. If they are, it is too bad that they are hooked up with those old fogies in the National League."[28]

Cincinnati (74–65)

Regular Lineup	AVG	OBP	SLG	R	RBI	SB
Mike Donlin, lf	.351	.420	.516	110	67	26
or Joe Kelley, lf, ut	.316	.402	.418	85	45	18

Cy Seymour, cf	.342	.382	.478	85	72	25
Cozy Dolan, rf	.288	.340	.356	64	58	11
Jake Beckley, 1b	.327	.384	.447	85	81	23
Harry Steinfeldt, 3b	.312	.386	.481	71	83	6
Tom Daly, 2b	.293	.332	.407	42	38	5
or George Magoon, 2b	.216	.314	.259	6	9	2
Tommy Corcoran, ss	.246	.267	.329	61	73	12
Heinie Peitz, c	.260	.331	.318	45	42	7
or Bill Bergen, c	.227	.252	.266	21	19	2
Leading Pitchers	**W**	**L**	**PCT**	**IP**	**H**	**ERA**
Noodles Hahn	22	12	.647	296	297	2.52
Bob Ewing	14	13	.519	246.7	254	2.77
Jack Sutthoff	16	9	.640	224.7	207	2.80
Ed Poole	7	13	.350	184	188	3.28
Jack Harper	8	9	.471	135	143	4.33
Bill Phillips	7	6	.538	118.3	134	3.35

The Reds managed to sign only one player away from the American League—Jack Harper of the St. Louis Browns. The Browns didn't put up much of a fight to retain Harper's services. Harper had reportedly received $5,000 for the 1902 season when he signed to play for the Browns. His 1903 salary with the Reds was to be $3,000. When Browns manager Jimmy McAleer was asked to comment on the report that Harper had signed with the Reds, he stated only that Harper had not signed with the Browns and was therefore free to sign with any club he wished. After the season closed McAleer told a reporter, "I look for Jack Harper to have a good season next year. He is a fine fellow and deserves success. However, on what he showed me he wasn't worth retaining at an advanced rate of pay."[29]

One of Herrmann's major contributions to the peace negotiations was volunteering to forego his rights to Sam Crawford and letting the Tigers have him without a struggle. At the time Herrmann probably figured he was set in the outfield. Even without Crawford, he had three good outfielders in Joe Kelley, Cy Seymour, and Mike Donlin. Kelley had long been considered one of the finest outfielders in the game, while Seymour and Donlin had played well while they were with the Orioles and, during the second half of 1902, with the Reds. Herrmann's sacrifice, however, turned out to be much greater than he initially realized. While Kelley, Seymour, and Donlin were all good hitters and fast runners, they shared one common shortcoming—in the field none of them was up to fighting off the sun that glared down on the right fielder in Cincinnati.

Donlin started the 1903 season in right field, having "won" the job by default. Kelley knew he couldn't play a sun field, and he was pretty sure Seymour wasn't up to it either. That left Donlin. Most aspects of the game came easily to Donlin. He was fast, had a great arm, and could hit from the day he first picked up a bat. There was one part of the game, though, that didn't come so easily to him. That was the daily grind. Donlin wasn't the kind of player who showed up for practice each day determined to focus on the weak points in his game and ready to work hard to improve his play. For Donlin, the ability was there or it wasn't, end of story.

Hanging tough on a fly ball coming at him out of the sun wasn't part of Donlin's skill set when the season opened on April 16. It still wasn't part of his game in early June when, after continually misjudging, muffing, and just plain missing fly balls sent his way, he told a reporter he would gladly give up a part of his salary to get out of right field.[30] A few days after Donlin made that statement, Kelley granted his wish, shifting him to left field. Donlin's fielding average at the time of the move was around .870.

The new right fielder was Cozy Dolan, a journeyman outfielder recently acquired from the White Sox in a trade. Dolan seemed to be the answer to the Reds' sun field problem. Over the remainder of the 1903 season he fielded everything that came his way without seeming to have any difficulty with the sun. In September Grillo praised Dolan's work, saying, "It has been many years since the Reds had anyone who could play that ugly sun field in right as well as he does and not let down in his batting."[31]

Unfortunately, Dolan wasn't able to sustain that performance. Before the 1904 season was a month old he, too, began losing fly balls in the sun, costing the team several games because of his errors. Dolan tried his best, at one time trying the "old Indian trick" of applying a black substance to the area below his eyes. The trick may have helped some, but he remained inconsistent as a right fielder until replaced in July by Jimmy Sebring, who was acquired from the Pirates. Sebring played well, but turned out to be only another short-term solution to the Reds' sun field problem. It was not until 1907 that the team found a man who could play adequately in Sam Crawford's old position.[32]

The Stars Said "Goodbye": Brooklyn

As in the previous two years, the Superbas were hit hard by the American League raids. The team that took the field for Brooklyn in 1903 bore little resemblance to the team that won the 1900 pennant. Only shortstop Bill Dahlen and left fielder Jimmy Sheckard remained from that team. Gone from the 1902 club were catcher Duke Farrell, outfielder Cozy Dolan, and pitchers Wild Bill Donovan, Frank Kitson, Jim Hughes, and Doc Newton. Even Wee Willie Keeler, a Brooklyn native who had turned down higher salary offers the first two years of the baseball war, left the team for more money in 1903.

It was a sad development for Brooklyn fans, and it is difficult not to feel some sympathy for Brooklyn president Charlie Ebbets and manager/vice president Ned Hanlon. During the baseball war the Brooklyn franchise seemed to find itself in a position quite similar to that of a current small- or mid-market team. The team's revenues weren't great enough to pay competitive salaries to all of the team's stars. Hanlon followed a strategy that would seem very familiar to modern baseball fans. Each season he came to terms with his younger, lower-salaried players and pleaded for a hometown discount from his older, established stars. The more ambitious and discontented players left first. The defectors from the 1900 team—Joe McGinnity, Lave Cross, and Fielder Jones—all felt they had been treated unfairly by Ebbets or, in Cross's case, by other National League owners. The players who departed after the 1901 season were veterans who wanted to earn higher salaries while they were still able to play. By the end of the 1902 season, the disparity between the salaries Hanlon was willing to pay and those offered by other teams had become too great for the Brooklyn stars to ignore.

Late in the 1902 season Wild Bill Donovan and Hanlon discussed Donovan's 1903 salary. They came to a verbal agreement on a number, but Hanlon procrastinated in presenting Donovan with a written agreement. In the meantime, the Tigers offered to pay Donovan several hundred dollars more than Hanlon had offered. Donovan told Hanlon he had a better offer from the Tigers but would sign with the Superbas if Hanlon matched the Detroit offer. When Hanlon refused, Donovan signed with the Tigers. Hanlon became angry with Donovan, but Donovan's response was simply that he dealt fairly with Brooklyn and would have been a fool to turn down Detroit's offer.

Frank Kitson's experience was very similar to Donovan's. He received an offer of $4,500 from Detroit, a much higher figure than he was receiving from the Superbas in 1902. Kitson said he preferred to stay in Brooklyn and would not sign with the Tigers until the Superbas had a chance to match the offer, which of course they refused to do.[33]

Wee Willie Keeler received an offer from Ban Johnson on behalf of the American League that was far better than anything Hanlon had offered. Keeler accepted the offer. When Hanlon complained that Keeler had not been fair to the Superbas, Willie responded, "I have stayed here [in Brooklyn] two years now at a loss of $1,800 just because I was told that it was to my advantage to play before the people of my town.... I think I have done my share and I guess no one will blame me if I hustle a bit for Willie and his interests."[34]

By mid–September of 1902 Hanlon had become very discouraged by the salary demands of his players. Abe Yager of the *Brooklyn Eagle* reported that Hanlon had not made any effort to sign players for two weeks. Hanlon told Yager, "The salary demands by each individual is such that if he had his way the Brooklyn club would be a fit candidate for bankruptcy courts at the end of next year, if not before the season is half over." Hanlon hinted to Yager that if he had his way the Brooklyn club would field a team made up mostly of minor league players. Then Hanlon "would take off his coat and start in as he did in 1894 and develop a team that in a couple of years would be a winner, whereas the other clubs would be finding the high-priced stars going back and be compelled to begin again to strengthen their clubs." Hanlon thought the Superbas might still make a profit playing through the season with a small payroll, while it would surely lose money by paying large salaries.[35]

Brooklyn (70–66)

Regular Lineup	AVG	OBP	SLG	R	RBI	SB
Sammy Strang, 3b	.272	.376	.333	101	38	46
Jimmy Sheckard, lf	.332	.423	.476	99	75	67
John Dobbs, lf-cf*	.236	.324	.316	69	63	23
Jack Doyle, 1b	.313	.383	.387	84	91	34
Bill Dahlen, ss	.262	.373	.342	71	64	34
Judge McCredie, rf	.324	.397	.347	40	20	10
or Doc Gessler, rf	.247	.366	.338	20	18	9
or Tom McCreery, of–1b**	.246	.332	.317	28	20	11
Tim Flood, 2b	.249	.291	.311	27	32	14
or Dutch Jordan, 2b	.236	.289	.285	27	21	9

Lew Ritter, c	.236	.290	.317	26	37	9
or Fred Jacklitsch, c	.267	.389	.364	31	21	4
Leading Pitchers	**W**	**L**	**PCT**	**IP**	**H**	**ERA**
Oscar Jones	19	14	.576	324.3	320	2.94
Henry Schmidt	22	13	.629	301	321	3.83
Ned Garvin	15	18	.455	298	277	3.08
Roy Evans	5	9	.357	110	121	3.27
Bill Reidy	6	7	.462	104	130	3.46

*Includes record with Chicago
**Includes record with Boston

Hanlon and Ebbets would soon follow the plan outlined to Yager, but for the 1903 season Hanlon tried his best to put together a contending team. He signed three veteran players who were no longer in great demand (Sammy Strang, Jack Doyle, and Fred Jacklitsch), and he re-signed Ned Garvin, who had joined the Superbas in August of 1902 after being given his release by the White Stockings. He tapped the Eastern League for Lew Ritter and Dutch Jordan, two veteran minor leaguers. As the season progressed he tried to fill gaps in the team by picking up Johnny Dobbs, Doc Gessler, and Tom McCreery, three men who played well at times in other years but were fringe major leaguers in 1903.

With only these players the Superbas would have been about on a par with the league's three weakest teams—the Beaneaters, Cardinals, and Phillies. But Hanlon had long benefited from ties to the West Coast, where he had discovered several fine players. In 1903 he figuratively struck gold there. He picked up two good pitchers—Henry Schmidt and Oscar Jones—who proved more than up to the task of pitching in the National League. Without the two ex–California League pitchers, the Superbas' pitching staff would have ranked among the worst in the league. With them the team had solid, if not great, pitching.

Schmidt was already a veteran pitcher by 1903. He was 30 years old and had been pitching professionally since 1893. During the 1890s the most prominent feature of minor league baseball was instability at both the team and league level. Schmidt's career reflected that instability. He played for a different team almost every year and at times with two different clubs. In the spring of 1898 he attracted some attention when he beat the best two National League teams, the Orioles and Beaneaters, in pre-season games. In 1901 Schmidt caught on with the Oakland Clamdiggers of the California League. He had a losing record that season, but in 1902 he became one of the league's top pitchers. California League seasons lasted about eight months in those days. Schmidt appeared in 64 of the 180 or so games his team played that season, winning 35 and losing 20.[36]

In Schmidt's first game with the Superbas he outpitched Christy Mathewson, although in truth "outpitched" didn't exactly describe his effort. He beat Matty, 9–7, on Opening Day. The Giants had runners on second and third with one out in the ninth inning, but Schmidt got out of the frame by striking out a batter for the second out and closed out the game by inducing a weak pop-up. He lost a rematch with Matty a few days later, when both pitchers were in better form. Two runs scored on an error by Dahlen as the Giants won, 2–1. Schmidt's next three games were shutout victories, two coming against the Phillies and the other against the Beaneaters. By June 25, Schmidt was 10–5, and had become a favorite of Brooklyn fans and baseball writers around the league.

Schmidt had a peculiar pitching style, which he complemented with a bit of downhome showmanship. After Schmidt beat the Cardinals, 5–2, in early June, a St. Louis reporter said, "After Schmidt got warmed up he was nearly the whole show. He wound himself up by revolving his arm three or four times, and let drive with a bunch of curves which looked like Chinese puzzles to most of the Cardinals." A Philadelphia writer described his delivery in a similar way: "Mr. Schmidt is quite a pitcher. Now and then he winds himself up like a Dutch windmill before turning the ball adrift, and he has a fine idea of distance and direction."[37]

In one of his victories over the Cardinals, Schmidt was so dominant he began telling the batters what pitch he planned to throw. "Here's a straight one, bet you a cent cigar you can't hit it," he supposedly told one batter, and kept up a similar banter with other St. Louis batters, who still were unable to hit his pitches with any effect.[38] Although he was born in Texas, Schmidt evidently learned English as a second language. His sentences were frequently put together in a grammatical structure that sounded more German than English. When the Superbas came out of a team slump in August, Schmidt assured Abe Yager, "When the team is right yet the team plays good ball already."[39]

Schmidt went into a slump in July and early August. On August 13 his record was 13–13. Yager attributed his troubles in part to concern about his wife, who had remained in Oakland and was facing a serious operation.[40] Whatever was bothering Schmidt's pitching, he evidently overcame it over the last seven weeks of the season. He won his last nine decisions in the 1903 campaign, finishing with a 22–13 record.

The contract Schmidt signed with the Superbas for 1903 did not contain a clause reserving his services for the following year. By the end of the schedule Schmidt was homesick for his family. His old team, the Oakland Clamdiggers, made him a generous offer if he would return to them in 1904. Schmidt decided to accept their offer. He never again played with a major league team. Thus, his major league career consisted of one season in which he was a 20-game winner, had a win-loss percentage of .629, and finished with a nine-game winning streak.

Hanlon's other pitching recruit from the West Coast was Oscar Jones. Unlike Schmidt, Jones was a youngster with little baseball experience. The 1903 season was only his third as a pitcher. Reportedly, he had never pitched prior to being pressed into service with the San Bernadino team in 1901. Although he had only a fastball when he began pitching, he was very effective, winning most of his games and mastering the curveball as he gained experience. In 1902 he pitched for Los Angeles in the California League. He led the league in wins, going 36–25.[41]

Jones won his first five games with the Superbas. He was the team's steadiest pitcher until Schmidt started his unbeaten streak in mid–August. He was a good hitter, batting .256 in 1903, largely because he was a very fast runner. Yager said Jones seldom went hitless in a game because his speed enabled him to beat out bunts. While Jones generally lacked the eccentricities that drew the writers' attention to Schmidt, he had an unusual habit. Reportedly, when he disagreed with an umpire's call, he would turn a backflip on the mound.[42]

A Painful Season: Boston

For Vic Willis and Togie Pittinger the 1903 season was one of recuperation and pitching in pain. The Beaneaters had been able to finish high in the 1902 pennant race because Willis and Pittinger were willing to become part of what was essentially a three-man rotation. The third spot in the rotation was shared by the remainder of the Beaneater staff. Willis pitched 410 innings in 1902, Pittinger 389.

Several other pitchers had worked that many innings in a season after the pitching distance was increased to 60'6" in 1893. Two of them—Cy Young and Joe McGinnity—had done so without any lasting effect on their pitching arms. Kid Nichols managed to carry a workload of that magnitude throughout most of the nineties but began showing its effects as the decade ended. The others had lost effectiveness in succeeding seasons and/or seen their careers ended prematurely with sore arms. Both Willis and Pittinger made it past their burdensome 1902 season, but both suffered in 1903.

Willis was the Beaneaters' highest-paid pitcher in 1902, the team's "ace." With the high salary came the implied responsibility of shouldering a heavy pitching burden. Manager Al Buckenberger leaned heavily on Willis throughout the 1902 season, not only relying on him to lead the team's three-man rotation, but at times also bringing him in to close out tough games.

For the first two months of the 1902 season, Willis was the lone consistently effective Beaneaters' pitcher. He owned four of the team's first six victories; six of its first twelve. On June 12 the Beaneaters were in fourth place with a 19–22 record. Willis' record was 11–4, the rest of the staff 8–18. As late as July 8, when the Beaneaters had a 34–27 record and had just finished a nine-game winning streak, Willis had played a part in more than half of his team's victories. His record on that day stood at 16–6, with two saves. Willis continued to pitch well after that, but lost more games than he won because of his team's lackluster offense. He finished the 1902 season with a 27–20 record. He had started 46 of his team's 141 games and finished 45 of his starts. As if that wasn't enough, he relieved in five games, winning one, losing one and saving three.

Pittinger started the 1902 season slowly, losing his first two starts and pitching only six innings in his third game, a 13–9 win. For a three-week period in late May and early June he was briefly dropped out of Buckenburger's three-man rotation, making one start and two relief appearances during that time. His record was 4–7 going into a June 14 start against Pittsburgh. In that game he held the Pirates to one hit, shutting them out, 3–0. That put him back into the rotation. Over the remainder of the season Pittinger seemed to thrive on the heavy workload. Including his one-hitter against the Pirates, he had fourteen games in which he held the opposition to six hits or fewer. He won 23 of his last 32 decisions, becoming the team's most effective pitcher after mid–July. His overall record was 27–16, tying Willis for second place in wins behind the Pirates' Jack Chesbro.

That was 1902—a season of success and good times. The 1903 campaign was more like the day after a wild night out on the town. For Willis the pain was nearly constant, coming in the form of poor outings, low-hit games resulting in losses, and a recurrence of the back discomfort that had ruined his 1900 season.

He began the season by losing five of his first six decisions. One of those losses was by a 10–7 score when he allowed 17 hits and three walks to the weak-hitting Phillies. He pitched well in the other games, however. In one of his losses he allowed only three hits, in another only six hits in ten innings. He also had a game in which he surrendered just two hits in nine innings but didn't get the decision. On June 12 he lost to the Cardinals, leaving the game after four innings and trailing, 8–0. His poor pitching was due to the return of his back pains.[43]

Boston (58–80)

Regular Lineup	AVG	OBP	SLG	R	RBI	SB
Charlie Dexter, cf	.223	.323	.280	82	34	32
Fred Tenney, 1b	.313	.415	.396	79	41	21
Duff Cooley, lf	.289	.342	.378	76	70	27
Pat Carney, rf	.240	.297	.298	37	49	10
or Joe Stanley, rf-cf-lf	.250	.306	.331	40	47	10
Pat Moran, c	.262	.331	.406	40	54	8
Ed Abbaticchio, 2b	.227	.306	.290	61	46	23
Ed Gremminger, 3b	.264	.313	.376	57	56	12
Harry Aubrey, ss	.212	.264	.249	26	27	7
Leading Pitchers	**W**	**L**	**PCT**	**IP**	**H**	**ERA**
Togie Pittinger	18	22	.450	351.7	396	3.48
Vic Willis	12	18	.400	278	256	2.98
John Malarkey	11	16	.407	253	266	3.09
Wiley Piatt	9	14	.391	181	198	3.18

Willis missed the next three weeks, came back to pitch poorly in two games, then sat out another two weeks. He seemed to have recovered physically when he returned to the rotation the last week of July, but he was still suffering badly from rotten luck. It seemed as if the only way he could win a game was by completely dominating the other team. His record was 8–8 over the remainder of the season. In five of his eight wins, he allowed either one or no runs and the other three wins were by scores of 3–2, 5–3, and 5–4 in ten innings.

For Pittinger the drop-off from 1902 was less dramatic, the pain less severe. Pittinger's 1903 season included a short spell on the sidelines due to a sore arm and was characterized by markedly inconsistent performances throughout the season. He won his first four games and pitched well through May. In early June he complained of pain in his pitching arm, though he continued to pitch after a ten-day rest period.[44]

Unlike Willis, who threw hard and whose best pitch was an overhand drop, Pittinger threw from different arm slots, his repertoire including an underhand raise ball similar to McGinnity's famed "Old Sal."[45] His pitching style evidently enabled Pittinger to withstand the heavy workload somewhat better than Willis. Nevertheless, when he took the mound Boston fans had no idea what to expect. Pittinger pitched a number of low-hit games, but he also had several days in which he resembled a batting practice pitcher. He had twelve games in which he allowed six or fewer hits. On the other hand, he had nine games in which he allowed at least nine runs. For the year he led the National League in losses, runs allowed, hits allowed and bases on balls. He also gave up the most home runs, but his league-leading total of twelve dingers seems pretty negligible to a modern-day fan.

Tragedy and Disappointment: Philadelphia

On a hot Sunday afternoon in August, the Phillies were stumbling through a doubleheader with Boston. They were in the fourth inning of the second game, having blown the opener, losing, 5–4, in 12 innings. Just outside the left field stands two drunken men grew tired of the derogatory taunts coming from a gang of children who had been following them. One of the men grabbed a little girl by the hair. She screamed.

Inside the park, fans along the left field foul line heard the screams. They ran to the railing of the gallery hanging over the street to see what was happening. More and more fans pushed against each other trying to get a view. Strained by the weight of the crowd, the railing gave way and the joints that supported the gallery snapped. Two hundred feet of gallery, along with many fans, fell 30 feet to the ground. As the gallery collapsed, several hundred people stranded further up in the hanging stands sought to escape, jumping on top of others, who were already lying on the street. Seven people died in the accident, more than 200 sustained injuries.[46]

It was a tragic incident that symbolized a bleak season for the Phillies' franchise. The 1903 campaign was a rebuilding year, with a new manager and lots of new players, mostly fringe major leaguers no longer desired by their former teams. Chief Zimmer had left the Pirates to try his hand as a manager. He took over a team with a rookie and second-year player sharing the catcher's duties (Frank Roth and Red Dooin), a former catcher bringing his iron glove to first base (Klondike Douglass), two banjo-hitting utilitymen competing for second base (Roy Brashear and Bill Hallman), a right fielder who couldn't catch a fly ball (Bill Keister), and a shortstop who was about to prove that his fine rookie season was an aberration (Rudy Hulswitt).

The Phillies did catch a break early in the season when Kid Gleason decided he wanted to play in Philadelphia, near his Camden, New Jersey, home, rather than in New York. Gleason filled the hole at second base. Zimmer's pitching didn't seem too bad, but his two best pitchers, Chick Fraser and Bill Duggleby, tended to put runners on base, which wasn't a good thing given the Phillies' inferior fielding. The Phillies didn't make a large number of physical errors by Deadball Era standards; they just watched many catchable balls go for hits and made lots of mental errors when opposing teams ran the bases aggressively.

Fans of bad baseball teams often maintain their interest by looking for signs of hope for the future, usually in the form of promising young players. Therefore, for Phillies fans Rudy Hulswitt's performance in 1903 must have been particularly discouraging. As a rookie in 1902, Hulswitt seemed likely to become one of the National League's star players. He had been on the verge of making the major leagues since 1899, when he was given a trial with the Louisville Colonels. He came close again in 1901, being cut by the Cleveland Blues just before the season started, with predictions that he had the makings of a good major league player. After joining the Phillies in 1902, he made a quick impression. In the opening series against the Superbas, he played so well that Brooklyn reporter Abe Yager wrote that he "was shaping up as one of the finds of the year." When Cincinnati writer J. Ed Grillo had a chance to see Hulswitt play, he echoed Yager's assessment. "Hulswitt, the new shortstop of the Phillies, judging from the game he played yesterday, has not been overestimated by the many newspapers that have sung his praises," Grillo said. "This young man acquitted himself in the finest kind of a manner yesterday."[47]

Philadelphia (49–86)

Regular Lineup	AVG	OBP	SLG	R	RBI	SB
Roy Thomas, cf	.327	.453	.365	88	27	17
Kid Gleason, 2b	.284	.326	.367	65	49	12
or Bill Hallman, 2b-3b	.212	.271	.288	20	17	2
Harry Wolverton, 3b	.308	.342	.383	72	53	10
Bill Keister, rf	.320	.352	.445	53	63	11
or John Titus, lf-rf	.286	.340	.404	38	34	5
Shad Barry, lf	.276	.321	.344	75	60	26
Klondike Douglass, 1b	.255	.308	.297	43	36	6
Rudy Hulswitt, ss	.247	.288	.329	56	58	10
Frank Roth, c	.273	.304	.359	27	22	3
or Red Dooin, c	.218	.254	.255	18	14	9
Leading Pitchers	W	L	PCT	IP	H	ERA
Bill Duggleby	13	16	.448	264.3	318	3.75
Chick Fraser	12	17	.414	250	260	4.50
Tully Sparks	11	15	.423	248	248	2.72
Fred Mitchell	11	16	.407	227	250	4.48
Jack McFetridge	1	11	.083	103	120	4.89

Hulswitt had good range and was able to make difficult plays with ease. Two days after Grillo praised his abilities, Hulswitt saved a game against the Reds with a great defensive effort. "Hulswitt made a remarkable stop of Corcoran's sharp grounder over second base," Grillo wrote. "He was so hurried that he did not have time to straighten up to make the throw to first. He cut the ball loose while stooping over." Grillo called the play "perhaps one of the most sensational seen on the local grounds this season."[48] As a batter, Hulswitt had a solid year. His .272 average with 18 extra-base hits ranked him near the top of the league among shortstops.

When the 1903 season opened, however, Hulswitt didn't seem like the same player. He was hesitant on ground balls and at times looked lost on routine plays. After one of Hulswitt's misplays contributed to a Phillies loss, a reporter wrote: "Rudolph Hulswitt's lately acquired habit of backing up his own plays, so to speak, brought disaster in the fourth.... With one out Doyle bumped a grounder on which Rudolph backed up for a few more bounds. Each bound meant at least two leaps for Captain Jack, and he was there when the ball arrived."[49] Two runs scored as a result of the play.

Hulswitt's early-season troubles that year seem to have been mostly a temporary fielding slump. Near the end of the season a Pittsburgh writer described him as "a fast and heady player both at bat and in the field."[50] But Hulswitt batted only .247 in 1903 and fell to .244 in 1904. His 81 errors in 1903 were the most of any National League shortstop, and his fielding averages were below the league norm in both 1903 and 1904. Late in the 1904 season the Phillies drafted Mickey Doolan, an outstanding fielder. Doolan became the Phillies' regular shortstop in 1905 and was one of the league's top fielding shortstops for the next nine years. Hulswitt was traded to a minor league team during the offseason of 1904–05. He later returned to the majors, playing for Cincinnati and the St. Louis Cardinals from 1908 to 1910, but the promise he showed as a young player went largely unfulfilled.

At Least the Grandstand Didn't Collapse: St. Louis

The Cardinals were still trying to recover from the mass exodus of their best players after the 1901 season. Not much was expected of the 1903 team, except the enthusiasm and hustle of young players trying to make the big leagues. "The Cardinal team this year contains but few players who can be classed as 'stars,'" a hometown reporter noted, "but the nine will be made up of a lot of youngsters who are out to make a reputation for themselves and who realize that the only way to do this is to play gilt-edge ball."[51] The writer and the fans had no way of knowing the Cardinals' rebuilding process would last about two decades. The difficulty of the process, however, was demonstrated in some of the events that occurred during the 1903 season.

St. Louis (43–94)

Regular Lineup	AVG	OBP	SLG	R	RBI	SB
John Farrell, 2b	.272	.336	.356	83	32	17
Patsy Donovan, rf	.327	.370	.378	63	39	25
or Jack Dunleavy, rf-p	.249	.306	.295	23	10	10
Homer Smoot, cf	.296	.342	.396	67	49	17
Dave Brain, ss	.231	.270	.319	44	60	21
George Barclay, lf	.248	.278	.310	37	42	12
Jimmy Burke, 3b	.285	.326	.329	55	42	28
Jim Hackett, 1b	.228	.272	.311	24	36	2
or Otto Williams, ss-ut*	.211	.242	.252	24	22	14
Jack O'Neill, c	.236	.288	.280	23	27	11
or Jack Ryan, c	.238	.273	.282	18	10	2
Leading Pitchers	**W**	**L**	**PCT**	**IP**	**H**	**ERA**
Chappie McFarland	9	19	.321	229	253	3.07
Three-Finger Brown	9	13	.409	201	231	2.60
Clarence Currie*	5	14	.263	181.3	190	3.82
Mike O'Neill	4	13	.235	145	184	3.79

*Includes record with Chicago

It takes good judgment and a measure of luck to build a good team, even out of promising material. In 1903 the Cardinals didn't seem to have a whole lot of either.

We've already seen that two young stars of the 1902 Cardinals—outfielder George Barclay and pitcher Mike O'Neill—fell victims to disease and injury. Their failure hurt the 1903 team, which had hoped for solid seasons from both.

The 1903 crop of youngsters included a couple of pretty good players, but for the most part manager Patsy Donovan was stuck with a collection of versatile youngsters who didn't quite fit in any one position in the majors. Two of Donovan's pitching recruits had been good hitters in the minors who filled in at other positions when they weren't pitching. One of them, Jim Hackett, was a big guy who had been among the better pitchers in the Class B Three-I League in 1902. It turned out that, despite his size, Sunny Jim's fastball had little zip, traveling about the right speed for batting practice in the major leagues. Donovan tried Hackett on the mound for a month before putting him on first base, where Hackett showed some power but couldn't make consistent contact.

Another pitching recruit, Jack Dunleavy, had pretty good stuff but often couldn't control it. Dunleavy was a fast runner and a good fielder, and he was the kind of gritty competitor fans like. Donovan used him as a fourth outfielder and a reserve pitcher. Dunleavy eventually proved inadequate at both positions but played three years in St. Louis, eventually taking over Donovan's right field job.

Before the season started Donovan traded his 1902 shortstop, Otto Krueger, to the Pirates for Jimmy Burke. Donovan evidently intended to play Burke at shortstop. Burke had other plans. He refused to report to training camp, saying he did not want to play the position. Burke's aversion to playing short may have been a result of the miserable fielding record he compiled when tried there previously. Donovan talked to Burke and agreed to play the recalcitrant veteran at third base. Donovan was forced to use Otto Williams, a long-shot prospect from the Southern Association, and Dave Brain, a career third baseman, at shortstop. Neither was able to do the job, although Brain hit well enough to stay in the National League until 1908.

Based on their 1903 records, Donovan's pitching staff didn't seem like a very capable group. Donovan gave nine pitchers a chance to show their stuff but didn't seem to get much in the way of results. The Cardinals' pitchers had the second-highest ERA in the league, with only the Phillies doing worse. But more patience with some of their 1903 pitchers might have paid big dividends for the Cardinals. Three members of Donovan's staff eventually won 20 games.

One of them, Bob Wicker, turned the trick in 1903. Wicker had spent the 1902 season with the Cardinals. His win-loss record had been only 5–12, but his ERA of 3.19 was not bad and he had struck out 4.6 men per nine innings, the fifth-highest average in the league. Wicker pitched only one game for the Cardinals in 1903. He relieved in the sixth inning of a contest the Cardinals eventually lost, 7–6, in ten innings. He allowed only four hits in the five innings he pitched and the run scored off him in the tenth inning was unearned. Although he would have been the losing pitcher by current scoring rules, the official scorer gave the loss to the Cardinals' starting pitcher. In his game summary the next day a St. Louis reporter said, "Dame Rumor has it that Wicker is to be released to Philadelphia. The latter is a hot weather pitcher, and if yesterday's exhibition goes for anything, he will be cutting a swath in another month."[52] The reporter was wrong about the team seeking Wicker's services—he was traded to Chicago rather than Philadelphia—but his advice to hold onto Wicker was right on target. Wicker went 20–9 with the Cubs in 1903.

The man the Cardinals got from Chicago in exchange for Wicker was Bob Rhoads, who didn't do much while he was in St. Louis. Donovan gave him a chance to earn a place on the Cardinals' staff, but Rhoads had only borderline stuff in 1903. The Cardinals released him the last day of August, partly because he hadn't been very effective and partly to save money. Rhoads was signed immediately by the Cleveland Blues. While he was with Cleveland, Rhoads learned to throw a pretty good spitball and became one of the Blues' better pitchers for several years. In 1906 he went 22–10 with a 1.80 ERA.

The third eventual 20-game winner on the Cardinals' 1903 staff was the best. Mordecai "Three-Finger" Brown was 26 in 1903, but he did not have a lot of professional experience. He was already 24 when he broke into the minor leagues in 1901 with the Class D Terre Haute Hottentots. Although his 25–8 record would certainly have attracted attention from higher-level teams, he probably made a bigger impression in September when the low-level Hottentots beat the Cardinals, 10–8, in an exhibition game. In the last three innings of the game, Brown fanned five Cardinals in a row, getting the last batter in the seventh inning, three batters in the eighth, and the leadoff hitter in the ninth.[53]

In 1902 Brown pitched for Omaha in the Class A Western League, putting up a 27–15 record. Donovan, probably remembering Brown's exhibition performance of the previous season, purchased his contract from Omaha after the 1902 season ended.

Brown got off to a good start with the Cardinals in 1903. In his major league debut he threw a one-hit shutout against the Cubs in a rain-shortened five-inning game. He beat Pittsburgh, 10–5, in his second outing, but he started taking his lumps after that. The Pirates scored 11 runs in seven innings the second time they saw him. Mordecai won only one game between April 25 and May 25, while losing five. In his only victory during that time, a reporter observed, "Brown did the pitching for Donovan's team, and looked like easy money. He was easy, too, and the Boston boys will feel sore for a month to think he got away with the game."[54] His fifth loss was a 13–4 pounding by the Giants in which he again gave up 11 runs in seven innings.

The future looked pretty dark for Brown at that time. He had tried to pitch through pain in his pitching shoulder but could no longer go on. Donovan told him to rest his arm in hopes the pain would go away. When the Cardinals went on an eastern trip in mid–June, Brown was left behind in St. Louis. He became depressed. He failed to show up at League Park for practice and began talking about going back to Omaha.[55] By the end of June, however, his shoulder began to feel better.

When the Cardinals returned home for a doubleheader on July 4, Donovan sent Mordecai into the first game to relieve Jack Dunleavy, who gave up three runs in the first two innings. Brown pitched well, giving up just two runs over the remainder of the game. Five days later he started and lost to the Giants, 4–2. It was his first start against Christy Mathewson in a matchup that would become legendary.

Brown's next win didn't come until mid–August, after eight straight losses, though he generally pitched well—wins weren't easy to come by for the 1903 Cardinals. Brown ended the season on a high note, winning six of his last eight games. His record that year was only 9–13, but his 2.60 ERA ranked eighth in the National League, not a mean feat considering how poorly the Cardinals fielded. He was viewed as a possible future star. But in December of 1903 the Cardinals were offered Jack

Taylor in a deal that included Brown. Taylor wasn't a possible future star; he was one of the best pitchers in the league. The Cardinals agreed to the deal. Taylor won 20 games for them in 1904, although he also lost 19 games. By 1906 he was back with the Cubs. Brown, of course, was on his way to a career that eventually resulted in his election to the Baseball Hall of Fame.

Poor Control: Mike Donlin

Mike Donlin was immensely talented. He was one of the fastest men in baseball when he played; he hit for average and power; he often made sensational catches in the field. His arm was so strong that his big league debut came as a pitcher. His batting statistics for the period in which he played—1899 to 1914—rank him with the very best players of his generation. He had the sixth-highest batting average of any player who played at least five years during that period. The players with better averages are considered among the top players in the Baseball Hall of Fame: Ty Cobb, Nap Lajoie, Tris Speaker, Eddie Collins, and Honus Wagner. Donlin also had the sixth-highest slugging percentage over that period and the tenth-highest on-base percentage. Again, only members of the Hall of Fame did better.

Donlin, of course, is not in the Hall of Fame. The principal reason for that is he lacked control. His control problem didn't involve pitches or even his throws from the outfield, although those did tend to go astray at times. Mike's problem was he couldn't control himself. On the field he couldn't resist attempting the sensational play. All too often he got thrown out trying to stretch a hit, steal a base, or move up a base when he had very little chance of being safe. Off the field he couldn't control a tendency to drink too much or to behave badly once he became inebriated. His desire for the spotlight caused him to give up baseball for the stage for two years at the height of his career. As a result of a series of suspensions, injuries, a two-year sabbatical, and six months of jail time, over the 16-year period between his first major league season and his last Donlin played in only 1,049 games and had only five seasons in which he appeared in more than 100 games.

As might be expected with Donlin, his entry into major league baseball occurred in an unusual fashion. In late 1898 and early 1899 Mike made headlines in local newspapers while pitching for several Northern California teams. The local correspondent for *The Sporting News* sent the paper's editor a picture of Donlin and a lengthy article that included box scores of every game Donlin had played. The editor, A. J. Flanner, gave the information to Pat Tebeau, the manager of the St. Louis National League team, who was intrigued by what he saw.

Tebeau went to see his boss, St. Louis owner Frank DeHaas Robison. "Here's a man we want," Tebeau said. "He is not only the best pitcher in the California League, but according to these scores and the clipping I have read from the San Francisco papers, its leading batter and speediest baserunner. He plays center field one day and pitches the next. He is surely worth a trial."[56] In keeping with his character, the brash young Donlin, who was being paid $50 per month in California, demanded $300 a month to come to St. Louis. Tebeau agreed to pay his price.[57]

Mike Donlin was a great hitter, but his off-field pursuits limited his baseball accomplishments (Library of Congress).

As soon as Donlin arrived, Tebeau knew he had found a gifted player. But the first task was to figure out what to do with him. Mike's first appearance was on the mound. He pitched three innings of relief against the tough Boston Beaneaters, allowing only one hit and one run. In his next appearance, however, he had trouble locating the plate.

Tebeau had already discovered during practice sessions that Mike could hit pretty well, and was anxious to find a spot for him in the field. As we shall see, that was a lot easier said than done. The team's shortstop was having a terrible year, so Tebeau tried Mike there. In his first game Mike did all right. He had two putouts and four assists, and made no errors. After that there were no putouts and no assists, just errors—two in the next game, three in the third. Mike struggled so badly in the third game that Tebeau changed places with him in the fifth inning by going to short while Donlin moved to first. Mike made his fourth error of the game while playing first base.[58]

Mike stayed in the lineup for a while at first base, but with every team using the tactics of "scientific baseball"—lots of bunting and aggressive baserunning—that position was not then a safe place to hide a fielding liability. Mike's poor play led to a fight with a teammate and another position change, this time to center field.[59]

There Donlin's speed helped to partially overcome deficiencies in fielding grounders and judging fly balls hit directly at him. He stayed in the lineup, however, principally because he hit better than any other candidate for the job. In his rookie season, coming straight from a low-level minor league team, Mike hit .323 with 15 doubles, six triples, and six home runs in 266 at-bats. He stole 20 bases. He hit several long-distance drives, including one that sailed about 430 feet and was considered the longest hit of the season by any National Leaguer.[60] His batting average was among the top 25 percent in the National League and his slugging percentage was the ninth-best. On the other hand, in 51 games as an outfielder, his fielding average was .873.

Off the field, besides the fight with a teammate that occurred at a train station, Donlin was involved in an incident in which he and three older teammates beat up an obnoxious traveling salesman in one of the disreputable districts of St. Louis.[61] After the season ended *The Sporting News*, which had acted as sort of a booster for him during the season, lamented that Mike had not played up to his potential because he had failed to take care of himself. "Mike is making the mistake that many others have made," the paper said. "Instead of trying to improve in fielding and learning how to bunt a la [Jesse] Burkett, he seems satisfied to get through a game in any old way so as to get with the gang for a time. If he keeps up the convivial pace he set in St. Louis, he'll drop out of the National League in another season."[62]

Donlin started the 1900 season as a reserve outfielder, behind Burkett, Emmet Heidrick, and Patsy Donovan, who had come to St. Louis during the offseason. He soon began playing almost regularly due to injuries to Heidrick and Donovan. By late June he seemed close to winning a regular job. Then another off-field incident impinged upon his career.

At 4 a.m. on a Sunday morning Donlin was returning from a drinking spree. While he and a teammate were waiting for a bus in "The Badlands," the nickname for a disreputable section of the city, they decided to go into a nearby bar. Inside, Donlin made a joking comment to an older fellow who didn't appreciate Mike's sense of humor. Either the older guy or a younger friend took out a knife and started slicing away at Donlin, slashing his face, throat, and hands in the process. The doctor who tended to him said the throat wound was near the jugular vein and would have been fatal had it been a little deeper.[63] Always indomitable, Donlin was back in the lineup after a few weeks, playing both the outfield and first base.

In his second season, despite improved pitching throughout the league, Mike once again stood out as a hitter. Although he played only a few games more than half the schedule, he finished third in the National League in home runs with ten. His slugging percentage was the fourth-highest in the league; his batting average the tenth-highest. Although his fielding had improved, it was likely that in 1901 he would still have to battle for playing time with the Cardinals. Therefore, when John McGraw offered him a chance to jump to the American League, Mike was eager to make the change. With McGraw's Orioles in 1901, Donlin played more than 100 games for the first time in his career. He finished second in the league in batting, with a .340 average, and was eighth in slugging percentage (.475). Under McGraw's tutelage, he became a more patient batter, finishing third in on-base percentage (.409).

In the all-important deportment category, the 1901 season was fairly quiet for Mike. In May he was fined and suspended for a few days for shouting obscene comments at an umpire after a game, but by Donlin's standards that was small change. He made up for the oversight during the offseason.

In March of 1902 he became involved in another fight after a night of drinking. Legally, this one proved to be far more serious than his previous escapades. After coming out of a bar, Donlin encountered a young lady named Minnie Fields, with whom he had some sort of relationship. Fields was with a male companion and another woman. Donlin exchanged words with Fields and then blows with the companion. During the fight he struck Fields in the face. When he went to court over the incident, Donlin encountered a combination even more harmful than Fields and her companion—an incompetent lawyer and a hanging judge. His lawyer didn't attempt to defend him, choosing instead to ask for the mercy of the court. The court—that is, the judge—was not inclined to be merciful. He sentenced Donlin to six months in jail.[64]

While Mike was serving time in jail, he was released by the Orioles. Of course, since he was a star athlete, there was no shortage of people who were willing to forgive his transgressions and help him find the path to peace and tranquility. In this case the Good Samaritans were the Cincinnati Reds, who were only thinking about Mike's well-being. Well, maybe also to a very small extent, about his potent bat. In May the Reds signed him, with a flexible reporting date based upon his release from jail.

Mike joined the Reds in late August, ready to tell anyone within earshot that he was a changed man. Although at first his baseball skills were somewhat rusty, he was soon playing his game by hitting the ball hard, running the bases a little too aggressively, making sensational catches in left field, and mixing into his baseball stew a generous portion of errors and misplayed balls. That fall he moved to Cincinnati and seemed to have overcome his problem with alcohol. "He goes everywhere, gets into congenial crowds, but will touch nothing but water," reported a Cincinnati writer.[65]

Donlin's good behavior lasted through the 1903 season, allowing Cincinnati fans to experience the full range of his abilities on the baseball field. The best part came when he swung the bat. He just missed winning the batting championship, his .351

average finishing slightly behind Honus Wagner's .355. He finished third in slugging percentage and fifth in on-base percentage. He was second in the league with 110 runs scored and stole 26 bases. His season batting totals were quite impressive.

There is, of course, more to baseball than just swinging the bat. We have already discussed Donlin's struggles in the Cincinnati sun field. He did better after he switched to left field, using his speed to make a number of outstanding catches, but he still wasn't exactly a candidate for a Gold Glove (if they had had such an award then). He finished the season with a fielding average of .900 in the outfield. There was also Donlin's baserunning, which was often quite exciting, both in a positive and a negative way. To get the full flavor of Donlin's game, it helps to look beyond season statistical totals by sampling the game summaries:

> Against St. Louis, on May 4: "Mike Donlin was a decided factor in the contest. He started off by handing St. Louis a tally when he muffed Smoot's fly in the first inning, but he more than redeemed himself for the blunder in the fifth, when, with Seymour on first and two men out, he sent the ball on a long journey to right center and circled the bases, winding up the trip with a regular [King] Kelley slide to the plate. In the eighth he made a star play, when, after catching Weaver's difficult line drive, he whipped the ball to first in time to double up Williams, who had started for second thinking Donlin would not reach Weaver's drive. The throw was a long and perfect one, the ball traveling at terrific speed."
>
> The next day, May 5, still against St. Louis: In the sixth, Donlin bunted and beat it out. Beckley bunted, was safe on an error. Morrisey sacrificed. "Corcoran grounded to [third baseman] Brain, who threw Donlin out at the plate, that is, after Mike had been chased up and down a while, and Magoon's fly ended the round without scoring."
>
> A poor play by Donlin. But on the plus side: "Donlin's catch of Brain's foul fly in the seventh was one of the best bits of fielding done on the local grounds this season by an outfielder. He made a long run for the ball, got it not more than five feet from the stand, and then dashed into the rail."
>
> Against New York, May 15: Donlin came to bat in the fifth with runners on second and third, one out. He doubled, scoring both runners. Then: "Mike was caught asleep somewhere in [shortstop] Dunn's territory and was easily disposed of."
>
> Against Brooklyn, June 8: "In the first, Donlin's hit to right and Seymour's single looked like a good starter, and when Kelley sacrificed it looked like a certainty that one or more runs would be scored. Donlin tried to score on Morrisey's little tap to [pitcher] Schmidt, however, and died at the plate. Morrisey stole second, but Corcoran's fly to Sheckard ended the inning."
>
> June 10, still against Brooklyn: In the Superbas seventh, "Strang, the first man up, got a free pass to first. He took second on Sheckard's fly to Donlin, who threw wild to first in trying to make a double play. Strang scored on Dobb's single to center."
>
> Against Boston, June 30: "The throwing away of hits by the Reds began in the first inning. Donlin opened festivities with a double that Dexter misjudged. Seymour flied out, after which Donlin attempted to pilfer third and was thrown out."[66]

There were many more such adventures and misadventures by Donlin throughout the season. Although he continued to exhibit poor judgment in the field and on the bases from time to time, we shouldn't lose track of the fact that the good far outweighed the bad. After all, a player doesn't score 110 runs by being thrown out on the basepaths all the time. When the 1903 season ended, both the Reds' management and the team's fans were looking forward to seeing what he would do in 1904.

Unfortunately for the Cincinnati folks, 1904 was a year in which Donlin's restless nature reasserted itself. The trouble started in Pittsburgh on the Reds' first road trip. The Reds won the first game as Donlin made three fine plays in the outfield. The next day he seemed to fall asleep on the bases, being "caught so far off second base as to make his position positively ridiculous."[67] He was taken out of the game shortly afterwards. After that game a Pittsburgh writer reported that during a night of drinking Donlin had loudly complained about the way manager Joe Kelley treated him. "He stated during one lucid interval during the evening that he wasn't going to try to play ball, for when he did make a good play Kelley accused him of trying to make easy plays look hard," the reporter said.[68]

Over the next two months Donlin played his usual exciting game, giving Cincinnati fans perhaps even more thrills and chills than usual. He was hitting the ball as hard as ever, but he seemed to be making slightly more misjudgments than normal. On June 28 he misplayed a ball in the third inning that gave St. Louis a run and made a wild throw in the tenth that added to the Cardinals' total after the lead run had already scored. A Cincinnati reporter commented, "The way Donlin hovered around left field in the game shows that either his legs are kind of wobbly or he is over-weight, for he had to exert himself to full extent in chasing fly balls."[69]

A few days later, after the Reds began a road trip, the team announced that Donlin was being suspended for 30 days after another drinking incident, this time in St. Louis. The Reds explained that Mike had become intoxicated several times during the season, but that Kelley had tried to deal with him on a personal level, choosing not to report the infractions. That approach had not worked and Kelley had reached the point where he just wanted Donlin off the team.[70]

Having already put themselves in a poor negotiating position, the Reds found that a number of teams were willing to purchase Donlin, but no one was willing to part company with a player or players even approaching Donlin's value. They worked out a three-way deal that sent Donlin to the Giants. In exchange the Reds got Jimmy Sebring, a pretty good young player, but nowhere near the hitter Donlin was. When Donlin reached New York, he found that McGraw intended to work him into the lineup slowly, not wishing to break up a winning combination.

As a result of the time off and McGraw's policy of easing him into the lineup, Donlin's numbers with New York were much lower than those he put up with Cincinnati. He hit .356 with the Reds, only .280 with the Giants. His on-base percentage dropped accordingly, although his slugging percentage was only slightly lower. Despite the drop-off with the Giants, Mike still had the second-best batting average in the league (.329) and the third-best on-base and slugging percentages (.383 and .457, respectively).

Donlin stayed with the Giants, more or less, until 1911. He had a great season in 1905, playing for the team McGraw considered his best ever. He hit .356 and scored 124 runs. In October of that year he punched a waiter in a restaurant after arguing with him over a bottle of champagne, then turned on a friend who tried to calm him down.

In February of 1906 he and a group of fellow drunks mistreated a black porter aboard a train. One of Donlin's companions had a gun that Donlin grabbed and aimed at the porter, telling the porter he would show him how guns are used in the Wild

West. The incident ended with Donlin spending a night in jail and appearing in court, but he avoided any serious jail time.[71]

Before the 1906 season was very old Donlin suffered a badly broken ankle sliding into a base. He missed all but 37 games of that season. In the spring of 1907, Donlin clashed with Giant management over who was responsible for the doctor bills covering his 1906 injury.[72] He ended up holding out the entire season, eventually going on the Vaudeville circuit with his wife, actress Mabel Hite.

He returned to the Giants for the 1908 season—the season the Giants finished second because of "Merkle's Boner." Although he might have slowed down some because of the ankle injury, he still retained his hitting ability. He had the second-best batting average in the league (.334) and the second-highest slugging percentage (.452).

After that season Donlin went back on the Vaudeville circuit, skipping both the 1909 and 1910 seasons. He returned to the Giants in 1911 but was exiled to Siberia—or rather, traded to the dreadful Boston Rustlers (the then-current nickname for the Beaneaters)—after only 12 games. He was a part-time player for the Rustlers the rest of that season. He moved on to Pittsburgh in 1912, sat out the 1913 season, and finished out his career pinch-hitting for the Giants in 1914. Even with all the time off chasing his Vaudeville dream he was able to bat higher than .300 during those years, except in 1914. Donlin was never much of a pinch-hitter, so he managed only a .161 average for the Giants in his final season.

After his last major league season Donlin returned to Vaudeville, although he did have a couple of short stints with minor league teams. He soon made his way to Hollywood where he appeared in quite a number of movies over the next two decades. For the most part, he played minor supporting characters and made bit appearances. He died of a heart attack in 1933 at the age of 55.[73]

A Quiet Hero: Deacon Phillippe

John Wayne hadn't been born when Deacon Phillippe reached the National League, but Phillippe fit the image that Wayne later projected in his movies. He was the strong, silent type: The guy who didn't say a lot, but who was ready to act when he was needed; the guy who stepped forward in tough times.

Phillippe was a quiet person who preferred the company of other men with reserved personalities. Off the field he went hunting with friends such as Honus Wagner, another man who shunned the big city's bright lights. His best friend on the Pirates was Sam Leever, who had been a school teacher. Phillippe tended to be steady rather than flashy. He acquired the nickname "Deacon" because of his reticent nature and strait-laced life style.[74] On the baseball diamond he was a man of strength. He possessed one of the best fastballs in the National League and complemented it with a sharp-breaking overhand curveball. His hallmark was consistency. He put the ball over the plate, challenging the batter to hit the ball if he could. As a rookie in 1899 he walked 1.79 batters per nine innings, the sixth-best total in the league. After that he got better. Over the next eight seasons he ranked either first or second in that category, five times finishing first.

Phillippe's first professional team was the Minneapolis Millers of the Western League. In his initial season with the Millers, 1897, they were a bad team. Deacon went 7–12 that year. Somehow he managed to catch the eye of Barney Dreyfuss, the Pirates' owner, who prided himself on his ability to uncover promising young players. Dreyfuss followed Phillippe's work through the 1898 campaign when the Millers went from being bad to being terrible. The Millers' two busiest pitchers after Phillippe had records of 9–28 and 10–38. Phillippe stood out among the Millers' pitchers with a 22–18 record, but Dreyfuss said he would have rated Deacon the league's best pitcher even if he hadn't won a single game.[75] As the owner of the Louisville Colonels, he purchased Phillippe's contract after the 1898 season.

With Louisville, Phillippe was part of the rejuvenation of a woebegone second-division team. As a rookie in 1899 he helped the Colonels improve to 75–77 by going 21–17, the best win-loss record on the team. When the Louisville and Pittsburgh teams were combined as part of the consolidation of 1900, Deacon suddenly found himself on a pennant contender and a member of the best pitching staff in the league. The Pirates had three pitchers who were twenty-game winners in 1899. Jesse Tannehill won 24 games in 1899, after winning 25 in 1898. Sam Leever went 21–23 but was a real workhorse, starting 39 games and relieving in 12. He had three saves as a reliever. The 1900 Pirates also had Rube Waddell, who had a 7–2 record after joining Louisville for the last few weeks of the 1899 season.

The young Pirate team fought down to the wire for the pennant in 1900 but lost to the Superbas. A big part of the team's strength was the pitching staff. A quick look at the staff's numbers might suggest that Phillippe was only its second- or third-best pitcher. Waddell led the league with a 2.37 ERA. Phillippe and Tannehill both had 20 wins, the second-highest total in the league, but Tannehill's win-loss record was 20–6, while Phillippe's was 20–13. Sam Leever had only a 15–13 record, but his 2.71 ERA was lower than Phillippe's 2.84.

A closer examination of the record shows, however, that at least one important person—manager Fred Clarke—considered Phillippe to be the ace of the Pirate staff, the guy Clarke wanted to pitch the big games. Clarke arranged his team's rotation so that Phillippe was scheduled to pitch against the toughest teams on the schedule. Phillippe made 17 starts against the three other first-division teams. No other Pirate pitcher started more than 12. Eleven of Phillippe's 20 wins came against first-division teams.

The 1901 pitching statistics told a similar story. The Pirates won the pennant this time, beating out the Phillies by 7½ games. Tannehill led the league with a 2.18 ERA, Phillippe was second at 2.22 and Chesbro was not far behind at 2.38. Chesbro had the best win-loss percentage in the league with a record of 21–10, .677; Phillippe was second at 22–12, .647; and Tannehill was third with 18–10, .643. While the results were similar, once again Phillippe was the guy Clarke sent out to the mound most often against the tough teams. Phillippe started 20 games against first-division teams, Tannehill started 13 and Chesbro 12. Against those teams Phillippe was 11–8, Tannehill was 7–5 with a no-decision, and Chesbro was 6–7, including one victory in relief of Tannehill.

The pattern was altered somewhat in 1902, the season the Pirates raced to a 30–6 mark by May 30, and won the pennant by 27½ games. That year the starts against first-division teams were divided pretty evenly among the Pirates' five starters. Chesbro led with 14, Phillippe had 13, Tannehill 11, Doheny ten, and Leever nine. Then again some people felt at the time that there was only one first-division team in the National League in 1902—the Pirates. The other seven teams comprised the second division.

The 1903 season brought another change in Clarke's use of his starters. Chesbro and Tannehill had jumped to the American League. Clarke began the season with three veteran starters he could depend on—Phillippe, Leever, and Doheny. He used the three regularly during the first two months of the season while slipping several other men into the fourth and sometimes fifth spots in his rotation.

Doheny's off-field problems led to increasingly longer intermittent absences from the rotation, starting in late June. Roaring Bill Kennedy, who became the fourth starter, also missed a lot of time, first because of an injury and later because of ineffectiveness. Over the course of the year the Pirates' pitching held up primarily because both Phillippe and Leever had outstanding seasons, Phillippe going 25–9 and Leever posting an even better mark of 25–7. While Clarke might have given Phillippe one or two extra starts against first-division teams, he was in no position to manipulate his pitching staff like he did in the first three years after the consolidation. In those years he had more pitching depth than any other major league team. In 1903 he was continually scrambling to find a pitcher who might give his team a chance to win.

In early August, when Barney Dreyfuss issued a challenge to Ban Johnson calling for a post-season series between the American and National league champions, the Pirates were still a relatively healthy team. By the time the season drew to a close that was no longer the case, especially with regard to the pitching staff.

Kennedy missed most of August and September with a sore arm. When he returned in mid–September he made two ineffective relief appearances before losing the last game of the season to New York, 4–1. At that point Kennedy had pitched a total of 15 innings since mid–August. Doheny pitched his last game on September 7. When the season ended, he was in a mental institution in Massachusetts. With about ten days left in the season, Sam Leever aggravated his ailing pitching shoulder while trying out a new shotgun in a trapshooting match. As a result, when the first World Series started, Phillippe was the only veteran pitcher who was healthy.

The banged-up pitching staff wasn't manager Fred Clarke's only problem. Shortstop Honus Wagner had a sore arm and a pulled leg muscle, second baseman Claude Ritchey had a sore arm, third baseman Tommy Leach was recovering from a swollen finger, and utilityman Otto Krueger had not yet recovered from a beaning. Clarke, the team's regular left fielder, was still nursing a sore leg.[76]

Entering the series, the Pirate team resembled one of John Wayne's military units after it had just survived an enemy attack. For Clarke that meant it was time to turn to the Pirates' strong, silent man for leadership. As he had before, Deacon Phillippe answered the call.

Phillippe started the opening game of the series on October 1, opposing Cy Young. He quickly established mastery over the Boston batters. He struck out five of the first seven men he faced, fanning the side in the second inning. He ended the game with ten strikeouts. He allowed only six hits and walked none as the Pirates beat Boston, 7–3. The Americans' runs all came late in the game after the Pirates had taken a seven-run lead.

Clarke started Leever, his other top pitcher, in Game Two. Leever lasted one inning, giving up two runs before being relieved by young Bucky Veil. Bill Dinneen held the Pirates to only three hits as Boston evened the series at one game apiece.

Having used three pitchers in the first two games, Clarke was apparently reduced to two choices for his Game Three starter: Veteran Roaring Bill Kennedy, who was still rebuilding his arm strength after a long layoff, or rookie Gus Thompson, who had gone 2–2 with an unimpressive 3.56 ERA after the Pirates purchased his contract from Class A in August. Clarke didn't like either of those choices. Instead, he asked Phillippe to pitch Game Three on one day's rest. Naturally, Deacon agreed to do it. Despite the short rest Phillippe was possibly more effective than he had been in the opening game. This time he held Boston to four hits and three walks while striking out five batters in a 4–2 victory.

The series moved from Boston to Pittsburgh for Game Four. Sunday, October 4, was a travel day. Monday turned out to be a rainy day, so the fourth game wasn't played until Tuesday, October 5. That gave Phillippe two days of rest. Once again, Clarke chose to pitch Phillippe on short rest rather than to risk going with any of his other pitchers. For eight innings Deacon again proved to be too much for the Boston batters, although he was not as overpowering as before, striking out only one batter. He held a 5–1 lead and had given up only four hits going into the ninth inning, but in that final frame the Americans caught up with him. They rapped out five hits, scoring three runs and leaving two men on base when the final out was recorded. Despite the last-inning scare, Phillippe had won three games for the Pirates, who led the series, 3–1, and needed only two more victories to win the best-of-nine series.

By now Clarke had reached the point where he had to start someone other than Phillippe. Old Roaring Bill Kennedy went to the mound on October 7, his thirty-sixth birthday. In what would be his last major league game, he gave it a good shot. He held Boston scoreless through the first five innings.

In the sixth inning the Pirates' normally reliable defense collapsed behind him. Clarke dropped a fly ball, Wagner dropped a throw on a potential force out and later made a bad throw, and Kennedy gave up a walk, a single and two triples. Boston scored six runs in that inning and added four more off Kennedy in the seventh.

Pirates ace Deacon Phillippe starred in the first modern World Series, winning three games (National Baseball Hall of Fame Library, Cooperstown, New York).

Thompson mopped up in the last two innings, allowing one more run. Meanwhile, Cy Young had little trouble with the Pirates, cruising to an 11–2 triumph.

The next day, October 8, Sam Leever dragged his sore arm out to the mound for Game Six. He gutted his way through the entire game, allowing ten hits, giving up two bases on balls, and hitting a batter in a 6–3 loss. The series was now tied at three games each.

On Friday, October 9, a brisk wind was blowing when Clarke arrived at Exposition Park. He announced that the game would be postponed because it was too windy to play. The postponement gave Phillippe three days of rest when he started on October 10. The game was Deacon's fourth in ten days. His opponent was Young, who was also making his fourth appearance over that time span. Cy had opposed Deacon on Opening Day, relieved Hughes in the third inning of Deacon's second win, and then beaten Kennedy on the day after Deacon's third win. Young won this duel between the aces of the two pitching staffs. Boston hit five fly balls into the overflow crowd and added six singles to beat Phillippe decisively, 7–3.

The series moved back to Boston for Game Eight. Once again rain intervened to give Clarke an excuse to pitch Phillippe. On October 13, he started his fifth game in 13 days, pitching this time with two days' rest. He pitched surprisingly well considering his October workload. He allowed just eight hits and didn't walk a batter. The Americans scored two runs in the fourth inning on a triple, an error, a sacrifice, and a single. They added another in the sixth on a triple into the crowd and a single. Bill Dinneen, pitching his fourth game in the series, held the Pirates to four hits and racked up seven strikeouts. The 3–0 victory was Dinneen's third of the series and gave Boston the world's championship, five games to three.

Although Phillippe's team lost the series and Bill Dinneen won as many games as he did, Phillippe's valiant effort is widely recognized as the foremost performance of the first modern World Series.[77]

Seven

1903, American League

Paying More, Getting Less

In the third and final year of the baseball war, the American League again came out ahead of the National League in the recruiting contests. But the newer league's advantage was much smaller than during the first two years. The American League signed 19 players away from the older league, while 15 players jumped in the other direction.

Most of the top players who changed leagues went to the American League. But the younger league's new stars came at high prices and some of the players the American League had signed in earlier years were now demanding higher salaries in their new contracts. Several of the contracts given to the 1903 American League jumpers would have been unimaginable four years earlier, when a salary of $3,000 was the most a player could hope for, and part of that would be for serving as team captain. The cost of winning the recruiting race became apparent during the 1903 season when the Cleveland club lost money despite attracting good crowds both at home and on the road.[1]

The National League, meanwhile, had begun attracting talented players back into its fold. John McGraw took a half-dozen top players back to the older league when he left Baltimore. He signed several other prominent players for 1903. Sam Mertes was one of the better hitters in the major leagues. John Warner and Billy Gilbert were both solid players. Had the peace agreement not dictated otherwise, Ed Delahanty would have played in New York in 1903 and George Davis would have been a Giant rather than a White Sox player reporting to the Polo Grounds each day. Cincinnati picked up Mike Donlin, signed Jack Harper away from the Browns, and might have kept Sam Crawford if there had not been peace between the two major leagues. Good players, such as Doc Casey, Kid Gleason, and Ned Garvin, signed with National League teams because of conflicts with their American League clubs. So both economics and competitive realities made it in the American League's interest to pursue peace during the winter of 1902–03.

The American League made one concession in the peace agreement that had a deep impact upon its future. The two leagues both wanted to have the same rules. Since 1901 the National League had been playing under the new "foul-strike rule," the rule used today in which the first two foul balls are counted as strikes and a foul bunt counts as strike three. Most of the American League owners disliked the rule. The National League representatives on the rules committee were adamant, however, about retaining the rule. Eventually the American League representatives dropped their objections, agreed to the rule and accepted the change reluctantly. For several years some of them continued to agitate for a return to the old rule.[2]

1903 American League Standings

Team	W	L	Pct.	GB
Boston	91	47	.659	—
Philadelphia	75	60	.556	14.5
Cleveland	77	63	.550	15
New York	72	62	.537	17
Detroit	65	71	.478	25
St. Louis	65	74	.468	26.5
Chicago	60	77	.438	30.5
Washington	43	94	.314	47.5

A majority of the players who jumped to the American League in 1903 went to two teams—the New York Highlanders and the Detroit Tigers. The Highlanders had inherited what was left of the Baltimore franchise, but Ban Johnson certainly didn't want to introduce his league to the nation's largest city by fielding the rag-tag group of players who played for the Orioles during the second half of 1902. Therefore, he placed all of the ex–Pittsburgh players, as well as Willie Keeler and Herman Long, with the Highlanders.

The Tigers had become almost as disorganized and demoralized by the end of the 1902 season as the Orioles had been—and with much less help from McGraw. (The ex–Oriole manager had tried his best to disrupt the Detroit team by taking Roscoe Miller away from them and trying to lure Kid Elberfeld.) Johnson gave the Tigers Wild Bill Donovan and Frank Kitson, who had been Brooklyn's top two pitchers. The Tigers had signed Sam Crawford during the summer of 1902 and added two journeyman ex–National Leaguers—outfielder Billy Lush and pitcher Mal Eason—just before the 1903 season started.

A Nebraska Cyclone in Boston

The Boston Americans didn't change much over the winter. The team lost catcher John Warner to the Giants but signed Duke Farrell from Brooklyn to replace him. There wasn't a great deal of difference in playing ability between those two catchers, but Farrell's personality was probably a better fit for the Boston team. The Americans had several Irish players and Warner had a reputation for harboring anti–Irish sentiments. For depth manager Jimmy Collins added Jack O'Brien, an outfielder purchased from Milwaukee of the Western League, and Norwood Gibson, a pitcher from Kansas City of the same league. O'Brien had previously played for Washington in the National League and for both Washington and Cleveland in 1901. Gibson had been one of the best pitchers in college baseball while at Notre Dame and was considered a bright prospect despite a losing record in the Western League in 1902.

Perhaps the most important change occurring over the winter was in the condition of Tom Hughes' right arm. Hughes had injured his arm while pitching for Baltimore in 1902. The Americans acquired him in July of that season, after McGraw's departure. They were willing to take on his expensive contract, despite the injury, because if Hughes could bounce back to his previous form he would be a valuable addition to the club.

Hughes first attracted widespread attention in 1900 while pitching for Omaha in the Western League. (This wasn't Ban Johnson's Western League, but a Class B league that took the name the American League had just abandoned.) Early in the season he pitched several low-hit games in a row and won his first seven games, acquiring the nickname "the Nebraska Cyclone."[3] His contract was purchased by the Chicago Orphans after Omaha's season ended.

Hughes' major league debut came in Philadelphia just as a tropical storm was approaching the city from the south. Chicago sportswriter Hugh Fullerton decided to trumpet Hughes' arrival by alluding to the coming storm. "For two days the weather bureau has been warning Philadelphians that a cyclone was coming," Fullerton wrote, twisting the facts a bit. "This afternoon the cyclone struck town. It was not the one expected, but a Chicago cyclone, fresh from Omaha, Cyclone Hughes, newest of all Tom Loftus' pitchers, and he would have swept everything before him but for the errors of omission and commission by his new comrades on the Chicago ball club."

Fullerton's write-up was a bit overdone, since "the Nebraska Cyclone" was lucky to escape the game with a 6–6 tie. But two veteran baseball men said after the game that Hughes looked like a good pitcher, having shown great speed, good control and a fine fast-breaking curveball.[4] Hughes made two more starts in 1900, winning one and losing one.

The next season Hughes found himself playing with the sad group of players dubbed the "Remnants" by Chicago writers. His 10–23 record with the Remnants didn't seem to be that of a world-beater, but baseball people knew he was a talented young pitcher. Pitching 308 innings in his first full season, Hughes fanned 225 batters, an average of 6.57 per game. No pitcher in the league struck out more per game than Hughes, not even teammate Rube Waddell, who averaged 6.2 per game. In August Hughes struck out 12 Cincinnati batters, including five in a row, while shutting out the Reds, 2–0.

During the season Hughes pitched three long extra-inning games. On June 16 he went 14 innings against the Giants in a game that ended in a 4–4 tie. He allowed 11 hits in that game while striking out 11. On July 31 he matched up against Noodles Hahn in another 14-inning affair. He lost the game, 5–4, but struck out 15 Reds. A third extra-inning affair was labeled "one of the best games ever."[5] On September 21, he threw 17 shutout innings against the Boston Beaneaters, outlasting his future teammate, Bill Dinneen, 1–0. He allowed only eight hits, while striking out 13 batters. Over the winter, Hughes jumped to the American League, signing with the Baltimore Orioles.

Modern pitching coaches would shudder at the thought of allowing a 22-year-old power-pitching phenomenon to throw 308 innings, including three marathon games such as Hughes pitched. Of course, there is no way of showing a connection between young Hughes' 1901 workload and the difficulty he had getting his arm in shape during the spring of 1902. As late as May 11, Orioles catcher and coach Wilbert Robinson told reporters, "Hughes still has a slight stiffness in his arm, which makes him fear to exert it as much as he might."[6]

Shortly after that, however, Hughes began airing it out. On May 17 he fanned six Senators in a 7–5 victory. Four days later he went ten innings against Detroit, losing, 4–2, but striking out eight Tigers. Coming back against the Tigers on two days' rest, he threw a four-hit shutout on May 24. In his next three starts, one of which came on one day's rest, Hughes was ineffective, allowing 13, 14 and 15 hits.

On June 8, Hughes slipped on the mound delivering a pitch to Elmer Flick, straining a tendon in his arm. The injury sidelined Hughes until July 18, when he started a game for his new team, the Americans, pitching in obvious pain for several innings before being relieved.[7] He started two more games over the next six weeks, lasting only a couple of innings in each. He pitched regularly the last month of the season but was not very effective.

At the beginning of the 1903 season Hughes didn't seem much better than he had been the last month of 1902. Boston played a doubleheader on the Opening Day of their 1903 season. Hughes relieved Cy Young in the ninth inning of the second game with the score tied, 7–7. He gave up three runs to lose, 10–7. Three days later, he relieved George Winter in the eighth inning of a 7–4 loss to the Philadelphia Athletics. This time he showed enough to get a start against the A's two days later and shut them out, 4–0.

Evidently, for the first few weeks of the season Hughes was somewhat reluctant to test his arm too severely. Boston writer Tim Murnane complained that Hughes had become too fond of his slow curve. When Hughes beat Washington, 6–4, on May 4, Murnane noted, "Hughes let up in the middle of the game as he is apt to do, but Captain Collins got to Mr. Hughes and after that it was a case of fastball with an occasional curve and drop. The result was that Boston held the lead quite handily."[8]

For most of the season Collins arranged his pitching rotation so that Cy Young and Bill Dinneen went to the mound every three or four games, while Hughes, Winter, and Gibson shared the intervening starts. Gradually Hughes started getting more starts than either Winter or Gibson, while starting almost as frequently as Young and Dinneen. The reason Collins began preferring Hughes was simply that Hughes had started pitching almost as well as Young and Dinneen. On May 26, in his first start in ten days, Hughes lost to the White Sox, 3–2, but gave up only seven hits in a well-pitched game. That loss brought his record to 2–3. He didn't lose again until July 10, winning six games in a row. He struggled for a couple of weeks but finished the season strong, winning 11 of his last 13 decisions.

Hughes' effective pitching took on added importance because a lack of pitching depth was one of the principal reasons the Americans had failed to win the pennant during the preceding two seasons. Hughes' recovery gave the team three top-notch pitchers, while Winter and Gibson provided pitching depth not matched by any other team.

Boston (91–47)

Regular Lineup	AVG	OBP	SLG	R	RBI	SB
Patsy Dougherty, lf	.331	.372	.424	107	59	35

Jimmy Collins, 3b	.296	.329	.448	88	72	23
Chick Stahl, cf	.274	.338	.375	60	44	10
or Jack O'Brien, cf	.210	.262	.302	44	38	10
Buck Freeman, rf	.287	.328	.496	74	104	5
Freddy Parent, ss	.304	.326	.441	83	80	24
Candy LaChance, 1b	.257	.303	.328	60	53	12
Hobe Ferris, 2b	.251	.287	.366	69	66	11
Lou Criger, c	.192	.256	.306	41	31	5

Leading Pitchers	**W**	**L**	**PCT**	**IP**	**H**	**ERA**
Cy Young	28	9	.757	341.7	294	2.08
Bill Dinneen	21	13	.618	299	255	2.26
Tom Hughes	20	7	.741	244.7	232	2.57
Norwood Gibson	13	9	.591	183.3	166	3.19
George Winter	9	8	.529	178.3	182	3.08

The team's other core players, the guys who had kept them in the pennant races until September in 1901 and 1902, continued to play well. When explaining the team's success, contemporary writers tended to start by praising the American's infield. In late August, a *Chicago Daily News* reporter wrote, "One of the most remarkable features of the club manager James Collins has gathered around him is that infield. There isn't another in the league, and possibly in the country, to compare with it."[9]

All four of Boston's infielders were outstanding fielders. First baseman Candy LaChance and second baseman Hobe Ferris were only average hitters, at best. Third baseman Collins hit for a good average and was one of the top power hitters in the league. He put himself in the all-important number two spot in the batting order in 1903, where he emphasized the hit-and-run game over the sacrifice. Freddy Parent enjoyed his best season with the bat in 1903. A small man, standing only 5'7" and barely weighing 150 pounds, he imitated Pittsburgh's Wee Tommy Leach by pounding the ball like a big slugger. He hit .304 in 1903 and had by far the most extra-base hits of his career. He tied for seventh in the league in doubles and for fourth in triples. He finished eighth in RBIs.

Boston's outfield was probably below average defensively, but it provided much of the team's punch. Left fielder Patsy Dougherty was the team's leadoff batter. He hit .331, stole 35 bases, and led the league with 107 runs scored. Right fielder Buck Freeman, the team's cleanup batter, was the most feared long-ball hitter of the era. In 1903 he finished third in the league in doubles, third in triples, and first in home runs. He had eight more extra-base hits than anyone else in the league, and his extra-base hits went for 190 bases, 28 more than the number two man in that category. Freeman led the league in RBIs with 104. The only outfield regular who didn't have a great year offensively was Chick Stahl, and that was mostly because Stahl missed half the season with an injury. While Stahl hit only .274, he scored 60 runs in the 77 games he played. Stahl's replacement, Jack O'Brien, was only an adequate fielder and batted below .200 for the entire time Stahl was out.

Behind the plate, the Americans received great defensive work from Lou Criger, whose throwing won several games. Never much of a hitter, Criger had trouble adjusting to the foul-strike rule, which was used for the first time in the American League in 1903. His average, which had ranged from .225 to .279 in his previous six major league seasons, fell to .192 in 1903.

Duke Farrell, who was to be the Americans' alternate catcher, broke his ankle after playing only a few games and didn't return to the lineup until September. Oddly, the 250-pound, lumbering catcher sustained the injury trying to steal second base. His eventual replacement, Jake Stahl, who came to Boston straight out of the University of Illinois, hit only .239, but with ten extra-base hits in 92 at-bats. Behind the plate, however, Stahl was still pretty raw. After watching him catch a few games, Murnane observed, "Stahl seems a bit clumsy for a real live catcher, and would be a handicap to the home team in that position."[10]

Although the Americans had talented players in every position, it is quite likely the team would not have won the pennant without its grand old man, Cy Young. Old Cy had another great season, ranking at or near the top in every important pitching category. He led the league in wins, with five more than any other pitcher. His 28–9 record resulted in the best win-loss percentage in the league (.757). He led the league in shutouts with seven and, as usual, gave up the fewest walks per nine innings (0.97). He was second in earned run average (2.08) and in opponents' on-base percentage (.276). He tied for the lead in complete games (34) and had the most innings pitched (341⅔). Young didn't try for strikeouts unless the situation dictated it, but he had the third-highest number of strikeouts (176) and ranked seventh in strikeouts per game (4.64). No pitcher had many saves in this era, but Young tied for the lead in that category. He made five relief appearances, in addition to his 35 starts, and had two saves, as well as two wins and a loss in relief.

During Young's first few years in the American League he accomplished at least one feat nearly every season seldom or never matched in baseball history. In 1903 Young stood out for his ability to outpitch his opponent in tough pitching duels. In mid–June he began a streak in which he tossed four straight shutouts. The last three shutouts were all by a 1–0 score, the only time that has been accomplished.[11]

As he had been for the previous two years, Young was the team's mainstay, the man who could be relied on to play well in good times and bad. The Americans faltered at the beginning of the 1903 season, struggling to stay at the .500 level until the end of May. Young had four of the team's first nine wins, and on June 26, when the team's record was 15–15, his personal record stood at 6–3. At that point the Americans began an eleven-game winning streak. Cy was an important part of that streak. He won two starts, picked up another victory in relief, and saved another game. The streak carried the team into first place, 1½ games ahead of Philadelphia.

The Americans and A's fought each other for the lead for the next two months, with Cleveland trailing behind in third place, close enough to overtake both of the leaders with a good-sized winning streak. The A's grabbed a slim lead for a while in late June, but the Americans regained first place and maintained a small lead until August 5, when the two teams met in back-to-back three-game series.

The Americans won five of the six games to move 6½ games ahead of the A's. Young beat Eddie Plank in one game but also had the American's only loss. The defining event of the two series was the disappearance of Rube Waddell after he lost the opening game, which was played in Philadelphia. After hiding out for nearly a week, Rube reappeared in Boston in time to pitch and lose the final game. By then his teammates were furious at him. The A's faded quickly after that, eventually finishing 14½ games behind the Americans, although still leading the Naps, who also stumbled through the last six weeks of the season.

After winning the American League championship, Boston, of course, met Pittsburgh in the first World Series. As recounted above, the most memorable performance in the series was turned in by Deacon Phillippe, who started five of the eight series games for the Pirates and pitched his team to a 3–1 edge before the Americans bounced back to win the next four games. For the victorious Americans Bill Dinneen led the way on the mound, winning three of the four games he pitched. Freddy Parent starred both in the field and at the bat. He hit .281, made a number of outstanding plays at shortstop, and led both teams in runs scored with eight, a World Series record that stood for 25 years.[12]

Not Enough Pixie Dust: Philadelphia

When baseball scribes gaze into their crystal balls each spring to divine how the oncoming season will unfold, they normally see a pennant race much like the previous one, with the reigning champion either repeating or finishing close to the top. In 1903 when they undertook that exercise, few baseball experts saw the A's winning the pennant—only two out of 35 writers responding to a poll picked the A's. Cleveland, New York, Boston, and St. Louis all drew more support. Most of the writers saw the A's finishing near the middle of the pack.[13]

Philadelphia (75–60)

Regular Lineup	AVG	OBP	SLG	R	RBI	SB
Topsy Hartsel, lf	.311	.391	.477	65	26	13
Ollie Pickering, cf	.281	.353	.346	93	36	40
Harry Davis, 1b	.298	.343	.44	77	55	24
Lave Cross, 3b	.292	.304	.356	60	90	14
Socks Seybold, rf	.299	.353	.462	76	84	5
or Danny Hoffman, lf	.246	.267	.347	29	22	7
Danny Murphy, 2b	.273	.295	.382	66	60	17
Monte Cross, ss	.247	.326	.319	44	45	31
Ossee Schreckengost, c	.255	.285	.353	26	30	0
or Doc Powers, c	.227	.242	.279	19	23	1
Leading Pitchers	W	L	PCT	IP	H	ERA
Eddie Plank	23	16	.590	336	317	2.38
Rube Waddell	21	16	.568	324	274	2.44
Chief Bender	17	14	.548	270	239	3.07
Weldon Henley	12	10	.545	186.3	186	3.91

We can't know why so few writers thought the A's would win or even contend for the pennant in 1903. After all, the only top player the A's lost was Dave Fultz, who ended up with the Highlanders. The A's also lost two pitchers, but neither was considered irreplaceable. Pete Husting's sore arm forced his retirement after the 1902 season, and Connie Mack made no effort to hold on to Fred Mitchell, who went to the crosstown Phillies. Mack replaced Fultz with Ollie Pickering, who had become a spare outfielder in Cleveland, and Danny Hoffman, who was considered a bright prospect. He replaced the two pitchers with three promising youngsters: Charles "Chief" Bender, Weldon Henley, and Andy Coakley.

Many writers noted that Fultz's absence would deprive the A's of a prolific run producer. And it is likely the writers thought Mack's pitching was too thin and were skeptical about the team's chances of winning with only two veteran starters—Rube Waddell and Eddie Plank. But it is also likely that, after a winter of pondering the events of 1902, the writers felt there was a little too much pixie dust associated with the A's 1902 triumph and that 1903 would not bring the same amount of good fortune.

The player who seemingly showered the A's dugout with pixie dust in 1902 was George Edward Waddell. That was a magical season for big Rube and the A's would not have won without him. The 1903 season, on the other hand, was one where his devilish side seemed to get the better of him. When Rube was on the mound, he generally pitched well, though he had more than his share of tough luck in 1903. When Rube wasn't pitching, however, he became a major distraction to the team and an almost constant irritant.

Before the season was over Rube had been suspended twice—once by Ban Johnson and once by Mack—had signed a revised contract for 1903 with good behavior clauses, was released by Mack after he ignored the good behavior clauses, and finally was re-signed by Mack, this time to a 1904 contract with new disciplinary clauses. By the end of August, when Waddell signed the 1904 contract, Mack was so weary of dealing with him that he let Rube take off the rest of the 1903 season.

Waddell's record in 1903 was actually pretty good; it just wasn't anywhere close to his outstanding 1902 record. Rube tied for third in the league in wins, with 21. He led the league in both total strikeouts (302) and strikeouts per nine innings (8.39). He was fourth in hits allowed per game (7.61), and was in the top ten in most other measures of pitching quality. And even though Rube's last appearance on the mound came on August 21, he still had the fourth-highest number of innings pitched.

One reason why the A's exceeded the baseball writers' expectations in 1903 was because the team now had three pitchers who would eventually enter the Baseball Hall of Fame: Waddell, Plank, and Bender. In 1903 Plank was as steady as Rube was unpredictable. His 23 wins were second only to Cy Young's 28 and his 336 innings pitched trailed only Young's 341⅔. Plank had 13 games in which he allowed six or fewer hits, plus a relief outing in which he allowed only three hits in 8⅓ innings. His longest winning streak was five games and his longest losing streak was four, both coming during the first few weeks of the season.

Although Bender was a 19-year-old rookie in 1903, he quickly became a solid part of the A's rotation. He worked 270 innings, ranking among the top ten in total strikeouts and strikeouts per game. He allowed only 7.97 hits per game, the eighth-best mark in that category.

Bender acquired the nickname "Chief" because of his Indian ancestry. His mother was part Chippewa Indian, his father was of German descent. He had left his family at the age of seven to attend a school for Indian boys in Philadelphia. When he was

12 years old he began attending the Carlisle Indian School, which became well known for its powerful football teams under Glenn "Pop" Warner. The Athletics had signed Bender in 1902 after one of Mack's agents saw him pitch for the Harrisburg Athletic Club.[14]

In 1903 veteran Harry Davis befriended the teenager, starting from the day the team left for spring training on a ship. Years later Bender said, "If it hadn't been for Harry Davis, who took me in tow, told me what to do and looked after me like a father, I think I might have died, or at least have been quite seasick.... I took his advice on anything and everything." One bit of advice Bender received applied to pitching. According to Bender, Davis told him, "Kid, whenever you get two strikes on a batter and no balls, throw the next one at his bean. Don't be afraid. You'll never hit anyone when you throw at 'em. But don't throw behind them or you surely will."[15]

When the season started, young Bender seemed intent upon applying Davis' pitching tip. After gaining a victory on Opening Day, pitching six innings in relief of Eddie Plank, Bender was given a start against the New York Highlanders. It's fair to say he made quite an impression. He not only shut out the Highlanders, holding them to four hits, he also intimidated them.

A Philadelphia reporter observed, "Bender used his speed to the best advantage possible. He was somewhat erratic, but this only augmented his effectiveness.... The New York players had a wholesome fear of his wicked inshoots, as he gave Ganzel a terrible shot in the back in the second inning. He also hit Williams and compelled most of the other batsmen to dodge some of his curves that went nearer their persons than the plate."[16] He continued to hit at least one batter in almost every start. In Chicago he opened the game by hitting Danny Green in the back, knocking Green out of the game. Later in the same game he clipped Cozy Dolan with a pitch.[17]

Over the course of the season Bender hit 25 batters, the most in the league. Although it is possible Bender was just wild inside during his rookie year, some other explanation seems more likely. In 1904 he hit only four batters, and the highest total over the rest of his career was 11. In addition to Davis' advice, Bender might also have been following the example of teammate Eddie Plank. In 1903 Plank was second to Bender in batters hit by a pitch, knicking 23. From 1902 through 1907 Plank hit at least 15 batters every year, topping out with 24 batters hit in 1905.

Too Many E's: Cleveland

In the spring of 1903 the *Cleveland Press* asked its readers to suggest a new nickname for the city's baseball team. The fans, enchanted by the play of star second baseman Napoleon Lajoie, chose the nickname "Napoleons," which was quickly shortened to "Naps." Cleveland's other major newspaper, the *Plain Dealer*, continued to use the nickname "Blues." Eventually "Naps" became the team's accepted nickname.[18]

The Naps were the "critics' choice" to win the pennant. The 1902 team had been transformed from the league's doormat into one of its top teams by the acquisition of several outstanding players as the season progressed. Although no major additions were made over the winter, most of the Cleveland players were young men just beginning their careers. Some improvement could be expected in 1903, and not much more would be needed for the team to win the pennant.

Cleveland (77–63)

Regular Lineup	AVG	OBP	SLG	R	RBI	SB
Harry Bay, cf	.292	.329	.364	94	35	45
Bill Bradley, 3b	.313	.348	.496	101	68	21
Nap Lajoie, 2b	.344	.379	.518	90	93	21
Charlie Hickman, 1b	.295	.325	.466	64	97	14
Jack McCarthy, lf	.265	.299	.352	47	43	15
Elmer Flick, rf	.296	.368	.413	81	51	24
or Jack Thoney, of	.205	.218	.254	10	9	7
John Gochnauer, ss	.185	.265	.240	48	48	10
Harry Bemis, c	.261	.295	.354	31	41	5
or Fred Abbott, c	.235	.270	.314	25	25	8
Leading Pitchers	**W**	**L**	**PCT**	**IP**	**H**	**ERA**
Addie Joss	18	13	.581	283.7	232	2.19
Earl Moore	20	8	.714	247.7	196	1.74
Bill Bernhard	14	5	.737	165.7	151	2.12
Red Donahue*	15	16	.484	267.7	287	2.59

*Includes record with St. Louis

But pennant-winners need some luck, as well as talent, and in 1903 the Naps came up a little short on both counts. The first sign that 1903 might not turn out to be such a great year came in January, when Lajoie came down with a severe illness, described in the press as pleurisy combined with pneumonia. By March he had recovered sufficiently to accompany the team on its spring training trip to New Orleans, but was able to engage in only light workouts until near the end of the training period. When the season started he played sporadically, appearing in only 15 of the team's first 25 games. When he did play, he wasn't the Lajoie of 1902, batting only .246 with little power and playing mediocre ball in the field.[19]

Lajoie's troubles played a part in the team's slow start—the Naps won only two of their first nine games and struggled to surpass .500 through the first week of June. Near the end of a long homestand in May, Lajoie started coming around. The day after a 5–4 victory over Washington on May 20, a *Plain Dealer* reporter wrote, "Captain Lajoie played one of his old-time games yesterday, accepting ten chances, many of them exceedingly difficult, without the semblance of an error."[20] Three days later Lajoie went 3-for-4 against Rube Waddell, his hits including a double that came within a foot of clearing the left field fence. He got his average above .300 by mid–June, and by the end of the month was at .333, tied for second in the league.

With Lajoie playing at his full potential the Naps were again a potent offensive team. When the season ended, Lajoie once again led the league in batting average and slugging percentage and finished third in on-base percentage. Four other Naps finished among the top twenty in batting average. Bill Bradley placed second in slugging; Hickman was sixth and Flick fourteenth. Bradley scored the second-highest number of runs in the league, Bay was fifth, Lajoie seventh, Flick eleventh. In RBIs,

Hickman had the second-highest total, Lajoie came in third and Bradley thirteenth. Harry Bay led the league in stolen bases and admiring comments about his speed.

When they put things together, the Naps could put on the kind of slugging shows fans love to see. They smashed "the longest hit on the grounds" in two different parks—Flick driving a ball far over the right field fence in Washington and Hickman clearing the center field fence in the Highlanders' new park.[21] Lajoie and Hickman went on a long ball binge (by Deadball Era standards) during a three-game series at St. Louis in late July. The two sluggers loved Sportsman's Park, one of the top hitters' parks of the era. In the first game, a 5–3 victory, the two each drove home runs over the left field fence. The next day the Naps lost, 9–5, but Lajoie was 3-for-4 with two doubles, while Hickman was 3-for-4 with a triple. In the third game, a 10–2 blowout, Hickman homered over the right field fence. His chief wrecking partner in this game was Bradley, who was 4-for-4 with three triples. Lajoie had two hits, but both were singles.

The Naps were not only strong at bat, they also had three of the best pitchers in the league. Earl Moore had the lowest ERA in the league. Bill Bernhard placed third and Addie Joss fifth. All three won a healthy percentage of their decisions: Bernhard had the third-best win-loss percentage (14–6, .700), Moore the fourth-best (19–9, .679), and Joss the eleventh-best (18–13, .581). Those three pitchers—three-quarters of the starting rotation—together had only 79 of the team's 140 decisions, which brings us back to the Naps' poor luck in 1903.

Not one of the team's three ace pitchers was able to throw a pitch in September. Bernhard went down first. On July 24 a line drive broke a finger on his pitching hand, ending his season. Manager Bill Armour tried to compensate for Bernhard's absence by going to a three-man rotation in August. That proved to be a mistake, as his pitchers were unable to hold up under the heavier workload.

On August 31 Moore, who two weeks earlier had won three complete-game victories in six days, complained of a sore arm after losing to St. Louis, 8–3. He missed the rest of the season. The next day Addie Joss came down with an illness that lasted through September. In place of these three stars the Naps finished the schedule with a pitching rotation of veteran Red Donahue, who had been acquired in August, three rookies purchased from the minors, and Bob Rhoads, who had been released by the Cardinals. They managed to go 14–13 in those games, but their pennant hopes, already starting to fade when Bernhard went out, quickly became little but a faint hope.

The Naps' failure to keep pace with Boston was due to more than bad luck. The Naps had some potent hitters and three top-notch pitchers, but they were deficient in an important area of the game: defense. They were a lousy fielding team even though four of the Naps were ranked among the best defenders at their positions. While Lajoie, Bradley, Bay and Flick were all outstanding fielders, elsewhere the team had serious problems.

Shortstop John Gochnauer set an American League record for errors with 98 in 1903. First baseman Charlie Hickman tied the record he set in 1902 with 40 errors. Gochnauer's record still stands, Hickman's error total was exceeded later in the decade by a Washington first baseman but is still the second-highest total in American League history. Fred Abbott, playing in only 71 games, led the league's catchers in errors with 19 and in passed balls with 17. Even Bradley, who was considered by some observers to be Jimmy Collins' equal as a third baseman, made more errors than any other American League third baseman in 1903. As a team the Naps finished dead last in fielding, with a .946 average, and made 25 more errors than any other team. Cleveland's pitchers were second in the league in ERA (2.66), and allowed only nine more earned runs than the top-ranked Boston pitching staff, but they ranked sixth in total runs allowed and gave up 66 more unearned runs than Boston pitchers.

Not Quite Ready: New York

Ban Johnson won a major concession in the peace agreement when the National League owners agreed to let the American League place a team in New York. At the time, Johnson acted as if his league's New York franchise was already a done deal, pending only a public announcement of the park location and Opening Day pitcher. The truth was, he was still searching for an ownership group and a place to build a park. He found both about six weeks before the season was scheduled to open.

The new owners did not exactly represent the cream of Manhattan society. They were Frank Farrell, a big-time gambler who owned a large number bars and pool halls, and William Devery, a Tammany Hall politician who had become wealthy running a protection racket while serving as the city's chief of police.

When John T. Brush learned that Johnson had won the right to put a team in Manhattan, he tried to block the intended move by acquiring the rights to every location even remotely fit for a new park. Johnson and Farrell outwitted Brush by picking a place located so far from the center of the city and so geologically forbidding that no one could conceive of using the site for a ballpark. The intended site featured a big slab of rock rising some 50 feet out of the ground at the top of a hill. With the help of hundreds of laborers and loads of dynamite, the new owners set out to have the park ready for Opening Day, which was scheduled for April 30, after the Highlanders had played six games on the road.[22]

When the big day arrived, the park still wasn't quite ready, but the Highlanders played anyway. Distances were shorter than normal due to a rope strung in the outfield. This was normal practice in 1903 for games where a large crowd was expected, such as on Opening Day. But this time if a player charged through the rope, he wouldn't be running into a crowd of fans. In right and center fields he would be plunging some 20 feet into a ravine that wound its way just back of the infield. The ravine, which was filled with rocks and boulders from the dynamite blasting, was nicknamed "The Pit." Any ball hit into The Pit was good for only two bases.[23] The Highlanders played six games in their semi-finished park before going on another road trip, this time for three weeks. Park construction forced the Highlanders to play 27 of their first 33 games on the road.

New York (72–62)

Regular Lineup	AVG	OBP	SLG	R	RBI	SB
Lefty Davis, lf	.237	.319	.263	54	25	11
Willie Keeler, rf	.313	.368	.367	95	32	24
Kid Elberfeld, ss*	.301	.365	.383	78	64	22

or Dave Fultz, cf	.224	.295	.271	39	25	29
Jimmy Williams, 2b	.267	.326	.392	60	82	9
John Ganzel, 1b	.277	.336	.378	62	71	9
Wid Conroy, 3b	.272	.322	.372	74	45	33
Herm McFarland, cf	.243	.333	.378	41	45	13
Monte Beville, c	.194	.252	.256	23	29	4
or Jack O'Connor, c	.203	.235	.231	13	12	4
Leading Pitchers	**W**	**L**	**PCT**	**IP**	**H**	**ERA**
Jack Chesbro	21	15	.583	324.7	300	2.77
Jesse Tannehill	15	15	.500	239.7	258	3.27
Clark Griffith	14	11	.560	213	201	2.70
Harry Howell	9	6	.600	155.7	140	3.53
Barney Wolfe	6	9	.400	148.3	143	2.97

*Includes record with Detroit

Johnson did a good job of putting the New York team together but ran into some rocks and boulders there, too. He gave prospective New York fans a team filled with proven winners. Most of the Highlanders were veterans who had played for pennant-winning teams in the past. Five came from the 1902 Pittsburgh champions (Jack Chesbro, Jesse Tannehill, Lefty Davis, Wid Conroy, and Jack O'Connor). Dave Fultz was a key player for the 1902 Athletics. Clark Griffith pitched for and managed the 1901 White Stockings. Herman Long played for five pennant winners in Boston and Willie Keeler for five between Baltimore and Brooklyn. Jimmy Williams had experienced a tough pennant race while playing for the Pirates in 1900, when they finished second to the Superbas.

The team looked pretty good on paper—only the Cleveland Naps had more support from the writers in their pre-season forecasting. In reality, the team was a little short of being pennant-winning material.

Shortstop Herman Long had been a fine player for more than a decade, but he hadn't been able to adjust to the new foul-strike rule. He hit only .188 in the 22 games he played for the Highlanders. Jack O'Connor was a smart, tough catcher, but at 37 he had seen his best years. O'Connor could also be hard-headed at times. He clashed with Griffith several times during the season and was suspended for not giving a full effort on key plays that lost a couple of games.[24] Lefty Davis, a fine player with Pittsburgh, reverted to his Brooklyn ways when he joined the Highlanders. Griffith gave him a thorough trial but released him after the 1903 season. Dave Fultz showed flashes of talent—he stole 29 bases in only 79 games—but had a poor season overall because of injuries.

Two of the team's highly paid players, Willie Keeler and Jack Chesbro, had seasons that were good when compared with other players' 1903 performances but seemed almost ordinary compared with the two stars' previous successes.

At the beginning of the season there was some doubt as to whether Keeler had fully recovered from a shoulder injury he suffered in a carriage accident during the offseason. Wee Willie got off to a slow start, which wasn't unusual for him. He was batting only .270 after the Highlanders' first 29 games but had scored 21 runs. He raised his average into the .280s shortly after that and stayed at about that level until

September, when a short hot spell raised his average close to where he finished the season, at .313.

As a team the Highlanders were a decidedly mediocre group, but Wee Willie almost certainly made them significantly better than they otherwise would have been. He was at the center of many of the team's scoring outbursts. He led the team both in runs scored (95) and in sacrifices (27), leading his teammates by a wide margin and finishing near the top of the league in both categories. The Highlanders had the fifth-best OPS (on-base plus slugging percentage) in the league, trailing the fourth-best Tigers by 30 points, but they outscored the Tigers by 12 runs. They were a lot like Griffith's 1901 White Stockings. Their offense often consisted of walks, bunts, and stolen bases. Wee Willie was usually in the middle of such rallies.

Examples of the Highlanders' ability to manufacture runs came on June 16–17, when they beat Chicago by identical 1–0 scores. In both games Keeler led off an inning with an infield scratch that resulted in a throwing error. In the first game he reached second on the error, went to third on a bunt by Fultz, and scored on a fly ball to the outfield. The next day he reached first on the error and went to second on a bunt single by Fultz. Keeler was forced at third on Kid Elberfeld's bunt, but Fultz scored from second when Jimmy Williams slapped a hit to right field.

Chesbro's 21–15 record paled in comparison with his 28–6 mark with the Pirates the previous year. But his 21 wins were third-highest in the league in 1903 and his .583 win-loss percentage was ninth-best. His season followed a rolling course of peaks and valleys, which was not unusual for the ace pitcher of a team that featured a mediocre offense and inconsistent defense. Chesbro pitched through two hand injuries and endured games in which routine fly balls and grounders eluded some of his fielders. Still, in 17 of his 36 starts he held the opposition to seven or fewer hits. He won five of his six starts in September as part of a late-season charge that almost carried the Highlanders past Cleveland into third place.

Kerosene: Detroit

The 1902 Tigers had been wracked by dissension. Several of the unhappy players were released over the winter, though discontent was so widespread that three or four dissatisfied players remained with the team. Over the winter the team suffered a sad loss when pitcher Win Mercer, who had been appointed manager for the 1903 season, committed suicide while on a barnstorming trip to the West Coast. To replace Mercer the Tigers hired Ed Barrow, who had just transformed the Toronto team of the Eastern League from a tail-ender to a pennant winner.

Later in his career Barrow would play a major role in building the great New York Yankee teams of the twenties, thirties and forties. In 1903 he might have been a good choice as the manager of a number of major league teams. Detroit wasn't one of those. Barrow was a big man who fancied himself as something of a fist fighter. He wasn't one of those namby-pamby guys who went out of his way to get along with other people; he was a "my way or the highway" kind of man.[25] That wasn't a particularly good match for the team he inherited, which had several players who might be described as "independent thinking" individuals. Bringing in Barrow as the manager of the 1903 Tigers was analogous to reducing a sizeable fire to a point where only hot embers remained, then throwing kerosene on it.

Detroit (65–71)

Regular Lineup	AVG	OBP	SLG	R	RBI	SB
Jimmy Barrett, cf	.315	.407	.391	95	31	27
Billy Lush, lf	.274	.379	.390	71	33	14
Sam Crawford, rf	.335	.366	.489	88	89	18
Charlie Carr, 1b	.281	.296	.374	59	79	10
Sport McAllister, ss-ut	.260	.297	.306	31	22	5
Heinie Smith, 2b	.223	.271	.283	36	22	12
Herman Long, ss–2b*	.213	.244	.260	27	31	14
Joe Yeager, 3b	.256	.303	.323	36	43	9
Deacon McGuire, c	.250	.306	.306	15	21	3
or Fritz Buelow, c	.214	.249	.307	24	13	4
Leading Pitchers	**W**	**L**	**PCT**	**IP**	**H**	**ERA**
George Mullin	19	15	.559	320.7	284	2.25
Wild Bill Donovan	17	16	.515	307	247	2.29
Frank Kitson	15	16	.484	257.7	277	2.58
Rube Kisinger	7	9	.438	118.7	118	2.96
John Deering*	7	7	.500	120.7	136	3.80

*Includes record with New York

Barrow's team was decent but not really a pennant contender. The Tigers had three fine pitchers in George Mullin, Wild Bill Donovan and Frank Kitson. Their outfield was arguably the best in the American League defensively, and was quite good offensively in 1903. Center fielder Jimmy Barrett and left fielder Billy Lush were the team's table-setters. Barrett, the Tigers' leadoff batter, led the league with a .407 on-base percentage. Lush, who often hit second, tied Nap Lajoie for the third-highest on-base percentage (.379).

Right fielder Sam Crawford led the league in triples and ranked second in batting average and fourth in slugging percentage. Following Barrett and Lush in the batting order, Crawford often came to the plate with men on base. He batted in 89 runs to rank fifth in the league. He might have driven in even more runs had he not been called upon to lay down 25 sacrifice bunts, which tied him for fourth in the league in that category, behind Lush, Willie Keeler, and John Gochnauer.

The Tigers had solid catching with veterans Jim McGuire and Fritz Buelow. Their weakness was the infield, which had been purged of three malcontents after the 1902 meltdown. That left three infield vacancies and Kid Elberfeld, a good shortstop who tended to become discontented over almost any little mishap.

The Tigers filled the first base vacancy with Charlie Carr, a minor league veteran who was a good fielder and hit well in 1903. The new second baseman was Heinie Smith, who came from the Giants in a trade for Kid Gleason. Smith was a borderline major leaguer who returned to the minors as a player-manager before the year ended. He played in the Eastern League until 1910, when he was 38 years old. Joe Yeager, a utility player in 1902, became the regular third baseman. Yeager spent most of the 1903 season learning the finer points of playing his position.

The Tigers were in the running for first place for the first six weeks of the 1903 season. That sounds good, but the same could be said of six other teams that year—at the end of May only 3½ games separated the first-place Boston Americans and the seventh-place New York Highlanders. Detroit's season started unraveling near the end of that month.

On Thursday, May 28, the Tigers lost the opening game of a series with St. Louis by bungling a rundown play between third and home. The team's execution of the play, which started with Elberfeld and involved the entire infield except the first baseman, was described as "sandlottish" by a Detroit writer.[26] On Friday, Elberfeld committed a costly error when he made a wild throw on a grounder that would have been the third out. The Browns scored a run on the play and added four more before the inning ended. Elberfeld's misplays in these two games came at inopportune times, but neither game was close, the Tigers losing by 7–2 and 7–3 scores.

The Tobasco Kid's contribution to defeat in Saturday's game was more direct. In a 2–1 loss, his misplays led to both St. Louis runs—one run scoring when Elberfeld held a relay throw while Jesse Burkett scored from first base, the other when Elberfeld threw wild to home plate attempting to get Emmet Heidrick on a ground ball.

After a day off to travel to Detroit, the two teams met again. On June 1, Elberfeld had a single in a five-run first inning. In the seventh inning he kicked some equipment around and threw his glove after a frustrating at-bat. On one pitch in the at-bat, a liner he hit down the left field line was called foul. Later in the same at-bat he was denied first base because he had made no effort to dodge a ball that hit him. In the ninth inning he booted a ground ball that might have become a game-ending double play. Later in the inning he made a half-hearted tag on a stolen base. The Browns scored three runs in the inning to pull out a 7–6 victory.[27]

The next day, June 2, Barrow announced that Elberfeld would be fined $200 and placed on indefinite suspension for his "careless and indifferent" play during the previous three days. In comments to the press Barrow implied that St. Louis manager Jimmy McAleer had somehow tampered with Elberfeld, even though there was no way McAleer could obtain Elberfeld's services under peacetime rules other than through an agreement with Detroit. Elberfeld threatened to sue the Detroit club to recover the $200. He said he would not play another game as a Tiger, adding that he would play in the outlaw Pacific Coast League if necessary.[28]

The general reaction throughout baseball to Elberfeld's suspension was that Barrow had overreacted. Joe Jackson of the *Detroit Free Press* said he thought Elberfeld's effort during the St. Louis games was about the same as his play in 1902 when Elberfeld was upset with the team. Jackson didn't think Elberfeld would try to lose on purpose. But Elberfeld was a moody player. He had been in a batting slump going into the St. Louis series, which Jackson felt was the cause of Elberfeld's poor fielding in the series, as well as his temper tantrum in the last game.

Another Detroit writer echoed Jackson's comment. "I do not suppose Barrow meant more than that Elberfeld had been losing games by indifferent play, including wild throws at critical points," he wrote. "If he [Barrow] intended to charge the shortstop with malicious throwing of games, Barrow will be very lonely in his belief."[29]

Tim Murnane of the *Boston Globe* wrote, "Ed Barrow is showing poor judgment in handling a great ballplayer like Elberfeld. Managers are plenty, but players like Elberfeld are scarce. Barrow has a record for losing his temper."

In an editorial, *The Sporting News* noted that Barrow and Elberfeld had been on the outs since spring training and that Elberfeld had wanted to change teams. "He has made costly errors at critical times and has shown an ugly disposition," the editor conceded, while insisting that Elberfeld "should not be accused of diamond dishonesty without the production of evidence that would justify his being placed on the blacklist."

Sy Sanborn of the *Chicago Tribune* said he knew little about the merits of Barrow's charges, but thought they were unwise. "Elberfeld is a great ballplayer in the eyes of the public and many managers," Sanborn wrote. "By making less of a spectacular affair out of his disciplining the player, Barrow could easily have negotiated a trade which would have removed Elberfeld from his own field and at the same time given him some equivalent. By advertising his own inability to handle Elberfeld, the Detroit manager damaged his own goods and lessened their value to others."[30]

Sanborn's comment summarized Barrow's situation accurately. Several clubs offered to take Elberfeld off Barrow's hands, but nobody was willing to offer much in return. On June 13 Elberfeld was traded to the Highlanders for Herman Long and Ernie Courtney. As we mentioned above, Long had been an outstanding shortstop for more than a decade but was no longer a valuable player. Courtney was a utility player.

With Elberfeld gone, the shortcomings of the Tigers' infield were magnified. The team finished the season without a regular shortstop. Long played the position long enough to confirm his inability to perform at an acceptable level and soon moved to second base. Nine different players tried their hand at the shortstop position before the season ended, including left fielder Billy Lush, pitcher Bill Donovan and two recruits from amateur teams.

Elberfeld's "careless and indifferent" play yielded a fielding average of .932 for the Tigers, along with a batting average of .341. The combined fielding average of his successors was .876. The two players who played most of the games after Elberfeld was traded, Long and Sport McAllister, hit .238 and .260, respectively. In his postseason assessment of the team, the *Free Press's* Jackson blamed the "experimental infield" for the Tigers' failure to finish in the first division. Jackson was referring not only to the unsettled condition of the shortstop position, but also Smith's mediocre play at second base and Yeager's inexperience at third.[31]

Seriously Off-Track: St. Louis

In 1903 the Browns were victims of two train wrecks, one figurative and the other literal. Coming off a second-place finish in 1902, the team was seen as a strong pennant-contender. It boasted an excellent defense and a deep pitching staff. The big question was whether or not it would hit.

During the first month of the season there was reason to believe the Browns would generate enough runs to win the pennant or come close. Three of the team's best hitters got off to good starts. Jesse Burkett hit .320 and scored 27 runs in the team's first 31 games. Big John Anderson hit .363 over the same span and Emmet Heidrick hit .307. The Browns were 17–14 in those games, just a game off the lead. Two of their better hitters, Charlie Hemphill and Bobby Wallace, were in slumps, and injured second baseman Dick Padden had played only six games.

With Hemphill and Wallace batting at their normal levels and Padden back in the lineup, the optimistic view held that the Browns would likely have enough punch to finish first or close to it. That didn't happen. Hemphill wasn't in a slump; he was unable to cope with the new foul-strike rule. Wallace was attempting to play through a case of tonsillitis. He had not been able to eat or sleep normally for several weeks when he had a minor operation in mid–June.[32] By then his batting average had shrunk to .219. Padden returned to the lineup for about a month before he reinjured himself, missing the rest of the season.

St. Louis (65–74)

Regular Lineup	AVG	OBP	SLG	R	RBI	SB
Jesse Burkett, lf	.293	.361	.377	73	40	17
Emmet Heidrick, cf	.280	.310	.395	55	42	19
Charlie Hemphill, rf	.245	.292	.300	36	29	16
or Joe Martin, rf*	.219	.252	.315	29	14	2
John Anderson, 1b	.284	.312	.385	65	78	16
Bobby Wallace, ss	.266	.309	.341	63	54	10
Hunter Hill, 3b	.243	.264	.297	30	25	2
Bill Friel, 2b	.228	.279	.305	46	25	4
Mike Kahoe, c	.189	.227	.258	26	23	1
or Joe Sugden, c	.212	.288	.228	18	22	4
Leading Pitchers	W	L	PCT	IP	H	ERA
Jack Powell	15	19	.441	306.3	294	2.91
Willie Sudhoff	21	15	.583	293.7	262	2.27
Ed Siever	13	14	.481	254	245	2.48
Clarence Wright**	6	15	.286	162.7	195	4.98

*Includes record with Washington
**Includes record with Cleveland

On June 24, after the Browns beat Philadelphia, 4–3, they were in third place, trailing Boston by 3½ games. They lost their next eleven games, falling from third place to seventh. Even after they broke that streak, the losses continued to pile up. By July 23 they had lost 21 of their last 25 games. Their pennant hopes were gone. Even worse, midway through the bad spell McAleer reached the end of his patience with the team.

In New York, as the losing streak was beginning, Red Donahue told McAleer he couldn't take his regular turn against the Highlanders because his arm was sore. McAleer told him to pitch anyway. When Donahue refused, McAleer suspended him without pay, telling him to return to the team when he was ready to pitch. Donahue left the team. He sent a telegram to St. Louis requesting his belongings, saying he would never play for the Browns again.[33] McAleer let Donahue hang in the wind for about a month before making a move.

As the losses mounted, McAleer began venting his frustrations in the press. In Philadelphia he told a reporter the Browns were "the worst quitters he ever saw." A St. Louis writer, after saying the team was playing good ball except for a nearly complete batting collapse, commented, "As a result of the quitting of the team, it is now all but in last place and pennant possibilities are not to be discussed. No wonder that Manager McAleer and Secretary Hedges are disgusted with the way things have been going and both would undoubtedly be willing to make changes if the team could be strengthened thereby."[34]

The changes began while the Browns were in their month-long downward spiral. First McAleer traded light-hitting infielder Barry McCormick to Washington for Joe Martin, a rookie who was batting .227 for the Senators and wasn't playing regularly for them. Shortly after that McAleer purchased the contract of third baseman Hunter Hill from a low-level minor league team. Then McAleer got rid of Donahue, trading him to Cleveland for Clarence Wright, who had been dropped from the Naps' rotation, and cash.

Over the last two months of the season the Browns played .500 ball, but McAleer continued his purge after the campaign ended. He traded John Anderson to New York for catcher Jack O'Connor, a player who otherwise might have been released by the Highlanders since he and Griffith could not get along with each other. Utility player Bill Friel was sent to a minor league team. The next spring Jack Powell was traded to New York after refusing to take a cut in pay. The reconstructed 1904 Browns again finished sixth, but lost ten more games than the 1903 team, its biggest weakness again being light hitting.

On August 28, after the Browns and Naps completed a series in Cleveland, the two teams boarded a special train headed for St. Louis, where they were to play each other the next afternoon. As the train was passing through Napoleon, Ohio, it ran into an open switch while traveling about 40 miles per hour. The engine jumped the rails. The players' sleeping cars were tossed around, the Cleveland car turning upside down and the Browns' car landing on its side.

Luckily, no one was seriously hurt, although a couple of Browns players suffered minor injuries. Pitcher Willie Sudhoff had a cut on his hand and sprained his wrist. Outfielder Emmet Heidrick received cuts on his legs and face. For the Naps, the only player injured in the wreck was Nap Lajoie, who bruised his knee. After a three-hour wait, a relief train came out to pick up the players. The game scheduled for August 29 was played as scheduled. Jack Powell, who had not been on the train, shut out the Naps, 4–0. As might be expected, neither team played a very energetic game.[35]

Playing Ugly: Chicago

Not a lot was expected from the White Sox entering the 1903 season, although few people thought they would finish as low as seventh place. The team had lost its manager, who was also a good pitcher (Clark Griffith), one of its best hitters (Sam Mertes), and its starting third baseman (Sammy Strang). Owner Charlie Comiskey also had to replace two starting pitchers who had not made it through the 1902 season

(Ned Garvin and Wiley Piatt). To replace all those productive veterans, Comiskey acquired pitcher Doc White and outfielder Cozy Dolan, plus a handful of Class A minor league players.

Then there was George Davis, probably the team's best player. In the spring Comiskey thought Davis would report to the White Sox before the season progressed very far. His backup plan was to obtain Harry Gleason, a utility player, from the Boston Americans. Comiskey had acquired Lee Tannehill, one of the minor leagues' top shortstops. He was going to move Davis to third base. Gleason would fill in at third base until Davis came to his senses and returned to the White Sox.

Chicago (60–77)

Regular Lineup	AVG	OBP	SLG	R	RBI	SB
Ducky Holmes, lf*	.270	.327	.330	66	26	35
or Bill Hallman, lf	.208	.320	.280	29	18	11
Fielder Jones, cf	.287	.348	.340	71	45	21
Danny Green, rf	.309	.375	.425	75	62	29
Jimmy Callahan, 3b	.292	.324	.387	47	56	24
Frank Isbell, 1b	.242	.266	.332	52	59	26
George Magoon, 2b	.228	.303	.278	32	25	4
or Tom Daly, 2b	.207	.304	.280	20	19	6
Lee Tannehill, ss	.225	.263	.276	48	50	10
Ed McFarland, c	.209	.264	.279	15	19	3
or Jack Slattery, c**	.207	.221	.239	9	20	2
Leading Pitchers	W	L	PCT	IP	H	ERA
Doc White	17	16	.515	300	258	2.13
Patsy Flaherty	11	25	.306	293.7	338	3.74
Roy Patterson	15	15	.500	293	275	2.70
Frank Owen	8	12	.400	167.3	167	3.50

*Includes record with Washington
**Includes record with Cleveland

Comiskey's plan went awry in two ways. First, after Boston gave him his release, Gleason refused to sign with Chicago on Comiskey's terms. Instead, he shopped around for a better deal. (He could do this because there was no National Agreement in place re-establishing the baseball trust—oops, make that Organized Baseball. That didn't come until the end of the season.) Gleason got the deal he wanted, but it came from Columbus of the American Association. Second, whether Comiskey liked it or not, Davis had already come to his senses. It made perfect sense from his perspective to do whatever the Giants asked him to do—which wasn't much—for more money than Comiskey would pay him to play baseball for the White Sox.

Davis' absence left Comiskey with a big problem—his infield was a mess. He had no third baseman. Tannehill, it turned out, wasn't as good a shortstop as advertised. Comiskey's second baseman (Tom Daly) had aged rapidly and no longer was a productive player. His first baseman, Frank Isbell, was a terrific fielder who was a mediocre hitter under the old foul-strike rule and a terrible hitter under the new rule.

Comiskey, through new manager Jimmy Callahan, tried a couple of experiments aimed at fashioning an acceptable infield. His first experiment was to move Isbell to third and put Cozy Dolan at first. Isbell showed excellent range at third base, which in his case was a bad thing. That gave him more opportunities to make a wild throw to first base, which he did on about one of every six chances.

Comiskey's next experiment, which lasted the rest of the season, was to put Callahan at third base. Callahan had been a pretty good pitcher for several years but pitched poorly the second half of the 1902 season. He was a good hitter and had thought about changing positions for a while. As a third baseman, Callahan continued to be a pretty good hitter. He seemed to possess the skills needed to play third base but, naturally, was extremely raw at the position. He made a lot of mental errors that didn't show up in the box score, as well as many physical errors that did.

The White Sox's infield deficiencies led to many ugly innings. For instance, on May 20 the Highlanders jumped off to a lead on a run manufactured by the Chicago infield. Lefty Davis started the game by popping a little blooper behind second that Tannehill misplayed. Willie Keeler followed with the obligatory bunt, which he directed at the new third baseman, Callahan. Both Davis and Keeler were safe when Callahan fell down trying to field the ball. Dave Fultz followed with another bunt—also obligatory under the tactics of the day—but botched it. He bounced it just off the third base side of the mound. The pitcher got the ball with plenty of time for a force out at third, but Callahan had started after the bunt and no one was covering the bag. The next batter hit an infield grounder that scored Davis from third.[36]

Although he improved somewhat on fielding bunts as he gained more experience, Callahan never mastered the skill. In mid–August a Cleveland reporter complimented pitcher Roy Patterson's fielding of bunts, adding the comment, "In fact, on bunts it was always Patterson that went after them, as Callahan is notoriously weak in handling them."[37]

Shortstop Tannehill had good range but a tendency to fumble the ball. In one of Sy Sanborn's game summaries, he noted, "Tannehill got his usual error, but this time no damage resulted."[38] It's likely Sanborn became a little too critical of Tannehill as the White Sox marched through their schedule booting game after game. Tannehill and the two second basemen who played beside him too frequently crossed signals when it came to covering second base. Sanborn usually blamed Tannehill for the miscue.

Tannehill would sometimes catch a ball with one hand when Sanborn thought a two-handed catch was in order. In one game Sanborn complained, "Tannehill was slow covering second almost every time one of Griffith's men attempted to steal. Once he made a grandstand catch on Davis, spearing the ball with one hand when the play ought to have been easy for him."[39] In another game, when a run scored after Tannehill dropped a relay throw attempting a one-handed catch, Sanborn remarked, "It is this habit of attempting lucky stabs instead of making every play as easy and sure as possible that stamps the minor leaguer."[40]

Sanborn's distemper in describing Tannehill's work can be partly excused when one considers the suffering the writer endured in having to sit through numerous exhibitions such as that of August 10, when the White Sox were drubbed, 10–2, by Cleveland. Sanborn's comment on that game: "The White Sox gave a listless, half-hearted exhibition from start to finish. Callahan forgot to cover third on a force hit, and then muffed Patterson's throw. Isbell failed to see easy bounders as they passed him, and

Tannehill spent most of his time in futile efforts to worry the baserunners, allowing at least two base hits by the maneuvers. On each occasion a run was scored by the hit."[41]

The Passing of a Great Player: Washington

When a team is bad—and the 1903 Senators were bad indeed—fans (and the media) sometimes vent their frustration on one or two players. Early in the season the object of the Washington fans' frustrations was Ed Delahanty. By the spring of 1903 Big Ed was well into the downward spiral that would soon take his life. He began spring training late because he hoped to persuade someone—the Senators, the Giants, the American League, anyone—to pay or forgive the debts he had incurred as a result of a winter spent at several racetracks. No one stepped forward, so the Senators agreed to reimburse $4,000 of advance pay Delahanty had received from the Giants. The money was to be repaid out of the annual $4,000 in salary the outfielder was to receive over the two years remaining on his contract.[42]

Washington (43–94)

Regular Lineup	AVG	OBP	SLG	R	RBI	SB
Charles Moran, ss	.225	.297	.298	41	24	8
Kip Selbach, lf	.251	.305	.356	68	49	20
Boileryard Clarke, 1b-c	.239	.273	.308	35	38	12
Jimmy Ryan, cf	.249	.290	.373	42	46	9
or Ed Delahanty, lf	.333	.388	.436	22	21	3
Watty Lee, rf-p	.208	.265	.277	17	13	5
or Scoops Carey, 1b	.202	.223	.240	8	23	0
Bill Coughlin, 3b	.245	.267	.302	56	31	30
Barry McCormick, 2b*	.216	.269	.275	27	39	8
or Rabbit Robinson, 2b-ss-of	.212	.279	.290	41	20	16
Malachi Kittridge, c	.214	.252	.245	8	16	1
or Lew Drill, c	.253	.331	.351	11	23	4
Leading Pitchers	**W**	**L**	**PCT**	**IP**	**H**	**ERA**
Casey Patten	11	22	.333	300	313	3.60
Al Orth	10	22	.313	279.7	326	4.34
Highball Wilson	7	18	.280	242.3	269	3.31
Davey Dunkle**	9	13	.409	190.3	207	4.16
Watty Lee	8	12	.400	166.7	169	3.08
Jack Townsend	2	11	.154	126.7	145	4.76

*Includes record with St. Louis
**Includes record with Chicago

When Big Del started working out, his weight was around 230 pounds, well over his preferred playing weight of about 190 pounds. He had lost some of the excess poundage by Opening Day, but he still moved about sluggishly. In the fourth inning of the Senators' first game he coaxed a walk from Jack Chesbro. He was pushed around to third with the help of a sacrifice and a single to left. When the next batter bunted to Chesbro, the pitcher grabbed the ball and fired to third, retiring big Del, who had decided against trying to score but couldn't get his body moving back to the base fast enough to avoid the putout. The next day he reached first after being hit by a pitch, but was quickly picked off by the pitcher. Later he let a routine fly ball drop in front of him for a gift base hit. Naturally, the fans in the bleachers were not shy about letting Del know how they felt about those miscues.[43]

The awkward baserunning and slow fielding characterized Delahanty's play for several weeks. In May a Washington writer commented, "Delahanty has been caught off bases about eight times already this season. Last week [Bill] Clarke was nipped while sleeping off second, and when he returned to the players' bench he declared he would soon be as clumsy as Delahanty in getting back to the sack when the pitcher was watching."[44] Writers around the league commented on Delahanty's lack of conditioning. When the Senators traveled to New York for an early-season series, a writer described Del as "looking untrained and overfed." On Del's first trip to Philadelphia, Charley Dryden of the *Philadelphia North American* informed his readers that, "The Fat Gentleman again appeared, thus assuring a performance that was highly moral and amusing, as well as instructive and entertaining."[45]

On his second trip to Philadelphia, Delahanty pulled a boner, failing to make a throw as an opposing baserunner scored from second base on a fly ball. The play elicited another sarcastic comment from Dryden: "This town is still glowing with excitement over Del's great feat yesterday of allowing Seybold to score from second on a fly to right field. Delahanty thought he had a record, but Mr. Loftus recalls that Bug Holliday turned the same trick at Cincinnati some years ago. Billy Hamilton ran home from second while Bug was resting after the catch." Delahanty's lame explanation of the play was that he thought Seybold was on third base, rather than second, and would score even if he made a throw.[46]

In mid–June, after Ducky Holmes was traded to Chicago, a Washington writer compared Holmes and Delahanty. "The latter is beyond doubt the better hitter, while Holmes is superior to Delahanty in fielding and baserunning. Del does not make many errors, but lots of balls hit fair that should be easy outs because Del cannot cover the ground."[47]

Delahanty still retained, however, the ability to crush a baseball. Upon his first appearance in Philadelphia he was greeted with a standing ovation by fans who remembered his slugging while he played for the Phillies. Rube Waddell was on the mound that day. Ever the showboat, Rube made a big display of motioning his outfielders to play deep, near the fences, when Del came to the plate. When Rube got around to pitching to him, Delahanty turned on one of his pitches, lining it along the left field foul line. The ball hit the fence so hard it rebounded almost all the way back to third base, where Del was standing when the ball was finally corralled.[48]

Delahanty tried to escape from his financial difficulties by turning to drink, a habit that had only emerged during the previous couple of years. In late June he went on a drinking binge while the Senators were in Detroit. He came close to having a mental breakdown. His family was asked to come over from Cleveland to help stabilize him. He seemed to have recovered when, on July 2, he boarded a train headed to New York, possibly intending to talk to John McGraw or John T. Brush about his situation. He became intoxicated during the trip and was ordered off the train near Niagara Falls. Shortly afterwards he fell off a bridge to his death in the Niagara River.[49]

After his death the baseball public began to focus on his immense talent rather than his recent shortcomings. All agreed he ranked among the greatest hitters of all time. The *Washington Post* baseball editor asserted that Delahanty was a shade above the others. "Unlike most heavy hitters, he was not impatient," the editor said. Delahanty was not a free swinger, like Lajoie, or fixated on hitting home runs, like Dan Brouthers. Instead, he was a patient, deliberate hitter. "Once he got a ball to his liking, and he usually waited until he did, he swung on it without apparent effort, and the result was generally a drive that was either safe or gave fielders all sorts of trouble to handle. Delahanty was also a place hitter. He could put the ball to either field, could hit it high or send it through the diamond at a rate that made it dangerous for basemen to play close in."[50]

The Man They Fought Over: George Davis

In July of 1903, as the American and National leagues were grappling over George Davis' future, Sy Sanborn of the *Chicago Tribune* remarked, "As a matter of fact the two leagues are not going to fight over George Davis alone. He is merely an incident, a sort of chip on the shoulder."[51] In a broad sense, Sanborn was right. The real issue was the peace settlement, and deeper still, John T. Brush's position of dominance among National League owners. The dispute over Davis's contract was but an incident Brush could use to push his own agenda. But for the "incident" to occur, there had to be a George Davis—a man who was both a very talented ballplayer and a somewhat devious and self-serving individual.

In 1903 Davis was all set to begin his fourteenth major league season. He had long been recognized as one of baseball's better players. His major league career had begun in 1890, the year of the Brotherhood War when twenty-four major league teams were signing players from wherever they could find them. Davis was nineteen when he joined the Cleveland Spiders, who were his

In 1903 George Davis was the focal point of an incident that almost re-ignited inter-league warfare (National Baseball Hall of Fame Library, Cooperstown, New York).

first professional team. His previous experience had been at the semi-professional level. He hit .264 for the Spiders in 1890, about ten points above the league average. The Spiders played him in the outfield, where he showed good range and led the league's outfielders in assists.

One of his teammates that year was Jim McAleer, who thought Davis possessed rare ability for a young player. Years later McAleer remarked that rookies inevitably display a lack of polish when they come to the major leagues without any significant minor league experience. "When you come right down to looking 'em all over, I don't recall but one player who came into the big league off the lots and didn't show it in some way. That was George Davis." When Davis came to the Spiders the other players expected to see a youngster who would require years of seasoning to become a finished player. Instead, McAleer said, Davis handled himself like a ten-year veteran. "Every move he made showed the natural player he was. The other members of the old Cleveland club will tell you the same thing. But George was one of a thousand."[52]

In his second year with the Spiders, Davis hit .289 and scored 115 runs, the sixth-highest total in the league. The next year, 1892, manager Pat Tebeau began using him as a type of super utility player. He played in 144 of the team's 153 games, but split his time between the outfield, third base and shortstop. The new defensive role may have affected his hitting. His batting average dropped to .241, slightly below the league average. He still managed to score 95 runs, however, and helped the Spiders win the second-half pennant of a split season. After that season he was widely considered the "best all-around player in America," which in modern terms meant that he was considered the National League's most versatile player.[53]

Following the 1892 season, which was a disaster financially for the National League, the owners decided the league's New York team needed to be strengthened for the good of the entire league. Cleveland owner Frank Robison was asked to contribute a player. He was first asked to send Patsy Tebeau, his manager and third baseman, to the Giants. When he demurred, saying that would be giving up too much, he was asked for Davis. Robison agreed. The Giants, in return, agreed to part with Buck Ewing, who had once been a great catcher, but now was a sore-armed first baseman/outfielder who was personally disliked by the Giants' new manager, John Montgomery Ward.[54]

Davis had his best years in New York. He played there for the next nine seasons, and batted better than .300 each year. From 1893 through 1895 he hit .355, .352, and .340, respectively. His best year may have been 1897, when he hit .353 and led the league with 135 runs batted in. Batting averages were higher in the 1890s than any other era, so in context Davis' numbers look less impressive than they might seem otherwise. But they were still good. And when Davis is compared with other players at the same position, rather than with the outfielders and first basemen who always dominate the offensive categories, they look even better. He played third base for the Giants until the middle of the 1896 season, when he moved to shortstop. Throughout the nineties and the first half of the next decade he ranked among the top three hitters at his position every year, usually placing either first or second.

Davis had some problems defensively as a third baseman. After the 1893 season there were rumors that he would be moved to the outfield because, according to one report, "Ward is not satisfied with Davis' slow, miserable throwing across the diamond."[55] No change was made, however, and Davis remained at third for another two-and-a-half seasons. In 1895 Davis played only 80 games at third base because of a sore arm, and in some of the games he played there he was not able to perform normally.

After Davis missed several games resting his sore arm, a reporter noted, "George Davis is back in the game, but it would be much better if he could be played in the outfield, where he could save his arm. George does not attempt to make the quick, snappy throws which frequently fall to the lot of third basemen and it is questionable if he will get his arm entirely back."[56] He seems to have played well defensively in the first half of 1896 before he moved to shortstop to make way for Bill Joyce, a third baseman who was acquired from Washington to become a player-manager for the Giants.

It evidently took Davis a year or so to master the intricacies of the shortstop position, but after that he was considered one of the top defensive shortstops — not quite on a par with Hughie Jennings, Herman Long, Bobby Wallace, or Bill Dahlen maybe, but still above average.[57] He hit better than any other player at the position, and was ranked as one of the game's best shortstops every year for over a decade.

Davis was twice appointed manager of the Giants. The first time came in 1895, when he was only 25 years old. After less than two months on the job, however, he asked to be relieved of his managerial duties, reportedly because he could not take the criticism that went with the job.[58] The Giants' record under Davis in 1895 was 16–17.

The second time came in 1900, when new Giants manager Buck Ewing complained that Davis was part of a clique that worked against him. Ewing charged that Davis had used a minor injury as an excuse to skip a western trip and used the time off to talk Freedman into firing Ewing.[59] After becoming manager in mid-season, Davis had his own problems with players who were not happy with the way he was running the team, despite the fact that the Giants went 39–37 under Davis after having had a losing record under Ewing. After the season he got rid of Kid Gleason, Dirty Jack Doyle, and Mike Grady, all of whom Davis accused of belonging to a disruptive clique.[60] Those losses, together with the defection of several players to the American League, left him with a relatively weak team. Under his leadership the Giants won 52 and lost 85 in 1901, finishing in seventh place, one game ahead of last-place Cincinnati.

After the 1901 season ended Davis was reported to have created "a stormy scene" in a meeting with team officials.[61] He signed with the Chicago White Stockings shortly after that. Freedman evidently made little effort to retain him. That might be understandable, considering Davis' poor record as the Giants' manager, even though he continued to be an outstanding player. What is somewhat surprising, though, is the negative response his signing received from a prominent member of the Chicago press corps. While Davis' signing with the White Stockings was still in the rumor stage, Hugh Fullerton of the *Chicago Tribune* filed a report about Clark Griffith's attempts to sign National League players. Fullerton wrote, "He [Griffith] claims George Davis, but I devoutly hope that Davis will never get into the American League, for he is a disgrace to the business."[62] Fullerton did not elaborate on that comment, so we cannot know the basis for it. It's possible he was referring to Ewing's charges against Davis.

Fullerton was not the only baseball writer bothered by some of Davis' actions. Shortly after Davis succeeded Ewing as New York's manager, a Pittsburgh writer observed, "Manager Davis is a great ballplayer, but he has worked without ambition.

Perhaps in his new role he can make the New Yorks play ball. Ewing found that an impossible task."

Three weeks later Tim Murnane of the *Boston Globe* noted sarcastically, "Since George Davis was made captain and manager of the New York team he has managed to be in the game every time."[63] Murnane's comment was both a reference to the Ewing affair and to a reputation Davis seems to have acquired for using minor injuries as an excuse to miss games. Another Pittsburgh writer made a similar comment during the 1901 season after third baseman Charlie Buelow sustained an injury. "The Giants will miss Buelow," he said, "and if George Davis takes his usual vacation before the injured man returns to his post the team will have hard work holding to its position."[64]

Davis had other habits that did little to encourage team cohesion. In August of 1901 the *Brooklyn Daily Eagle's* Abe Yager stated, "When a manager calls another player down for his own mistakes, it is no wonder his team cannot win. Davis made a glaring muff of a short fly from Dolan's bat in the eighth and, instead of taking his medicine, blamed Murphy because that player tried to get the ball, too, and stopped at the proper time when he saw that his manager was under it."

A month later a Pittsburgh writer reported, "The Giants are torn by internal dissensions, mostly owing to financial loans in which manager Davis is said to be interested."[65] Fullerton alluded to the same issue in the spring of 1902, after Davis joined the White Stockings: "I predict that the first time Davis borrows a bunch of dollars of Mertes (one of his tricks) and forgets to pay it back, there will be a ruction in the club that will keep even Comiskey guessing."[66]

Davis' reputation wasn't helped by the approach he chose to try to get back to New York. When he negotiated with Comiskey prior to signing with the White Stockings, Davis obtained the services of his old manager, John Montgomery Ward, who had obtained a law degree and built a successful law practice in New York. Ward wrote an "ironclad contract" that guaranteed Davis' salary with Chicago for the 1902 and 1903 seasons. Unlike the standard baseball contract, such agreements were usually written as personal services to be performed for the owner or the club.

When Davis decided to rejoin the Giants, he again appealed to Ward for help. Ward wrote another non-standard contract, this time with either Freedman or the Giants. To the press Ward disingenuously explained that the new contract was valid and took precedence over the Chicago contract because the reserve clause in Davis' 1901 baseball contract gave the Giants a prior claim on his services. Of course, a year earlier Ward had argued that the same reserve clause did not entitle New York to any future claim on Davis' services.[67] Newspapermen and many fans thought this explanation was just a little bit too slick.

After Davis defied the terms of the peace settlement and joined Brush in actions that almost led to renewal of the baseball war, criticism of his habits increased. A *Washington Post* writer declared that few tears would be shed if Davis were forced out of baseball altogether. "No player in recent years has been so severely 'knocked' by the boys who play the game as has George Davis," the writer said. "His personality is unattractive and his disposition almost unbearable according to the opinion of many ballplayers…. There is no question about Davis' playing ability, but he has not 'toted fair' with the two leagues and the magnates are quite put out over his stubbornness."[68]

After Davis rejoined the White Stockings in 1904, Sy Sanborn of the *Chicago*

Tribune wrote that Davis "seems to be entirely unconscious of the injury he has done Comiskey or of the fact that he has forfeited the respect of the public by his double-dealing and it is just possible that his moral deficiencies are such that he does not realize he has done anything outside of the pale of honesty."[69]

Although Davis had offended many sportswriters and fans by his conduct in 1903, he still retained his ability to play baseball very well. It wasn't long before writers and fans began to focus on his performance on the field rather than any personal shortcomings. A common comment early in the 1904 season was similar to one appearing in the *Washington Post:* "George Davis is covering a great deal of ground between second and third. He seems to be just as fast and useful as ever." Near the end of July a Philadelphia writer observed, "Those critics who didn't think much of George Davis as a ballplayer are referred to the position of the White Sox in the race. The shortstop has made a possible pennant winner of last year's tailender. Comiskey knew what he was doing when he said he'd have Davis or war."[70]

Davis was one of the stars of the pennant-winning "Hitless Wonders" in 1906. That was his last good season, although he played through 1909. He had one more year in professional baseball, as the manager of a last-place team in the Western League in 1911. He coached the Amherst College baseball team from 1913 to 1918. Then, as far as the baseball world was concerned, he dropped out of sight, and seemingly, out of mind. When the Baseball Hall of Fame was established in the mid-thirties, there were several elections in which Davis's contemporaries received at least momentary attention through the voting process. Although players with less impressive credentials than Davis received at least a smattering of votes, Davis was not named on even one ballot.

In 1968 Lee Allen, the official Hall of Fame historian, wrote an article in *The Sporting News* describing his efforts to track down the date and place of Davis' death.[71] Allen's article, which included a few salient facts about Davis' career, seemed to reawaken interest in him. Eventually he became the subject of a couple of articles in publications issued by the Society for American Baseball Research. In his book, *Whatever Happened to the Hall of Fame?*, Bill James argued that Davis was a better player than Joe Tinker. James compared the records of the two shortstops and concluded that in choosing Tinker, rather than Davis, for enshrinement in the Hall the electors had selected the wrong man. In 1998, the Veterans Committee decided Davis' record deserved to be honored. He was inducted into the Baseball Hall of Fame that year, along with executive Larry McPhail and outfielder Larry Doby.[72]

Bill Bradley, B. I.

The Cleveland third baseman of 1903 was Bill Bradley, B. I. He was a much different—make that a much better—player than Bill Bradley, A. I. In this case the "B. I." and "A. I." are short for "Before Injury" and "After Injury." In July of 1906 Bradley suffered a broken wrist when he was hit by a pitch. He missed the remainder of the 1906 season, and after that was never again the same hitter. Before the wrist injury Bradley had a batting average of .298 and a slugging percentage of .424, both very good figures for the years involved (1899 through 1906). Over the remainder of his career, which extended through the 1910 season and also included 73 games in the Federal League in 1914–15, he had a batting average of .216 and a slugging percentage of .266.[73]

For three years, from 1902 through 1904, Bradley was one of the top sluggers in the American League, and he was the best-hitting third baseman each of those years. His hitting declined in 1905 and 1906, possibly because of the aftereffects of a stomach ailment or perhaps due to the advent of the spitball. But among American League third basemen, only Jimmy Collins outhit him in 1905 and no other third baseman hit better in 1906. Therefore, since Bradley was an outstanding fielder, it is easy to make an argument that he was the best third baseman in the American League over the five-year period from 1902 through 1906.

Beginning as early as 1900 newspaper writers were comparing Bradley's fielding favorably with the "gold standard" for third basemen—that is, with Jimmy Collins. Because bunting was a central part of every team's scoring strategy, no team could hope to have a winning record without a good fielding third baseman. There were four American League third basemen who were normally named as being great fielders: Collins, Bradley, Lave Cross, and Bill Coughlin. Of the National League third basemen, only Tommy Leach was often mentioned with that group.

From time to time a reporter would become impressed with the fielding prowess of one of this group and claim that he was the best ever. When that occurred Tim Murnane of the *Boston Globe* could be counted on to remind all interested parties that Collins was the greatest of them all. Therefore, when in June of 1903 Murnane published an article in which he conceded that Bradley was about as good as Collins, other writers took note. Murnane's article is interesting because of its detailed analysis of the fielding styles of the Cleveland and Boston third basemen, as well as its comments about the other leading fielders at third. Murnane wrote:

> When Joe Cantillion went on record some time ago, saying that Bradley of the Cleveland club was the greatest thing that ever happened around a third base, the friends of Collins, Cross and Leach took exceptions, and I was among the number.
>
> Since then I have seen all those mentioned, except Cross, at work with plenty to do, and admit that I like Bradley better than ever. His fielding in the last Cleveland series in this city was simply phenomenal. His short field work outclassed anything that I ever saw on a ball field. On several occasions he went back of the pitcher and fielded the ball to first by some wonderful underhand throwing. Collins was putting up a great game at third in the same series. He was stronger than Bradley on fast ground balls to his left, and covered more ground back of the base. He handled thrown balls better, and made remarkable long-distance plays until one man looked fast where the other looked slow, when making a comparison.
>
> Bradley made more fuss, and naturally would catch the crowd, while Collins made all plays in perfect position, and depended wholly on his hands. No false motions could be detected in Collins' playing, while Bradley made one think that he was playing in great luck.
>
> Bradley got away from the mark first, while Collins had the surest hands. Collins is the same year in and year out, and never has off spells. If Bradley keeps up the style of game he put up in this city it would be a toss-up between the two great players.
>
> Leach was here with Pittsburgh and had plenty of work, but was shy several points of being a Collins or a Bradley. He is small and looks good, but has not the reach of the other two when all are out for the goods.

Before suffering from illness and injuries, Bill Bradley ranked with the top third basemen in baseball (National Baseball Hall of Fame Library, Cooperstown, New York).

Lave Cross is all that the place calls for, and, while not quite as fast as the other three, is fully as sure from all angles. Cross depends on his big mitt for blocking the ball, making sure of first stopping it, and then throwing accurately to first from most any position.

Leach and Bradley play the prettiest game to look at from the grand stand, while from a player's point of view Collins and Cross would make the team feel stronger. Cross and Collins are the most accurate throwers. I doubt if Collins has made half a dozen poor throws on the home grounds in three years, or since the American grounds were opened here.

In all the games that Lave Cross has played here in the same time two real poor throws are all that he has made. Both Bradley and Leach have made four times that number in the same time. In one game here last week Leach made two throws ten feet short of first base, and Bradley keeps his first baseman continually digging out the short throws. Bradley sends the most difficult ball to handle, while Cross throws the most perfect one for the baseman. Collins, too, keeps the ball on a line unless when hurried on a short hit and forced to throw underhanded. I think both Collins and Cross are at times worried a bit about the teams they handle, especially Collins, for during the last two years I have seen him fall into a trance several times and go at a ball out of form, something he would not do in a thousand years if his mind was wholly on his ball playing....

Speaking of third basemen, [Billy] Lauder in shape [not injured], [Harry] Wolverton, [Barry] McCormick, Coughlin and [Harry] Steinfeldt are a good second to the big quartet, while the other major league men are fifty percent shy of the real thing.[74]

As Bradley's batting average started to shrink toward the end of the decade, he began bunting much more frequently. In 1907 he laid down 46 sacrifice bunts. In 1908, when sacrifice flies were recognized as sacrifice hits and lumped with sacrifice bunts, Bradley was credited with 60 sacrifices, the second-highest total in baseball history.[75]

The great play of Bill Bradley, B. I. remained in the minds of at least a few baseball writers who lived into the mid-thirties. When the Baseball Hall of Fame ballot was distributed to the electors for the first election in 1936, it contained a tentative list of thirty-two players the voters might choose to select. Among the third basemen three names were suggested: Jimmy Collins, Pie Traynor, and Bill Bradley.[76]

Count Your Cows: Kid Elberfeld

Almost any reference to Kid Elberfeld is likely to mention his temper or surly behavior. His career was peppered with fines, suspensions, and ugly incidents, both on the field and off. Some examples:

Summer, 1899: Playing for Detroit, then in the Class A Western League, Elberfeld went to the entrance door for players at Bennett Field. He knocked on the door but the groundskeeper didn't respond fast enough to suit him. Elberfeld kicked the door open and broke the lock. When the groundskeeper complained to team president Van Derbeck, he was told to get a new lock.[77]

August 1899: Upset over a call by umpire Haskell, Elberfeld assaulted him, giving him a black eye and a bloody lip. After being pulled away from the umpire, Elberfeld continued to curse at him, hoping to provoke another fight. Ban Johnson fined Elber-

Kid Elberfeld was noted for his hot temper and surly disposition (Library of Congress).

feld $100 and suspended him for the remainder of the season. When Johnson was told that Elberfeld's mother was a widow and relied on Elberfeld for some of her support, he lifted the suspension.[78]

Either 1899 or 1903: Sam Crawford and Elberfeld played together in Cincinnati and Detroit. One day the two and some of their teammates were sitting in a hotel dining room. The hotel's waiters ignored the players for some twenty minutes while they served other diners at nearby tables. Elberfeld soon lost patience. Crawford later explained what happened next: "Elberfeld says, 'I'll get you some waiters, fellows.' Darned if he didn't take one of the plates and sail it way up in the air, and when it came down on that tile floor it smashed into a million pieces. In that quiet, refined dining room it sounded like the Charge of the Light Brigade." Elberfeld's antic got the immediate attention of three or four waiters.[79]

June 1901: Against the Athletics, Elberfeld tried to score from third on a grounder to second base. Elberfeld came in with spikes high, tearing the glove off catcher Mike Powers' hand and "taking a chunk out" of his leg. For the rest of the series Philadelphia baserunners slid hard into second base every time Elberfeld covered the bag. When the series was over, Elberfeld was out for almost two weeks—because of illness, the Tigers said; others said it was to recover from the retaliatory beating he had taken.[80]

May/June 1903: As described above, Elberfeld sulked and played poorly for several weeks, leading to his suspension and eventual trade by the Tigers. The Highlanders were happy to get him, and he played well for them.

July 1903: While in St. Louis with the Highlanders, Elberfeld was arrested for assaulting a waiter. According to the waiter, Elberfeld had called him a thief. When the waiter refused to wait on him, Elberfeld threw a bottle at him and hit him in the jaw.[81]

August 1906: In the first inning of a game Elberfeld was hit in the arm by a pitch. Umpire Silk O'Loughlin refused to award him first base, saying he had purposely been hit by the pitch. Elberfeld argued the call but went to the bench after the at-bat ended. After sitting there for a few moments, he grabbed a bat and headed toward O'Loughlin while yelling at him. He was stopped by other New York players and St. Louis catcher Branch Rickey. After some coaxing they got him away from the plate and out of the park.[82]

September 1906: On an attempted steal of third base Dan Murphy was called safe on a close play. New York players surrounded umpire O'Loughlin, protesting the decision. Elberfeld approached O'Loughlin aggressively, and O'Loughlin waved him away. The umpire's gesture infuriated Elberfeld, who rushed at O'Loughlin, attempting to kick him. O'Loughlin backed up and ordered Elberfeld out of the game. Elberfeld ran up to O'Loughlin again, making six deliberate attempts to spike him on the feet. Then he grabbed O'Loughlin's arm and tried to push him back. O'Loughlin wiggled free from Elberfeld's grasp and summoned the police, who escorted Elberfeld to the New York bench. When O'Loughlin insisted that Elberfeld leave the park, Elberfeld again went after the umpire. He was restrained by a teammate, broke free, and was again stopped by the police.[83]

July 1907: Behaving somewhat like he had in 1903, when manager Ed Barrow suspended him and then traded him to New York, Elberfeld was suspended by New York president Frank Farrell for "indifferent work in the field and at the bat." This time he was reinstated, and in 1908 appointed manager of the Highlanders.[84]

Undated: In his book *Before They Were the Bombers,* Jim Reisler described an incident that occurred on Elberfeld's farm near Chattanooga, Tennessee. It was customary at the time for cattle to roam free. Each farmer identified his cattle by its brand. Elberfeld and a neighbor disputed the ownership of a calf whose brand had faded. The two men took the dispute to a court, which ruled in the neighbor's favor. A few weeks later the calf became sick and died. Many of Elberfeld's neighbors suspected the calf had been poisoned and most of those thought they knew who was responsible.[85]

"Socks": Ralph Seybold

Suppose you're Buck Ewing, Cincinnati's manager in 1899. It's late July, your veteran team has been struggling all season, and the city's three newspapers are debating who should succeed you as manager next year. The boss, John T. Brush, has started talking about rebuilding the team by recruiting a flock of youngsters. Yet, while you know winning the pennant is probably only a forlorn hope, you aren't that far behind the third- and fourth-place teams. In fact, your team has started a nice winning streak, and you know this seemingly lost season could still be rescued. Then this new outfielder, fresh from a Class B team, jumps off the train. He looks like he spent the entire train ride in the dining car. He's got a bigger belly than half of the bartenders in town. Are you going to bench one of your veteran outfielders, who are all playing pretty well right now, for that guy?

Well, if you've been looking at the Philadelphia Athletics' stats in this book, you would make the educated guess that the new guy, Ralph "Socks" Seybold, would do all right if he got a chance to play regularly. The real Buck Ewing showed Seybold to a spot at the end of the bench. Then the Reds went on a fourteen-game winning streak, which still left them in fifth place in the twelve-team league. When they lost five of their next six games, he decided to put Seybold into a few contests.

From Ewing's perspective, it undoubtedly made sense to stick with his veterans while the team was on a hot streak. From Seybold's perspective, it made no sense at all. Seybold had a tendency to put on weight when he wasn't playing, and he gained lots of weight while occupying the Reds' bench. He had been in a hot streak when he left his minor league team, but nearly a month on the bench cost him his timing. When he got into the lineup, he had a couple of bad games in the field and didn't hit very well.

One of the local baseball writers immediately pronounced him a failure. "Seybold has demonstrated in the three games he has played with the Reds that minor league stars do not always pan out in the big organization," he wrote. "In the first place there is nothing about Seybold's appearance that would indicate he is a ballplayer. He might be able to hold a job in the big league if he were a sticker of the Delahanty-Lajoie caliber, but unless he is a terrific hitter he will never do for the reason that he is slow on his feet and is not a quick thinker."[86]

Seybold played 22 games for the Reds in 1899. He hit only .224 and was sold to Brush's other team, the Indianapolis Hoosiers. The reporter who dismissed Seybold as a career minor leaguer was J. Ed Grillo, who normally was very perceptive in baseball matters. About the only thing he got right about Seybold was that he didn't look like a ballplayer.

Socks was one of those players who was chronically overweight and looked every pound of it. Baseball writers commonly mentioned his size. When the Athletics became known as the "White Elephants" in 1902, it seemed natural for reporters to link the symbol with the team's big right fielder. After Seybold hit a long home run in St. Louis, the hit was described as follows: "In the seventh inning, Seybold, who is accused of being the 'white elephant' about whom McGraw did so much talking, landed his bat with his 300 pounds back of it gently on the nose of the ball. This time [Jesse] Burkett did not even take the trouble to chase the leather, as it was sailing high and ticketed for one of the bleacher seats."[87]

In another game, this time against Cleveland, Seybold hit a grounder at first baseman Charlie Hickman, another heavily built gentleman. Charles Dryden of the *Philadelphia North American* described the incident. "Another exciting event," wrote Dryden, "was a sort of tub race between Mr. Seybold and Mr. Hickman in the second. Socks pasted a grounder, which Hickman fielded well back on the line. [Pitcher Earl] Moore started for the bag but Captain Larry [Lajoie] yelled to Hickman, 'Take it yourself.' The earth shook as Socks and Hick thundered toward the sack from opposite directions, while the folks in the upper pavilion held fast to their seats. Socks beat him to it."[88]

Dryden's description seemed to imply that Seybold was a slow runner, but such was not the case. Once he got his weight moving, Socks could move at a pretty good clip. He didn't steal many bases, but he could cover his outfield position pretty well. He also had soft hands. In 1903 he caught 80 fly balls before making his first error of the season.[89]

A sense of his fielding abilities can be gained from a description of a catch he made against the Tigers. "Elberfeld met one that he sent screeching towards the fence, between right and center. Seybold cut across lots on a long run. Close to the fence he made one last leap forward, shoved out his ungloved hand, head high, and whirled around. The fact that he turned instead of following, was the only way in which the spectators knew that he had completed the most sensational play of the local season." Seybold finished the play by throwing to second base to double up a baserunner who thought he had no chance of catching the ball. His catch came just a little over a year after he made a similar bare-handed grab against the Orioles.[90]

What Seybold did best, of course, was hit. He was one of the American League's top sluggers from 1901 through 1907. He finished in the top ten in slugging percentage in each of those years, and was among the league leaders in home runs in six of them. His hitting also furnished material for sportswriter Dryden. Columbia Park, the A's home field, had an advertisement on the left field fence that promised to give ten dollars and a case of scotch to any player hitting a home run over the sign. In 1903 Seybold accomplished the feat two days in a row. A few days later, while the A's were in Cleveland, Socks was handed an envelope with the firm's return address on it. Enclosed was a check for twenty dollars. Dryden described the scene for his readers. "With the check came a letter complimenting Socks on his prowess with the bat, and hoping he would keep up his luck. Seybold replied that if things broke nicely for him the firm would have to lay a pipe line from the distillery to Columbia Park in order to save freight charges on the prizes."[91]

Don't Tread on Griff: Clark Griffith

Clark Griffith was born in a log cabin in southwestern Missouri in 1869. His father died in a hunting accident two years later. By the time he was 11 years old, young Clark had begun laying traps for small animals, such as skunks, raccoons, and opossums. He could sell the furs of those animals for a dollar or so in a nearby town. Often Clark would go out at night hunting raccoons with his dog, Major. After Major treed a raccoon, Clark would climb the tree and shake the limb the raccoon was on until the animal fell. Major would then attack the raccoon, fighting it until Clark could descend from the tree and finish it off with a club.

One night Major treed what looked to Clark like an unusually big raccoon. Clark climbed the tree with his club, reaching the limb holding the animal. He shook the limb as hard as he could but couldn't shake the animal loose. Suddenly the animal jumped to the top of the tree, snarling and spitting at Clark. When Clark started climbing higher, the animal jumped at him. Clark hit it with his club, and it fell to the ground where Major started fighting it. When Clark got to the ground, he noticed that Major was not doing very well in the struggle. At first Clark couldn't do too much to help Major for fear of hitting the dog, rather than the animal, with his club. Eventually he found an opening and managed to hit the animal on the head.

After tending to Major, he swung the dead animal over his back and headed home. On the way he met a farmer who asked him what he was carrying. "A great big coon," said young Griffith, "the biggest coon I ever did see." The farmer took a closer look. "Coon, hell," the farmer said. "Son, that ain't a coon. You got a wildcat." Years later, when Griffith related the story to a sportswriter, he mentioned that the wildcat weighed 60 pounds, about the same as he weighed at the time. The sportswriter printed the story, ending it with the observation that "Clark Griffith had actually whipped his weight in wildcat!"[92]

A familiar image of Griffith is that of the white-haired owner of the Washington Senators, the "Friend of Presidents," a long-time member of the baseball establishment who was highly respected for playing a major role in the early success of the American League. In the early 1900s, the Clark Griffith who moved about the major league diamonds seemed a lot closer in nature to the small boy who fought a wildcat than to the mature gentleman of later decades.

Griffith started his professional baseball career with Bloomington of the Tri-State League in 1888. He was 10–4 with Bloomington. His pitching in an exhibition game against Milwaukee was impressive enough that Milwaukee's manager, Jim Hart, who later became an owner of the Chicago National League team, bought him from Bloomington. Griffith became Milwaukee's top pitcher in 1889. In 1890 he won 27 while losing only seven, leading to his purchase by Charles Comiskey, the manager of the St. Louis Browns of the American Association. Griffith was 11–8 with the Browns before being traded to the Boston Red Stockings in the same league, where he was 3–1. Then Griffith came down with a sore arm just as the American Association and the National League combined, dropping four of the American Association teams in the process. In the scramble for jobs that followed, Griffith was allowed to drift back to the minor leagues.

During the next two years Griffith found employment on the West Coast. In 1892 he pitched for Tacoma, which beat its competition so handily fans lost interest in the pennant race. The league collapsed in August. Shortly afterwards Tacoma's manager received a telegram inviting the team to represent Missoula, Montana, in the independent Montana State League. The manager told his players he didn't think a town as small as Missoula could afford to pay the salaries it was offering; therefore, he was declining the offer. At that point the 22-year-old Griffith stepped forward, saying the players had little to lose by accepting the offer. He said he wanted to accept it. The players shouted their agreement and followed Griffith to Missoula.

When the players arrived in Missoula, they found themselves in a bustling mining town of saloons and gambling places. After Griffith's first game, a 6–0 win, the miners celebrated by passing the hat for their baseball heroes, collecting $700 for Griffith and lesser amounts for the other players. The following weekend brought a grudge match with Missoula's bitter rival, Helena. Reportedly more than $100,000 was bet on the game. Griffith took a 4–3 lead into the ninth inning. With the tying run on third, Missoula's catcher let a pitched ball get past him. As he dashed to the backstop to get the

In his later years Clark Griffith was the baseball establishment's "friend of Presidents." Here he is pictured with FDR and his adopted sons, Jimmy and Billy (Library of Congress).

ball, the run scored. After grabbing the ball, he looked up into the barrels of a half-dozen drawn pistols. "Son, don't let that happen again," one of the pistol-wielders said. At that point the catcher decided he didn't feel up to continuing the game. After Missoula's regular catcher, who was out of the lineup because he was nursing a terrible hangover, agreed to replace him, Missoula won the game, 5–4.

In 1893, the month of August brought another crisis for Griffith. He had a great season for Oakland, winning 30 games, but the owner wasn't able to meet his payroll. Griffith led a rebellion by the players, who told the owner they would not play another game until they received the back pay they were owed. The owner refused to pay and the entire league soon disbanded. Again out of a job, Griffith supported himself for a few weeks by performing on stage at a local honky-tonk musical hall. Then his former Milwaukee manager, Jim Hart, came to his rescue. In September he wired Griffith, telling him to come to Chicago. Griffith got into three games with Chicago, losing two of them but pitching well enough to stay with the team in 1894.[93]

With Chicago, Griffith became one of the better pitchers in the National League. He won 20 games or more each year from 1894 through 1899. Standing only 5'6" and weighing about 155 pounds, he didn't have much of a fastball. He relied on a variety of slow curves and good control, and continually played mind games with batters. He became known for slashing the ball with his spikes, a Chicago writer noting that he "has a habit of half-soling and heeling his shoes with the ball during play."[94]

He not only threw slow pitches, he worked slowly. Batters often grew impatient waiting for him to get around to throwing a pitch. He was always looking for an advantage against the hitter. In one game on a hot, dry July afternoon in Chicago, the prairie wind was blowing steadily toward the batter. With Honus Wagner at bat, Griffith began kicking up dust around the mound. Then, as the wind carried a cloud of dust toward the plate, Griffith would send in a pitch through the dust cloud, forcing Wagner to peer through the dust while searching for the ball. The trick seemed to work well, though Wagner managed to foul off the ball a few times. Then the elements conspired against Griffith. A fine rain began falling, quelling the dust and enabling Wagner to get a good look at a pitch, which he lined for a base hit.[95]

The Chicago teams of the mid- and late-nineties had several players with a mischievous bent of mind. Griffith was one of them. On a visit to Washington in 1894, catcher Pop Schriver agreed to try to catch a ball dropped from the Washington Monument, a feat many thought would end by injuring the person trying to make the catch. Schriver was able to hold on to a ball on his second try. Griffith witnessed the catch. He was at the top of the monument dropping the ball for Schriver.[96]

In 1898 John T. Brush wrote a "rowdy ball resolution" that he wanted all National League players to sign. In it the players were to pledge not to use indecent language during games. Griffith was the spokesmen for Chicago players, who refused to sign the document. "The paper sent is an insult to every player," Griffith said. "Further, we refuse to sign anything that John T. Brush is connected with, whether it is right or wrong."[97]

Before the 1900 season started, Griffith announced that he and teammate Charlie Dexter were planning on leaving the club on May 20 to go to Cape Nome in Alaska. They were going to mine for gold. "Griffith is reading up on mining and on Cape Nome," a reporter said, "besides engaging in a lively correspondence with railroad agents." May 20 came and went, but Griffith remained with the Orphans. Perhaps that was because he thought he had a better scheme for getting rich.

In July he announced that pitcher Virgil Garvin would challenge champion boxer Terry McGovern to a match at 133 pounds. Garvin was 6'3", but was very thin—Griffith claimed he weighed 140 pounds. Griffith was willing to bet $1,000 that McGovern could not knock out Garvin within six rounds. Garvin was wiry and quick, and said he had considerable experience as a boxer. Griffith went so far as to post $500 as a bond for the match, which never came off.[98]

By the end of the 1890s Griffith had become active in organizing a players' union. He clearly did not feel good about the way the National League owners were running the league, especially after they dropped four teams prior to the 1900 season. Just before that season began, former owner John B. Day, who had been given a sinecure as chief of umpires for the league, declared that the only thing necessary to make a success of the season was for the players to behave decently. Griffith fumed when he heard Day's statement. "What ought to be done," Griffith said, "is to appoint a chief to watch the magnates and prevent them from bringing the game into disrepute. I never knew a player whose behavior was not lady-like in comparison with the acts of these magnates."[99] During the winter of 1901, Pittsburgh owner Barney Dreyfuss asked Hart if it was true that Griffith had jumped to the American League. Hart said he didn't know. Dreyfuss replied, "Well, he's an anarchist, anyway, and would disrupt that league if they took him."[100]

Griffith was an active member of the Players' Protective Association, which was formed during the 1900 season. He was elected vice president of the organization and was a member of the committee that presented the association's demands to the owners at the National League's winter meeting in December. The players asked that the clause reserving a player's service to a club be limited to five years, the "farming system" be abolished, a player's consent be obtained before he could be traded or sold, limits be set on the number of times and duration of suspensions without pay, and a committee of arbitration be established with equal representation by player representatives. Many baseball writers thought these demands were a little extreme. The owners thought they smacked of socialism and dismissed them without serious consideration.[101]

Before these meetings began, Griffith had been working with Ban Johnson and Charles Comiskey in their efforts to put the American League on equal footing with the National League. After the National League owners summarily rejected petitions from both the players and the American League, Griffith called the two men and told them, "There's going to be a new major league, if you can get the backing. Because I can get the players." He spent the rest of the winter meeting with players, eventually persuading more than 20 National Leaguers to jump to the American League. Griffith, of course, signed with the White Stockings as a player-manager.[102]

In his new role Griffith became a much more serious person—not on the mound, where he had always been a fierce competitor, but in his general approach to the game. With the Orphans, Griffith had been a pain to his managers, always ready to complain, always looking for a way to be annoying. A Chicago writer once compared Griffith and a couple other Orphans to errant schoolboys who delighted in bending the rules.[103] With the White Stockings Griffith, the erstwhile "anarchist," was the man in charge—in effect, the schoolmaster. He focused his energies on preparing the team to play winning baseball and managing the games. In June a Chicago writer noted the change in Griffith's behavior, saying Comiskey was the only person not surprised by Griffith's transformation from an "indifferent" pitcher—by which he meant one who resisted any attempt by his managers to overwork him—to one of the league's hardest workers.[104]

Griffith's rebel tendencies had not completely disappeared, however. To some extent they were re-directed at American League umpires. To those umpires there was little to choose from between Griffith and John McGraw when it came to obnoxious behavior on the field. Griffith was thrown out of five games in 1901, one more than McGraw, and was suspended for five days. In late August, after the game in which Katoll and Shugart were suspended, an exasperated Ban Johnson vented his frustration to a reporter. "I lay all this trouble with the umpires to those National Leaguers, Griffith and McGraw. They have stirred up all this trouble previously unknown to the American League." Collins and others like him had caused no trouble, Johnson said. "These two, however, are so anxious to make a reputation as pennant winners they manage things so that the men run loose and create the trouble."[105]

As a pitcher Griffith had his best major league season in 1901. His 24–7 record gave him the best win-loss percentage in the league. He also was a fireman of sorts, in the fashion of the day, which was to bring in the staff ace when dire necessity and the pennant race called for it. He inserted himself into five games as a relief pitcher, winning three, saving one, and finishing out a losing game after the starting pitcher was ejected by the umpire. His win total was the third-highest in the league, exceeded only by Cy Young and Joe McGinnity, and his ERA was the fourth-lowest in the league.

The 1901 season was Griffith's last big winning season. He was 15–9 in 1902, but his season was cut short by a stomach ailment. He was 14–11 with the New York Highlanders in 1903. Perhaps his biggest season with the Highlanders was 1905, when he co-invented, along with John McGraw, the role of spot starter-relief ace. That season he was 9–6, with an ERA of 1.67. He made 18 relief appearances, saving three games, while winning five and losing three in relief.

Chapter Notes

Preface

1. Lawrence S. Ritter, *The Glory of Their Times: The Story of the Early Days of Baseball Told by the Men Who Played It*, Quill ed. (New York: William Morrow, 1992), p. 34.

Chapter One

1. David Nemec, *The Great Encyclopedia of 19th Century Major League Baseball* (New York: Donald I. Fine, 1997), pp. 629–36; Burt Solomon, *Where They Ain't: The Fabled Life and Untimely Death of the Original Baltimore Orioles, the Team that Gave Birth to Modern Baseball* (New York: Free Press, 1999), pp. 137–157.
2. *Sporting News*, Nov. 11, 1899, p. 3; Dec. 16, 1899, pp. 1, 3.
3. *Sporting News*, Dec. 23. 1899, p. 3; Jan. 13, 1900, p. 1; Mar. 17, 1900, p. 5.
4. *Sporting News*, Mar. 17, 1900, p. 1; Apr. 14, 1900, p. 2.
5. *Sporting News*, Apr. 15, 1899, p. 4; Mar. 10, 1900, p. 1; Mar. 17, 1900, p. 5; Mar. 31, 1900, p. 4.
6. *Chicago Tribune*, Apr. 1, 1900, p. 17; Apr. 15, 1900, p. 17; Apr. 29, 1900, p. 18.
7. *Philadelphia Public Ledger*, May 21, 1900, p. 18.
8. *Boston Globe*, Jun. 14, 1900, p. 4.
9. *Chicago Tribune*, Jul. 8, p. 18.
10. *Boston Globe*, Jun. 3, 1900, p. 39; Jun. 17, 1900, p. 22; Sep. 24, 1900, p. 5; *Chicago Tribune*, May 13, 1900, pp. 17–18; Aug. 5, p. 18; *Brooklyn Daily Eagle*, Aug. 26, 1900, p. 10; *Sporting News*, Sep. 1, 1900, p. 5.
11. *Chicago Tribune*, Oct. 7, 1900, p. 19.
12. *Brooklyn Daily Eagle*, Apr. 3, 1900, p. 14; May 22, 1900, p. 16; *Sporting News*, Apr. 14, 1900, p. 1.
13. Lyle Spatz, *Bad Bill Dahlen: The Rollicking Life and Times of an Early Baseball Star* (Jefferson, NC; McFarland, 2004), pp. 1–2, 206–8.
14. *Brooklyn Daily Eagle*, Apr. 22, 1900, p. 8.
15. *Boston Globe*, Jun. 24, 1900, p. 33; *Chicago Tribune*, Jul. 29, p. 18.
16. *Brooklyn Daily Eagle*, Aug. 6, 1900, p. 10; Aug. 9, 1900, p. 10.
17. *Brooklyn Daily Eagle*, Sep. 1, 1900, p. 6; Sep. 8, 1900, p. 3; Sep. 9, 1900, p. 8; Sep. 11, 1900, p. 15.
18. *Brooklyn Daily Eagle*, Oct. 2, 1900, p. 17.
19. *Sporting News*, Apr. 14, 1900, p. 5.
20. *Pittsburgh Chronicle-Telegraph*, Apr. 26, 1900, p. 2; Jun. 7, 1900, p. 2; Jun. 27, 1900, p. 2.
21. Alan H. Levy, *Rube Waddell: The Zany, Brilliant life of a Strikeout Artist* (Jefferson, NC: McFarland, 2000), pp. 50–68.
22. *Pittsburgh Chronicle-Telegraph*, Jul. 31, 1900, p. 2.
23. *Brooklyn Daily Eagle*, Jun. 8, 1900, p. 16.
24. *Pittsburgh Chronicle-Telegraph*, Aug. 6, 1900, p. 2; Aug. 10, 1900, p. 2; Sep. 5, 1900, p. 2.
25. *Sporting News*, Jul. 8, 1899, p. 6.
26. *Philadelphia Public Ledger*, Aug. 1, 1900, p. 14.
27. *Sporting News*, Jun. 9, 1900, p. 4.
28. *Boston Globe*, Apr. 24, 1900, p. 7.
29. *Boston Globe*, May 21, 1900, p. 5.
30. *Boston Globe*, Jun. 13, 1900, p. 4.
31. *Boston Globe*, Jun. 20, 1900, p. 8.
32. *Sporting News*, Aug. 4, 1900, p. 1; Nov. 3, 1900, p. 4.
33. *Sporting News*, Jul. 14, 1900, p. 4.
34. *Chicago Tribune*, Apr. 4, 1900, p. 6; Apr. 8, 1900, p. 18.
35. *Pittsburgh Chronicle-Telegraph*, May 7, 1900, p. 2.
36. *Chicago Tribune*, Jun. 24, 1900, p. 18.
37. *Chicago Tribune*, Sep. 21, 1900, p. 8.
38. *Chicago Tribune*, Jul. 8, 1900, p. 18; Jul. 15, 1900, p. 18.
39. *Chicago Tribune*, Jul. 25, 1900, p. 9.
40. Frederick Ivor-Campbell, Robert L. Tiemann, and Mark Rucker, eds., *Baseball's First Stars* (Cleveland: Society for American Baseball Research, 1996), p. 14; *Sporting News*, Jun. 26, 1897, p. 4.
41. *Sporting News*, Apr. 14, 1900, p. 2.
42. *Sporting News*, Mar. 17, 1900, p. 5; Mar. 31, 1900, p. 4.
43. *Pittsburgh Chronicle-Telegraph*, Jul. 5, 1900, p. 2; Sep. 13, 1900, p. 2.
44. *New York Sun*, Jul. 14, 1900, p. 5.
45. *Sporting News*, Feb. 19, 1898, p. 4.
46. *Sporting News*, Nov. 18, 1899, p. 2; Jerold Casway, *Ed Delahanty in the Emerald Age of Baseball* (Notre Dame, IN: University of Notre Dame Press, 2004), p. 166.
47. *Sporting News*, Sep. 15, 1900, p. 5.
48. *Pittsburgh Chronicle-Telegraph*, Jul. 23, 1900, p. 2.
49. *Sporting News*, Dec. 9, 1899, p. 2; Oct. 13, 1900, p. 2.

50. *Cincinnati Commercial Tribune*, Jun. 9, 1901, p. 10.
51. *Brooklyn Daily Eagle*, Aug. 7, 1901, p. 11.
52. *Brooklyn Daily Eagle*, Jun. 21, 1901, p. 13.
53. *Sporting News*, Jul. 2, 1898, p. 6.
54. *Sporting News*, Oct. 30, 1897, p. 4.
55. *Sporting News*, Jan. 7, 1899, p. 5.
56. *Sporting News*, Dec. 20, 1902, p. 2.
57. Solomon, *Where They Ain't*, pp. 14–18; 28–35; 58–72.
58. *Sporting News*, Mar. 6, 1897, p. 6; Sep. 25, 1897, p. 4; Dec. 10, 1898, p. 6.
59. *Sporting News*, Oct. 27, 1900, p. 5.
60. *Sporting News*, Dec. 1, 1900, p. 5.
61. W. B. Hanna, "The Twenty-Five Greatest Players," *Baseball Magazine*, Jun. 1924, pp. 299–300.
62. *New York Times*, Feb. 1, 1936, p. 10; John Thorn, et. al., eds., *Total Baseball: The Official Encyclopedia of Major League Baseball, 4th ed.* (New York: Viking Press, 1995), p. 253.
63. Billy Evans, "Baseball's Thirteen Best Hitters," *Esquire*, Jun. 1942, pp. 62, 106–7; "The All-Time All-Star Team of the American League," *Sport*, Sep. 1958, pp. 10–11; "The All-Time All-Star Team of the National League," *Sport*, Oct. 1958, pp. 42–3; Bill James, *The New Bill James Historical Baseball Abstract* (New York: Free Press, 2001), p. 843.
64. *Sporting News*, Jan. 7, 1899, p. 2; Jul. 1, 1899, p. 5.
65. *Sporting News*, Jun. 17, 1899, p. 5.
66. *Sporting News*, Mar. 10, 1900, p. 2.
67. *Cincinnati Commercial Tribune*, May 18, 1900, p. 5.
68. *Pittsburgh Chronicle-Telegraph*, Aug. 28, 1900, p. 2.
69. *Sporting News*, Jul. 16, 1892, p. 3; Jul. 23, 1892, p. 6; Jul. 30, 1892, p. 3; Aug. 6, 1892, p. 3; Aug. 20, 1892, pp. 1, 3; Jul. 22, 1893, p. 1.
70. *Sporting News*, Jul. 22, 1893, p. 1.
71. Don Doxsie, *Iron Man McGinnity: A Baseball Biography* (Jefferson, NC: McFarland, 2009), pp. 18–31; *Sporting News*, Jan. 27, 1894, p. 2.
72. *Sporting News*, Feb. 10, 1894, p. 5; Jan. 19, 1895, p. 5; Mar. 28, 1896, p. 2.
73. *Sporting News*, Mar. 14, 1896, p. 4.
74. *Sporting News*, Jun. 13, 1896, p. 1; Oct. 24, 1896, p. 2.
75. *Sporting News*, May 4, 1895, p. 4; Nov. 27, 1897, pp. 2, 5.
76. *Sporting News*, Jun. 4, 1898, pp. 1, 5; Jul. 9, 1898, p. 5.
77. *Sporting News*, Feb. 11, 1899, p. 1; Jun. 17, 1899, pp. 4, 5; Sep. 2, 1899, p. 1; Jan. 20, 1900, p. 1.
78. Doxsie, *Iron Man McGinnity*, pp. 32–5; *Sporting News*, Mar. 19, 1904, p. 2.
79. *Sporting News*, May 21, 1898, p. 1; May 28, 1898, p. 4; Jul. 2, 1898, p. 3.
80. *Sporting News*, Apr. 29, 1899, p. 1; May 6, 1899, p. 5; Jul. 8, 1899, p. 4.
81. *Baltimore Sun*, Jun. 2, 1899, p. 6; Don Jensen, "Joseph J. McGinnity," in Tom Simon, ed., *Deadball Stars of the National League* (Dulles, VA: Brassey's, 2004), p. 42.
82. *Sporting News*, May 26, 1900, p. 4.
83. *Sporting News*, Apr. 2, 1898, p. 3; *Boston Globe*, Aug. 29, 1900, p. 4.
84. *Milwaukee Journal*, May 4, 1901, p. 12; Sep. 1, 1901, p. 4.
85. *Sporting News*, Feb. 8, 1896, p. 3.
86. *Sporting News*, Feb. 24, 1900, p. 1.
87. *Sporting News*, Apr. 23, 1898, p. 4.
88. *Chicago Tribune*, Jun. 2, 1903, p. 15.
89. *Sporting News*, Apr. 1, 1899, p. 2; *Brooklyn Daily Eagle*, Apr. 25, 1900, p. 16.
90. *Brooklyn Daily Eagle*, Sep. 7, 1900, p. 13; Oct. 9, 1900, p. 16.

Chapter Two

1. Eugene Murdock, *Ban Johnson: Czar of Baseball* (Westport, CT: Greenwood, 1982), pp. 45–49.
2. *Pittsburgh Chronicle-Telegraph*, Apr. 6, 1901, p. 12; Apr. 9, 1901, p. 14.
3. Levy, *Rube Waddell*, pp. 75–77.
4. *Pittsburgh Chronicle-Telegraph*, Jul. 21, 1900, p. 2; *Cincinnati Commercial Tribune*, Jul. 2, 1900, p. 5.
5. *Pittsburgh Dispatch*, Apr. 22, 1901, p. 8.
6. *Sporting News*, Aug. 10, 1901, p. 4.
7. *Pittsburgh Dispatch*, Jun. 20, 1901, p. 8; *Cincinnati Commercial Tribune*, Aug. 5, 1901, p. 7.
8. *Pittsburgh Dispatch*, Sep. 29, 1901, p. 13.
9. Dennis DeValeria and Jeanne Burke DeValeria, *Honus Wagner: A Biography* (New York: Holt, 1996), pp. 94–95.
10. *Pittsburgh Dispatch*, Jul. 29, 1901, p. 8; Aug. 12, 1901, p. 9; *Brooklyn Daily Eagle*, Sep. 14, 1901, p. 2.
11. *Pittsburgh Dispatch*, May 28, 1901, p. 10.
12. *Philadelphia Public Ledger*, Jul. 1, 1901, p. 16.
13. *Brooklyn Daily Eagle*, Jul. 9, 1901, p. 13; Aug. 1, 1901, p. 8; *Cincinnati Commercial Tribune*, Jul. 18, 1901, p. 7.
14. *Brooklyn Daily Eagle*, Jun. 7, 1901, p. 13.
15. *Boston Globe*, Aug. 15, 1900, p. 5.
16. *St. Louis Globe-Democrat*, Aug. 2, 1901, p. 11.
17. *Sporting News*, Aug. 10, 1901, p. 4; Sep. 21, 1901, p. 4.
18. *St. Louis Globe-Democrat*, Sep. 2, 1901, p. 4.
19. *Chicago Tribune*, Apr. 1, 1901, p. 8; *Pittsburgh Chronicle-Telegraph*, Apr. 24, 1901, p. 12.
20. *Sporting News*, Oct. 20, 1900, p. 5.
21. Ritter, *Glory of Their Times*, pp. 21–3.
22. *Sporting News*, Apr. 30, 1898, p. 4; Jul. 30, 1898, p. 1.
23. *Sporting News*, Jul. 15, 1899, p. 5.
24. *Sporting News*, Oct. 7, 1899, p. 5.
25. *Sporting News*, Nov. 25, 1899, p. 2.
26. DeValeria and DeValeria, *Honus Wagner*, pp. 92–110.
27. *Sporting News*, Jul. 29, 1899, p. 5; Aug. 31, 1901, p. 1.
28. *Sporting News*, Sep. 8, 1900, p. 1; *Brooklyn Daily Eagle*, Sep. 10, 1900, p. 15.
29. *Chicago Tribune*, Apr. 4, 1900, p. 6; Apr. 22, 1900, pp. 18.
30. *Sporting News*, Sep. 28, 1901, p. 7.
31. *Sporting News*, Nov. 6, 1897, p. 3; Gregg Dubbs, "Jim Sheckard: A Live Wire in the Dead Ball Era," *Baseball Research Journal*, 1980, p. 134.
32. *Sporting News*, Oct. 16, 1897, p. 7.
33. *Brooklyn Daily Eagle*, Oct. 15, 1900, p. 16.
34. *Brooklyn Daily Eagle*, May 25, 1901, p. 8.
35. *Pittsburgh Chronicle-Telegraph*, Apr. 24, 1900, p. 2.
36. *Sporting News*, Dec. 30, 1899, p. 2.
37. *Sporting News*, Nov. 30, 1900, p. 4.

38. *Sporting News*, Aug. 17, 1901, p. 4; *St. Louis Globe-Democrat*, Aug. 17, 1901, p. 7.
39. *Brooklyn Daily Eagle*, Jul. 3, 1901, p. 13.
40. *Sporting News*, Oct 28, 1899, p. 2; *Cincinnati Commercial Tribune*, Jul. 1, 1901, p. 6; *Pittsburgh Dispatch*, Aug. 4, 1901, p. 13.
41. *Cincinnati Commercial Tribune*, Sep. 29, 1901, p. 10.
42. *Sporting News*, Oct. 24, 1903, p. 2.
43. *Boston Globe*, Jul. 18, 1900, p. 7; *Pittsburgh Chronicle-Telegraph*, Jul. 20, 1900, p. 2.
44. *St. Louis Republic*, May 24, 1901, p. 5.
45. *Cincinnati Commercial Tribune*, Jun. 4, 1901, p. 7.
46. Ritter, *Glory of Their Times*, p. 176.
47. *Cincinnati Commercial Tribune*, Jun. 7, 1901, p. 7.
48. *Sporting News*, Oct. 12, 1901, p. 1.
49. *Boston Globe*, Jun. 2, 1901, p. 4; *Brooklyn Daily Eagle*, Jul. 23, 1901, p. 10.
50. *Sporting News*, Jun. 22, 1901, p. 5; *Boston Globe*, Aug. 20, 1901, p. 4; *New York Press*, Aug. 31, 1901, p. 5; Oct. 6, 1901, p. 9; Ray Robinson, *Matty: An American Hero* (New York: Oxford University Press, 1993), p. 33.
51. Levy, *Rube Waddell*, p. 129.
52. Ritter, *Glory of Their Times*, pp. 25, 49.
53. *Sporting News*, Jan. 12, 1901, p. 5.
54. *Sporting News*, Jun. 2, 1900, p. 4; May 25, 1901, p. 5.
55. Ritter, *Glory of Their Times*, p. 25.
56. *Philadelphia Public Ledger*, Sep. 13, 1900, p. 14; *Brooklyn Daily Eagle*, May 27, 1900, p. 10.
57. *Chicago Tribune*, Jun. 7, 1901, p. 6.
58. *Chicago Tribune*, Jul. 15, 1901, p. 8; Jul. 16, 1901, p. 4.
59. *Sporting News*, Aug. 3, 1901, p. 5.
60. *Chicago Tribune*, Aug. 25, 1901, p. 19; Aug. 26, 1901, p. 8.
61. *Sporting News*, Sep. 14, 1901, p. 4.
62. *Sporting News*, Dec. 28, 1901, p. 3; Jan. 11, 1902, p. 5.
63. *Baltimore Sun*, Aug. 28, 1899, p. 6; Sep. 18, 1899, p. 6; Charles C. Alexander, *John McGraw* (Lincoln: University of Nebraska Press, 1995), pp. 66–67; *Sporting News*, Sep. 9, 1899, p. 1.
64. *Sporting News*, Mar. 13, 1897, p. 1; Jul 31, 1897, p. 1; Feb. 19, 1898, p. 5; Dec. 3, 1898, p. 1; Sep. 30, 1899, p. 5; Jun. 9, 1900, p. 7.
65. Thomas J. Schlereth, *Victorian America: Transformations in Everyday Life* (New York: HarperCollins, 1991), p. 288; U.S. Department of Commerce, Bureau of the Census, *Historical Statistics of the United States*, 1949, pp. 45–8.
66. *Sporting News*, Feb. 9, 1901, p. 1; Sep. 28, 1901, p. 4.
67. *Washington Post*, May 15, 1902, p. 9; Jun. 14, 1902, p. 9.
68. *Philadelphia Public Ledger*, Sep. 10, 1902, p. 6.
69. Figures on National League players of 1900 were calculated using birth and death dates listed in *Total Baseball*.
70. *Cincinnati Commercial Tribune*, May 20, 1901, p. 6; Sep. 15, 1901, p. 7; *Philadelphia Public Ledger*, Apr. 17, 1901, p. 18; *Pittsburgh Dispatch*, Sep. 30, 1901, p. 8.
71. *Chicago Tribune*, Sep. 7, 1900, p. 8; *Sporting News*, Feb. 22, 1902, p. 1.
72. *Cleveland Plain Dealer*, Aug. 20, 1902, p. 6; *Washington Post*, May 10, 1903, p. A10; *New York Press*, Aug. 4, 1901, p. 5.
73. *Washington Post*, May 11, 1902, p. 8.
74. Cindy Thomson and Scott Brown, *Three Finger: The Mordecai Brown Story* (Lincoln: University of Nebraska Press, 2006), pp. 11–12.
75. *Philadelphia North American*, Sep. 18, 1904, p. 11; *Sporting News*, Jun. 26, 1897, p. 5.

Chapter Three

1. *Sporting News*, Jun. 22, 1901, p. 6.
2. *Sporting News*, Jan. 1, 1898, p. 2; May 21, 1898, p. 1; Sep. 3, 1898, p. 5.
3. *Sporting News*, Sep. 9, 1893, p. 1; Sep. 22, 1900, p. 7; *Washington Star*, Aug. 27, 1901, p. 7.
4. *Sporting News*, Oct. 6, 1894, p. 4; Jul. 22, 1899, p. 1; Apr. 7, 1900, p. 1; Feb. 23, 1901, p. 6.
5. *Chicago Tribune*, May 16, 1901, p. 6; *Detroit Free Press*, Jul. 9, 1901, p. 10.
6. *Sporting News*, Sep. 22, 1900, p. 7; Feb. 23, 1901, p. 6.
7. *Sporting News*, Feb. 23, 1901, p. 6.
8. *Detroit Free Press*, Jun. 13, 1901, p. 10.
9. *Chicago Tribune*, Apr. 15, 1901, p. 6; Jun. 27, 1901, p. 6; Jul. 24, 1901, p. 6; Aug. 22, 1901, p. 4; Aug. 24, 1901, p. 6.
10. *Milwaukee Journal*, Apr. 11, 1901, p. 12.
11. *Chicago Tribune*, Aug. 22, 1901, p. 4; Aug. 23, 1901, p. 4; *Washington Post*, Aug. 22, 1901, p. 8.
12. *Chicago Tribune*, Jul. 30, 1901, p. 4.
13. *Chicago Tribune*, Sep. 22, 1901, p. 17.
14. *Boston Globe*, May 16, 1901, p. 8; Jun. 10, 1901, p. 8.
15. *Boston Globe*, Jun. 1, 1901, p. 5.
16. *Boston Globe*, Jun. 15, 1901, p. 8; Jul. 1, 1901, p. 10; *Sporting News*, Nov. 16, 1901, p. 1.
17. *Detroit Free Press*, Apr. 26, 1901, pp. 1, 10; Apr. 27, 1901, p. 10; Apr. 28, 1901, p. 8; Apr. 29, 1901, p. 8; *Detroit Evening News*, Apr. 26, 1901, p. 11.
18. *Baltimore Sun*, May 21, 1901, p. 6; *Philadelphia Public Ledger*, May 9, 1901, p. 16.
19. *Sporting News*, Jun. 26, 1897, p. 1; Sep. 11, 1897, p 7.
20. *Sporting News*, Dec. 31, 1898, p. 1.
21. Alexander, *John McGraw*, pp. 68–70; 73–75.
22. *Sporting News* Oct. 22, 1898, p. 3.
23. *Sporting News*, Aug. 24, 1901, p. 7; Sep. 14, 1901, p. 4.
24. *Baltimore Sun*, Aug. 8, 1901, p. 6.
25. *Baltimore Sun*, Aug. 22, 1901, p. 6.
26. *Baltimore Sun*, May 18, 1901, p. 6; Jun. 3, 1901, p. 6; Jun. 14, 1901, p. 6; Jun. 15, 1901, p. 6; Aug. 6, 1901, p. 6; Aug. 23, 1901, p. 6; Sep. 4, 1901, p. 6.
27. Nemec, *Great Encyclopedia of 19th Century Major League Baseball*, pp. 670, 676; *Sporting News*, Nov. 18, 1899, pp. 5, 7; *Washington Star*, Jun. 6, 1901, p. 9.
28. *Cleveland Plain Dealer*, May 13, 1901, p. 13.
29. *Cleveland Plain Dealer*, May 10, 1901, p. 8.
30. *Cleveland Plain Dealer*, May 2, 1901, p. 6; Jul. 24, 1902, p. 6; *Milwaukee Sentinel*, Jul. 9, 1901, p. 4.
31. *Sporting News*, Dec. 2, 1899, p. 6; *Chicago Tribune*, Apr. 1, 1900, p. 17; Apr. 9, 1900, p. 4; May 4, 1900, p. 4.
32. *Chicago Tribune*, May 27, 1901, p. 6; Aug. 15, 1901, p. 4.

33. *Cleveland Plain Dealer*, Aug. 30, 1901, p. 3; Sep. 8, 1901, Sec. 2, p. 3; May 6, 1902, p. 3; May 27, 1902, p. 6; Oct. 2, 1903, p. 8.
34. *Milwaukee Sentinel*, May 14, 1901, p. 4.
35. *Milwaukee Sentinel*, Jun. 13, 1901, p. 4; Jun. 14, 1901, p. 4.
36. *Cleveland Plain Dealer*, Aug. 22, 1902, p. 6.
37. *Sporting News*, Jul. 8, 1899, p. 5; *Boston Globe*, May 10, 1903, p. 4; *St. Louis Republic*, Apr. 8, 1901, p. 3; *Washington Star*, Jun. 8, 1901, p. 7.
38. J. M. Murphy, "Napoleon Lajoie: Modern Baseball's First Superstar," *The National Pastime*, Vol. 7, No. 1, 1988, pp. 8–20; *Sporting News*, Sep. 5 1896, p. 5.
39. *Sporting News*, Aug. 21, 1897, p. 5; Sep. 4, 1897, p. 1; Mar. 26, 1898, p. 2; *Boston Globe*, Jun. 4, 1900, p. 5.
40. *Sporting News*, May 21, 1898, p. 5; Jul. 16, 1898, p. 5; Nov. 25, 1899, p. 5.
41. *Sporting News*, Aug. 27, 1898, p. 7.
42. *Detroit Free Press*, Apr. 23, 1901, p. 10.
43. *Cleveland Plain Dealer*, Jun. 12, 1902, p. 6.
44. *Boston Globe*, Jul. 17, 1902, p. 5.
45. *Detroit Free Press*, May 5, 1901, p. 11.
46. *Sporting News*, May 5, 1900, p. 5; *Boston Globe*, Jun. 25, 1900, p. 2; *Philadelphia Public Ledger*, Jul. 23, 1900, p. 14; Jul. 26, 1900, p. 12.
47. *Sporting News*, Jun. 3, 1899, p. 1.
48. *Baltimore Sun*, Jul. 14, 1899, p. 6; *Washington Post*, May 19, 1902, p. 8.
49. *Sporting News*, Jul. 7, 1900, p. 4.
50. *Baltimore Sun*, Aug. 19, 1901, p. 6.
51. *Sporting News*, Sep. 7, 1901, p. 7.
52. *Sporting News*, Sep. 21, 1901, p. 4.
53. *Sporting News*, Jul. 27, 1901, p. 4; Aug. 24, 1901, p. 5.
54. *Detroit Free Press*, Jul. 30, 1901, p. 9.
55. *Detroit Free Press*, Jul. 14, 1901, p. 8.
56. *Detroit Free Press*, Jul. 20, 1901, p. 8.
57. *Detroit Free Press*, Jul. 28, 1901, p. 8; Aug. 11, 1901, p. 8; Aug. 14, 1901, p. 3.
58. Reed Browning, *Cy Young: A Baseball Life* (Amherst: University of Massachusetts Press, 2000), pp. 84–5, 90–1.
59. Browning, *Cy Young*, pp. 110–1; *Sporting News*, Mar. 1, 1902, p. 4; Sep 19, 1903, p. 4.
60. *Washington Post*, Sep. 27, 1903, Sec. 3, p. 8.
61. *Boston Globe*, May 15, 1904, p. 45.
62. *Sporting News*, Sep. 9, 1893, p. 5; Jun. 3, 1896, p. 5; Apr. 10, 1897, p. 4.
63. *Washington Post*, Apr. 30, 1903, p. 8.
64. *Sporting News*, Mar. 21, 1896, p. 3; Mar. 26, 1898, p. 2; *Washington Post*, Apr. 28, 1903, p. 9; Browning, *Cy Young*, pp. 96–98.
65. James, *The New Bill James Historical Baseball Abstract*, pp. 846–51.
66. Browning, *Cy Young*, pp. 210–15.

Chapter Four

1. *Philadelphia Public Ledger*, Apr. 22, 1901, p. 16; *Chicago Tribune*, May 18, 1901, p. 6.
2. *Sporting News*, Aug. 3, 1901, p. 4.
3. *Baltimore Sun*, Jul. 27, 1901, p. 6.
4. *Milwaukee Sentinel*, Jul. 27, 1901, p. 4; *Pittsburgh Dispatch*, Aug. 12, 1901, p. 9; *Boston Globe*, Sep. 11, 1901, p. 2.
5. *Sporting News*, Dec. 28, 1901, p. 8; *Boston Globe*, Apr. 13, 1902, p. 28.
6. *Boston Globe*, Apr. 6, 1902, p. 6; *Philadelphia Inquirer*, Apr. 22, 1902, p. 5; *St. Louis Globe-Democrat*, May 7, 1902, p. 13.
7. *Baltimore Sun*, Jul. 8, 1902, p. 6; Jul. 9, 1902, p. 6.
8. *Pittsburgh Post*, Jun. 2, 1902, p. 6; *Cincinnati Commercial Tribune*, Jun. 2, 1902, p. 8.
9. *Pittsburgh Post*, Jun. 30, 1902, p. 6.
10. *Pittsburgh Post*, Sep. 22, 1902, p. 6; Oct. 5, 1902, Sec. 2, p. 2.
11. *Pittsburgh Post*, Aug. 31, 1902, Sec. 2, p. 2.
12. *New York Press*, Sep. 10, 1902, p. 4.
13. *Brooklyn Daily Eagle*, Apr. 21, 1902, p. 8.
14. *Sporting News*, Aug. 2, 1897, p. 1; Jun. 25, 1898, p. 5; *Brooklyn Daily Eagle*, Jul. 22, 1900, p. 10.
15. *Sporting News*, Apr. 16, 1898, p. 1.
16. *Sporting News*, Jun. 17, 1899, p. 5; Sep. 23, 1899, p. 5.
17. *Cincinnati Commercial Tribune*, Jun. 15, 1901, p. 7.
18. *Brooklyn Daily Eagle*, Jul. 26, 1901, p. 10; Aug. 23, 1901, p. 12.
19. *Sporting News*, Apr. 28, 1900, p. 4.
20. *Brooklyn Daily Eagle*, May 28, 1902, p. 13; Jun. 9, 1902, p. 8.
21. *Sporting News*, Jan. 14, 1905, p. 6.
22. Robert L. Tiemann and Mark Rucker, eds., *Nineteenth Century Stars* (Manhattan, KS: Ag Press for the Society for American Baseball Research, 1989) p. 79; Harold Kaese, *The Boston Braves* (New York: Putnam's, 1948), pp. 76–7; *Sporting News*, Feb. 21, 1903, p. 2.
23. *New York Times*, Dec. 24, 1935, p. 20; Feb. 1, 1936, p. 10; Thorn, et. al., *Total Baseball*, pp. 249, 253.
24. *Chicago Tribune*, May 18, 1902, p. 10.
25. *Sporting News*, Apr. 19, 1902, p. 5; Feb. 7, 1903, p. 2.
26. *Cincinnati Commercial Tribune*, Aug. 18, 1902, p. 7; Aug. 20, 1902, p. 7.
27. *Chicago Tribune*, Apr. 17, 1902, p. 6.
28. Levy, *Rube Waddell*, pp. 94–5.
29. *Sporting News*, Dec. 19, 1901, p. 1; Nov. 2, 1901, p. 1.
30. *Chicago Tribune*, May 5, 1902, p. 6.
31. *Chicago Tribune*, May 11, 1902, p. 10; *Boston Globe*, Jun. 13, 1902, p. 5.
32. Ritter, *The Glory of Their Times*, pp. 39–40.
33. Gil Bogen, *Tinker, Evers, and Chance: A Triple Biography* (Jefferson, NC: McFarland, 2000), pp. 42–4.
34. *Sporting News*, Nov. 2, 1901, p. 2.
35. *Sporting News*, Dec. 7, 1901, p. 4.
36. *St. Louis Globe-Democrat*, Apr. 20, 1903, p. 5; Jun. 11, 1903, p. 15; Sep. 10, 1904, p. 5; *Cincinnati Commercial Tribune*, Aug. 30, 1903, p. 12.
37. *Boston Globe*, Jun. 6, 1902, p. 4; *Cincinnati Commercial Tribune*, Jun. 23, 1902, p. 8.
38. *St. Louis Globe-Democrat*, Aug. 23, 1903, Ed. Sec., p. 9.
39. *Sporting News*, Nov. 5, 1904, p. 4.
40. *Brooklyn Daily Eagle*, Apr. 24, 1902, p. 13.
41. *St. Louis Globe-Democrat*, Apr. 27, 1902, Sec. 3, p. 14.
42. *Philadelphia Public Ledger*, Jun. 24, 1901, p. 18.
43. *Boston Globe*, Jun. 24, 1902, p. 5.
44. *New York Press*, May 14, 1902, p. 5.
45. *Cincinnati Commercial Tribune*, May 18, 1902, p. 11; May 19, 1902, p. 8.

46. *Cincinnati Commercial Tribune*, May 20, 1902, p. 8.
47. *New York Press*, May 20, 1902, p. 5.
48. *New York Press*, Jul. 10, 1902, p. 5.
49. *Brooklyn Daily Eagle*, Apr. 18, 1902, p. 13.
50. *Cincinnati Commercial Tribune*, Aug. 17, 1902, p. 10.
51. Kaese, *Boston Braves*, pp. 77–78.
52. *Sporting News*, May 8, 1897, p. 5; Jun. 19, 1897, p. 6.
53. *Sporting News*, Jul. 31, 1897, p. 6.
54. Kaese, *Boston Braves*, pp. 82–3.
55. *Sporting News*, Apr. 2, 1898, p. 5.
56. *Sporting News*, May 14, 1898, p. 5; Oct. 8, 1898, p. 5.
57. *Pittsburgh Dispatch*, Apr. 17, 1902, p. 10.
58. *Pittsburgh Dispatch*, May 5, 1901, p. 12.
59. *Sporting News*, Nov. 5, 1904, p. 1.
60. Mark Armour, "Thomas William Leach," *Deadball Stars of the National League*, p. 158.
61. *Sporting News*, Jun. 7, 1902, p. 5; *Cincinnati Commercial Tribune*, Apr. 16, 1900, p. 5.
62. *Sporting News*, Sep. 16, 1899, p. 1.
63. *Sporting News*, May 19, 1900, p. 1.
64. *Pittsburgh Chronicle-Telegraph*, Aug. 8, 1900, p. 2.
65. Ritter, *Glory of Their Times*, pp. 66–7.
66. *Cincinnati Commercial Tribune*, Apr. 9, 1900, p. 5.
67. *Cincinnati Commercial Tribune*, May 11, 1900, p. 5; May 12, 1900, p. 5.
68. *Cincinnati Commercial Tribune*, Apr. 1, 1901, p. 7; Sam Crawford, "What I Think About Baseball," *Baseball Magazine*, Feb. 1916, p. 40.
69. *Cincinnati Commercial Tribune*, Apr. 28, 1901, p. 9; May 5, 1901, p. 11; Jul. 20, 1901, p. 7; *Philadelphia Public Ledger*, Jun. 14, 1901, p. 14.
70. Philip J. Lowry, *Green Cathedrals: The Ultimate Celebration of Major League and Negro League Ballparks* (New York: Walker, 2006), pp. 64–5; Bill Lamberty, "Samuel Earl Crawford," *Deadball Stars of the American League*, p. 537.
71. *Cincinnati Commercial Tribune*, Aug. 20, 1902, p. 7; Aug. 28, 1902, p. 7; Aug. 31, 1902, p. 11.
72. F. C. Lane, "The King of Sluggers," *Baseball Magazine*, Feb. 1916, pp. 55–7.
73. Dewey and Acocella, *Biographical History of Baseball*, p. 317.
74. Joe Dittmar, "William Aloysius Bergen," *Deadball Stars of the National League*, p. 277.
75. *Cincinnati Commercial Tribune*, May 21, 1902, p. 8.
76. *Cincinnati Commercial Tribune*, Jun. 16, 1901, p. 9.
77. *Brooklyn Daily Eagle*, May 22, 1904, News/Cable Sec., p. 7.
78. *Cincinnati Commercial Tribune*, Jun. 16, 1901, p. 9.
79. *Cincinnati Commercial Tribune*, Aug. 21, 1902, p. 7.
80. *Cincinnati Commercial Tribune*, Jul. 19, 1903, p. 11.
81. Lee Allen, *The Cincinnati Reds 1948* (Kent, OH: Kent State University Press, 2006), p. 69.
82. *Sporting News*, Nov. 18, 1899, p. 2.
83. *Sporting News*, Apr. 24, 1897, p. 6.
84. *Sporting News*, Oct. 2, 1897, p. 1.
85. *Sporting News*, Mar. 26, 1898, p. 1; Aug. 27, 1898, p. 5; Sep. 10, 1898, p. 5.
86. *Sporting News*, Feb. 4, 1899, p. 5; Mar. 18, 1899, p. 2.
87. *Sporting News*, Apr. 1, 1899, p. 5; Apr. 29, 1899, p. 1; Jul. 1, 1899, p. 4.
88. *Sporting News*, Jul. 8, 1899, p. 5.
89. *Cincinnati Commercial Tribune*, Jul. 13, 1900, p. 5.
90. *Cincinnati Commercial Tribune*, Jul. 16, 1900, p. 5.
91. *Pittsburgh Chronicle-Telegraph*, Aug. 4, 1900, p. 2.
92. *Boston Globe*, May 23, 1901, p. 5.
93. Dan Levitt, "Frank George 'Noodles' Hahn," *Deadball Stars of the National League*, p. 234.
94. *Cincinnati Commercial Tribune*, Jun. 5, 1901, p. 7.
95. *Cincinnati Commercial Tribune*, Oct. 8, 1901, p. 7.
96. *Cincinnati Commercial Tribune*, Aug. 29, 1903, p. 7.
97. *Cincinnati Commercial Tribune*, Jul. 13, 1904, p. 7.

Chapter Five

1. *Philadelphia North American*, Sep. 28, 1902, p. 11.
2. *Philadelphia Public Ledger*, Jun. 16, 1902, p. 14.
3. *St. Louis Globe-Democrat*, Sep. 27, 1903, Sp. Sec., p. 3.
4. Norman Macht, *Connie Mack and the Early Years of Baseball* (Lincoln: University of Nebraska Press, 2007), pp. 275–7; Levy, *Rube Waddell*, pp. 94–100.
5. *Sporting News*, Jan. 10, 1903, p. 7.
6. *Philadelphia Public Ledger*, Sep. 3, 1902, p. 6; Sep. 5, 1902, p. 6.
7. *Sporting News*, Feb. 6, 1904, p. 4.
8. *St. Louis Globe-Democrat*, Jun. 15, 1902, Sec. 3, p. 12; *Baltimore Sun*, Jul. 19. 1902, p. 6; *Detroit Free Press*, Apr. 16, 1903, p. 10.
9. *St. Louis Globe-Democrat*, Jun. 11, 1902, p. 13.
10. *St. Louis Globe-Democrat*, May 10, 1902, p. 15; Sep. 1, 1902, p. 9.
11. *Sporting News*, Dec. 7, 1901, p. 4.
12. *Sporting News*, Oct. 4, 1902, p. 4.
13. *Sporting News*, Dec. 13, 1902, p. 3.
14. *Boston Globe*, Apr. 28, 1902, p. 8; May 23, 1902, p. 5.
15. *Washington Post*, Sep. 24, 1902, p. 9.
16. *St. Louis Post-Dispatch*, Jun. 9, 1902, p. 6.
17. *Sporting News*, Aug. 2, 1902, p. 4.
18. *Chicago Tribune*, Apr. 27, 1902, p. 11.
19. *Chicago Tribune*, Apr. 24, 1902, p. 6.
20. *Boston Globe*, Jun. 1, 1902, p. 44.
21. *Philadelphia Public Ledger*, Jun. 23, 1902, p. 16.
22. *Boston Globe*, May 8, 1902, p. 44.
23. *Sporting News*, Oct. 11, 1902, p. 1.
24. *Chicago Tribune*, Aug. 29, 1902, p. 2.
25. *Chicago Tribune*, Jun. 27, 1902, p. 13; Sep. 21, 1902, p. 9.
26. *Cleveland Plain Dealer*, Jun. 9, 1902, p. 6.
27. *Cleveland Plain Dealer*, May 31, 1902, p. 8.
28. *Cleveland Plain Dealer*, Jun. 5, 1902, p. 6; Jul. 24, 1902, p. 6; Aug. 23, 1902, p. 6; *Sporting News*, Sep. 20, 1902, p. 6.

29. *Washington Post*, Sep. 14, 1902, p. 8.
30. Casway, *Ed Delahanty*, p. 187.
31. *Philadelphia Public Ledger*, Jul. 9, 1902, p. 14.
32. *Washington Post*, Apr. 2, 1902, p. 9.
33. *Washington Post*, Apr. 30, 1902, p. 8; May 13, 1902, p. 9; Jun. 5, 1902, p. 9; Jun. 27, 1902, p. 9.
34. *Washington Post*, Jul. 10, 1902, p. 9; Jul. 20, 1902, p. 9; *Chicago Tribune*, Jul. 20, 1902, p. 9.
35. *Washington Post*, Jun. 29, 1902, p. 9.
36. *Washington Post*, Jul. 16, 1902, p. 9.
37. *Detroit Free Press*, Jun. 28, 1902, p. 10.
38. *Detroit Free Press*, Jul. 6, 1902, p. 7.
39. *Detroit Free Press*, Jun. 26, 1902, p. 3.
40. *Detroit Free Press*, Jul. 13, 1902, p. 8.
41. *Detroit Free Press*, Jul. 18, 1902, p. 3; Jul. 23, 1902, p. 3.
42. *Detroit Free Press*, Aug. 24, 1902, p. 8;
43. *Detroit Free Press*, Aug. 14, 1902, p. 3; Sep. 1, 1902, p. 8.
44. *Detroit Free Press*, Aug. 3, 1902, p. 8.
45. *Sporting News*, Jan. 17, 1903, p. 4; *Detroit Free Press*, Aug. 12, 1902, p. 10.
46. *Detroit Free Press*, Sep. 22, 1902, p. 8.
47. *Sporting News*, Jun. 14, 1902, p. 1; Alexander, *John McGraw*, pp. 85–93.
48. *Baltimore Sun*, Aug. 3, 1902, p. 6.
49. *Baltimore Sun*, Jul. 30, 1902, p. 6.
50. *Baltimore Sun*, Aug. 20, 1902, p. 6; *Washington Post*, Aug. 24, 1902, p. 9.
51. *Detroit Free Press*, Jun. 3, 1902, p. 10; *Baltimore Sun*, Jul. 28, 1902, p. 6; Jul. 30, 1902, p. 6.
52. *Baltimore Sun*, Aug. 27, 1902, p. 6.
53. Stanton Hamlet, "James Joseph Collins," *Deadball Stars of the American League*, pp. 403–4.
54. *Sporting News*, Jul. 20, 1895, p. 5.
55. *Sporting News*, Jul. 20, 1895, p. 5; Aug. 3, 1895, p. 3.
56. *Sporting News*, Nov. 16, 1895, p. 1.
57. *Sporting News*, Apr. 18, 1896, p. 6; Apr. 25, 1896, p. 4.
58. *Sporting News*, Jan. 21, 1899, p. 2.
59. *Sporting News*, Apr. 9, 1898, p. 2.
60. *Sporting News*, Jan. 22, 1898, p. 3.
61. *Sporting News*, Oct. 9, 1897, p. 2; Feb. 25, 1899, p. 3.
62. Hanna, "The 25 Greatest Players," pp. 299–300.
63. "All-Time All-Star Team of the American League," pp. 10–11; James, *New Bill James Historical Baseball Abstract*, p. 555.
64. *Sporting News*, May 25, 1895, p. 5; Aug. 3, 1895, p. 5; Nov. 2, 1895, p. 6.
65. *Sporting News*, Dec. 30 1899, p. 1.
66. *Chicago Tribune*, May 12, 1900, p. 6.
67. *Cleveland Plain Dealer*, Apr. 18, 1901, p. 6.
68. *Washington Post*, Apr. 10, 1902, p. 8.
69. *Chicago Tribune*, Sep. 28, 1902, p. 9.
70. *Washington Post*, May 10, 1903, p. A12.
71. *Washington Post*, Jul. 24, 1903, p. 9.
72. Brian McKenna, "Dave Fultz," Baseball Biography Project at //sabr.org/bioproject.
73. *Sporting News*, Jun. 25, 1898, p. 1; Jul. 2, 1898, p. 7.
74. *Sporting News*, Jul. 30, 1898, p. 5; Sep. 24, 1898, p. 5.
75. McKenna, "Dave Fultz."
76. *Detroit Free Press*, Jul. 14, 1901, p. 8.
77. *Cleveland Plain Dealer*, Aug. 9, 1902, p. 6.
78. *Philadelphia Public Ledger*, Sep. 5, 1902, p. 6.
79. *Philadelphia Public Ledger*, Oct. 2, 1902, p. 6.
80. Scott Longert, *Addie Joss: King of the Pitchers* (Birmingham, AL: EBCO Media, 1998), pp. 31–3
81. Longert, *Addie Joss*, pp. 42–5; *Brooklyn Daily Eagle*, Sep. 24, 1901, p. 15; *Sporting News*, Mar. 29, 1902, p. 7.
82. *Cleveland Plain Dealer*, Apr. 27, 1902, Sec. 2, p. 2.
83. *Cleveland Plain Dealer*, May 5, 1902, p. 3.
84. Alex Semchuck, "Adrian Joss," *Deadball Stars of the American League*, p. 654.
85. *Sporting News*, Dec. 6, 1902, p. 3.
86. Longert, *Addie Joss*, pp. vii-viii.

Chapter Six

1. Murdock, *Ban Johnson*, pp. 60–3; *Sporting News*, Dec. 20, 1902, pp. 1–2.
2. *Sporting News*, Jan. 17, 1903, p. 6.
3. *Sporting News*, Jan. 17, 1903, p. 5.
4. *Sporting News*, Jan. 17, 1903, pp. 4–5; *Sporting Life*, Jan. 17, 1903, pp. 3–5.
5. *Sporting News*, Jan. 17, 1903, p. 6.
6. *Sporting News*, Jan. 24, 1903, p. 1.
7. Casway, *Ed Delahanty*, pp. 244–52.
8. *St. Louis Globe-Democrat*, Mar. 29, 1903, p. 14; *Sporting News*, May 9, 1903, p. 1; *Chicago Tribune*, Jul. 4, 1903, p. 6.
9. *Chicago Tribune*, Jun. 26, 1903, p. 8.
10. *Chicago Tribune*, Jun. 27, 1903, p. 6.
11. *St. Louis Globe-Democrat*, Jun. 28, 1903, p. 15.
12. *Chicago Tribune*, Jun. 30, 1903, p. 13; Jul. 4, 1903, p. 6.
13. *Chicago Tribune*, Jul. 4, 1903, p. 6; *New York Times*, Jul. 17, 1903, p. 8.
14. *Chicago Tribune*, Jul. 5, 1903, p. 11; *Boston Globe*, Jul. 5, 1903, p. 30.
15. *Sporting News*, Jul. 18, 1903, p. 1.
16. *Brooklyn Daily Eagle*, Jul. 16, 1903, p. 10; *New York Times*, Jul. 21, 1903, p. 7; *St. Louis Globe-Democrat*, Jul. 26, 1903, Ed. Sec., p. 9.
17. DeValeria and DeValeria, *Honus Wagner*, pp. 110–1.
18. *Pittsburgh Post*, Jun. 7, 1903, Sec. 2, p. 2.
19. *Cincinnati Commercial Tribune*, Jun. 9, 1903, p. 10.
20. *Pittsburgh Post*, Jul. 29, 1903, p. 5; DeValeria and DeValeria, *Wagner*, p. 134; *Sporting News*, Jan. 4, 1917, p. 1.
21. *Sporting News*, Jun. 20, 1903, p. 4.
22. *Cincinnati Commercial Tribune*, Jun. 12, 1903, p. 10.
23. Doxsie, *Iron Man McGinnity*, pp. 70–3; *New York Times*, Aug. 2, 1903, p. 12; Aug. 9, 1903, p. 14.
24. *New York Times*, Sep. 1, 1903, p. 8; *New York Sun*, Sep. 1, 1903, p. 6.
25. *Boston Globe*, Apr. 29, 1903, p. 5.
26. *Boston Globe*, Jun. 30, 1903, p. 5; Aug. 13, 1903, p. 7; *Philadelphia North American*, Jul. 19, 1903, Sp. Sec., p. 1; *Sporting News*, Nov. 7, 1903, p. 1.
27. *Boston Globe*, May 24, 1903, p. 37.
28. *Sporting News*, Sep. 20, 1902, p. 1.
29. *St. Louis Globe-Democrat*, Sep. 9, 1902, p. 13; *Washington Post*, Oct. 1, 1902, p. 8.
30. *Cincinnati Commercial Tribune*, Jun. 12, 1903, p. 10.
31. *Cincinnati Commercial Tribune*, Sep. 17, 1903, p. 7.

32. *Cincinnati Commercial Tribune*, May 12, 1904, p. 8; May 14, 1904, p. 8; Jul. 13, 1904, p. 7; Aug. 28, 1904, p. 9.
33. *Sporting News*, Sep. 6, 1902, p. 5.
34. *Sporting News*, Jan. 24, 1903, p. 2.
35. *Sporting News*, Sep. 20, 1902, p. 1.
36. *Brooklyn Daily Eagle*, Apr. 12, 1903, p. 7.
37. *St. Louis Globe-Democrat*, Jun. 5, 1903, p. 13; *Philadelphia North American*, May 5, 1903, p. 1.
38. *Brooklyn Daily Eagle*, Jun. 5, 1903, p. 12.
39. *Brooklyn Daily Eagle*, Aug. 4, 1903, p. 15.
40. *Brooklyn Eagle*, Jul. 27, 1903, p. 12.
41. *Brooklyn Eagle*, Apr. 12, 1903, p. 7.
42. *Brooklyn Eagle*, Jul. 28, 1903, p. 13; *Detroit Free Press*, Sep. 6, 1903, Sec. 2, p. 4.
43. *Boston Globe*, Jun. 13, 1903, p. 6.
44. *Boston Globe*, Jun. 6, 1903, p. 5; Jun. 22, 1903, p. 3.
45. *Boston Globe*, Jun. 15, 1902, p. 4.
46. *Philadelphia North American*, Aug. 9, 1903, pp. 1, 10; *Sporting News*, Aug. 15, 1903, p. 5.
47. *Brooklyn Daily Eagle*, Apr. 22, 1902, p. 13; *Cincinnati Commercial Tribune*, May 13, 1902, p. 8.
48. *Cincinnati Commercial Tribune*, May 15, 1902, p. 8.
49. *Philadelphia North American*, May 5, 1903, p. 5.
50. *Pittsburgh Post*, Sep. 12, 1903, p. 10.
51. *St. Louis Globe-Democrat*, Apr. 15, 1903, p. 12.
52. *St. Louis Globe-Democrat*, Apr. 18, 1903, p. 15.
53. *Sporting News*, Sep. 21, 1901, p. 4.
54. *St. Louis Globe-Democrat*, May 13, 1903, p. 15.
55. *Sporting News*, Jun. 20, 1903, p. 4; Dec. 19, 1903, p. 4.
56. *Sporting News*, Aug. 12, 1899, p. 4.
57. *Sporting News*, Jul. 29, 1899, p. 4.
58. *Sporting News*, Aug. 5, 1899, p. 4.
59. *Sporting News*, Aug. 12, 1899, p. 4; Aug. 26, 1899, p. 4.
60. *Sporting News*, Sep. 2, 1899, p. 4.
61. *Sporting News*, Sep. 9, 1899, p. 4.
62. *Sporting News*, Oct. 21, 1899, p. 4.
63. *Sporting News*, Jun. 30, 1900, pp. 1, 4.
64. *Sporting News*, Mar. 22, 1902, p. 1; Mar. 29, 1902, p. 6.
65. *Cincinnati Commercial Tribune*, Sep. 14, 1902, p. 7; *Sporting News*, Oct. 25, 1902, p. 1.
66. *Cincinnati Commercial Tribune*, May 5, 1903, p. 10; May 6, 1903, p. 10; May 16, 1903, p. 10; Jun. 9, 1903, p. 10; Jun. 11, 1903, p. 10; Jul. 1, 1903, p. 3.
67. *Cincinnati Commercial Tribune*, Apr. 23, 1904, p. 8.
68. *Sporting News*, Apr. 30, 1904, p. 4.
69. *Cincinnati Commercial Tribune*, Jun. 29, 1904, p. 7.
70. *Cincinnati Commercial Tribune*, Jul. 6, 1904, p. 7.
71. *Sporting News*, Oct. 28, 1905, p. 6; Feb. 17, 1906, p. 6.
72. *Sporting News*, Feb. 2, 1907, p. 1.
73. Michael Betzold, "Turkey Mike Donlin," *Baseball Research Journal*, Vol. 29, pp. 80–3; Rob Edelman, "Turkey Mike Donlin in the Movies," *Baseball Research Journal*, Vol. 30, pp. 73–5.
74. Mark Armour, "Charles Louis 'Deacon' Phillippe," *Deadball Stars of the National League*, pp. 157–8.
75. *Sporting News*, Sep. 30, 1899, p. 4.
76. DeValeria and DeValeria, *Honus Wagner*, pp. 121–135.
77. Robert Peyton Wiggins, *The Deacon and the Schoolmaster*, (Jefferson, NC: McFarland, 2011), pp. 133–47; *Pittsburgh Post*, Oct. 2, 1903, p. 12; Oct. 3, 1903, p. 12; Oct. 4, 1903, Sec. 2, p. 2; Oct. 7, 1903, p. 8; Oct. 8, 1903, p. 8; Oct. 9, 1903, p. 8; Oct. 11, 1903, Sec. 2, p. 2; Oct. 14, 1903, p. 8.

Chapter Seven

1. *Sporting News*, Oct. 31, 1903, p. 1.
2. *Sporting News*, Feb. 28, 1903, p. 1.
3. *Sporting News*, Jun. 2, 1900, p. 5; Jun. 9, 1900, p. 1.
4. *Chicago Tribune*, Sep. 8, 1900, p. 8.
5. *Chicago Tribune*, Sep. 22, 1901, p. 17.
6. *Baltimore Sun*, May 12, 1902, p. 6.
7. *Baltimore Sun*, Jun. 9, 1902, p. 6; *Boston Globe*, Jul. 19, 1902, p. 5.
8. *Boston Globe*, May 5, 1903, p. 2.
9. *Boston Globe*, Aug. 25, 1903, p. 5.
10. *Boston Globe*, Jul. 11, 1903, p. 5.
11. Browning, *Cy Young*, p. 129.
12. Dan Desrochers, "Alfred L. 'Freddy' Parent," *Deadball Stars of the American League*, p. 416.
13. *Cleveland Plain Dealer*, Apr. 20, 1903, p. 3; *Detroit Free Press*, Apr. 19, 1903, Sec. 2, p. 4.
14. William C. Kashatus, *Money Pitcher: Chief Bender and the Tragedy of Indian Assimilation* (University Park: Pennsylvania State University Press, 2006), pp. 5–28.
15. *Sporting News*, Dec. 31, 1942, p. 4.
16. *Philadelphia Public Ledger*, Apr. 28, 1903, p. 10.
17. *Philadelphia North American*, May 13, 1903, p. 5; Jun. 3, 1903, p. 5.
18. John Philips, *The 1903 Naps* (Cabin John, MD: Capital, 1989), p. 6.
19. *Sporting News*, Jan. 31, 1903, p. 2; Mar. 21, 1903, p. 1; *Cleveland Plain Dealer*, May 25, 1903, p. 6.
20. *Cleveland Plain Dealer*, May 21, 1903, p. 8.
21. *Cleveland Plain Dealer*, Jul. 7, 1903, p. 8; Jul. 22, 1903, p. 6.
22. Jim Reisler, *Before They Were the Bombers: The New York Yankees' Early Years, 1903–1915* (Jefferson, NC: McFarland, 2002), pp. 25–9, 47–8.
23. *New York American*, May 1, 1903, p. 10; *Washington Post*, May 2, 1903, p. 9.
24. *New York Press*, Jun. 12, 1903, p. 5; *St. Louis Globe-Dispatch*, Aug. 23, 1903, p. 12.
25. Edward Grant Barrow with James M. Kahn, *My Fifty Years in Baseball* (New York: Coward-McCann, 1951), pp. 21–2, 52, 60–1.
26. *Detroit Free Press*, May 29, 1903, p. 10.
27. *Detroit Free Press*, May 30, 1903, p. 10; May 31, 1903, p. 8; Jun. 2, 1903, p. 10.
28. *Detroit Free Press*, Jun. 3, 1903, p. 10; Jun. 4, 1903, p. 10.
29. *Detroit Free Press*, Jun. 7, 1903, Sec. 2, p. 4; *Sporting News*, Jun. 13, 1903, p. 5.
30. *Sporting News*, Jun. 6, 1903, p. 4; *Boston Globe*, Jun. 6, 1903, p. 5; *Chicago Tribune*, Jun. 7, 1903, p. 11.
31. *Detroit Free Press*, Oct. 4, 1903, Sec. 2, p. 4.

32. *St. Louis Globe-Democrat*, Jun. 20, 1903, p. 15; Jun. 25, 1903, p. 14.
33. *St. Louis Globe-Democrat*, Jul. 15, 1903, p. 13; Jul. 27, 1903, p. 11.
34. *Philadelphia North American*, Jul. 19, 1903, Sp. Sec., p. 1; *St. Louis Globe-Democrat*, Jul. 5, 1903, Ed. Sec., p. 8.
35. *St. Louis Globe-Democrat*, Aug. 30, 1903, p. 15; *Sporting News*, Sep. 5, 1903, p. 4.
36. *Chicago Tribune*, May 21, 1903, p. 8.
37. *Cleveland Plain Dealer*, Aug. 11, 1903, p. 6.
38. *Chicago Tribune*, Jul. 25, 1903, p. 9.
39. *Chicago Tribune*, Jun. 28, 1903, p. 9.
40. *Chicago Tribune*, Aug. 15, 1903, p. 8.
41. *Chicago Tribune*, Aug. 11, 1903, p. 4.
42. Casway, *Ed Delahanty*, pp. 244–53.
43. *Washington Post*, Apr. 23, 1903, p. 9; Apr. 24, 1903, p. 9.
44. *Washington Post*, May 10, 1903, p. A10.
45. *New York Times*, May 1, 1903, p. 7; *Philadelphia North American*, May 9, 1903, p. 5.
46. *Philadelphia North American*, Jun. 4, 1903, p. 5.
47. *Washington Post*, Jun. 15, 1903, p. 8.
48. *Washington Post*, May 9, 1903, p. 8.
49. Casway, *Ed Delahanty*, pp. 259–75.
50. *Washington Post*, Jul. 12, 1903, Sec. 2, p. 11.
51. *Chicago Tribune*, Jul. 5, 1903, p. 11.
52. *Sporting News*, Jul. 22, 1905, p. 6.
53. *Sporting News*, Mar. 4, 1893, p. 1.
54. *Sporting Life*, Mar. 4, 1893, p. 3.
55. *Sporting News*, Oct. 21, 1893, p. 1.
56. *Sporting News*, Jul. 20, 1895, p. 4.
57. *Sporting News*, Mar. 19, 1898, p. 6.
58. *Sporting News*, Jun. 8, 1895, p. 1.
59. *Pittsburgh Chronicle-Telegraph*, Jul. 14, 1900, p. 2.
60. *Sporting News*, Oct. 20, 1900, p. 5.
61. *Cincinnati Commercial Tribune*, Oct. 11, 1901, p. 7.
62. *Sporting News*, Oct. 19, 1901, p. 1.
63. *Pittsburgh Chronicle-Telegraph*, Jul. 16, 1900, p. 2; *Boston Globe*, Aug. 17, 1900, p. 12.
64. *Sporting News*, Jun. 15, 1901, p. 5.
65. *Brooklyn Daily Eagle*, Aug. 23, 1901, p. 12; *Pittsburgh Dispatch*, Sep. 6, 1901, p. 9.
66. *Sporting News*, Apr. 5, 1902, p. 3.
67. Nicole DiCicco, "George Stacey Davis," *Deadball Stars of the American League*, p. 487.
68. *Washington Post*, Apr. 26, 1903, p. B8.
69. *Sporting News*; Mar. 19, 1904, p. 2.
70. *Washington Post*, Jun. 10, 1904, p. 8; *Philadelphia North American*, Jul. 31, 1904, p. 9.
71. *Sporting News*; Aug. 17, 1968, p. 6
72. Bill James, *Whatever Happened to the Hall of Fame? Baseball, Cooperstown, and the Politics of Glory* (New York: Simon & Schuster, 1995), pp. 195–205; 214–15.
73. Scott Longert, "Bill Bradley," *The National Pastime*, Vol. 16, 1996, pp. 127–8.
74. *Boston Globe*, Jun. 28, 1903, p. 35.
75. Steve Constantelos, "William Joseph Bradley," *Deadball Stars of the American League*, pp. 642–3.
76. *New York Times*, Dec. 26, 1935, p. 24.
77. *Sporting News*, Aug. 12, 1899, p. 7.
78. *Sporting News*, Aug. 5, 1899, p. 1.
79. James, *New Bill James Historical Baseball Abstract*, p. 636.
80. *Detroit Free Press*, Jun. 4, 1901, p. 10; *Boston Globe*, Jun. 26, 1901, p. 8.
81. *St. Louis Globe-Democrat*, Jul. 10, 1903, p. 13.
82. *New York Times*, Aug. 9, 1906, p. 14.
83. *New York Times*, Sep. 4, 1906, p. 10.
84. Terry Simpkins, "Norman Arthur 'Kid' Elberfeld," *Deadball Stars of the American League*, pp. 705–6.
85. Reisler, *Before They Were the Bombers*, p. 67.
86. *Sporting News*, Aug. 26, 1899, p. 1.
87. *St. Louis Globe-Democrat*, Aug. 3, 1902, p. 15.
88. *Philadelphia North American*, Jun. 12, 1903, p. 5.
89. *Cleveland Plain Dealer*, Aug. 16, 1903, p. 8.
90. *Detroit Free Press*, May 21, 1903, p. 10.
91. *Philadelphia North American*, Jun. 30, 1903, p. 5.
92. *Washington Post*, Jan. 17, 1938, p. 14.
93. *Washington Post*, Jan. 19, 1938, p. 17; Jan. 20, 1938, p. X18.
94. *Sporting News*, May 7, 1898, p. 5.
95. *Chicago Tribune*, Jul. 18, 1900, p. 9.
96. *Sporting News*, Sep. 1, 1894, p. 1.
97. *Sporting News*, Apr. 16, 1898, p. 1.
98. *Chicago Tribune*, Apr. 1, 1900, p. 17; Apr. 13, 1900, p. 4; Jul. 19, 1900, p. 9; Jul. 24, 1900, p. 9.
99. *Chicago Tribune*, Apr. 15, 1900, p. 6.
100. *Chicago Tribune*, Mar. 7, 1901, p. 6.
101. *Brooklyn Daily Eagle*, Jun. 11, 1900, p. 16; *Boston Globe*, Dec. 13, 1900, p. 8; Dec. 15, 1900, p. 4.
102. *Washington Post*, Jan. 24, 1938, p. X14; *Chicago Tribune*, May 2, 1901, p. 6.
103. *Sporting News*, Apr. 7, 1900, p. 5.
104. *Chicago Tribune*, Jun. 2, 1901, p. 19.
105. *Boston Globe*, Aug. 25, 1901, p. 4.

Bibliography

Newspapers and Periodicals

Baltimore Sun, 1899–1902
Boston Globe, 1900–03
Brooklyn Daily Eagle, 1900–03
Chicago Tribune, 1900–03
Cincinnati Commercial Tribune, 1900–03
Cincinnati Enquirer, 1902
Cleveland Plain Dealer, 1901–03
Cleveland Press, 1901
Detroit Evening News, 1901
Detroit Free Press, 1901–03
Milwaukee Journal, 1901
Milwaukee Sentinel, 1901
New York American, 1902–03
New York Press, 1901–03
New York Times, 1900–03
Philadelphia Inquirer, 1900–03
Philadelphia North American, 1902–03
Philadelphia Public Ledger, 1900–03
Pittsburgh Chronicle-Telegraph, 1900–01
Pittsburgh Dispatch, 1900–03
Pittsburgh Post, 1902–03
St. Louis Globe-Democrat, 1900–03
St. Louis Republic, 1901
St. Louis Post-Dispatch, 1902
Sporting Life, 1897–1903, *passim*.
The Sporting News, 1892–1903
Washington Post, 1901–03
Washington Star, 1901–02

Books

Alexander, Charles C. *John McGraw*. Lincoln: University of Nebraska Press, 1995.
Alexander, Charles C. *Our Game: An American Baseball History*. New York: Henry Holt, 1991.
Allen, Lee. *The Cincinnati Reds 1948*. Kent, OH: Kent State University Press, 2006.
Barrow, Edward Grant, with James M. Kahn. *My Fifty Years in Baseball*. New York: Coward-McCann, 1951.
Bogen, Gil. *Tinker, Evers, and Chance: A Triple Biography*. Jefferson, NC: McFarland, 2003.
Browning, Reed. *Cy Young: A Baseball Life*. Amherst: University of Massachusetts Press, 2000.
Casway, Jerold. *Ed Delahanty in the Emerald Age of Baseball*. Notre Dame: University of Notre Dame Press, 2004.
DeValeria, Dennis, and Jeanne Burke DeValeria. *Honus Wagner: A Biography*. New York: Henry Holt, 1996.
Dewey, Donald, and Nicholas Acocella. *The Biographical History of Baseball*. New York: Carroll and Graf, 1995.
Doxsie, Don. *Iron Man McGinnity: A Baseball Biography*. Jefferson, NC: McFarland, 2009.
Evers, John J., and Hugh S. Fullerton. *Touching Second: The Science of Baseball*. Chicago: Reilly and Britton, 1910.
Fleitz, David L. *Ghosts in the Gallery at Cooperstown*. Jefferson, NC: McFarland, 2004.
Hittner, Arthur D. *Honus Wagner: The Life of Baseball's "Flying Dutchman."* Jefferson, NC: McFarland, 1993.
Ivor-Campbell, Frederick, Robert L. Tiemann, and Mark Rucker, eds. *Baseball's First Stars*. Cleveland: Society for American Baseball Research, 1996.
James, Bill. *The New Bill James Historical Baseball Abstract*. New York: Free Press, 2001.
_____. *Whatever Happened to the Hall of Fame? Baseball, Cooperstown, and the Politics of Glory*. New York: Simon & Schuster, 1995.
_____, and Jim Henzler. *Win Shares*. Morton Grove, IL: Stats Publishing, 2002.
Jones, David, ed. *Deadball Stars of the American League*. Dulles, VA: Potomac Books, 2006.
Kaese, Harold. *The Boston Braves*. New York: Putnam's, 1948.
Kashatus, William C. *Money Pitcher: Chief Bender and the Tragedy of Indian Assimilation*. University Park: Pennsylvania State University Press, 2006.
Levy, Alan H. *Rube Waddell: The Zany, Brilliant Life of a Strikeout Artist*. Jefferson, NC: McFarland, 2000.

Longert, Scott. *Addie Joss: King of the Pitchers.* Birmingham, AL: EBCO Media, 1998.

Lowry, Philip J. *Green Cathedrals: The Ultimate Celebration of Major League and Negro League Ballparks.* New York: Walker, 2006.

Macht, Norman. *Connie Mack and the Early Years of Baseball.* Lincoln: University of Nebraska Press, 2007.

Mack, Connie. *How to Play Ball.* Chicago: Brewer, Barse, 1908.

Mayer, Ronald A. *Christy Mathewson: A Game-By-Game Profile of a Legendary Pitcher.* Jefferson, NC: McFarland, 1993.

Murdock, Eugene. *Ban Johnson: Czar of Baseball.* Westport, CT: Greenwood, 1982.

Nemec, David. *The Great Encyclopedia of 19th Century Major League Baseball.* New York: Donald I. Fine Books, 1997.

Philips, John. *The 1903 Naps.* Cabin John, MD: Capital, 1989.

Reisler, Jim. *Before They Were the Bombers: The New York Yankees' Early Years, 1903–1915.* Jefferson, NC: McFarland, 2002.

Ritter, Lawrence S. *The Glory of Their Times: The Story of the Early Days of Baseball Told by the Men Who Played It.* New York: Morrow, 1985.

Robinson, Ray. *Matty: An American Hero.* New York: Oxford University Press, 1993.

Schlereth, Thomas J. *Victorian America: Transformations in Everyday Life.* New York: HarperCollins, 1991.

Simon, Tom, ed. *Deadball Stars of the National League.* Dulles, VA: Brassey's, 2004.

Solomon, Burt. *Where They Ain't: The Fabled Life and Untimely Death of the Original Baltimore Orioles, the Team That Gave Birth to Modern Baseball.* New York: Free Press, 1999.

Spatz, Lyle. *Bad Bill Dahlen: The Rollicking Life and Times of an Early Baseball Star.* Jefferson, NC: McFarland, 2004.

Thomson, Cindy, and Scott Brown. *Three Finger: The Mordecai Brown Story.* Lincoln: University of Nebraska Press, 2006.

Thorn, John, Pete Palmer, and Michael Gershman, eds. *Total Baseball: The Official Encyclopedia of Major League Baseball,* 4th ed. New York: Viking, 1995.

Tiemann, Robert L., and Mark Rucker, eds. *Nineteenth Century Stars.* Manhattan, KS: Ag Press for The Society for American Baseball Research, 1989.

U. S. Department of Commerce, Bureau of the Census. *Historical Statistics of the United States, 1789–1945.* Washington, DC: U.S. Government Printing Office, 1949.

Wiggins, Robert Peyton. *The Deacon and the Schoolmaster.* Jefferson, NC: McFarland, 2011.

Articles

Ahrens, Art. "Emmet Heidrick: Forgotten St. Louis Star." Bob Tiemann, ed., *Mound City Memories: Baseball in St. Louis.* Cleveland: Society for American Baseball Research, 2007.

"The All-Time All-Star Team of the American League." *Sport,* Sept. 1958, pp. 10–11.

"The All-Time All-Star Team of the National League." *Sport,* Oct. 1958, pp. 42–3.

Betzold, Michael. "Turkey Mike Donlin." *Baseball Research Journal* 29, pp. 80–3.

Crawford, Sam. "What I Think About Baseball." *Baseball Magazine,* Feb. 1916, p. 40.

Dubbs, Gregg. "Jim Sheckard: A Live Wire in the Dead Ball Era." *Baseball Research Journal,* 1980.

Edelman, Rob. "Turkey Mike Donlin in the Movies." *Baseball Research Journal* 30, pp. 73–5.

Evans, Billy. "Baseball's Thirteen Best Hitters." *Esquire,* June 1942, pp. 62, 106–7.

Hanna, E. B. "The 25 Greatest Players." *Baseball Magazine,* June 1924, pp. 299–300.

Lane, F. C. "The King of Sluggers." *Baseball Magazine,* Feb. 1916, pp. 55–7.

Longert, Scott. "Bill Bradley." *The National Pastime* 16 (1996): 127–8.

Murphy, J. M. "Napoleon Lajoie: Modern Baseball's First Superstar." *The National Pastime* 7, no. 1 (1988): 8–20.

Internet Sites

http://baseballhall.org
http://www.baseball-reference.com
http://www.la84.org
http://www.retrosheet.org
http://sabr.org/bioproject

Index

Abbaticchio, Ed 215
Abbott, Fred 241, 242
Alexander, Grover Cleveland "Pete" 114
Allen, Lee 151, 259
American League standings 81, 156, 233
Anderson, John 53, 81, 103, 161, 191, 249, 250
Anson, Adrian "Cap" 35, 39, 87, 131, 142
Armour, Bill 190, 242
Arndt, Harry 178, 179
Aubrey, Harry 215

Babb, Charlie 203
Baltimore Chop 32
Baltimore Orioles (American League) 94–96, 176–80; team statistics 95, 176, 177
Baltimore Orioles (National League) 5, 6, 10, 12, 21, 32, 33, 41, 44, 66, 94, 99, 108, 109, 124–25, 180, 184–85, 187, 244
Baltimore Patriots 177–180
Bannon, Jimmy 180
Barclay, George 134–36, 218, 19
Barnes, Ross 108
Barrett, Jimmy 25, 26, 60, 89–91, 145, 173, 174, 246
Barrow, Ed 245–48, 264
Barry, Shad 19, 137, 217
Baseball Hall of Fame 1, 5, 7, 11, 12, 26, 35, 45, 66, 79, 116, 128, 133, 148, 163, 183, 192, 221, 239, 259, 262
Baseball-reference.com 3
Bay, Harry 169, 170, 241, 242
Bean, Joe 139
Beaumont, Ginger 15, 47, 48, 68, 121, 122, 200
Beck, Erve 99, 100, 129, 174
Beckley, Jake 7, 25, 60, 72, 78, 121, 123, 129, 144, 207, 209, 225

Bemis, Harry 169, 241
Bender, Charles "Chief" 238–40
Bergen, Bill 60, 125, 130, 149, 150, 209
Bernhard, Bill 18, 51, 91, 92, 117, 120, 157, 169, 170, 192, 241, 242
Berra, Yogi 137
Beville, Monte 244
Bill James Electronic Baseball Encyclopedia 3
Bostock, Lyman 108
Boston Americans 86–88, 164–66, 233–38; team statistics 87, 164, 235, 236
Boston Beaneaters 6–9, 18–20, 57, 58, 127–29, 214–16; team statistics 19, 57, 58, 127, 128, 215
Bowerman, Frank 27, 60, 72, 139, 195, 203
Bradley, Bill 22, 58, 65, 99, 169–70, 241, 242, 259–62
Brain, Dave 218, 219, 225
Bransfield, Kitty 15, 47, 48, 121, 122, 144, 200
Brashear, Roy 134, 216
Breitenstein, Ted 25, 104, 152
Bresnahan, Roger 7, 94–96, 120, 138, 177, 200, 203
Brodie, Steve 81, 94–96, 139
Brooklyn Superbas 5–14, 53–55, 123–27, 210–13; team statistics 10, 11, 53, 124, 211, 212
Brouthers, Dan 142, 255
Brown, Mordecai "Three-Finger" 79, 80, 208, 218, 220–21
Browne, George 137, 138, 140, 202
Browning, Reed 112, 113
Brush, John T. 23–28, 61, 82, 95, 125, 129, 130, 140–41, 144, 146, 147, 152, 193–98,

208, 243, 254, 255, 258, 265, 269
Buckenberger, Al 214
Buelow, Charlie 258
Buelow, Fritz 55, 89–91, 173, 174, 246
Burke, Jimmy 83, 90, 103, 104, 118, 218, 219
Burkett, Jesse 7, 8, 21, 56, 68, 79, 161–63, 191, 223, 247, 249, 266
Butler, Ike 178

Callahan, Jimmy 23, 58, 83–86, 167, 168, 251, 252
Camp, Walter 186
Cantillion, Joe 260
Carew, Rod 108
Carey, George "Scoops" 63, 171, 184–86, 253
Carlton, Steve 154
Carney, Pat 127, 215
Carr, Charlie 246
Carrick, Bill 27–28, 59, 97, 171
Casey, James "Doc" 53, 89–91, 174, 175, 206, 232
Castro, Luis 157
Chadwick, Henry 142
Chance, Frank 7, 22, 59, 78, 121, 131–33, 203, 206–08
Chesbro, Jack 7, 15, 48–50, 122, 123, 127, 133, 199, 214, 228, 229, 244, 245, 253, 254
Chicago Orphans/Remnants/Cubs 6–9, 22, 23, 58, 59, 130–33, 205–08; team statistics 22, 23, 58, 59, 131, 206
Chicago White Stockings 82–86, 166–68, 250–53; team statistics 82, 83, 166, 167, 251
Childs, Clarence "Cupid" 22, 59
Childs, Pete 57, 137

Cincinnati Reds 6–7, 9, 23–27, 60, 61, 129, 130, 208–10; team statistics 25, 60, 129, 130, 208, 209
Clarke, Bill "Boileryard" 19, 58, 97, 98, 171, 172, 186, 253, 254
Clarke, Fred 7, 8, 15, 16, 22, 47–50, 61, 63, 93, 121, 122, 125, 199–203, 228–231
Clarkson, John 116
Clemens, Roger 114, 126
Cleveland Blues/Naps 98–102, 168–70, 240–43; team statistics 99, 169, 241
Cleveland Spiders 5, 6
Clingman, Bill 22, 23, 97
Coakley, Andy 239
Cobb, Ty 2, 35, 108, 148, 183, 221
Colcolough, Tom 104
Collins, Eddie 35, 221
Collins, Jimmy 7, 18, 19, 58, 82, 87, 88, 95, 96, 107, 164, 65, 180–84, 233, 235, 236, 242, 260, 262, 271
Comiskey, Charlie 79, 102, 103, 119, 152, 166–68, 177, 178, 196, 198, 250–52, 258, 259, 267, 270, 271
Congalton, William "Bunk" 131
Conigliaro, Tony 66
Connolly, Tom 96
Conroy, Wid 63, 90, 103, 118, 121, 122, 199, 200, 244
Cooley, Duff 15, 57, 127, 215
Corbett, Young 23, 159
Corcoran, Tommy 25, 26, 78, 129, 130, 209, 217, 225
Coughlin, Bill 80, 96, 97, 171, 172, 253, 260, 262
Courtney, Ernie 248
Crawford, Sam 7, 25–27, 60, 73, 129, 133, 144–48, 195, 209, 210, 232, 233, 246, 264
Criger, Lou 21, 55, 87, 164, 236
Crockett, Daniel "Davey" 89, 110, 111
Cronin, Jack 26, 89, 90, 120, 139, 202, 203
Cross, Lave 10, 12, 53, 54, 91, 92, 107, 118, 124, 157, 210, 238, 260, 262
Cross, Monte 17, 51, 136, 153, 156–58, 238
Cuppy, Nig 87
Currie, Clarence 218
Cushman, Ed 115

Dahlen, Bill 10–11, 53, 124, 210–212, 257

Daly, Tom 10–11, 53, 72, 119, 126, 166, 167, 209, 251
Davis, Alfonzo "Lefty" 47, 69, 70, 121–23, 199, 243, 244, 252
Davis, George 7, 27, 28, 59, 70, 138, 141, 166, 167, 194–98, 232, 251, 255–59
Davis, Harry 63, 92, 93, 157, 185, 238, 240
Day, John B. 270
Dean, Dizzy 154
Decker, George 77
Deegan, William "Dummy" 79
Deering, John 246
Delahanty, Ed 7, 8, 12, 17–19, 29, 30, 39, 51, 52, 65, 66, 70, 72, 78, 106, 118, 119, 133, 136, 138, 141, 153, 170, 171, 172, 186, 194–96, 232, 253–55, 265
DeMontreville, Gene 10, 12, 53, 57, 58, 109, 127
Denzer, Roger 59
Detroit Tigers 89–91, 173–76, 245–48; team statistics 89, 174, 246
Detroit Wolverines 123
Devery, William 243
Dexter, Charlie 59, 131, 132, 215, 225, 269
Dillon, Frank "Pop" 89–91, 111, 174
Dinneen, Bill 18, 19, 58, 127, 164, 165, 166, 230, 231, 234–36, 238
Dobbs, Johnny 60, 129, 131, 133, 211, 212
Doby, Larry 259
Doheny, Ed 27–28, 48, 122, 123, 200–202, 229
Dolan, Joe 92–93
Dolan, Patrick "Cozy" 124, 126, 209, 210, 240, 251, 252, 258
Donahue, John "Jiggs" 162
Donahue, John "Red" 8, 18, 51, 136, 162, 241, 242, 249–50
Donahue, Tim 22, 65, 78
Donlin, Mike 21, 55, 94–96, 108, 129, 130, 176, 200, 208–10, 221–27, 232
Donovan, Patsy 21, 55–57, 134, 135, 182, 218–20, 223
Donovan, Wild Bill 45, 53, 55, 78, 124, 210, 211, 233, 246, 248
Dooin, Charles "Red" 137, 216, 217
Doolan, Mickey 218
Dougherty, Patsy 164, 165, 235–36,
Douglass, William "Klondike" 17, 137, 216, 217
Dowd, Tommy 53, 87, 164

Dowling, Pete 99, 102
Doyle, Jack 27, 59, 131, 137, 139, 140, 171, 173, 211, 212, 217, 257
Dreyfuss, Barney 6, 69, 122, 123, 130, 197, 198, 200, 228, 229, 270
Drill, Lew 171, 253
Dryden, Charlie 254, 266
Duffy, Hugh 7, 58, 102–04
Duggleby, Bill 51, 120, 136, 137, 157, 216, 217
Dungan, Sam 97, 98
Dunkle, Davey 253
Dunleavy, Jack 218–20
Dunn, Jack 11, 13, 94, 95, 109, 138, 139, 203, 204, 225
Dwyer, Frank 175, 176

Eason, Mal 59, 128, 233
Ebbets, Charlie 188–90, 196, 198, 210, 212
Elberfeld, Norman "Kid" 26, 60, 89–90, 141, 173–75, 189, 195–97, 233–43, 245–48, 262–66
Ely, Fred "Bones" 8, 15, 48, 50, 92, 93, 118, 119, 123, 171, 172
Evans, Billy 35
Evans, Roy 139, 212
Everitt, Bill 97, 98
Evers, Johnny 133, 206–08
Ewing, Bob 209
Ewing, Buck 7, 26, 28, 35, 152, 256–58, 265

Falkenberg, Cy 199, 201
Farming (players) 23–25
Farrell, Charles "Duke" 10, 12, 53, 77, 124, 125, 149, 210, 233, 237
Farrell, Frank 243, 264
Farrell, John 96–98, 134, 218
Ferris, Hobe 87, 88, 164, 236
Fields, Minnie 224
Fisher, Chauncy 59
Fisher, Cherokee 115
Flaherty, Patsy 251
Flanner, A. J. 221
Flick, Elmer 7, 12, 17, 18, 29, 51, 106, 107, 119, 120, 136, 146, 153, 156, 157, 168–70, 235, 241, 242
Flood, Tim 124, 126, 211
Fogel, Horace 138–40
Foreman, Frank 95
Foster, Clarence "Pop" 59, 97
Foutz, Frank 95
Fox, Bill 60
Fraser, Charles "Chick" 18, 51, 91–94, 117, 120, 136, 137, 157, 216, 217
Freedman, Andrew 6, 7, 27,

Index

61, 120, 130, 140, 173, 177, 208, 257, 258
Freeman, John "Buck" 18–20, 58, 87, 88, 108, 164, 165, 236
Friel, Bill 103, 161, 162, 249, 250
Frisbee, Charlie 27, 28
Frisk, Emil 26, 90
Fullerton, Hugh 7, 234, 257, 258
Fultz, Dave 53, 92, 102, 141, 157, 186–89, 195, 238, 239, 244, 245, 252

Galvin, James "Pud" 114
Ganzel, John 22, 23, 59, 240, 244
Garvin, Virgil "Ned" 23, 58, 102, 103, 166–68, 212, 232, 251, 270
Gatins, Frank 54
Gear, Dale 96–98
Geier, Phil 26, 60, 92, 105
Gershman, Michael 3, 35
Gessler, Henry "Doc" 211, 212
Gibson, Norwood 233, 235, 236
Gilbert, Billy 77, 102, 103, 140, 176–78, 202–04, 232
Gleason, Harry 164, 251
Gleason, William "Kid" 27, 59, 89–91, 107, 111, 173, 174, 191, 216, 217, 232, 246, 257
Gochnauer, John 107, 169, 241, 242, 246
Grady, Mike 27, 59, 97, 257
Green, Danny 22, 59, 68, 131, 166, 240, 251
Green, Ed 115
Gremminger, Ed 127, 215
Griffith, Clark 7, 23, 45, 58, 82–88, 102, 116, 133, 167, 168, 180, 244, 245, 250, 252, 257, 267–71
Grillo, J. Ed 144–46, 155, 204, 208, 210, 217, 265
Grove, Lefty 114
Guerrero, Pedro 36

Hackett, Jim 218–19
Hahn, Frank "Noodles" 25, 42, 48, 60, 129, 130, 150–55, 209, 234
Hallman, William H. "Bill" 103, 251
Hallman, William W. "Bill" 51, 137, 216, 217
Hamilton, Billy 7, 19, 36, 57, 68, 127, 254
Hanlon, Ned 7, 9, 11–14, 20, 21, 33, 42, 44, 45, 52–55, 65, 69, 123–27, 130, 131, 145, 184, 199, 201, 204, 210–13

Hanna, E. B. 183
Harley, Dick 60, 89, 129, 173, 174, 206
Harper, Jack 56, 161, 162, 209, 232
Hart, Bill 99
Hart, Burt 95, 96
Hart, Jim 77, 132, 133, 196, 197, 208, 267, 269, 270
Hartman, Fred 83–84, 134
Hartsel, Tully "Topsy" 58, 131, 157, 188, 238
Harvey, Ervin "Zaza" 84, 85, 99, 101, 102, 191
Haskell, John B. 85, 262
Hawley, Emerson "Pink" 27, 28, 37–43, 59, 102, 103
Hayden, Jack 92–94, 107
Hearne, Hughie 124, 126
Hedges, Robert 250
Heidrick, Emmet 21, 56, 66–68, 78, 161, 223, 247, 249, 250
Heilbronner, Louis 57
Heismann, Crese 178–80
Hemphill, Charlie 55, 87, 88, 161, 249
Henley, Weldon 238, 239
Herrmann, August "Garry" 147, 194, 195, 197, 208, 209
Hickman, Charlie 27, 28, 59, 107, 138, 164, 165, 169, 170, 241, 242, 266
Hill, Hunter 249–50
Hite, Mabel 227
Hoffer, Bill 81, 99
Hoffman, Danny 238, 239
Hogriever, George 103
Holliday, James "Bug" 254
Holmes, James "Ducky" 89–91, 173–75, 251, 254
Hornsby, Rogers 184
Howell, Harry 11, 13, 53, 94, 95, 177, 178, 244
Hoy, William "Dummy" 79, 82, 84, 100, 129
Huelsman, Frank 80
Hughes, Jim 11, 53, 55, 124, 126, 210
Hughes, Tom 59, 77, 131, 165, 176, 177, 231, 234, 235, 236
Hulswitt, Rudy 137, 216–18
Husting, Pete 90, 103, 157, 158, 160, 164, 165, 239

Iburg, Herman, "Ham" 137, 144
Indianapolis Hoosiers (Western League) 23, 24, 26, 79, 92, 95, 125, 143, 265
Irwin, Charlie 25, 32, 53, 54, 124
Isbell, Frank 83, 84, 166, 251, 252

Jacklitsch, Fred 137, 212
Jackson, Jim 95, 96, 139
Jackson, Joe 174–76, 247, 248
James, Bill 114, 184, 259
Jennings, Hughie 5, 7, 10, 11, 51–53, 77, 137, 180, 184, 257
Johnson, Ban 1, 46, 52, 58, 85, 96, 98, 107, 118, 120, 123, 129, 133, 173, 175, 177, 193, 197, 198, 211, 229, 233, 234, 239, 243, 244, 262, 264, 270, 271
Johnson, Randy 114
Johnson, Walter 114
Jones, Bert 21
Jones, Davy 1, 131–33, 161, 206
Jones, Fielder 10, 11, 53, 82, 84, 100, 108, 166, 167, 210, 251
Jones, Jim 139
Jones, Oscar 212, 213
Jones, Tom 178
Jordan, Dutch 211, 212
Joss, Addie 169–70, 189–92, 241, 242
Joyce, Bill 44, 257

Kahoe, Mike 25, 26, 145, 161, 249
Katoll, Jack 83–86, 178, 271
Keefe, Tim 116
Keeler, Willie 1, 5, 7, 10–14, 30–36, 53, 54, 66, 69, 78, 104, 124, 133, 142, 181, 210, 211, 233, 243–46, 252
Keister, Bill 21, 55, 94, 95, 108–110, 171, 172, 176, 216, 217
Kelley, Joe 5, 7, 10, 11, 33, 53, 54, 69, 112, 119, 120, 124, 126, 130, 133, 155, 176, 177, 208–10, 225, 226
Kelley, Mike "King" 225
Kennedy, Bill 11, 13, 14, 43–45, 53, 55, 199–02, 229–31
Kihm, George "Dummy" 79
Killen, Frank 39
Killilea, Henry 194
Kisinger, Charles "Rube" 246
Kitson, Frank 11, 13–14, 53, 55, 124, 125, 210, 211, 233, 246
Kittridge, Malachi 57, 58, 127, 253
Kling, Johnny 59, 121, 131, 132, 206, 208
Krueger, Otto 56, 134, 200, 202, 219, 229

Lachance, George "Candy" 99, 164, 236
Lajoie, Napoleon "Larry" 2, 7,

12, 17, 18, 29, 30, 33, 39, 51, 82, 88, 91, 92, 94, 104–108, 117, 120, 121, 133, 138, 144, 147, 157, 169–71, 179, 187, 188, 221, 240–42, 246, 250, 255, 265, 266
Lane, F. C. 147–48; court case 94, 117, 119, 120, 157, 165, 169, 172, 177
Lange, Bill 143
Lanigan, Ernest 82, 93, 104, 110
Lauder, Billy 139, 187, 203, 262
Leach, Tommy 14–15, 47, 48, 50, 61, 63, 69, 73, 75, 121–23, 143, 144, 193, 199, 200, 229, 236, 260, 262
Lee, Watty 96–98, 118, 171, 253
Leever, Sam 15, 48–49, 72, 116, 122–23, 200–02, 227–31
Leitner, George "Dummy" 79, 180
Lewis, Ted "Parson" 19, 58, 87, 95, 101, 164
Loftus, Tom 8, 23, 76–78, 132, 172, 186, 234, 254
Long, Herman 18–20, 57, 78, 127–29, 142, 181, 233–44, 246, 248, 257
Louisville Colonels 5, 6, 15, 61, 63, 69, 75, 84, 89, 93–94, 125, 180, 181, 185–87, 216, 228
Lowe, Bobby 19, 20, 57, 58, 127, 131–33, 142, 206
Lundgren, Carl 131, 133, 206
Lush, Billy 127, 233, 246, 248

Mack, Connie 1, 16, 39, 91–94, 118, 120, 156–60, 188–89, 239, 240
Macmillan's *Baseball Encyclopedia* 2, 3
Maddux, Greg 114
Magoon, George 32, 60, 109, 129, 209, 225, 251
Malarkey, John 128, 215
Maloney, Billy 102–03, 162
Manning, Jimmy 38, 96–98, 118
Martin, Joe 249–50
Mathews, Bobby 115, 116
Mathews, Eddie 184
Mathewson, Christy 2, 7, 48, 49, 60, 61, 70–73, 77–78, 92, 114, 139, 40, 154, 183, 195, 202–06, 212, 220
McAleer, Jimmy 68, 98–99, 101, 162–64, 185, 209, 247, 249, 250, 256
McAllister, Lewis "Sport" 89, 174, 176, 246, 248

McBride, Algie 25, 59
McCarthy, Arch 176, 188
McCarthy, Jack 22, 58, 99, 102, 169, 170, 241
McCarthy, Tommy 77, 181
McCloskey, John 180, 181
McCormick, Barry 22, 59, 131, 16, 162, 250, 253, 262
McCredie, Walter "Judge" 211
McCreery, Tom 53, 68, 124, 126, 211, 212
McFarland, Charles "Chappie" 218
McFarland, Ed 17, 18, 51, 119, 136, 166–68, 251
McFarland, Herm 83, 84, 178, 244
McFetridge, Jack 217
McGann, Dan 21, 56–57, 120, 134, 139, 176, 177, 203
McGinnity, Joe 7, 11, 13, 14, 28, 37–43, 45, 53, 55, 88, 94–96, 111, 116, 120, 139, 177, 202–06, 210, 214–15, 271
McGovern, Terry 159, 270
McGraw, John 1, 5, 7, 10, 21, 22, 35, 41, 52, 55, 65, 66, 77, 82, 85, 94–96, 108, 109, 118, 120, 130, 134, 138–41, 158, 172, 173, 175–77, 179, 181, 187, 194–96, 198, 202–05, 224, 226, 232–34, 254, 266, 271
McGraw, Minnie 77
McGuire, James "Deacon" 10, 12, 32, 53, 119, 124, 126, 173, 174, 246
McIntryre, Matty 92, 93
McJames, James "Doc" 11, 53, 55, 78
McKechnie, Bill 150
McPhail, Larry 259
Mendoza, Mario 149
Menefee, John "Jock" 23, 59, 131, 206
Mercer, Win 7, 27, 28, 59, 97, 173–75, 182, 245
Mertes, Sam 22, 23, 58, 82–84, 140, 166, 195, 202, 203, 232, 250, 258
Mesner, Steve 150, 151
Meyers, John "Chief" 72
Miller, Dakin "Dusty" 131
Miller, Roscoe 89–91, 111, 139, 140, 173–75, 202, 233
Milwaukee Brewers 43, 58, 59, 81, 85, 102–104; team statistics 103
Mitchell, Fred 87, 158, 160, 165, 217, 239
Moore, Earl 99–101, 169, 170, 188, 241, 242, 266
Moran, Charles 253
Moran, Pat 127, 215

Morrisey, Jack 225
Morton, John 186
Mullin, George 173–75, 246
Murnane, Tim 43, 105, 106, 113, 119, 138, 167, 171, 181, 198, 207, 235, 237, 248, 258, 260
Murphy, Danny 157, 238, 258, 264
Murphy, Ed 56, 134

Nance, William "Doc" 89, 90
Nash, Bill 181
National League: contraction 1, 5–7, 81, 84, 89, 90, 97; standings 9, 46, 47, 120–21, 198, 199
Nelson, Ray 60
New York Giants 6–10, 27, 28, 59, 60, 138–41, 202–05; team statistics 27, 59, 60, 138–39, 202, 203
New York Highlanders 193, 195–97, 243–45; team statistics 243, 244
Newton, Doc 25, 26, 60, 124–26, 210
Nichols, Art 56, 64, 68, 134
Nichols, Charles "Kid" 7, 18, 19, 45, 58, 114, 127, 135, 173, 214
Niekro, Phil 114
Nops, Jerry 13, 94, 95

O'Brien, Jack 97, 99, 233, 236
O'Brien, John 109
O'Brien, Tom 15, 47, 78
O'Connor, Jack 15, 47, 48, 112, 121–23, 199, 244, 250
O'Day, Hank 153
O'Hagan, Hal 132
O'Loughlin, Francis "Silk" 264
O'Neill, Jack 134, 135, 218
O'Neill, Jim 136
O'Neill, Mike 134–36, 218, 219
O'Neill, Steve 136
Orth, Al 18, 51, 119, 136, 171, 253
Owen, Frank 251

Padden, Dick 56, 83, 161, 191, 249
Parent, Freddy 87–88, 164, 165, 236, 238
Patten, Casey 26, 60, 96, 97, 171, 253
Patterson, Roy 83–86, 167, 168, 180, 251, 252
Pfiester, Jack 199
Phelps, Ed 199, 200
Philadelphia Athletics 91–94, 156–161, 238–40; team statistics 92, 157, 238
Philadelphia Phillies 6–8, 17,

18, 51, 52, 136–38, 216–18; team statistics 17, 18, 51, 137, 217
Phillippe, Charles "Deacon" 15, 48, 69, 116, 122, 123, 200, 201, 227–231, 238
Phillips, Bill 25–27, 60, 130, 209
Phyle, Bill 60
Piatt, Wiley 18, 51, 78, 86, 92, 167, 168, 180, 215, 251
Pickering, Ollie 99, 101, 169, 238–39
Pittinger, Charles "Togie" 58, 128, 214–16
Pittsburgh Pirates 6, 7, 9, 14–17, 47–50, 121–23, 199–202; team statistics 15, 47, 48, 122, 200
Plank, Eddie 92, 93, 157–60, 161, 237–40
Players' Protective Association 270
Poole, Ed 122, 130, 209
Potter, James 197
Powell, Jack 21, 42, 56, 57, 161–164, 249, 250
Powers, Michael "Doc" 92, 157, 238
Prentiss, George 78
Preston, Walt 180
Pulliam, Harry 186–87, 197, 198

Quinn, Joe 25, 97, 98, 128

Radbourn, Charles "Old Hoss" 115, 116
Raymer, Fred 59, 131
Reidy, Bill 102, 103, 162, 212
Reisler, Jim 265
Reitz, Heinie 77
Renteria, Edgar 66
Retrosheet.org 3
Rhines, Billy 41
Rhoads, Bob 133, 220, 242
Rickey, Branch 23, 264
Ritchey, Claude 15, 47, 48, 121, 122, 200, 201, 229
Ritter, Lawrence S. 73, 133
Ritter, Lew 212
Robinson, Wilbert 5, 7, 10, 21, 41, 55, 63, 94, 95, 109, 177–80, 235
Robinson, William "Rabbit" 253
Robison, Frank DeHaas 5, 68, 115, 116, 135, 193, 197, 208, 221, 256
Robison, Stanley 5, 112, 135
Rogers, Colonel John I. 117, 169, 196
Rose, Pete 34
Roth, Frank 216, 217
Rusie, Amos 38, 61

Ruth, Babe 35, 108, 148, 157, 183
Ryan, Jack 56, 134, 218
Ryan, Jimmy 22, 171, 253
Ryan, Nolan 38

St. Louis Browns 161–64, 248–50; team statistics 161, 249
St. Louis Cardinals 5–7, 9, 21, 22, 55–57, 133–36, 218–21; team statistics 21, 56, 134, 218
Sanborn, Ira "Sy" 130–31, 167, 198, 248, 252, 255, 258
Schaefer, William "Germany" 131
Scheibeck, Frank 99
Schmidt, Henry 212, 213, 225
Schmidt, Mike 184
Schreckengost, Ossee 55, 73, 87, 96, 157, 158, 164, 238
Schriver, William "Pop" 56, 269
Scott, Ed 25, 26, 60, 75, 99, 145, 146
Seaver, Tom 114
Sebring, Jimmy 199, 200, 210, 226
Selbach, Kip 27, 36, 37, 59, 138, 176, 178, 179, 253
Selee, Frank 7, 19, 58, 98, 127, 131–33, 141, 142, 181, 183, 205–08
Seybold, Ralph "Socks" 26, 60, 92, 93, 107, 157, 238, 254, 265, 266
Seymour, Cy 28, 59, 94, 95, 120, 129, 130, 133, 177, 207, 209, 225
Shay, Danny 26
Sheckard, Jimmy 10, 12, 14, 53, 54, 65–67, 69, 120, 124, 146, 176, 177, 203, 210, 211, 225
Sheridan, John 159, 177
Shields, Charlie 178
Shugart, Frank 83, 85, 271
Siever, Ed 89, 174–76, 249
Sisler, George 35
Skopec, John 84
Slagle, Jimmy 7, 17, 18, 29, 30, 52, 57, 131–33, 206
Slattery, Jack 251
Smith, Aleck 72, 178
Smith, Elmer 27, 28, 77
Smith, George "Heinie" 63, 139, 246, 248
Smith, Harry 47, 102, 118, 122, 199, 200
Smoot, Homer 134, 218, 225
Somers, Charles 87, 169, 170
Spahn, Warren 114
Sparks, Tully 102, 103, 164, 165, 217

Speaker, Tris 35, 183, 221
Stahl, Charles "Chick" 19, 58, 87, 88, 107, 164, 165, 236
Stahl, Jake 237
Stallings, George 89, 91, 106, 118
Stanley, Joe 215
Staub, Rusty 36
Stein, Ed 44
Steinfeldt, Harry 25, 60, 78, 130, 153, 209, 262
Stimmel, Archie 60
Strang, Sammy 59, 138, 166, 211, 212, 225, 250
Strobel, Charles 190–91
Sudhoff, Willie 21, 56, 105, 161, 162, 249, 250
Sugden, Joe 83, 84, 161, 162, 249
Sullivan, Bill 19, 58, 83, 84, 166
Sutthoff, Jack 209
Syndicate baseball 5, 6

Tannehill, Jesse 15, 48, 49, 122–23, 127, 199, 228, 229, 244
Tannehill, Lee 251–253
Taylor, Jack 23, 42, 59, 76, 131, 133, 146, 206, 208, 221
Taylor, Luther "Dummy" 60, 79, 138, 139, 168, 202, 203
Tebeau, Pat 21, 68, 106, 221–23, 256
Tenney, Fred 18, 19, 57, 64, 121, 127, 132, 141–43, 171, 183, 215
Thielman, Henry 130
Thomas, Roy 17, 18, 29, 30, 51, 68, 137, 138, 217
Thompson, Gus 230–31
Thompson, Sam 36
Thoney, Jack 241
Tinker, Joe 131–33, 206–08, 259
Titus, John 217
Townsend, Jack 51, 136, 171–73, 253
Traynor, Pie 184, 262
Tucker, Tommy 142

Van Derbeck, George 262
Van Haltren, George 27, 59, 203, 204
Vaughn, Henry "Farmer" 153
Veil, Bucky 201, 230

Waddell, Rube 7, 15, 16, 47–49, 59, 73–78, 102, 131, 156, 157, 159–61, 176, 189, 192, 228, 234, 237–39, 241, 254
Wagner, Al 61
Wagner, Earl 142
Wagner, Honus 7, 14–17, 47,

48, 50, 61–63, 66, 69, 105, 118, 121, 122, 147, 185, 200, 201, 221, 225, 227, 229, 230, 269
Waldron, Irv 97, 103, 104
Walker, Dixie 36
Wallace, Bobby 7, 21, 50, 56, 109, 161–63, 191, 249, 257
Walsh, Ed 192
Ward, John Montgomery 33, 44, 256, 258
Warner, Glenn "Pop" 240
Warner, John "Jack" 60, 138, 140, 164, 195, 202–04, 232, 233
Washington Nationals (National League) 5–7
Washington Senators 96–98, 170–73, 253–55; team statistics 97, 171, 253
Watkins, W. T. 144
Wayne, John 227, 229
Weaver, Art 225
Weaver, Earl 29
Weimer, Jake 206
Weyhing, Gus 13, 14
White, G. Harris "Doc" 49, 51, 137, 251
Wicker, Bob 134, 206, 219–20
Wilhelm, Irvin "Kaiser" 199, 201
Williams, Jimmy 15, 20, 47, 65, 94, 95, 109, 175, 177, 178, 180, 240, 244, 245
Williams, Otto 218, 219, 225
Williams, Walter "Pop" 131, 133
Willis, Vic 7, 18, 19, 58, 92, 127–28, 144, 214, 215
Wilson, Hack 143
Wilson, Howard "Highball" 160, 253
Wiltse, Lewis "Snake" 49, 92, 93, 157, 158, 178–80
Winter, George 87, 164, 165, 235, 236
Wolfe, Barney 244
Wolverton, Harry 17, 22, 51, 64, 65, 78, 136, 171, 172, 217, 262
Wood, Bob 60, 99, 100, 169
Wright, Clarence "Gene" 169, 249, 250

Yager, Abe 124, 137, 211–13, 217, 258
Yeager, George 139
Yeager, Joe 53, 89–91, 174–76, 246–48
Yerkes, Stan 134, 135
Young, Cy 1, 2, 7, 21, 45, 55, 58, 82, 87, 88, 91, 101, 111–16, 133, 160, 161, 164–66, 183, 191, 214, 229, 231, 235–37, 239, 271
Young, Nick 93

Zimmer, Charles "Chief" 15, 47, 48, 121, 122, 143, 199, 216

www.ingramcontent.com/pod-product-compliance
Lightning Source LLC
Chambersburg PA
CBHW081158230426
43666CB00016B/2850